ELIZABETH GASK

Mrs. Gaskell, pastel by Samuel Laurence, 1854

WINIFRED GÉRIN

ELIZABETH GASKELL

A BIOGRAPHY

OXFORD
AT THE CLARENDON PRESS
1976

Oxford University Press, Ely House, London W.1

OXFORD LONDON GLASGOW NEW YORK
TORONTO MELBOURNE WELLINGTON CAPE TOWN
IBADAN NAIROBI DAR ES SALAAM LUSAKA ADDIS ABABA
KUALA LUMPUR SINGAPORE JAKARTA HONG KONG TOKYO
DELHI BOMBAY CALCUTTA MADRAS KARACHI

ISBN 0 19 812070 2

© *Oxford University Press 1976*

*Printed in Great Britain
at the University Press, Oxford
by Vivian Ridler
Printer to the University*

TO THE MEMORY OF

MARY STOCKS

WHO LOVED MRS. GASKELL
AND WHO WAS, LIKE HER,
A MANCUNIAN BY ADOPTION
AND
A CHAMPION OF
NOBLE CAUSES

PREFACE

MRS. GASKELL was notably hostile to any form of biographical notice being written of her in her lifetime. She considered all such attempts as highly impertinent, and consistently refused to facilitate any inquiries undertaken with that intent.

I disapprove so entirely of the plan of writing 'notices' or 'memoirs' of living people [she wrote to an applicant for data only a few months before her death], that I must send you on the answer I have already sent to many others; namely an entire refusal to sanction what is to me so objectionable and indelicate a practice, by furnishing a single fact with regard to myself. I do not see why the public have any more to do with me than to buy or reject the wares I supply to them.

I am sorry to seem uncourteous to a friend of Dr. Morell's and Professor Nichol's; but it is not *you*, but the impertinent custom, of which I want to show my disapprobation.

I never had anything to do with 'any public works of usefulness'—but suppose I had? What respect could you have had for a person who distinctly flew in the face of the precept 'Let not thy left hand' etc,—.

I would gladly give you any information or help of any kind that I thought justifiable, even at the cost of a good deal of trouble to myself. But I will not, in the present instance, because I consider it *un*justifiable, and I may add that *every* printed account of myself that I have seen have [*sic*] been laughably inaccurate. Pray leave me out altogether.[1]

Presumably her experience of writing the *Life* of her friend Charlotte Brontë made her extremely reluctant to countenance a similar undertaking with herself as subject.

The objection was sustained by her family after her death. No family letters or biographical data were made available to the would-be biographer, with the result that the character and literary reputation of Mrs. Gaskell were left to the gossip-writers, and knowledge of her life drawn from the personal impressions of the casual acquaintances who knew her purely on the social plane. Of such were the recollections of admiring contemporaries, like Mary Howitt, Mary Cowden Clarke, Edna Lyall; while close friends like Eliza Bridell-Fox and Mme Mohl contented themselves with publishing personal impressions without great substance.

[1] *GL* 571, 4 June ?1865.

In 1906 the firm of Smith, Elder & Co., Mrs. Gaskell's publishers, wishing to bring out a definitive edition of her works, including the fugitive pieces published in the periodical press, obtained permission from her literary executors—her daughters Meta and Julia Gaskell— to empower Professor A. W. Ward to edit the texts and supply a biographical notice to accompany it, the whole to be known as the Knutsford Edition. Professor Ward was authorized to proceed, and his notice was the first to cover, even if only cursorily, the whole range of Mrs. Gaskell's life, under instruction from her daughters. Despite its omissions and occasional errors of fact, it remains of considerable value as correlating Mrs. Gaskell's work with the facts of her life.

Among the fullest of the personal memorials was the work published in 1908 by Margaret Shaen, a niece of Mrs. Gaskell's great friends the Winkworths—*Memorial of Two Sisters*—which while principally concerning them had a good deal to say about Mrs. Gaskell.

In 1909 Clement Shorter, the noted Brontë editor and biographer, was invited by the General Editor of the English Men of Letters Series to devote a volume to Mrs. Gaskell, and obtained conditional consent from Meta Gaskell to supply him with information, on the understanding that he submitted his completed text for her approval. The material collected by Shorter from every available source filled two impressive volumes of typescript (preserved in the Brotherton Library, University of Leeds), but the degree of Meta Gaskell's supervision of his work may be judged by her letter to him of 25 November 1909 in which she said: 'I am trusting to your promise to let me read over your MS of the English Men of Letters book before it is put into type, as this might possibly save some erroneous statements. I feel specially keen about this because of a mistake made in Mr. Secombe's[2] introduction.'

The project was never completed, for what reasons can only be surmised. Meta Gaskell died in October 1913, and left instructions with her executors and solicitors, Worthington and Padmore to burn all documents relating to her mother. On Shorter's application to be allowed access to them, he met with a refusal. Among these documents, it must be supposed, were not only Mrs. Gaskell's letters to Meta and Julia, but to her husband, since none of these has ever come to light.

For the great good fortune, however, of Gaskell scholars, the letters to her eldest daughter, Marianne, Mrs. Thurston Holland, were preserved by her and have been recently made available by her grand-

---

[2] Thomas Secombe had recently edited *Sylvia's Lovers* (1910).

daughter, Mrs. Trevor Jones, to whom is owed a great debt of gratitude. The letters constitute quite the most valuable and biographically revealing of the total collection of some 600 surviving letters written by Mrs. Gaskell, addressed to a wide circle of correspondents, and eventually published in 1966.

Following on Shorter's abortive attempt to publish a Life and Letters of Mrs. Gaskell (on the pattern of his Brontë volumes) Jane Whitehill, of Cambridge, Mass., attempted the task. Working in close conjunction with J. A. Symington, the Brontë editor, on the plan formulated by Shorter, and using the relevant biographical data collected by him, she completed two typescript volumes of 186 and 130 pages respectively of a 'Life and Letters'. In the event, only the material constituting the third volume, the correspondence of *Mrs. Gaskell and Charles Eliot Norton*, was published in 1930 by the Oxford University Press.

Ill fortune has indeed dogged prospective Gaskell biographers and all attempts at presenting a complete over-all picture of her life based on authentic material has had to wait the long-delayed publication of the letters, sorely depleted as the collection is by the successive destructions enjoined by her executors.

Elizabeth Haldane's *Mrs. Gaskell and her Friends*, published in 1930 without access to the family letters and relying only on those to outside correspondents, was a brave attempt to make bricks without straw.

The first full-scale work on Mrs. Gaskell—which is more an examination of her work than of her life—was that of A. B. Hopkins of Baltimore in 1952. Like its predecessors, it had to rely heavily on the friendships and correspondence outside Mrs. Gaskell's family, with Dickens, George Smith, Charles Eliot Norton, notably. Mrs. Gaskell was such a voluminous letter-writer, and had such a wide circle of friends, and was so free from constraint with those she loved and trusted, that she revealed herself as fully in such letters as in those to her family. What was inevitably missing from such a narration, was the thread connecting *un*connected relationships and events—in Mrs. Gaskell's case the very thread of life.

Now that Professors Chapple and Pollard have restored the balance, as it were, to our one-sided knowledge of Mrs. Gaskell, by their scrupulously researched and edited volume of *The Letters of Mrs. Gaskell* (Manchester University Press, 1966),[3] the time has come to present her life anew, as it could never have been done before.

[3] Referred to throughout the text as *GL*.

It is not that any sensational revelations have come to light, nor even a valid reason for the family's rooted aversion to having her life written. But we now can have a view of Mrs. Gaskell temperamentally as well as intellectually capable of the wit and charm of *Cranford*, of the wide and deep perception of *Wives and Daughters*, of the pathos of the *Life of Charlotte Brontë*, and yet also harassed like other women with over-wrought nerves, with morbid fears, with impatience of restraint, with a pleasure in dress, with a passion for travel; a very complete human being in short; always candid, invariably outspoken, an enemy of humbug in every form, delightfully fresh in her reactions—whether it be to a May morning or to the Great Exhibition of 1851.

The present biography is, therefore, the first to be written in the light of this new knowledge. It is based on widely researched studies into Mrs. Gaskell's background, and the influences that shaped her mind and art.

In the hundred and ten years that have passed since her death, criticism of her work and assessment of her achievement have far outstripped studies of her life, and these have greatly varied. Mrs. Gaskell's place in the Pantheon of Letters has even now not been fully established. When she died, the literary press was unstinting in its praise and her position as one of the major novelists of her day was unquestioned. Reporting her death in the November 1865 issue of the *Athenaeum*, the writer rated her as 'if not the most popular, with small question, the most powerful and finished female novelist of an epoch singularly rich in female novelists'. It is not a claim that posterity has endorsed. Mrs. Gaskell was not first and foremost a craftsman. A busy woman with a family to rear and a social conscience, she did not subordinate all other considerations to her writing; her work was the handmaid of her conscience. At every level, however, even in her contributions to the periodical press, her writing was so faithful a reflection of her personal problems as always to be instinct with life. It was the human dilemma that absorbed her in what she wrote. She had not always time to recon-sider the shape or form.

She cannot, therefore, be ranked as a compeer of Jane Austen; her art is not sustainedly perfect, witty, and polished. Her imagination has not the cosmic range of Charlotte or Emily Brontë, nor has her mind the depth of George Eliot's. Nevertheless, what her admirers can claim is that her range of experience was wider than any of theirs, her art and life were more completely integrated, and she had at her best a special quality of radiance, the reflection of her own happy mind. The intensely personal character of her work, relating directly as so much of it does to her own experience, will, it is hoped, gain in interest and meaning and importance for the readers of her novels the better her life is known. And towards that objective, the present biography has been written.

W. G.

ACKNOWLEDGEMENTS

WITHOUT the publication in 1965 of the *Letters of Mrs. Gaskell* under the joint editorship of Professor Chapple and Professor Pollard of Hull University, the present work could not have been attempted with any more hope of thoroughness than the few which preceded it. My first thanks are, therefore, due to the editors, whose scholarship has gathered together from every available source the widely scattered originals of the letters, and animated the text with the fullest possible data concerning the people and places that constituted Mrs. Gaskell's world. In thus supplementing their text with a General Biographical Index they have made the task of the biographer not only easier, but far more enjoyable. Thanks to them, the Gaskell territory has been fully signposted for future investigators. My debt to the editors does not end there; and I would like to acknowledge the generous and whole-hearted consent they gave me to quote fully from their text, thus obviating for me the long task of tracing the originals for myself.

The editing of the Gaskell letters could not have been the complete triumph it is, however, but for the generous decision of the copyright holder of the family letters, Mrs. Gaskell's great granddaughter Mrs. Trevor-Jones, to place the entire correspondence at the editors' disposal; a decision which allowed the edition to aim at completeness; and a gesture for which all Gaskell students and lovers must cordially thank her. In addition to such general thanks I owe Mrs. Trevor-Jones my personal and heartfelt gratitude for her delightful hospitality and generous permission to make use of her mostly unreproduced family portraits to illustrate this book.

A considerable body of Gaskell material was collected by Clement Shorter for his projected but never completed life of Mrs. Gaskell, and I am extremely grateful to David Masson, Librarian of the Brotherton Library, Leeds, for making the Shorter Collection available to me, and for helping me in every possible way during my work there.

I would also like to thank Mrs. Barbara Smith, Assistant Librarian of Manchester College, Oxford, for her expert guidance through the college's rich collection of Unitarian literature, which permitted me to follow the varied and learned career of Mrs. Gaskell's husband. I am also much indebted to the help and kindness of the Revd. William Strachan,

Unitarian minister of Knutsford, for making his registers and Gaskell collection available to me, and in particular for lending me his own, and by now very rare, copy of Mrs. Gaskell's *Diary* of her children's early years.

To Manchester University Library I have several debts of gratitude to acknowledge; particularly for allowing me access to their collection of Charlotte Brontë's letters to Mrs. Gaskell, and for allowing reproductions of the portraits of Elizabeth Stevenson in their possession.

I am very grateful to Mr. J. G. Sharps, a collector of Gaskell letters, and author of an admirable work on *Mrs. Gaskell's Observation and Invention*, for allowing me to quote from letters from her brother in his possession.

Mrs. Gaskell's great sensitivity towards her surroundings, whether beautiful like her Knutsford countryside, or crushing like the Manchester slums of her day, laid a double obligation on me to visit for myself every place connected with her life; and in the general gratitude I feel towards those who guided me through the Gaskell country, the present owners of the Gaskell home at Plymouth Grove among others, I want to thank my friend Violet Ratcliffe who made a summer visit to Silverdale so memorable; and Miss Lethbridge who allowed me to go all over Mrs. Gaskell's last beautiful home, The Lawn, at Holybourne, and gave me the contemporary photograph that figures in this book. And, finally, Mrs. E. M. Gordon, for generously lending me the last portrait of Mrs. Gaskell for reproduction here.

W. G.

CONTENTS

LIST OF PLATES

I am myself and nobody else, and can't be
bound by another's rules

ELIZABETH GASKELL

CHAPTER I

THE DOUBLE HERITAGE

EXCEPT that they were both born north of the Trent—and both came of confirmed dissenting families—there was little resemblance in the origins and backgrounds of Elizabeth Gaskell's parents. William Stevenson, her father, came from Berwick-on-Tweed, the son and brother of naval men seeing active service during the French Revolutionary wars, with a long family connection with the sea. Her mother, Elizabeth Holland, was on the contrary born of yeoman stock as far inland as could be, in the heart of rural Cheshire.

The imprint of these dual influences remained apparent in their daughter. Throughout her life, the call of the sea was so irresistible that she would say the ancestors of the Stevensons were surely Norsemen, and that the blood of the Vikings ran in her veins.[1] Quite as powerful was the emotional pull on her sensibilities of natural beauty, of the countryside in which she was reared, the restorative properties of which in the end became necessary for her health.

Whatever the high degree of civility—'civility' in the eighteenth-century sense of the word—to which she attained, and despite or because of the immense charm of manner noted by all who met her, she remained throughout her varied and travelled life a North Country woman, strong in her moral convictions, forthright in expression. This essential quality in her make-up is not conveyed by Richmond's crayon drawing, but the portrait by Samuel Laurence eloquently sums it up.

William Stevenson's parents, Post-Captain Joseph Stevenson (1719-99) and Isabella Thomson, cousin of the poet James Thomson, were natives of Berwick where William was born on 26 November 1772, the second of a family of four boys, whose immediate brothers, Joseph and John, became officers in the Royal Navy. Both died young in the French wars, one in a Dunkirk jail and the other drowned while attempting to escape from jail. Such incidents touching the immediate family circle brought home the history of their times to William's daughter as no

[1] Anne Thackeray Ritchie, Preface to *Cranford* (edn. of 1891), p. x.

history-book could have done. The French Revolution was a recurring subject in many of her tales.[2] William's youngest brother, Robert, became a surgeon, and his children were later to be Elizabeth Gaskell's only relatives on her father's side.[3]

William was the product of the romantic and scientific age into which he was born, liberal in politics, aristocratic in tastes, experimental in ideas. He seems to have inherited two of the characteristics of the natives of Berwick: Scottish hard-headedness and the English love of the sea. 'Berwick', as the Recorder of the city said on the occasion of the visit of Charles I in 1623, was

a town neither wholly regulated by English or Scottish laws, but by customs and usages in some things differing from both, yet rather inclined to English laws, and more affecting Scotch fashions and language, as being oftener saluted by the rescript of the one, and seeing and hearing of the other . . .[4]

That William retained a Scottish accent throughout his life was, therefore, not surprising; it was a trait he shared with his daughter's eventual husband and one that she liked to bestow on her male fictional characters.

William's roving disposition was early apparent, and his truancies from school (he attended Berwick Grammar School) an inveterate habit. They were invariably directed towards the city ramparts from where he could see the sea. Already at eight he was his mother's main problem: 'The children', she wrote to her husband stationed off Cork, in the only letter between them to be preserved, 'are all well and give me no trouble, except William who hardly ever attends school and is constantly running about the walls.'[5] It was not mere schoolboy indolence that led him astray, but a keen curiosity in the spectacle of the sea, to which he and his brothers were so deeply drawn.

It was not for the sea, however, that his father intended him, but for the pacific life of the ministry. The family were Dissenters at a time when Dissent was anathema in academic circles, and debarred him from a scholar's place at either university. William Stevenson affiliated himself, moreover, to the Unitarians who, of all unorthodox communities, were the least tolerated by the Establishment. It was certainly not worldly advancement he was seeking when he trained for the Unitarian ministry— first at Daventry Academy in 1787, moving with it on its transfer to

[2] See notably *My Lady Ludlow*, 'My French Master'.
[3] *GL* 183.
[4] *Notes for the Guidance and Information of the Freemen of the Borough of Berwick-upon-Tweed* (1968), p. 5.
[5] *Annual Biography and Obituary*, 1830.

Northampton, and finally at Manchester Academy as a divinity student. From there he emerged in 1792 as a qualified minister, in his twentieth year. At one stage, possibly during the holidays, he went as a travelling tutor with a young student, a Mr. Edwards, to Bruges, where the events of the French Revolution overtook him and drove him home at the beginning of 1793. The experience, though brief, had improved his knowledge of French, in which, as well as in Italian, he later proved himself a proficient scholar.

On his return to England he was appointed resident preacher to Dobb Lane Unitarian Chapel at Failsworth near Manchester, and it was from there, preaching about the countryside on Sundays, as was the custom with the Dissenters—and teaching classics at Manchester Academy in the week—that he met his future wife, Elizabeth Holland.

His arrival in the Hollands' district of Cheshire, as a visiting preacher to be hospitably welcomed to their home on Sundays, can be pictured from his daughter's re-creation of the scene in her pastoral novel *Cousin Phillis*, written nearly seventy years after the event. The marriage between William Stevenson and Elizabeth Holland, the fourth daughter and sixth child of Samuel Holland of Sandlebridge in Cheshire, took place at Over Peover Church (the Hollands' parish church) on 1 December 1797. By then, however, William had already abandoned his vocation as preacher and his post as classics tutor at Manchester Academy. Such a decision, taken on the eve of marriage, argues no common character.

He had, so he declared, developed conscientious scruples at receiving payment for propagating the Gospel, and he had abandoned the ministry and a certain livelihood before having any other to put in its place. For teaching he felt a similar distaste, especially the teaching of the classics. How unorthodox his views on this subject were, and how little self-interested, can be judged by his treatise directed against the classics in education, *Remarks on the Very Inferior Utility of Classical Learning*, published in 1795. After which it is hardly surprising to learn that he turned against university lecturing in favour of a totally different occupation—experimental farming.

One of his closest friends from Berwick days was James Cleghorn, who had made a success of scientific and experimental farming over the border. Following Cleghorn's example, if not actually moved by his advice, William Stevenson apprenticed himself to an East Lothian farmer. East Lothian was then pioneering agricultural studies, and the first Chair for Agriculture in the British Isles was founded in Edinburgh at this time.

After a training of six months, he rented his own smallholding at Laughton Mills, in the immediate vicinity of Edinburgh.

The failure of the enterprise after four years (attributed to the French wars and successive bad harvests) threw him back upon his former resources for a livelihood and decided him in 1801 to sell up and to move into Edinburgh itself. Of Laughton he carried away only two mementoes —his son John born 27 November 1798, and an incurable skin disease brought on by his inordinate consumption of salmon out of season, which despite his handsome bearing disfigured him for life.

Being now a married man with a child to support, he sought the relative security of settled employment, and set up a lodging-house for students in Drummond Street, skirting the university, where he earned additional fees as a university coach. The work did nothing to satisfy William's tastes or fill his pockets, and he turned to writing. Having views to voice and information to diffuse on many subjects—from navigation to topography—he found an outlet in the literary periodicals of the day for which Edinburgh was famous. Within a year of settling in the city Stevenson became editor of the *Scots Magazine* (1803) and contributed regularly as a reviewer of new works to the *Edinburgh Review*, the *Westminster Review*, the *Gentleman's Magazine*, and the *Farmer's Journal*, of which his friend James Cleghorn was the editor. The journalistic habit thus formed was to remain the one constant factor throughout the remainder of his unsettled life.

In the cultural society of Edinburgh where intelligence ranked higher than fortune, William Stevenson evidently made his mark, as his friend Mrs. Fletcher later recorded, remembering him from those early days with love and reverence.[6] The entertainment offered at the evening gatherings was of the simplest kind, tea or coffee handed round replacing a set meal, and good conversation and music affording the true refreshment of the evening. 'People did not meet to eat', recorded Mrs. Fletcher, 'but to talk or listen.'[7] In that predominantly Whig society, William Stevenson sufficiently distinguished himself to come to the notice of Lord Lauderdale. This marked the turning-point in his career.

In the spring of 1806 the new Whig administration under Fox appointed Lord Lauderdale Governor-General of India in succession to the late Marquis of Cornwallis, and Lord Lauderdale invited Stevenson to accompany him as his private secretary—a post of honour and security coveted by many. It would be out of character for William Stevenson to

[6] *Autobiography of Mrs. Fletcher* (Edinburgh, 1875), p. 271.
[7] Ibid.

be tempted by such considerations, but to his restless mind the adventurous life it promised must have appeared like the realization of his dreams. It was natural to him to seek his objective afar rather than at hand, and the appointment to India looked like fulfilling the unsatisfied curiosity of years, in the scope it offered his talents and the field it provided for his experimental ideas. By the time he left Edinburgh on Lord Lauderdale's invitation he was thirty-four. The Drummond Street home, the last of many Scottish homes, dismantled, its contents crated for shipment from Leith to London, and with his wife and eight-year-old son John, Stevenson sailed southward in his patron's wake. To be near Lord Lauderdale, who lived in Mayfair, pending the grand exodus to India, Stevenson also lodged in Mayfair, regardless of expense.

The shock to the uprooted family when this bright future suddenly vanished before their eyes was cruel and bewildering. For they soon learnt that the Government's appointment of Lord Lauderdale was not confirmed by the East India Company, and without that confirmation it was void. The whole project had to be abandoned and Stevenson found himself overnight not only a placeless man but one who had lost his bearings.

Lord Lauderdale, however, was not without a conscience. In compensation for Stevenson's loss, he recommended him for a government sinecure, the post of Keeper of the Records at the Treasury. The minutes of the meeting held in the Treasury Chambers at Whitehall on 20 May 1806 show that the appointment of Mr. Stevenson had already been decided by that date. He was to enter on his functions on 5 July at a starting salary of £200 a year; in due course it would rise to £350 a year.

Stevenson remained at this pettifogging post for the next twenty-three years. After the dazzling mirage of India it must have seemed a drab occupation, but he came to be recognized as an 'intelligent and efficient officer'[8] sedulous in his attention to business, much respected by his fellows. No inkling of his dissatisfaction reached his superiors and he became a model civil servant on all counts. Though nothing could altogether compensate for his lost opportunity, he had, like Charles Lamb, more hours of leisure than of employment, and so the residue of his unsatisfied dreams could spend itself in writing. He became a prolific pamphleteer and gazetteer, contributing to all the foremost periodicals of the time and resuming contacts with the literary and scientific circles he had frequented[9] in his Edinburgh days. The list of his productions

[8] Treasury Minutes. Book 29/87 P.R.O. Memorial of William Stevenson.
[9] *Annual Biography and Obituary*, 1830. Obituary of William Stevenson.

is as impressive as it is varied. He published works on such unrelated subjects as *A System of Land Surveying* (1805 and 1810), *A General View of the Agriculture of Surrey* (1809), and a companion volume on the agriculture of Dorset in 1812. In the *Gentleman's Magazine* (1814) his editorial remarks on Campbell's and Yorke's *Lives of the Admirals* filled several numbers. The sea still held its place in his affections, and in 1824 he published a major work, *The Historical Sketch of Discovery, Navigation and Commerce*. He became responsible for most of the subject-matter in the *Annual Register*. The heterogeneous accumulation of knowledge gained in his many previous employments brought him belated returns now, though he never really achieved his full potential. Only vicariously were his ambitions fulfilled. In due course his son went to sea, and the daughter—born late to him in London—inherited not only the many gifts he possessed but a stability of character he wholly lacked, and achieved a name in literature he had in vain pursued. The family set up house in Lindsey Row in Chelsea, and there Elizabeth Cleghorn Stevenson, as she was called after her mother and after her father's oldest friend, was born on 29 September 1810. She was the eighth, and last, of her parents' children, the only one except the first-born to survive infancy. These successive losses, it can readily be supposed, contributed to the mother's early death. She survived the birth of her last child by only thirteen months, dying on 29 October 1811.

Mr. Stevenson had moved house in the summer after Elizabeth's birth for the greater comfort of his enlarged family, but he did not go far. He moved to 3 Beaufort Row which was just round the corner, still with a full view of the river. The death of his wife after barely three months in the new home left him a bewildered man with a year-old infant on his hands.

While a neighbour, a Mrs. Whittington, took care of the infant, Elizabeth Stevenson's family in Cheshire reacted at once. Her brother, Swinton Holland, who was a partner in the firm of Baring Bros., had warned them of the illness and approaching death, and one of her sisters from Knutsford, Mrs. Lumb, had travelled up to Chelsea to nurse her and then to take charge of the bereaved widower. The news of the death when it reached Knutsford was received with the most practical good sense imaginable by the youngest member of the family, Mary Anne, Mrs. Lumb's daughter, herself a girl of twenty at the time. Her letter to her mother written on the occasion has survived,[10] and it tells us some-

[10] From the copy in the Shorter Collection, Brotherton Library, Leeds.

thing of the sort of people to whom the orphaned Elizabeth was to be entrusted.

The Heath—Nov. 1 1811

My dear Mother, I was greatly shocked to hear from my Aunt Katie's letter of the death of my poor Aunt Stevenson. You had mentioned her in your last letter to me as being far from well; but I had no idea her complaints were in the least degree dangerous, and was therefore quite unprepared for the melancholy intelligence, which came to us yesterday. Poor little Elizabeth! What will become of her? She has almost been the constant subject of my thoughts ever since—and it is about her I have taken up my Pen, to write to you. Do you not think she could come to us? If you have never for a moment thought of this plan, I dare say the mention of it will surprise you; but do not read my Letter over too hastily, for I assure you my scheme will require your attention. The first thing to be thought of is whether *you* will have any objection to her coming here, and the next if Mr. Stevenson dare trust his little girl under my care. Should both these questions be answered in the negative, every further obstacle is, *I think*, entirely removed, though you will, I dare say, find several; which makes me regret I cannot see you, and talk about it, for I am certain I should have it in my power to remove any doubts you may have as to the success of the plan. You will say she is at present too young, and a year or two hence it will be more advisable to have her, but I can not agree with you on this point—for my own gratification I had much rather have a Child the age of Elizabeth, to begin with, than an older, who may have been used to different ways to what they would have here—She is at present quite an Infant—perhaps not even able to walk—this latter circumstance, if the case, will render her a less troublesome companion on a journey than if she were always wanting to be on her feet, and when she were once here, I am sure she may soon be able to run about herself. Charles[11] at her age, I remember, could amuse himself pretty well, and every day you know would lessen that objection. I call it an objection, for I know you will remind me of the *time and attention* such a charge will oblige me to sacrifice. I know it (for I have, I think, thought of everything); but can I not rise early in a morning, and by giving up some of my more trifling employments, such as practising for my own amusement only, working fancy-work, and by giving over keeping plants, surely I may find time for all that is needful. You may smile at my good resolutions of being so industrious, when they have so often failed; but when I shall have such a stimulus to my exertions, I do not hesitate to say *I am sure* I shall have resolutions enough to perform all I promise.

I have measured between the Bed on my side and the Door, and I find there is ample room for a pretty *large* Crib (which I will pay for) but should you think it will crowd the room too much, or having the child in the room in the night, will disturb you *in the least*, I will most joyfully take my little Charge up into the Garret and sleep there.

---

[11] Presumably Charles Holland, born 1799, her cousin.

With regard to *her clothes*, you need not give yourself any trouble about them. I will not say I can entirely plan them all myself; but the *sewing part* I will engage to perform. I have got quicker with my Needle even since you left, and I am certain having the care of Elizabeth's Clothes will do me a great deal of good; it will teach me more about contriving and planning, which is what I least acquainted with of anything in the work-line.

My allowance is so handsome that it has enabled me to procure for myself things which I have not the least occasion for, and which for the future I intend to be without, and I shall have double pleasure, when I shall have little Elizabeth to share a part with me.

Do, my dear Mama, give *at least* your consent to my proposal—Should Mr. Stevenson have any fears, tell him I will perform the part of mother to Elizabeth to the very best of my power.

Your affectionate Daughter, Mary Anne Lumb

(Pray keep this letter to yourself)

M. A. Lumb

Mary Anne Lumb was a cripple and had been herself in need of care all her life. As an infant she had jumped from her nurse's arms at an open window on seeing her mother approach the house, and had injured her back permanently. At the time she urged the adoption of her little cousin she was nearly of age and could in fact substantiate her offer to keep Elizabeth at her own expense. She was in receipt of an independent income under her father's will, and would shortly inherit the full legacy.

The proposal, therefore, to assume the care of Elizabeth, without it having the character of a legal adoption, was so unexceptionable that Mr. Stevenson could offer no better alternative for his orphaned daughter. Elizabeth was born delicate, like the rest of the Stevenson children, and clearly her best chance of survival was to be reared in the country. Mrs. Lumb acted on her daughter's impulsive proposal and Mr. Stevenson found no reason to oppose it. So Elizabeth Stevenson was conveyed north in charge of the Mrs. Whittington who had already shown herself benevolently disposed towards the child, and settled in her aunt Lumb's house on the edge of Knutsford Heath, by general consent of all parties. Cherished by her aunt and cousin, petted by the grandparents at Sandlebridge, her infant maladies prescribed for by her uncle Peter, she blossomed into a beautiful child.

Ill-fortune, however, continued to pursue Mary Anne Lumb, with whom the whole plan of Elizabeth's adoption had originated. As she approached her majority in the spring of the following year, 1812, she travelled to Halifax with her mother to see the family solicitors about her inheritance and the necessity of making a will. It was fully her intention to benefit her little cousin Elizabeth by dividing her inheritance between her mother and herself. But it was not to be. Arrived at Halifax she was taken ill suddenly and died within the day, of 'Spasms' as it was reported. The comment of friends that Mary Anne's death would not only deprive Mrs. Lumb 'of her sole companion and chief object of affection but also perhaps greatly abridge the means of rendering her future life comfortable',[12] would seem to indicate that Mary Anne's death occurred *before* she entered into her inheritance, and that her mother, who was not a beneficiary under her husband's will, would therefore receive no part of it. The need for economy in Mrs. Lumb's home—even if it were the 'elegant economy' generally practised by the ladies of Knutsford—is accounted for by this circumstance. Mary Anne's allowance would, of course, cease with her death.

The tragedy also left Elizabeth Stevenson doubly the poorer: she would grow up without knowing the cousin to whose tenderness she owed her happy home, and by whose generosity her future would have been ensured. Only from hearsay and the bereaved mother's report of her daughter's singular sweetness of character would Elizabeth be able to judge of her loss; as a tribute of gratitude and love in years to come, she called her own first child Marianne in memory of her cousin.

Of Elizabeth Stevenson's two dissimilar heritages, it was undeniably, and paradoxically, the country influences of her mother's family and not the intellectual urban influences of her father, that predominated. Although she spent most of her adult life in Manchester and other cities, she remained a countrywoman at heart.

[12] Edward Hall Collection, M-1006(d) 205. Wigan Central Library.

CHAPTER II

A PROVINCIAL CHILDHOOD

In Elizabeth's childhood the little town of Knutsford, sixteen miles from Manchester, was not so exclusively in 'the possession of the Amazons' as the future author of *Cranford* would have us suppose. While her care in infancy rested naturally with her aunt—'Oh there will never be one like her!' she wrote of her in later life—and her aunt's youngest sister Abigail Holland who shared the house with her after the death of Mary Anne, the first stimuli to exertion, observation, and adventure came decidedly from the men of her family.

The Hollands were a prolific family, rooted in the soil of Cheshire for centuries past, who had expanded into every walk of life by the time Elizabeth Stevenson knew them. There were in particular her three uncles who had each made his way in the world in a distinctive manner: Dr. Peter Holland, the eldest (born 1766), was the local surgeon and devoted his life to his fellow townsfolk in Knutsford; Samuel (born 1767) was a quarry-owner, with large works at Liverpool and Portmadoc, from where she would first discover the coastline and mountain scenery of Wales; and Swinton, already mentioned, the London banker, partner in Baring Bros., was to give her her first glimpses of London society. By these men and their backgrounds her childhood would be far more powerfully influenced, her ultimate destiny directed—possibly even her affections attached—than by her own father. As they were all married, married twice in each case, with large families of children, she would never lack for playmates. At one time she could count on the companionship of fifteen contemporary cousins, without reckoning the younger generation that followed in due course. All the memories of her youth would be brightened by their presence.

The nearest to her both topographically and in affection was, necessarily, her uncle the doctor, who lived in the Church House, a handsome bow-windowed house overlooking the churchyard, at the top end of the little town, in close proximity to Mrs. Lumb's home across the common. In the carefree days before lessons had to be considered, Elizabeth—

Lily as she was early called—was privileged to drive with her uncle on his country rounds and see the homes of his patients—the country gentry, the farmers, and the cottagers—who made up his far-flung practice. It was an experience whose effects are recognizable enough in her books in which the stored-up observation of that past way of life is so memorably used. Evidently she used her ears as well as her eyes, for she developed a faultless ear for dialogue—the terse, pithy, often humorous style of speech that characterizes the medical men in her books, notably Dr. Gibson and Mr. Harrison. Four years before she had arrived at Knutsford, Dr. Holland had been thrown from his gig and received an injury that left him lame for life; but though he suffered and was often irritable in consequence, he was not the less active and was totally dedicated to his work. The imprint of his upright character was as deep as it was lasting: he was for her always the model of the practical, active man.

Next to him as an early influence on her childhood was her grandfather, Samuel Holland the elder, her mother's father. He lived out at Sandlebridge, 4 miles from Knutsford on the Macclesfield road, in a notable house, part farm building and part manor, which had come into the Holland family by marriage in 1718 and was to remain in it for the next two hundred years. It stood at the crest of the highway as it rose from the mill dam and the blacksmith's forge of Little Warford in the hollow below, a deep, double-fronted house two storeys high, with fourteen bedrooms and a great loft running the whole length of the roof. Though there was no drive, the entrance gates were flanked by stone pillars 'surmounted by great stone balls about 6 or 7 feet apart', as Elizabeth herself subsequently described them, the said pillars having entered local and even national history because of their connection with Clive of India. Clive, as Elizabeth recorded, 'was a great friend of my mother's family' and during his schooldays at Knutsford (where he lodged with his tutor Dr. Eaton, minister of the Presbyterian chapel there) he used to visit regularly at the Hollands' home, and 'put my great-grandmother into a terrible fright by jumping from one [of the stone balls] to the other; and when I was a child his exploits were traditional in the neighbourhood, and spoken of under the breath as something too daring to be told aloud'.[1]

The Hollands were of strong Dissenting stock, and Samuel Holland combined the life of land-agent farmer (commanding 300 acres of land) with that of preacher, in the manner described later by his granddaughter in *Cousin Phillis*. That he was actually portrayed in the character of

[1] GL 43, letter to Geraldine Jewsbury, 2 Apr. 1849.

'Farmer Holman' his grandson, later Sir Henry Holland, confirmed.[2] He was a devout man living not only on nature's bounty but in close spiritual touch with nature's God, whose laws he interpreted according to his own strong preconceptions, unbeholden to any parson. He was a friend of Josiah Wedgwood with whose family several of the Hollands intermarried. Short as was Elizabeth's own experience of her grandfather who died when she was six, his personality was a part of the place, and powerful enough to impress her long after his death.

To Sandlebridge she was brought from Knutsford each spring and summer as a young child, and to Sandlebridge she constantly returned in adult life, after marriage, and, in due course, with her own children, so deeply had she learnt to love the place. It so completely epitomized the peace of the countryside for her that whenever a scene of pastoral beauty was to be evoked in her novels, it was Sandlebridge she described. Writing from the house some years later to a sister-in-law, she said:

Fancy me sitting in an old fashioned parlour, 'doors and windows opened wide', with casement window opening into a sunny court all filled with flowers which scent the air with their fragrance—in the very depth of the country—5 miles [sic] from the least approach to a town—the song of birds, the hum of insects the lowing of cattle the only sounds—and such pretty fields and woods all round . . . We are up with the birds, and sitting out on the old flag steps in the very middle of fragrance. . . . There are chickens, and little childish pigs, and cows and calves and horses, and *baby horses*, and fish in the pond, and ducks in the lane, and the mill and the smithy . . . The house and walls are over-run with roses, honey-suckles and vines . . . I sat in a shady corner of a field gay with bright spring flowers . . . with lambs all around me . . . I don't get much writing done here . . . for one can't think any thing but poetry and happiness.[3]

Mrs. Lumb's house, the home where Elizabeth spent the first continuous twelve years of her life, stood at the top of Knutsford facing the heath—hence its name Heathside—somewhat in isolation from the centre, through which ran, from top to bottom, the narrow thoroughfare called King Street, in which and off which in lanes and alleys were crowded the several inns, bow-fronted shops, offices, and dwellings that made up the busy little town. At the top of King Street, amid cottage gardens and flowering shrubs, Knutsford dissolves, as it were, into the parkland. Wrought-iron gates announce the approaches to Tatton Park, the 'Stately Home' of the Egerton family, bestowed by the first Elizabeth

[2] Sir Henry Holland, *Recollections of a past life* (London, 1877).
[3] *GL* 4, 12 May 1836.

on Keeper Egerton for his services to the Crown, which so appropriately and handsomely endows the quiet little place with that patent of gentility after which the society of Elizabeth Gaskell's *Cranford* so unremittingly strove.

Heathside itself was a large, irregular, red-brick Queen Anne house with high chimney-stacks, built on the very verge of the heath that encircles the town, with pleasure gardens and kitchen gardens behind and pasture enough to yield sustenance for a couple of cows, poultry, geese and ducks, and a shaggy pony. Elizabeth's first impressions of the world were thus the rural sights and sounds, the rural scents, of her country home, which throughout her life wherever she happened to be remained the criteria of happiness for her. 'I was brought up in a country town,' she wrote to Mary Howitt, 'and . . . when spring days first come and the bursting leaves and sweet earthy smells tell me that "Somer is ycomen in," I feel a stirring instinct and long to be off into the deep grassy solitudes of the country.'[4]

Outside the immediate family orbit, the strongest single influence on her childhood was certainly religion as she was taught it in the little primitive Unitarian Chapel in Brook Street, at the remotest (and also most hidden) end of the town from her home up on the Heath. She was taken there regularly by her aunt Lumb. The informality of the worship and the antique charm of the interior, with its box-pews, oak galleries, white-washed walls, and diminutive windows of diamond-paned lights, unchanged since its opening in 1698, succeeded in capturing rather than in stifling an imagination as fervent as it was inquisitive. Elizabeth Gaskell described it in her novel *Ruth*:

The chapel was up a narrow street, or rather *cul-de-sac* . . . on the outskirts of the town, almost in fields. It was built . . . when the Dissenters were afraid of attracting attention or observation, and hid their places of worship in obscure and out-of-the-way parts of the towns . . . The chapel had a picturesque and old-world look, for luckily the congregation had been too poor to rebuild it, or new-face it, in George the Third's time. The staircases which led to the galleries were outside, at each end of the building, and the irregular roof and worn stone steps looked grey and stained by time and weather. The grassy hillocks, each with a little upright headstone, were shaded by a grand old wych-elm. A lilac-bush or two, a white rose-tree, and a few laburnums, all old and gnarled enough, were planted round the chapel yard; and the casement windows of the chapel were made of heavy-leaded, diamond-shaped panes, almost covered with ivy, producing a green gloom, not without its solemnity, within. The ivy was the home

[4] *GL* 8, May 1838.

of an infinite number of little birds, which twittered and warbled, till it might have been thought that they were emulous of the power of praise possessed by the human creatures within, with such earnest, long-drawn strains did this crowd of winged songsters rejoice and be glad in their beautiful gift of life. The interior of the building was plain and simple . . . When it was fitted up, oak-timber was much cheaper than it is now, so the wood-work was all of that description . . . The walls were whitewashed and were recipients of the shadows of the beauty without; on their 'white plains' the tracery of the ivy might be seen, now still, now stirred by the sudden flight of some little bird.[5]

What Elizabeth Stevenson learnt at Brook Street Chapel, thanks to the enlightened minister, the Revd. Henry Green, with whom and whose family she formed a lifelong friendship, was a rule of charity and hope that accorded well with her own cheerful temperament. It was also something that she saw daily practised in the homes of her Holland kindred, so that unlike many of her tormented contemporaries she was not subjected to a gospel of fear that left her at war with her own generous and compassionate nature. In a censorious age she was singularly uncensorious.

The first change that might have affected her circumstances occurred when she was four and her distant father married again in 1814. Had he keenly wanted his daughter home, or had his bride felt a particular need for a child about the house, Elizabeth would, no doubt, have been dispatched to London and her aunt Lumb would have been unable to do anything about it. But this, it appears, was not the case, and the new Mrs. Stevenson quickly produced children of her own. A son, William, was born in 1815, and a daughter, Catherine, a year later.

The new Mrs. Stevenson had been Miss Catherine Thomson, whose brother, Dr. Anthony Todd Thomson, was a fashionable and popular physician of Scots origin with a house in Sloane Street and a Chelsea practice, in the exercise of which he made the acquaintance of Mr. Stevenson of the Treasury. It was he who had brought Elizabeth into the world, and his connection with and influence on the destiny of Elizabeth did not end there. In 1820 he himself made a second marriage, with a Miss Katherine Byerley of Warwick, whose sisters kept a select boarding school for girls to which in due course, and doubtless on his recommendation, Elizabeth was sent. This was not, however, until she was twelve years old; up to that time she lived uninterruptedly at Knutsford.

---

[5] *Ruth*, ch. 14, pp. 150–1. (All page-references to Mrs. Gaskell's novels and short stories are to the Knutsford edition published by Smith, Elder in 1906.)

Her father does not appear to have visited her. Within three years of her departure north, he was taken up with the reorganization of his life occasioned by his second marriage. The new Mrs. Stevenson came from a rather more socially pretentious background than did his first dear wife, and Elizabeth being as yet so young—and admirably cared for by the Hollands—there was no immediate need to seek her out. Time enough when she was of an age to benefit by the new Mrs. Stevenson's example. With the new duties and interests provided nearer home by the births of the two children, the obligation, or inclination, to visit his absent child was removed still further from his thoughts.

Elizabeth's own brother John, however, visited her at Knutsford on more than one occasion. The memory of those visits was long cherished by the old aunts and uncles and the tales of his reckless exploits fondly repeated in the family. He was everything a small girl could wish: strong, spirited, kind. He was early destined for the Royal Navy, like his grandfather and his uncles, John and Joseph Stevenson, but strangely enough, perhaps for want of a patron to find him a presentation, he had no entry, and had to go into the Merchant Navy with the East India Company's fleet of ships.

How often he visited Knutsford or how seldom matters little; what matters is that a living contact was established between the brother and sister and that they grew so close in affection and intimacy that the sister's tastes and feelings became sufficiently known to the brother—twelve years younger though she was—for him to encourage and develop them. Their relationship was all the easier because, despite the disparity in age, his role was not that of parent or guardian. The tone he assumed towards her in his letters was that of genial, bantering playmate, exacting of her confidence and love, but also dearly loved by him. They shared perhaps the same need for affection after the loss of their mother, and sensed that in a special way they belonged to each other.

The few remaining letters of John Stevenson plainly show this relationship: he not only knew that she liked to write, but urged her to do so. Firstly it was a journal he wished her to keep—having noted the sharpness and precision of her powers of observation—and then, when she sent him part of a story, he encouraged her to go on with it. His comments on these first writings, though already dating from her sixteenth year, show that it was no new subject between them. 'I am very glad to hear that you have begun a Journal', he wrote from Blackwall on 8 June 1827, 'and have no doubt it will be a very amusing as well as interesting one—at least I know you can if you like, make it so—I shall hope to have

B

good long extracts from it.' Two years earlier he had written a letter to
Mrs. Lumb from India in which he seemed to complain of Elizabeth's
inadequacy as a correspondent; but she would, he argued, never be
short of matter if only she would keep a journal. A week after writing
from Blackwall he wrote again from the ship *Recovery* off Gravesend,
on 17 June 1827, asking her to send him 'good long extracts from her
log', as anything she wrote would be of interest to him.[6]

It was the occasion of John's first voyage in 1822, when Elizabeth was
twelve, that brought her back for the first time to Chelsea to say good-bye
to him. The memory of that parting and the sorrow it brought was so
keen that it remained with her into adult life, long after subsequent
meetings and partings appear to have been forgotten. When her own
children asked to be told about her seaman brother it was the most vivid
recollection of him she could give,[7] and she regretted she could recall so
little else. That he returned several times to England in the course of the
next six years, and saw her on each visit, is clear from his surviving letters.
The affection and the bantering tone were sustained to the end. Ploughing
up the river on his last voyage home in the teeth of contrary winds, he
accused her whistling of hampering the ship's progress.[8]

Nothing in that first visit to her father, a virtual stranger to her, and
to her new stepmother, was to bring consolation to Elizabeth for the loss
of her brother. After he was gone she found no one to replace him. The
memories of that visit, and of all the subsequent visits to Chelsea, which
as the years passed became regular annual obligations, brought no
comfort to her. She did not hesitate to report on them years afterwards:

Long ago I lived in Chelsea occasionally with my father and stepmother, and
very, *very* unhappy I used to be; and if it had not been for the beautiful, grand
river, which was an inexplicable comfort to me, and a family of the name of
Kennett, I think my child's heart would have broken.[9]

Strong words to use of any experience, and surprising when applied to
a paternal home. William Stevenson may have been a kind father, certainly
he was a cultured one, with tastes that should have accorded well with
the growing sensibilities of his eldest daughter, but his day-long absences

[6] The letters of John Stevenson here summarized are derived from J. G. Sharps, *Mrs.
Gaskell's Observation and Invention* (Fontwell, 1970), pp. 17, 120, to whom the originals
now belong. See also Jane Coolidge, manuscript material for a Life of Mrs. Gaskell,
Brotherton Library, Leeds.

[7] Letter from Marianne Gaskell to C. K. Shorter, Gaskell Collection, Brotherton Library,
Leeds.

[8] Summary of a letter from John Stevenson to his sister in the possession of J. G. Sharps.

[9] *GL* 616, fragment of a letter to Mary Howitt, undated.

from home at his office left Elizabeth virtually with the sole companionship of her stepmother and her stepbrother and sister. Towards them she felt so little sense of kinship that she spoke of them rarely, and when grown up only slightingly: of Catherine it was 'my little miss of a $\frac{1}{2}$ sister,[10] and twenty-five years passed after that before she sought her out again.

Towards her stepmother her feelings were altogether more acute; it was not indifference she felt, but intense dislike. That Mrs. Stevenson possessed some of the more disagreeable traits characterizing Mrs. Gibson in *Wives and Daughters* can hardly be doubted, the lack of candour and the affectation in particular. Elizabeth's love of truth, and the total frankness and straightforwardness of her own nature, were such as to alienate from her anybody who lacked such attributes. It may also be, however, that jealousy played its part in influencing her judgement so early and so completely against her father's second family. She confessed frankly in the diary she kept later about her elder children that jealousy was a part of her love for them. How wounded were her feelings by her father's absorption in his second family can readily be imagined. She wanted to love him, indeed she is reported to have greatly loved him, and was the more hurt at not being the chief object of his love in return. Her sense of deprivation of maternal love increased rather than diminished with the years, and was further intensified, one suspects, by the failure not only of the second Mrs. Stevenson but of her own father to fill the void. 'I think no one but one so unfortunate as to be early motherless can enter into the craving one has after the lost mother', she wrote later.[11]

Repeatedly, in her writings, she recurred to the theme of motherless girls—Mary Barton, Ruth, Mollie Gibson—and ascribed all their misfortunes to this initial loss. Driven in upon herself by the lack of sympathy where she most needed it, she sought consolation where she could, not in people but in the beauty of nature that, whether in the country or in London, was all about her at that time. She derived great comfort from the 'beautiful, grand river' to which, in those days before the Embankment was built, access was immediate by the shallow wooden steps that led down to the strand through the shaded tree-lined road before the house in Chelsea. Only a low wooden barrier divided her from the shore where, at low tide, she could wander and watch the shipping, and think of her brother John whose presence would have made up for so much.

[10] *GL* 3, Dec. 1833.
[11] *GL* 614, Feb. 1849, to George Hope, on receipt of letters from her mother addressed formerly to him.

This may not have been the sort of behaviour to conciliate her step-mother. Elizabeth was, admittedly, not of an age when girls are angels; in her own daughters she was to note the passing phase of 'temper' in adolescence, and Mrs. Stevenson's later reference to the general 'improve-ment'[12] in Elizabeth suggests that there had been room for it. For what-ever reasons, and perhaps there were already financial ones, Elizabeth was sent back to Knutsford that same summer.

In her Knutsford home she was inevitably surrounded by old people, and the chief influences on her expanding, eager mind were those of a past generation. While this was not lost upon her keenly observant faculties, and cannot be regretted since it gave the world her accumulated memories of them in *Cranford*, intellectually she was undernourished, as she realized later. Thanking her publisher in later years for a reprint of Brooke's novel, *The Fool of Quality*, originally published in 1766, she told him 'I know and like the Fool of Quality of old. I was brought up by old uncles and aunts, who had all old books, and very few new ones; and I used to delight in the Fool of Quality, and have hardly read it since.'[13]

To be ranked among the 'aunts', by reason of their seniority in age, were her elderly cousins, the children of Dr. Holland's first marriage, the redoubtable Mary Holland (the reputed prototype of 'Deborah Jenkyns'), and her younger sister Lucy who was similarly identified with 'Miss Matty'. Their brother was the future Sir Henry Holland, Physi-cian in Ordinary to the queen, and the only other member of Elizabeth's family to distinguish himself. He was studying in Edinburgh during Elizabeth's early childhood, but he always made a point of returning home for the holidays. He cherished Knutsford all his life and was, of course, the inheritor of Sandlebridge. In 1816 when he set up his first practice in London, at a house in Mount Street, his sister Mary followed to keep house for him till he married. There she moved in circles undreamt of in Knutsford's wildest imaginings and acquired—and retained unchallenged—a reputation for grandeur and learning that permitted her to regulate the niceties of Knutsford society for the remainder of her life. Among the many contacts she made during her years in London she gained the friendship of Maria Edgeworth with whom she continued to correspond till the latter's death.[14] When Maria Edgeworth read *Mary Barton* in the last months of her life, in 1848, by a wholly unknown and

---

[12] See below, p. 38.   [13] *GL* 434, 29 June 1859.
[14] According to Marilyn Butler, *Maria Edgeworth* (Oxford, 1972), p. 227, she stayed with the Hollands in 1813.

anonymous author, she wrote to her old friend Miss Holland, not because she knew of her relationship to the author, but merely to express her critical approbation of a new work which she judged would satisfy her fastidious taste. A niece of Miss Holland's, visiting the old lady at Church House in 1846, found her re-reading the letters from Miss Edgeworth, of which there were 'drawers full' in the house, and enjoying anew their singular charm.[15] No pity need be wasted on young Elizabeth Stevenson if the model of elegant writing advocated by 'Cousin Mary' was to be sought in the works of Maria Edgeworth, with which Church House was stocked; not all the tasks imposed by that arbiter of taste would be as pleasant. As the letters of Mrs. Gaskell attest, 'Cousin Mary', who lived to the age of eighty-four, long outliving her famous kinswoman, remained an object of somewhat anxious veneration to the end.

Luckily for Elizabeth Stevenson there were cousins of the second generation of her own age to enliven the holidays, when the children of Swinton Holland—five boys and three girls—and of Samuel Holland from Wales returned to the family 'grass roots' at Knutsford and Sandlebridge. With those 'dear cousins', as she later wrote, were associated 'some of the happiest recollections of my childhood'.[16]

Knutsford was not only a country town, but a town so invaded by the country that it was barely begun before it ended. As Elizabeth later described it in *Wives and Daughters*, 'the little straggling town faded away into country on one side, close to the entrance-lodge of a great park' (p. 2). This was the already mentioned Tatton Park, whose 1,000 acres stretched away from the very top of King Street into miles of forest. Tatton Park with its orangery and twin meres was not open to the public in those days and was strictly 'preserved' ground. More accessible, however, were the ruined house and grounds of Old Tabley Hall, on the other side of Knutsford, on the road to Sandlebridge, where the glades were open to all and the lake was the scene of many a happy outing organized by the young Hollands. How vivid were the memories of the summer days spent there with her cousins can be judged by Elizabeth's account of them to Mary Howitt, long afterwards:

Near the little, clean, kindly country town, where . . . I was brought up there was an old house with a moat within a park called Old Tabley, formerly the dwelling-place of Sir Peter Leycester, the historian of Cheshire . . . Here on summer mornings did we often come, a merry young party, on donkey, pony, or even in a cart with sacks swung across—each with our favourite book, some with sketch-books, and one or two baskets filled with eatables. Here we rambled,

---

[15] A. W. Ward, Introduction to *Cranford*, p. xxi.   [16] *GL* 83, Nov. 1850.

lounged and meditated: some stretched on the grass in indolent repose, half reading, half musing with a posy of musk-roses from the old-fashioned trim garden behind the house, lulled by the ripple of the waters against the grassy lawn; some in the old crazy boats, that would do nothing but float on the glassy water, singing, for one or two were of a most musical family and warbled like birds: 'Through the greenwood, through the greenwood', or 'A boat, a boat unto the ferry', or some such old catch or glee. And when the meal was spread beneath a beech tree of no ordinary size (did you ever notice the peculiar turf under beech shade?) one of us would mount up a ladder to the belfry of the old chapel and toll the bell to call the wanderers home. Then if it rained, what merry-making in the old hall. It was galleried, with oak settles and old armour hung up, and a painted window from ceiling to floor. The strange sound our voices had in that unfrequented stone hall! The last time I was there during the fall of rain from one of those heavy clouds which add to a summer day's beauty, when every drop of rain is sun-tinged and falls merrily amongst the leaves, one or two of Shakespeare's ballads, 'Blow, blow thou winter wind', and 'Hark, hark the lark at Heaven's gate sings', etc. were sung by the musical sisters in the gallery above, and by two other musical sisters (Mary and Ellen Needham from Lenton near Nottingham) standing in the hall below. . . .[17]

Such pictures of freedom, summer magic, and companionship explain much in the character and emotional make-up of the future Mrs. Gaskell. Her childhood was enriching to a girl of her poetic temperament, responsive as she was to an exceptional degree to natural beauty—even to the quality of turf under trees.

What regular education she had before going to boarding school at the age of twelve followed the set curriculum of a past generation. The textbooks were unaltered since the time the Miss Hollands learnt their lessons: Goldsmith's *History of England*, Rollin's *Ancient History*, Lindley Murray's *Grammar*, Mrs. Chapone's *Letters on the Improvement of the Mind*, 'plenty of sewing and stitching'—and two French lessons a week. 'Those happy lessons!' she exclaimed in retrospect, recalling the circumstances of her exceptional good fortune in having a real Frenchman to teach her, a noble émigré at that, a M. Rogier, the prototype of the Monsieur de Chalabre of her autobiographical tale, 'My French Master'.[18]

M. Rogier,[19] like others of his countrymen who had sought asylum in England during the Terror and found himself faced with the immediate

[17] *GL* 8, May 1838.
[18] See 'My French Master', in vol. 2 of the Knutsford edition, pp. 507–8; also *My Lady Ludlow*, p. 27.
[19] For more details respecting M. Rogier see H. Green, *Knutsford, its Traditions and History* (London, 1859), pp. 134 ff.

necessity of earning a living, did so in the manner most natural to himself—and the least demanding of qualifications he did not possess—by teaching the French language and giving dancing lessons to the youthful élite of Knutsford and its immediate vicinity. The dancing lessons were, indeed, so eagerly sought after and so well attended as to warrant the hire of the splendid Assembly Rooms in the town's leading hostelry—the historic Royal George at the centre of King Street.

At a time when Knutsford lay on the main road south, and the passage of coaches brought prosperity to the town, and to the Royal George in particular, the elegance of the Assembly Rooms was a matter not only of local but of county pride. They were indeed, and still are today, beautiful in design, proportion, and lighting, with their high lozenged ceiling, Adam fireplaces, crystal candelabra, heavy crimson curtains, and the minute stage with room for two or three musicians, for an exhibition of 'Tableaux Vivants' (much in vogue at the time) or, as the author of *Cranford* tells us, for the performance of a conjurer. Next to the Assembly Rooms was a room for the chaperons and whist-players, a rotunda in shape and decorated in an equally elegant though somewhat more sober style, as befitted the graver character of those frequenting it.

Admitted on sufferance and a substantial fee twice a week, M. Rogier's classes were far from fulfilling the main *raison d'être* of the Knutsford Assembly Rooms, which was to serve as a setting for the county balls. How exclusive these were in Elizabeth's youth can be judged from the following:

Into those choice and mysterious precincts no town's person was ever allowed to enter; no professional man might set his foot therein; no infantry officer saw the interior of that ball or that card room. The old original subscribers would fain have had a man prove his sixteen quarterings before he might make his bow to the queen of the night; but the old original founders of the . . . assemblies were dropping off; minuets had vanished with them, country dances had died away, quadrilles were in high vogue—nay, one or two of the high magnates . . . were trying to introduce waltzing (as they had seen it in London, where it had come in with the visit of the Allied sovereigns), when . . . made his *début* on these boards. He had been at many splendid assemblies abroad; but still the little old ball-room attached to the George Inn in his native town was to him a place grander and more awful than the most magnificent saloons he had seen in Paris or Rome.[20]

Along with the dancing lessons were the twice-weekly lessons in French language and literature, so early assimilated by Elizabeth as to

[20] 'A Dark Night's Work', Knutsford edn., vol. 7, pp. 406–7.

form her taste for life. The lessons, if her account of them in 'My French Master' may be taken as biographically correct, were held at Heathside under the most agreeable circumstances:

... our life was passed as much out of doors as in-doors, both winter and summer — we seemed to have our French lessons more frequently in the garden than in the house; for there was a sort of arbour on the lawn near the drawing-room window, to which we always found it easy to carry a table and chairs, and all the rest of the lesson paraphernalia . . .[21]

The reflection that this scene casts on the good sense and liberal-mindedness of Mrs. Lumb explains something of her niece's love for her and total devotion to her memory. Nursing her in her last illness years later, and hearing 'her faint broken voice . . . thanking us for our kindness', Mrs. Gaskell commented: 'as if *we* could ever repay her thousand kind thoughts and deeds to us.'[22] She remembered her for her 'gentle loving voice and deep tender interest in those around her', qualities that sufficiently explain not only her gratitude towards such an aunt, but the development of those comparable qualities in herself— sympathy and selflessness—that resulted in great part from the upbringing she received.

[21] 'My French Master', p. 510.   [22] *GL* 5, 18 Mar. 1837.

CHAPTER III

THE FORMAL EDUCATION OF A WRITER[1]

THE year 1822, already made momentous for Elizabeth by the departure of her brother and her own first visit to London, was marked by yet further changes in her life. In August she was sent to the Miss Byerleys' boarding school in Warwickshire, which at that time was at Barford, 3 miles on the Stratford side of Warwick. As these ladies were related to Dr. Thomson, the decision to send Elizabeth there presumably came from her parents in London rather than from her aunts in Knutsford. The choice of the Miss Byerleys' school would, however, have been acceptable to the Hollands and the Stevensons alike, because of the Wedgwood connection that linked all three families. (Dr. Peter's first wife, Mary Willet, was a niece of Josiah Wedgwood's, as was Swinton Holland's first wife, who was her sister.)

The Miss Byerleys' father, Thomas Byerley, was a nephew of the first Josiah Wedgwood, who had adopted him and taken him into his firm, first as a traveller, then as manager of the London showrooms, and finally as manager of the works at Etruria. The Miss Byerleys' youth had, therefore, been informative and interesting, bringing them into contact with the artists and designers working for the firm, and with the aristocratic clientele that frequented their father's showrooms. The whole family were distinguished by their good manners. They lived over the showrooms in York Street, St. James's, and the girls grew up not only in a cultivated ambience but with a day-to-day knowledge of the conduct of business. This was an asset not possessed by many young women. In their circle to be in trade was no stigma, for their father's trade was regarded as in the same category as the fine arts. Josiah Wedgwood was received every year by Queen Charlotte to present to her the firm's latest collection of designs, and invariably came away from the palace with an order.

There were eight Miss Byerleys, born over an interval of fifteen years,

[1] The data concerning the Miss Byerleys contained in this chapter have been derived for the most part from Phyllis Hicks's *A Quest of Ladies* (Birmingham, 1949).

the eldest in 1786 and the youngest in 1801—of whom six became active in the conduct of the school. To their father's credit he gave them the best education the times afforded to girls, paying visiting masters for them and sending the most intelligent ones to boarding school. He had decided early on to set them up in a school of their own, and the plan was made possible by the generosity of Josiah Wedgwood, who left them £200 apiece.

By 1809 the three eldest Miss Byerleys, Frances, Maria, and Elizabeth, were of an age—twenty-three, twenty-two, and twenty respectively—to set up school and inherit their legacies. By then their father was resident at Etruria, and a Midlands situation for the school was found at Warwick. There the Wedgwoods had a substantial business connection with the Parkes family, Unitarians like themselves, of considerable influence in the town, and through their recommendation pupils were soon enlisted. A house was taken for the school in the High Street with enough rooms to board sixteen pupils, and the Miss Byerleys published their Prospectus in the Warwickshire press—*The Coventry Mercury*, *Aris's Birmingham Gazette*, *The Warwick Advertiser*—in the week of 15 January 1810. It read:

MISS BYERLEYS

BEG leave respectfully to acquaint their
Friends and Public, that their School
for YOUNG LADIES, in WARWICK, will be opened on
the 29th inst.

The charges for Board, exclusive of Washing, and for Instruction in English Reading, Spelling, Grammar and Composition, in Geography, and the Use of the Globes, and in Ancient and Modern History, are, Thirty Guineas per Annum, and Three Guineas for Entrance.

The Terms for Instruction in the French Language, Music, Drawing, Dancing, and Writing and Arithmetic, and for Washing, are inserted in a printed Paper, which will be delivered to any Persons who will do Miss BYERLEYS the Honour to ask for it.

To Day-Scholars the annual Charges for the general course of Instruction, will be Eight Guineas, but they are not required to pay any Entrance, and they will be instructed in French, Drawing, Music, Dancing, Writing and Arithmetic, upon the same Terms which are proposed for Boarders.[2]

One great advantage the Miss Byerleys had over many of their contemporaries in the field was that they could bring to the conduct of their venture a genuine business sense and a practical insight into the needs

[2] *A Quest of Ladies*, p. 14.

of young women of moderate means. Well educated themselves, they had more to offer their pupils than the 'accomplishments' in vogue at the time. They had travelled abroad with their father, and were proficient linguists, capable of teaching Latin, French, and Italian, even without the aid of visiting masters. As the younger Miss Byerleys, Katherine, Jane-Margaret, and Anne, in turn came of age, inherited their legacies, and joined their sisters, the curriculum of the establishment continued to expand.

The school was planned on liberal lines and there was nothing mean even in its appointments. The very china in daily use was a gift from Josiah Wedgwood; French was taught by an émigré Frenchman (to Elizabeth's continuing good fortune), dancing was in the care of another Frenchman, who undertook to teach Quadrilles in three lessons. Even before the Miss Byerleys had moved into their first quarters at Warwick, their cousin Josiah II had generously supplied the Broadwood grand piano that was a *sine qua non* in such educational establishments. Accomplishment with one instrument—piano, harp, guitar—was considered an essential requisite for any educated young woman at the time. When published music was so expensive, manuscript music albums in which to copy the popular music of the day were essential, and Elizabeth Stevenson had her music albums like the other girls. Two of them have been preserved.

Under the stimulus of Katherine Byerley, later Mrs. Todd Thomson, who became a writer of considerable success under the pen-name Grace Wharton, the teaching of English was thorough and the study of literature a priority. Her own initiation into letters was said to have been given her when, as a child, visiting her father at Etruria, she had been read to by Coleridge himself, an imperishable memory for anyone so favoured. Such an influence could not be lost upon the young Elizabeth Stevenson, whose earliest compositions, it is said, received much encouragement from her teacher.

The Miss Byerleys were dedicated teachers, Frances, Katherine, and Anne (who married a rich man called Samuel Coltman) continuing to serve the school even after marriage. Whether living in London like Mrs. Thomson, or in Warwick like Mrs. Parkes, or in Surrey like Mrs. Coltman, they remained in touch with the establishment, inviting the girls during the holidays, even taking them abroad with them, caring for those who had been ill by affording them a pleasant convalescence, and keeping the school up to date by reporting changes in fashion—both in teaching and dress—and new trends in accomplishments. The Miss Byerleys themselves made a point during the annual holiday of taking lessons in subjects in which they felt they were growing stale. They were, patently, born teachers, bringing good sense to bear on their work, and above all a sense of practicality and thoroughness. Their method was successful and the number of students increased.

After seven years at Warwick they could afford to take into account the increasing inconveniences of their situation there: some parents had taken exception to the location of the school in the High Street, a noisy thoroughfare opposite a public house, and without a garden; and in 1817 they moved to Barford, to 'a more elegant and convenient house', with stabling and a good garden that permitted the pupils more air and exercise.

Elizabeth Stevenson joined the school while it was at Barford, though successive biographers have continued to associate her with it only after its move to Stratford-upon-Avon in 1824. 'I was five years at Miss Byerley's,' she told her own eldest daughter years later when she contrasted Marianne's gay schooldays with her own, 'and never drank tea out of the house *once* let alone going to plays . . .'[3] To Walter Savage Landor, also, she mentioned having been five years at school in Warwickshire.[4] As she left school in 1827, this establishes her arrival at the Miss Byerleys in 1822.

She was extremely lucky in her surroundings. Barford House was charmingly situated in large gardens at the entry to the little town on the Wellesbourne road, facing parklands and meadows stretching to the horizon, just the type of rural scene in which she delighted. The house was built in a graceful Palladian style, with pedimented portico, flat roof crowned by a cupola, and a frontage of six windows, the ground floor ones reaching to the ground and interspersed with flat Corinthian columns. It was a gentleman's house, with a circular drive, coach-house, and extensive gardens behind, where any girl with a love of nature could learn to differentiate the names of British trees, of which a splendid variety abounded, under the most agreeable circumstances.

The school had its own pews at Barford Church, the little low-towered Norman church situated within easy walking distance from the school, where the Miss Byerleys are commemorated by two mural tablets to the memory of their young—and unsatisfactory—brother Francis (who died on the passage home from the West Indies in 1818) and of their youngest sister Charlotte who died at the school in 1817. It was at

---

[3] *GL* 97+ (p. 837), May 1851.
[4] *GL* 197, May 1854.

Barford Church that the marriage of Katherine Byerley and Dr. Thomson took place. Elizabeth Stevenson's memories of Barford Church remained so vivid that she could write of it years afterwards with detail in her story 'Lois the Witch'; '. . . there rose the little village church of Barford (not three miles from Warwick—you may see it yet), . . . the old low grey church could hardly come before her vision without her seeing the old parsonage too . . .'[5] For the school's walks there were the banks of the Avon, spanned by a sturdy stone bridge at the town's end, and flanked by pleasant meadows.

Potential story-teller that Elizabeth Stevenson was, what interested her in her school surroundings were the old and historic houses with which human dramas had been connected. Recalling some of these in after years to Mary Howitt, she said: 'As a schoolgirl I could not see much, but I heard of many places that I longed to know more about.' Mentioning Compton Wynyates, Charlecote Park, Shottery, she added: 'I am giving but vague directions, but I am unwilling to leave even in thought the haunts of such happy days as my schooldays were.'[6]

The removal from Barford to Stratford-upon-Avon took place on 7 May 1824, and was dictated once again by the need for larger premises, the school continuing to expand and prosper. It was the Miss Byerleys' good fortune that put a notable house on to the market at the very time they were looking for new premises. The house called Avonbank, from its situation on the banks of the river just by the church, was a Tudor building that had originally belonged to Shakespeare's cousin Thomas Greene, the Town Clerk of Stratford. He had bought it in 1604, but only entered into possession of it in 1611 when his dramatist cousin retired to Stratford and needed to occupy his own house, New Place, loaned to Greene up to then. To an educative establishment, with cultural pretensions, the possession of a historic house with such associations had considerable advantages. The house was, moreover, large, with twenty-three bedrooms, capable at one time of lodging sixty pupils, and delightfully situated on the lawns that ran down to the river, next door to Holy Trinity Church.

Though the Miss Byerleys were brought up Dissenters, Miss Maria—the Principal—made a point of renting pews in the established churches of the various parishes where her schools were situated, and at Stratford the girls attended Shakespeare's church and sat within sight of the chancel and his monument. When the young Elizabeth Stevenson's

[5] 'Lois the Witch', Knutsford edn., vol. 7, p. 111.
[6] GL 12, Aug. 1838.

eye strayed away from the preacher, as no doubt it did, to rest on the splendid Clopton Chapel in the north aisle, what she stored away in her memory, to be used years later, were not the records of Sir Hugh Clopton's civic virtues and benefactions to his town, but the romantic and truly Shakespearian drama of Charlotte Clopton who died in one of the plague years, allegedly the very year the poet was born, and was hurriedly buried in the vaults of Clopton Chapel. According to Elizabeth's informant, when the contagion struck down yet another member of the Clopton family and his corpse was carried down to be laid by hers, it was found that, Juliet-like, she had not died but had revived in her grave. She was found leaning against the wall in her grave-clothes, dead a second time, 'but not before, in the agonies of despair and hunger, she had bitten a piece from her white round shoulder', as Elizabeth subsequently related with Gothic relish.[7]

Her Stratford schooldays played their part in making a writer of her, since it was her article on 'Old Clopton Hall', sent to William Howitt in 1838 and published by him in his collection of *Visits to Remarkable Places* (1840), that brought her in touch with professional writers and gave her the first experience of appearing in print. The paper on Clopton may have been written while she was still at school; it was certainly the record of an authentic experience, since the opportunity to visit the Hall came through the invitation of a fellow pupil, whose home it then was, as Elizabeth later explained to William Howitt:

I was at school in the neighbourhood and one of my school-fellows was the daughter of Mr. W[yatt] who then lived at Clopton. Mrs. Wyatt asked a party of the girls to go and spend a long afternoon, and we set off one beautiful autumn day, full of delight and wonder respecting the place we were going to see.

Met in the hall by their hostess, the girls were given leave to 'ramble where they liked in or out of the house', so long as they took care 'to be in the recessed parlour by tea-time'. Elizabeth describes her adventure in wandering up 'the wide shelving oak staircase' and discovering a curiously carved old oak chest, filled with 'BONES'—whether human or animal she did not stay to distinguish in her panic; fleeing headlong down the oak staircase 'in partly feigned and partly real terror',[8] she regained the safety of the parlour.

Certainly a girl of Elizabeth Stevenson's developing tastes and romantic nature could not have been more fortunate in her school, where

---

[7] 'Clopton Hall' (in Howitt's *Visits to Remarkable Places*, London, Longman and Co., 1840).   [8] Ibid.

full scope was allowed to her intellect in surroundings of great natural beauty. She would all her life be peculiarly sensitive to her surroundings, depressed or elated according to whether they were ugly or beautiful, even to the extent that her health was sometimes affected. Returning to Shottery years later, she responded all over again to the old enchantment, describing the cottage where she was staying as

> . . . a very pretty, really old fashioned cottage . . . where one's head was literally in danger of being bumped by the low doors, and where all the windows were casements . . . where the scents through the open hall door were all of sweet briar and lilac and lilies of the valley: where we slept with our windows open to hear the nightingales' jug-jug, and where the very shadows in the drawing room had a green tinge from the leafy trees which over hung the windows.[9]

The Miss Byerleys made Elizabeth happy at a time in her youth when her family circumstances were far from happy, and gave her stimulating lessons and access to great literature; even more, they offered her a balanced education at a time when teaching was a one-sided affair for girls, and encouraged instead of crushed her imagination. She remained on affectionate terms with at least one Miss Byerley—Jane-Margaret—after leaving school, whom she spoke of as 'dear Miss Jane' and from whom she heard about the break-up of the Ruskin marriage—Mrs. Ruskin being a former pupil of the school, Effie Grey.[10] She also kept in touch with the Thomsons—Dr. Todd and his wife, the former Katherine Byerley—and their daughter Kate, who lived in London, and remained eager for news of them.[11] But perhaps the quality that she owed most to the teaching of Avonbank was her total absence of false gentility; an affectation all too common among young women of the time, and the one which she herself pilloried most memorably in the character of Mrs. Gibson in *Wives and Daughters*.

Elizabeth left school in the summer before her seventeenth birthday in June 1827, and almost immediately was caught up in an experience which was also of considerable educational value to her—a six-week holiday in Wales in the company of her Holland relatives. The discovery of that beautiful and unspoilt region had a lasting effect on her development, both as a person and as a writer, and it was to figure frequently in her books. Wales lay most conveniently to hand for the residents of her county when in need of change, rest, recuperation after illness, or retirement, and it was probably the purchase of the house near Portmadoc by her uncle Samuel Holland, the Liverpool quarry-owner, that led to

---

[9] *GL* 48, 29 May 1849.   [10] *GL* 20, 195.   [11] *GL* 3, Dec. 1833.

the first visit of the Knutsford Hollands. Elizabeth Stevenson went in
the company 'of 17 aunts and cousins and such like' in July 1827. Hearing
of the projected trip her father wrote to her (the only letter of his to be
preserved) on 2 July, urging her as her brother had before to keep
a diary of what she saw and remembered. By that time, at the end of her
five years at school, he knew his daughter more intimately than formerly,
and had, it is reported, taken a hand at coaching her himself in her
holidays.[12] From certain references in Elizabeth's later novels it is likely
that she sometimes shared the lessons of her 'little miss of a ½ sister', as
Margaret Hale did with her cousin in *North and South*, in the London
house that was at times her adoptive home. Mr. Stevenson was reputed
by then to have become proud of his elder daughter.[13]

Having made a considerable fortune, Samuel Holland II had acquired
a delightful house overlooking Portmadoc estuary—'Plas Penrhyn',
referred to throughout Mrs. Gaskell's correspondence by its initials only
as 'P.P.'—and proved himself to be a most genial host. Elizabeth became
a frequent and welcome visitor, as were her future girl friends with whom
'Uncle Sam' carried on 'regular flirtations'.[14] The link between uncle
and niece was further strengthened when, in due course, Elizabeth's
sister-in-law, Elizabeth Gaskell, married 'uncle Sam's' son, Charles
Holland, in December 1838. 'Uncle Sam's' family consisted of his wife,
Katharine, two sons, and three daughters, all older than Elizabeth, but
good friends throughout her life.

According to Elizabeth's reminiscences of that first trip to Wales the
party stayed a month at Aber, 5 miles from Bangor, from where they
moved up and down the coast, and across to Anglesey, and climbed in
Snowdonia. 'It is perhaps as well', she wrote later, 'that you should come
down gradually from mountains; not at once from Snowdonia to flat
Lancashire; I remember when I first came from spending a very happy
fortnight at Plâs Brereton (nr Caernarvon you know) to Liverpool
I used to get on a sort of knoll from which I could see the Welsh hills,
and think of the places beyond them again.'[15] She recalled Puffin Island
and Criccieth—'don't you think Criccaeth a wild pretty little fishing-
town?'—and observed that 'the pleasure of sketching is the reminding
you of the time you did it'.[16]

Her memory of Anglesey was not merely scenic but dramatic; she
took so keen an interest in an old naval character, Captain Barton by

[12] Mrs. E. H. Chadwick, *Mrs. Gaskell: Homes, Haunts, and Stories* (London, 1910),
p. 138.   [13] See below, p. 38, the letter of Mrs. Stevenson, 15 June 1829.
[14] *GL* 9, 17 July 1838.   [15] *GL* 9, 1838.   [16] Ibid.

name, that she wrote a story about him, based on fact. In due course she sent the tale to her brother whose comment has survived. Writing to her from Chelsea on 30 July 1828, on his last leave home, he said:

You have really made out a very pretty story of Captain Barton—it would almost make the foundation of a novel—it was indeed a narrow escape of Kitty's [probably Uncle Sam's daughter Kate] and must have given her a tremendous fright, though I have heard and read many stories of them, I never saw a quicksand and hardly believed them to be so dangerous as was generally spoken of . . .[17]

The danger of quicksands, that so early impressed Elizabeth through the narrow escape of her cousin Kate Holland,[18] served her later as subject for at least one dramatic story, 'The Sexton's Hero' (1847). The memory of Captain Barton remained vivid still in 1838 when she inquired after him from her sister-in-law, just returned from a visit to Beaumaris, and his name was to serve in another context when she used it for the protagonist of her first novel, *Mary Barton*. She remembered also visiting the ruined monastery on Puffin Island on which there was a telegraph station, and being much interested in the man in charge, 'who had fought in the *Victory* with Nelson', as she told her future sister-in-law. And she went on to remember the Puffins too, 'queer uncanny animals', and ended her nostalgic reminiscences by saying 'I *long* to be in those wild places again, with the fresh sea breeze round me, so thoroughly exhilarating'.[19]

The impact of Wales added another dimension to her love of nature. Brought up in the country as she was, the natural scenery around Knutsford had been a gentle delight; but the grandeur and mystery of the Welsh mountains and sea brought an extension of spiritual experience. Without ever attaining the same kind of communion with nature as Wordsworth or Emily Brontë, she developed a more familiar sort of intimacy, pining for it when parted from it and delighting in every reunion. She described the experience, with the *naïveté* appropriate not only to her heroine Ruth alone with her lover in the Alps, but also to her own youthful self on that first discovery of untamed nature in Wales, as

opening a new sense; vast ideas of beauty and grandeur filled her mind at the sight of the mountains, now first beheld in full majesty. She was almost overpowered by the vague and solemn delight; but by-and-by her love for them equalled her awe, and in the night-time she would softly rise, and steal to the

---

[17] Letter in the possession of J. G. Sharps.
[18] A further incident, involving the same cousin and the quicksands in Portmadoc estuary, is referred to in *GL* 7.   [19] *GL* 9, July 1838.

window to see the white moonlight, which gave a new aspect to the everlasting hills that girdle the mountain village . . . Ruth was up betimes, and out and away, brushing the dewdrops from the short crisp grass; the lark sung high above her head, and she knew not if she moved or stood still, for the grandeur of this beautiful earth absorbed all idea of separate and individual existence.[20]

[20] *Ruth*, ch. 5, pp. 64-5.

CHAPTER IV

THE LOST BROTHER AND FATHER

IN several of Elizabeth Gaskell's novels and short stories occurs the subject of a man lost at sea—generally a young man. He is lost without trace, witness, or explanation. His safe return after the passage of years is made the consoling—and unconvincing—solution of such happy plots as *Cranford*. Even where he is not reported lost, only absent at sea, like Will Wilson in *Mary Barton* and Frederick Hale in *North and South*, his return is made the occasion for inordinate rejoicing by his family. The return of Charlie Kinraid, reported drowned, in *Sylvia's Lovers* is used to even more dramatic effect, as the instrument of Fate in destroying the false happiness of his rival. The subject was patently one very close to Mrs. Gaskell's heart, the effect of a haunting recurrent dream following a traumatic experience. The experience, in her case, was real enough, and marked her for life. In 1828-9—the date cannot for obvious reasons be verified—her brother John Stevenson was lost on a voyage to India and never heard of again.

He left few traces of his short life. He was born on 27 November 1798, the eldest son of his parents, during the time they lived in East Lothian, but not even the entry of his birth in the parish register of Corstorphine where they lived has been preserved.[1] Where he was educated, except under his father's tuition, is not known. The first documentary evidence of his manhood relates to his twenty-first year when he received the Freedom of Berwick, an honour accessible to all men born natives of the town, or the sons of natives, as was John Stevenson. In his certificate of admission he is cited as a 'marriner in the service of the East India Company', but as the records of the Company show, he was not even a regular employee. On 1 March he entered into a covenant with them by which they licensed him to go to India 'as a free mariner', sailing in private vessels trading between England and India, on condition he obeyed the Company's regulations. His father put up a bond of £500 for

[1] Letter from Marianne, later Mrs. Thurston Holland, to C. K. Shorter, 1914. Shorter Collection, Brotherton Library, Leeds.

his good behaviour. His letters show that he made several voyages, and according to the *Bengal Directory* for 1824 he was then residing in Calcutta.[2]

He sailed on his maiden voyage to India in 1822 and subsequently came and went with some regularity (the voyage varied between eighteen months and two years) until his final departure. His few letters home to his sister were dated, as has been seen, 1825, 1827, and 1828. The last letters, dated from Beaufort Row on 30 July and 16 August 1828, express his disappointment at not getting up to Knutsford to see her before he sailed, and, striking a more melancholy note, his dissatisfaction with his situation, and desire to leave the service. He thought of settling for good in India. There is no evidence whatever about the circumstances of his loss. Whether this was at sea or after he landed and penetrated into the interior of the country, in search of that situation after which he half hankered, was never established. When asked by Clement Shorter in 1914, the daughters of Mrs. Gaskell could tell him nothing definite. According to them, her memory of him was very faint. All the information that Marianne, Mrs. Gaskell's eldest daughter, could give him was that 'when I was ten years old my mother told me that she could only just remember her brother—that he went to sea—I think also she said when she was quite a young girl, that she remembered coming up on a visit to her father from Knutsford to wish her brother good-bye. I think she must have been about twelve years old when she paid that visit.'[3]

The evidence of Mrs. Gaskell's novels and short stories would suggest that, far from forgetting her brother, his personality was so strongly imprinted on her memory as to serve as prototype for all the nautical characters she introduced. His very language, sea-slang as it obviously was, brings life and sparkle to such characters as Will Wilson in *Mary Barton*, Frederick Hale in *North and South*, Charlie Kinraid in *Sylvia's Lovers*.

Much as the future Mrs. Gaskell disliked, and even repudiated, suggestions of original sources for her tales and prototypes for her fictional characters, it is impossible to read those passages in her works describing the sea and seamen without associating them with her early experience of her brother; there is in them a too personal note of things seen and emotions felt to dissociate them from memory. Such passages occur particularly in *North and South*, where the relationship between sister and brother, separated for years and reunited after the girl has

[2] India Office Library, India Office Ledgers, ST 1216.
[3] Letter in Brotherton Library, Leeds.

passed childhood, echo the very circumstances of Elizabeth and John Stevenson up to her eighteenth year.

. . . even in her stay-at-home life, his wild career, with which she was but imperfectly acquainted, must have almost substituted another Frederick for the tall stripling in his middy's uniform, whom she remembered looking up to with such admiring awe. But in their absence they had grown nearer to each other in age, as well as in many other things.[4]

. . . all their intercourse was peculiarly charming to her from the very first . . . He understood his father and mother—their characters and their weaknesses, and went along with a careless freedom, which was yet most delicately careful not to hurt or wound any of their feelings. He seemed to know instinctively when a little of the natural brilliance of his manner and conversation would jar. . . .[5]

Even the physical traits of the fictional Frederick read like the description of a face remembered:

He had delicate features, redeemed from effeminacy by the swarthiness of his complexion, and his quick intensity of expression. His eyes were generally merry-looking, but at times they and his mouth so suddenly changed, and gave her an idea of latent passion, that it almost made her afraid.[6]

Even the recollection of her brother's letters, received at long intervals and from great distances, seems to infuse her description of Frederick's letters in the novel: 'There were the yellow, sea-stained letters, with the peculiar fragrance which ocean letters have.'[7]

Her interest in and familiarity with young nautical types present in the descriptions of Will Wilson in *Mary Barton*, and Brother Peter when young in *Cranford*, convey an over-all picture of a distinct personality, whose characteristics are constant: dashing, reckless, open-hearted, kind. 'Thinking has, many a time, made me sad, darling,' says Frederick in *North and South*; 'but doing never did in all my life . . . My precept is, "Do something . . . do good if you can; but at any rate, do something." '[8] There is an authentic ring in Frederick's reply to Margaret's question whether he can sail as well from London as from Liverpool: 'To be sure, little goose. Wherever I feel water heaving under a plank, there I feel at home. I'll pick up some small craft or other to take me off, never fear.'[9] The pet name 'little goose' is used again by Dr. Gibson addressing Molly in *Wives and Daughters*, and sounds like a family recollection. His rough-and-ready philosophy of good and evil also sounds like an authentic echo: 'Blot your misdeeds out . . . by a good deed, as soon as you can;

[4] *North and South*, p. 294.   [5] Ibid., p. 293.   [6] Ibid.
[7] Ibid., p. 124.   [8] Ibid., pp. 295-6.   [9] Ibid., p. 309.

just as we did a correct sum at school on the slate, where an incorrect one was only half rubbed out. It was better than wetting our sponge with our tears.'[10]

The news of her brother's loss must have reached the family some time at the end of 1828 or early in 1829, for it brought Elizabeth to London to give comfort to her father, and she had already been there some time when he suffered the fatal stroke from which he died in March 1829. This appears from the letter Mrs. Stevenson wrote to Mrs. Lumb after her husband's death.[11]

Her last contacts with her father were, therefore, darkened by the tragedy of her brother's loss. They may also have been clouded by her father's worsening financial position, of which the full implications could not be hidden from her. Despite his supplementary earnings from contributions to the literary magazines, Mr. Stevenson's salary at the Treasury proved insufficient for the calls upon it. In a letter to *Blackwood's* written many years later, his daughter recalled how, when hard-pressed to pay his second son's school fees, he had turned for help to them. 'My father', Elizabeth wrote in March 1859, 'was one of the earliest contributors to Blackwood's Magazine; and some Mr. Blackwood was, for auld acquaintance sake, extremely kind in assisting in the education of a half-brother of mine, since dead.'[12] In June 1827 his financial position was so bad as to oblige him—with his wife's consent—to sell the stocks constituting her dowry, a sum of £800. By the terms of the will drawn up immediately after this transaction he provided that this sum should be refunded to her, and if his estate could not meet it, he instructed his executor (his brother-in-law, Dr. Thomson) to sell his furniture and books to make up the deficiency. Only after the restitution to the widow of the borrowed sum was any provision to be made for his son John and daughter Elizabeth Cleghorn; and they would share equally with the widow and her children in whatever remained of the estate.

It was Elizabeth's 'beautiful conduct'[13] on this occasion that won her the commendations of her stepmother after Mr. Stevenson's death. Her acquiescence in the plan would necessarily leave her, after the break-up of the home, the sale of the furniture and the books (valuable as these may have been), with nothing—or at best with a negligible sum.

Mr. Stevenson's will is an altogether revealing document. While his early career sufficiently showed how little self-seeking he was in the

---

[10] *North and South*, p. 296.   [11] Shorter Collection, Brotherton Library, Leeds.
[12] *GL* 415, 5 Mar. 1859.
[13] Letter of Mrs. Stevenson to Mrs. Lumb, Shorter Collection, Brotherton Library, Leeds.

pursuit of a profession, it needs the evidence of the will to prove quite how unbusinesslike he was even to the end of his life. He left the will undated and unsigned and without witnesses, thus causing his widow almost insuperable difficulties to prove it. In appointing his brother-in-law his executor, he made the further mistake of calling him 'Alexander', and caused a confusion of identities which had to be clarified on oath before a magistrate. Only after witnesses had sworn to the bona fides of the will, by swearing to the handwriting being Mr. Stevenson's, and the identity of the executor was established, could probate be granted to the widow, on 15 June 1829.[14]

According to his official obituary[15] Mr. Stevenson suffered a first stroke on Friday, 20 March 1829, 'as he sat at tea with his family', suddenly losing his sight and becoming paralysed down his right side. He was carried to bed, but suffered a second stroke and died on Sunday, 22 March. Neither in the official obituary nor in the Treasury memoir of him was any mention made of his having at any time been a Unitarian, and his funeral took place in the Parish Church of Chelsea (at that time the new Parish Church of St. Luke's) on 27 March, and he was buried beside his first wife in the King's Road cemetery.

That Mr. Stevenson was a highly endowed, interesting, much-respected man there can be no doubt, and the terms in which his official obituary was couched show him to have been much appreciated by his colleagues and acquaintances. He was, according to this document, especially noted 'for being kind and benevolent, a zealous and active friend. Showing no pride of authorship, but disinterested, retired and modest in his habits, loving knowledge for its own sake'—a man, in short, so much after his daughter's heart that it is surprising that she did not love him more. With everything to unite them in natural disposition and intellectual tastes, the reason for the life-long coolness that persisted between them—if coolness it was that caused their long separation—is unlikely to have lain exclusively with either the father or the daughter. Some of the blame must surely be laid at Mrs. Stevenson's door.

That daily contacts with such a man would be highly stimulating to a girl of Elizabeth's developing tastes is evident, but her need at that age for affection was overwhelmingly greater than any pleasure she could derive from being her father's object of pride. His coaching her in Latin, French, and Italian may have given her keen enjoyment and brought them

---

[14] Copy of the will of William Stevenson, proved in the Prerogative Court of Canterbury, 15 June 1829. Somerset House.

[15] P.R.O., Treasury Minutes, 29/87: Memorial of William Stevenson.

into intellectual contact, but it could not itself bridge the emotional gap created by the habit of years, and her very silence on the subject of her father in later life would suggest that the gap was, indeed, never bridged.

Few authors have written more delightfully about fathers and daughters than the future Mrs. Gaskell: they live by the very naturalness of their presentation. Dr. Gibson and Mollie, Mr. Hale and Margaret, John Barton and Mary—they are memorable for their silences as much as for their words. Yet who would venture to assert that they are the image of the relationship existing between Elizabeth and her own father? The contrary, rather, would appear to be the case; that they represent the wish-fulfilment of a great emotional need. All the greater reason for her sense of desolation at his death, following so shortly on the loss of her brother.

On the very day that Mr. Stevenson's will was proved, his widow wrote to Elizabeth's aunt, Mrs. Lumb. The letter makes plain the rarity of Elizabeth's visits to her father and the equal rarity of his letters to Knutsford.

'Often did he intend writing to you about Elizabeth and frequently he spoke to me about her', wrote Mrs. Stevenson. As if in extenuation, she chose to focus upon the character of Elizabeth herself, as though the explanation for the relationship between the families lay there. 'Indeed both he and I considered her much improved altogether and although he said little I could easily see that he felt proud of his daughter. I do not recall at present that in any one instance he was either hurt or vexed about her.' Why, Mrs. Lumb might well ask herself, should he have been either? In the opinion of a stepmother he would appear to have some right to be so. And at once, as though to obliterate the impression her words made, Mrs. Stevenson added the corollary: 'Her conduct at the time of her Father's and my distress was certainly very beautiful and more like a person much older. Indeed she was a very great comfort to me my own girl being young and consequently not so thoughtful. I shall ever love Elizabeth as my own child.'[16] The words, that bring to mind the language of the fictional 'Mrs. Gibson' towards her stepdaughter, will have been heard before by Elizabeth Stevenson; she had long since taken their measure. How valueless she reckoned them may be judged by Mrs. Stevenson's further comment: 'I . . . trust that nothing will ever break that friendship which I trust is between us at this time, and also the love that she and her brother and sister have for each other.' The twenty-five year interval that Elizabeth allowed to elapse before seeking a renewal of acquaintance with her stepmother and sister supplies the effective answer to Mrs. Stevenson's wish.

[16] Letter in Shorter Collection, Brotherton Library, Leeds.

CHAPTER V

THE CHRYSALIS YEARS

WITH the death of her father, Elizabeth's connection with the household in Beaufort Row ended. Mrs. Stevenson herself moved from there in September. The immediate problem for Elizabeth was not so much where to go (she would always, the Hollands repeatedly told her, find a home at Knutsford and, indeed, she sought it there in every emergency), as what to do now. She was the poorer in every way by her father's death and she was far too spirited a girl not to think of seeking some way of making herself independent. But for the time being her London relatives—her uncle Swinton Holland, the banker, and her cousin Henry Holland, the doctor—stepped in and invited her to go to them to recover from her recent sorrows and to have a taste of London life. The early portraits of her suggest that their task would be both easy and agreeable.

Swinton Holland, who had been a 'Baltic merchant' until the French Revolution disrupted trade, was by that time a senior partner in Baring's Bank, with a house in Park Lane. His children, Edward (the future M.P. for Evesham), Frederick (later a Captain in the army), George, Caroline, and Louisa, were near contemporaries of Elizabeth's, and they remained close to her for the rest of their lives. Her recent bereavements would not incite or even entitle her to such gaieties as dances, the opera, or the theatre, but in her relatives' homes she could attend dinners and meet the inner circle of their acquaintance. At the house in Park Lane she had plenty of opportunity for doing so. To a girl of her keen powers of observation this was an education in itself, and one from which she profited to the full. At no time was the future Mrs. Gaskell at a loss in society, or ever otherwise than at her ease in making contact with strangers. The gift, which derived as much from intense interest in other people as from a lack of self-consciousness, was a precious asset that served her both in life and literature. Her sympathies, like her antipathies, were instant and strong, uncalculated and genuine. At the age of nineteen she was unlikely to judge people with all the ripeness of maturity, but the experience then afforded her gave her insights into codes and

conventions hitherto unknown to her. While she would never set herself
up as a censor of society, she would extract the last ounce of humour
from its follies.

It was said of her cousin Henry Holland, the fashionable physician
living at 25 Lower Brook Street, that he led as full a social life as a professional one. He was twice married and his second marriage, to Saba,
the daughter of Sydney Smith, assured his entry into the Whig society
of Holland House, as his lively memoirs relate. He frequently met Lord
Lauderdale, William Stevenson's erstwhile patron, but does not mention
whether Lauderdale ever met or interested himself in William Stevenson's
orphaned daughter. Like all her relations, Henry Holland was so reticent
or indifferent about his cousin's fame that he excluded all but the most
perfunctory references to her from his memoirs, so one source of evidence
about her début in London is denied us.

Before his years as a medical student in Edinburgh, Henry Holland
had been at school in Newcastle with a friend of the Holland family,
the Revd. William Turner, who combined a career in the Unitarian
ministry with schoolmastering, and the fact that Elizabeth went on from
London to spend the winter of 1829-30 at Newcastle in Mr. Turner's
home suggests an introduction arranged by Henry Holland. Mr. Turner,
who had been twice married, was by then a widower with one daughter,
Anne, living at home, and the arrangement appeared suitable enough
for their bereaved young relative. Mr. Turner was not only a trusted
friend of the Hollands, but related by marriage. His first wife, Mary
Holland, was a cousin of Elizabeth's mother; and his second wife, Jane
Willet, a niece of Josiah Wedgwood's, was a sister to Dr. Peter Holland's
first wife, Anne, and Swinton Holland's wife, Mary. Mr. Turner was,
therefore, the uncle of Elizabeth's cousins, Mary and Lucy Holland
(Dr. Peter's daughters). Mary had at one time lived with her uncle and
aunt in Newcastle. The connection was, therefore, no new one, and
Elizabeth would only be following in her cousins' footsteps if she finished
her education in the Turners' household. That it was incorrectly interpreted as affording her a place as companion or governess was later much
resented by her daughters. Meta Gaskell wrote to Clement Shorter in
1909 that it was said

that after her Father's death my Mother was sent out into the world to earn her
own living, and that she went to Mr. Turner of Newcastle in order to do so. The
fact was that her aunt Mrs. Lumb's house was always a real home to her, and that
she returned to live there like a daughter to her aunt. The relation between my
Mother and her Aunt was really of the closest and tenderest nature. Her stay in

Newcastle on two successive visits was just the ordinary visit of a girl to her connections. Visits in those days were very long when journies were so tedious. *In
each case* she went on to pay visits to friends of her Father's and Mother's in
Edinburgh.[1]

The change from Park Lane to the minister's small house on the outskirts of Newcastle (at 13 Cumberland Row) might not, on the face of it,
have been altogether to the taste of a high-spirited handsome girl with
a good leaven of worldliness in her; but the fact that Elizabeth voluntarily
returned to Mr. Turner's house during two successive winters, and that
she later wrote with love and veneration of the man and his home, suggests
that the household was to her liking and that she found in it the fulfilment
of a genuine need.

Mr. Turner's brand of Christianity was certainly of that social practical
type that appealed both to the compassionate side of her nature and to
her strong sense of justice. It offered her an outlet and a sense of direction,
at a time when these were lacking and she had not yet found her vocation
as a writer. The religion she was to evolve was not mystical or narrowly
dogmatic. It was deeply charitable, and it was in her nature to wish to
feed the hungry, to nurse the sick, and to educate the ignorant.

Neither at her aunt's house at Knutsford, nor at the Miss Byerleys'
school, had she met with standards of social conduct quite like Mr.
Turner's, and the extent to which she adopted them can only be judged
by her later attitudes. While she never obtruded her religion on others,
or, like so many of her contemporaries, used it to tyrannize over children
and domestics, or allowed it to crush the natural gaiety of her own spirits,
it is nevertheless apparent that the whole direction of her life was rooted
in religion. It is not surprising that when she married it was a clergyman
she took for her husband, a public-spirited humanitarian very much in
the tradition of Mr. Turner.

That Mr. Turner was the prototype for the Revd. Thurston Benson
in Mrs. Gaskell's *Ruth* has been vouched for by Sir Henry Holland.[2]
The resemblance in character and situation is close. Like Mr. Benson,
Mr. Turner was Unitarian minister of a Newcastle congregation (the
Hanover Square Congregation) and former headmaster of a boys' school
noted for its humanitarian principles. He was a man of rare goodness
and charm, as Elizabeth was to find; utterly unpretentious, single-
minded, simple as an Apostle in his way of life. He was active in
every project for improving the lot of the huge pauper population of

---

[1] Shorter Collection, Brotherton Library, Leeds.
[2] Sir Henry Holland, *Recollections of a Past Life.*

Newcastle and a pioneer in popular education. He was accessible to all, especially the destitute, and an organizer of relief during the strikes and famines of the 1830s and 1840s. The young George Stephenson was a pupil of his and never forgot the help he received from him. 'Mr. Turner was always ready to assist me with books, with instruments, and with counsel, gratuitously and cheerfully. He gave me the most valuable assistance and instruction; and to my dying day I can never forget the obligations which I owe to my venerable friend.'[3]

Mr. Turner lived to be ninety-five and eventually retired to Manchester where, among a devoted circle of friends, he counted the Gaskells. It was Mr. Gaskell who pronounced his funeral sermon and who told the story of the churchman who, while admitting the great goodness of Mr. Turner, regretted not expecting to see him in heaven—because of the deplorable fact that he was a Unitarian. The woman to whom this was said knew all about Mr. Turner's life. 'No,' she said, 'I confess I do not. He will be too much in the light of the throne for me to see him.'[4]

During her second winter spent at Mr. Turner's, the cholera epidemic of 1830-1 spread from the Continent to Newcastle and Elizabeth experienced at first hand some of the incidents she was to relate in her novel *Ruth*. Responsible for her safety, Mr. Turner sent her across the border to Edinburgh, in the charge of his daughter Anne, a girl considerably older than Elizabeth. According to Meta Gaskell she went to Edinburgh as the guest of old friends of her parents there.[5] But one such friend, Mrs. Fletcher, a noted hostess whose drawing-room in Castle Street had been one of the most attractive centres of Edinburgh intellectual society, no longer lived there. It was not until 1848 and the publication of *Mary Barton* that Mrs. Fletcher, then living in the Lake District, made the first approach to the daughter of her old friends, and gave Elizabeth those intimate details of the past pleasures of Edinburgh society that she incorporated in her novel *My Lady Ludlow*.

Very different was the Edinburgh that Elizabeth and Anne Turner found in the winter of 1831 when they sheltered there from the plague at Newcastle. Their outings appear to have been few and their circumstances very straitened, their acquaintances limited though eagerly sought out. If the account in *My Lady Ludlow* is based on personal experience, and there is every indication that it is so, she and Anne Turner led a dismal life in cheap lodgings with very little to entertain

[3] Quoted in Chadwick, *Mrs. Gaskell*, p. 147.   [4] Quoted ibid., p. 151.
[5] Meta Gaskell to Clement Shorter, 25 Nov. 1909, Shorter Collection, Brotherton Library, Leeds.

them. Staying in Edinburgh reputedly for health reasons, the young protagonist of the tale records how dreary she found 'the stiff walks in the streets, the decorum of which obliged me to tie my bonnet-strings neatly, and put on my shawl with some regard to straightness'.

> The evenings were the worst. It was autumn, and of course they daily grew longer; they were long enough, I am sure, when we first settled down in those grey and drab lodgings. . . . The House belonged to an old man, at one time a tutor to young men preparing for the University, in which capacity he had been known to Mr. Dawson. But his pupils had dropped off; and, when we went to lodge with him, I imagine that his principal support was derived from a few occasional lessons . . . and from letting rooms. . . .[6]

After suffering various inconveniences and annoyances at the hands of their eccentric landlord, the girls received an invitation to spend the evening at the home of their doctor, which calls from the narrator a comment that sounds too personal not to have applied to young Elizabeth Stevenson herself: 'if it had been to spend an evening at the dentist's, I believe I should have welcomed the invitation, so weary was I of the monotony of the nights in our lodgings.'[7]

The only tangible evidence of Elizabeth's stays in Edinburgh comes from the miniature painted of her in 'June 1830' by W. J. Thomson there, and the marble portrait bust executed by David Dunbar.

William John Thomson (1771-1845) was a regular exhibitor at the Royal Scottish Academy, and was, in all probability, a connection of Elizabeth's stepmother, née Catherine Thomson, and of Dr. Todd Thomson, her brother. Dr. Thomson was a native of Dumfries, where after Mr. Stevenson's death his widow retired, and where Elizabeth Gaskell later visited her. The records of the Royal Scottish Academy show that in 1834 Thomson painted Elizabeth again and exhibited her portrait, catalogued No. 171, under her married name, mis-spelt 'Mrs. Gaskill'. The continued connection would seem to indicate some relationship, since permission to paint an unmarried girl at the time would not readily be accorded to a stranger, and the Gaskells' financial position even after she was married would hardly have allowed them to commission a portrait from a successful artist. The Edinburgh portraits give a misleading impression, however, of Elizabeth's life at the time, suggesting a maturity she had not yet attained.

The friendship with Anne Turner stood her in good stead, when, in

---

[6] 'Round the Sofa', Introduction to *My Lady Ludlow*, p. 1.
[7] 'Round the Sofa', p. 4.

the autumn of 1831, she accompanied her on a visit to Manchester, where Anne Turner's sister, Mary Robberds, wife of the Unitarian minister of Cross Street Chapel, had settled. The move to Manchester, and the subsequent prolonged visit to the Robberds' home, proved to be the turning-point in Elizabeth's life, since it brought her the acquaintance of the man she married and settled her for good in Manchester.

An alien place it seemed to her at first sight, as she painfully remembered in describing its impact on her heroine in *North and South*; a place with an aggressive character that both repelled and stimulated her. How such a girl, refined, beautiful, educated, intelligent, would react to the challenge of such a place at such a time in its history appears the major problem at this juncture in Elizabeth Stevenson's life. Its interest lies precisely in what Manchester did for her against all probabilities; for it was undeniably due to Manchester that she found her vocation.

CHAPTER VI

THE MANCHESTER MARRIAGE

MARY TURNER's husband,[1] the Revd. John Gooch Robberds (1789–1854), a native of Norwich, had been minister of Cross Street Unitarian Chapel since 1811. The family lived in the Greenheys district of Manchester, a rural oasis of green fields and springing hedges on the outskirts of the city as it then was, its sweet air and tranquil shades contrasting forcibly with the complex of cotton mills and calico-printers' works that constituted the city centre. The impression Elizabeth then received was sharp enough to remain fresh in her memory fifteen years later when she described it in *Mary Barton*:

There are some fields near Manchester, well known to the inhabitants as 'Green Heys Fields', through which runs a public footpath to a little village about two miles distant. In spite of these fields being flat, and low, nay, in spite of the want of wood . . . there is a charm about them which strikes even the inhabitant of a mountainous district, who sees and feels the effect of contrast in these commonplace but thoroughly rural fields, with the busy, bustling manufacturing town he left but half-an-hour ago.[2]

The need for such a refuge from the noise, ugliness, and darkness in which the vast majority of Manchester people spent their working lives became a deeply appealing subject to Elizabeth, who was herself always so acutely affected by her environment.

Three years previously Mr. Robberds was given a junior assistant to help him in the ministry of Cross Street Chapel, the Revd. William Gaskell, a distinguished classical scholar, and a graduate of Glasgow University. He had trained for the Unitarian ministry at Manchester New College, then at York.

Born in 1805, immensely tall and ascetically thin, his striking figure was as much a part of the Robberds' home circle as if he had been a member of the family, and it was inevitable that he and Elizabeth Stevenson should be much thrown together. An indefatigable worker,

[1] Richard Wade, *The Rise of Nonconformity in Manchester* (Manchester, 1880).
[2] *Mary Barton*, p. 1.

both on his own account and on that of his fellow men, combining intellectual brilliance with the active life of teacher and preacher, he was both a university lecturer and a social worker. Despite his Scottish training, and his slightly Scottish accent, he was a Lancastrian, a native of Warrington, where his family had been established for a century. His father had been a prosperous manufacturer of sail canvas and had provided well for his family. William had two brothers and two sisters. His brother Samuel was a distinguished doctor, a specialist in mental diseases.[3] His sisters, Eliza and Anne, were as yet unmarried when Elizabeth Stevenson first met them. The widowed Mrs. Gaskell was by that time remarried, to the Revd. E. K. Dimock, Unitarian Minister of Warrington. The close links binding the Robberds and Gaskell families, and the proximity of Warrington to Manchester, soon drew Elizabeth into the orbit of the Gaskell connection, and while she became close friends with Eliza and Anne, William lost no time in falling in love with her. Within five months of arriving in Manchester and first meeting the Gaskells, Elizabeth found herself engaged. By March 1832, when she was home again, William went to Knutsford to be introduced to her beloved aunt Lumb—not as a prospective lover dependent on her consent, but as her already affianced husband. On the eve of his return to duty in Manchester, Elizabeth wrote to her future sister-in-law Eliza Gaskell an account of the visit. Every quality for which she later became known is already apparent in this first extant letter: her high spirits, the sparkle of her style, the zig-zag course of her reasoning, her honesty and want of all affectation, her fun and freedom of thought and expression—all the characteristic traits that so charmed her contemporaries.

You ought indeed, my dearest Eliza, to consider it a great proof of my love, that I can even meditate writing to you on William's last evening (See how impudent I've grown) but my conscience would reproach me for ever and a day if I let him go without my portion of thanks for your kind letter. He may finish his half at Ardwick, and as I shan't be there to see, he may say what scandal he likes of us all, and give me as bad a character as he chooses. N.B. I have been behaving very well, so don't believe a word to the contrary.

He has not seen half, no nor a quarter so much as I wished of my darling Aunt Lumb. I scarcely like to think of the cause now she is so much better, but the very morning after he came, she broke a small bloodvessel which alarmed us all very much indeed, and has confined her to bed ever since. William has, however, seen

---

[3] He became Medical Superintendent of Lancaster Asylum (1840), and was appointed by Lord Shaftesbury Commissioner in Lunacy (Obituary Notice).

1. Old Lindsey Row, Chelsea, drawing by W. W. Burgess, c. 1820

2. Cheyne Walk, Chelsea, drawing by W. W. Burgess, 1817

her several times, and though not nearly enough, yet I hope knows her a little bit. And you can't think what rude speeches she makes to me. To give you a slight specimen—'Why Elizabeth how could this man ever take a fancy to such a little giddy thoughtless thing as you' and many other equally pretty speeches . . . oh dear! I shall miss him sadly to-morrow . . . and I must look forward to the *28th of March 1832* when he has promised to come back again. Pray give my warmest thanks to your sister [Anne Gaskell] for her kind addition to your letter—and do you, dearest, pray write again to me, and that right speedily—tell me anything that interests you—and oh! don't forget how to fight with pillows and 'farm yard noises' when Edward heard you laughing so plainly. I can't write a word more now, seeing I have 150 things to say to this disagreeable brother of yours—so believe me—

Your very loving crony   E. C. Stevenson.[4]

William's letter, written two days later, reads:

My dearest Eliza—

I cannot think of keeping from you any longer the half of the letter, which was promised, from my better half although I have scarcely time to make it up into a whole. Though from Mrs. Lumb's unfortunate illness I was unable to see much of her, I saw sufficient to confirm the impression which I had received from Elizabeth and make me at once admire and love her. In the short interview which I was permitted to have with her she treated me in the kindest and most affectionate manner, and expressed the great pleasure which she felt that Elizabeth had been led to form an engagement with me. I also contrived, I believe, to get into the graces of aunt A.C. [Abigail Holland] who upon the whole I like very well, though she is not by any means to be compared with Mrs. Lumb. I have called Mrs. Lumb's illness unfortunate—and yet in one respect I can hardly deem it so. It served to present Elizabeth to me in a still more lovely and endearing light than I had before beheld her, and did more perhaps to knit our souls together than months could have done, without it. You can't imagine how lonely I feel without her. I must get over to K[nutsford] again next week, for one day at least. I am now writing with her rings on my fingers, wearing of which you seem to have cautioned as the summit of impudence, with her likeness lying before me, if likeness it can be called . . . Your most affectionate brother,

Wm. Gaskell[5]

That Elizabeth knew her own mind and was determined to marry him was evident; that he was even more resolute in carrying away the prize that had fallen into his lap appears in his joyful letters. She was not only lovely but gay, well-educated, and good; what more could he hope for? They were, in many respects, admirably matched: passionate devotees

---

[4] *GL* 1, 20 Mar. 1832.
[5] From the original letter in the Shorter Collection, Brotherton Library, Leeds.

C

of poetry, true nature-lovers, keen walkers, musical, artistic, liberal-minded—in his case a liberal in politics. They were both earnestly bent on bettering the conditions of the poor, though neither may then have anticipated quite how fully their lives would become involved in the social problems of their time and, in particular, of their town. Admittedly she tended towards exuberance and he towards gravity, and his vocation meant they must live in Manchester for good, but for the time being they were too much in love to notice such irrelevancies. Knutsford was only 16 miles away, and seemed compensation enough for the Manchester pall of smoke at that early time of joy in loving and being loved.

In default of a dowry of her own, Elizabeth could be assured, through the generosity of her aunt Lumb, of an annuity at her death of £80 a year. While William's stipend as an assistant minister could be but modest, he probably inherited some money from his father. Elizabeth Gaskell, who made herself the witty spokesman of a society almost wholly composed of persons practising 'elegant economy',[6] had never been accustomed to luxury and was not afraid of facing life as a clergyman's wife with very moderate means.

Up to 1837 Unitarians were still constrained by law to be married in a church of the Establishment, and Elizabeth Stevenson and William Gaskell were married in Knutsford Parish Church on 30 August 1832. She was not yet twenty-two, and William was just turned twenty-seven. Her uncle, Dr. Peter Holland, gave her away and her cousins, the daughters of his second marriage, Susan and Catherine Holland, were her bridesmaids. William's sister, Eliza, acted as his 'witness'.[7] Dr. Holland's house overlooking the church was well placed for the wedding breakfast that followed and as the setting for the local customs that Elizabeth later described to Mary Howitt. The Hollands were a greatly respected family in Knutsford and the whole community played its part in marking the occasion.

One of the customs, on any occasion of rejoicing, of strewing the ground before the houses of those who sympathise in the gladness with common red sand, and then taking a funnel filled with white sand, and sprinkling a pattern of flowers upon the red ground. This is always done for a wedding, and often accompanied by some verse of rural composition. When I was married, nearly all the houses in the town were sanded, and these were the two favourite verses:

> Long may they live,
> Happy may they be,

[6] See *Cranford*, p. 4.
[7] Registers of St. John's Parish Church, Knutsford.

> Blest with content,
> And from misfortune free.
>
> Long may they live
> Happy may they be,
> And blest with a numerous
> Pro - ge - ny.

Explaining how the custom originated in the Middle Ages with the annual celebration of the 'well-dressing' in the town, when real flowers were strewn before the house of the latest married bride, Elizabeth commented, 'you cannot think how pretty our dear little town looks on such occasions'.[8]

The honeymoon was spent in Wales, a region already beloved by Elizabeth. They were away a month, spending the first fortnight at Aber, 5 miles from Bangor. 'Dear Little Aber', William called it, and in her novel *Ruth* Elizabeth wrote of 'Abermouth'. From there they went on to Conway, Caernarvon, Llanberis, Beddgelert, and finally to Portmadoc to stay with Sam Holland at Plas Penrhyn, where they spent the remainder of their holiday. It was from there that they wrote, on 17 September, their light-hearted account of their journey to Eliza Gaskell. Eliza was, in their absence, getting their new home ready, which, like William's previous home with her, was to be in Dover Street.

My very dear Sister,

. . . We enjoyed our stay at dear little Aber very much indeed—and were not a little loth to leave it last Monday though hope was leading us on to still more beautiful and grander scenes. We went that day through some of the finest which Wales has to show. Our first stage was to Conway by coach as beautiful a ride as heart could desire. On the left we had Beaumaris and the Sea shining and sparkling in the morning light, and on our right the hills covered with the richest and warmest tints, and the air so fresh and pure, and Lily looking so very well, and two bugles playing all the way. Wasn't it enough to make one very happy? We went through the fine old castle of Conway . . .[9]

In the general euphoria of the hour Elizabeth managed to lose her feather boa, but they were not long downcast, for after Conway they 'proceeded on through the pass of Llanberis—and here boa and every-thing else, but my own Lily, was forgotten in the wondrous wildness and rugged grandeur of the scene'. It was William's first meeting with

---

[8] *GL* 12, 18 Aug. 1838.
[9] From the original letter in the Shorter Collection, Brotherton Library, Leeds.

the Samuel Hollands, and the first of many holidays spent with them. Of their home he wrote:

The scenery about here is very fine, and the view from the drawing-room windows quite glorious . . . Mrs. Holland is kindness itself—and Sam I like very much—and Ann I am quite in love with. My bonny wee wife—*My* bonny wee wife—grows I do think more bonny than ever. She is very much better than when we left K[nutsford] and I hope will go on gaining strength, though she maintains she is already as strong as a horse. And now as I want her to fill up the other half I must come to one or two little things, which I wish you to do. First, to buy the piano (a Broadwood), get some saucers for plants, heap up the earth around the celery, and while you do it keep the stalks of the outside leaves well together, to prevent the earth from getting between them . . . We can hardly tell you when we shall be home—but we are proposing being at K. at the beginning of next week.[10]

Elizabeth's letter filled up the sheet with her own particular flashing view of things:

My dearest Eliza, That most wicked brother of yours and husband of mine has left me such a wee wee bit of time to write all *my* news, and thanks having taken such a time to *his* eloquence that poor I must write helter-skelter. And first and foremost thanks upon thanks from the very bottom of my long heart, for yr letter which was *so* welcome, as we had been hoping for news from *our home*. It was very nice of you writing to *me*, your new *sister* too. . . . As you justly conjecture I *have* a *great* deal of trouble, in managing this obstreperous brother of yours, though I dare say he will try and persuade you the trouble is all on his side. I find he has been telling you I look very well, so I think that is a pretty broad hint that I am to tell you he is looking *remarkably* well which he really is. Mountain [air] seems to agree with us and our appetites admirably. You would be astonished to see our appetites, the dragon of Wantley, 'who churches ate of a Sunday, Whole dishes of people were to him, but a dish of Salmagunde' was really a delicate appetite compared to ours. If you hear of the principality of Wales being swallowed up by an earthquake, for earthquake read Revd Wm Gaskell—How very good you are to be staying at home by yourself while—here's post.

Your most affect: Sister E. C. Gaskell.[11]

The return to Manchester, via Knutsford, took them to their new house at 14 Dover Street, off the Oxford Road, which Eliza Gaskell had been getting ready for them, piano and all. William was as great a lover of music as his bride, and music became very much a part of their family life. In the years to come he showed himself, even more than his wife, an exacting listener to his daughters' performances.

[10] From the original letter in the Shorter Collection, Brotherton Library, Leeds.
[11] *GL* 2, 17 Sept. 1832.

On Elizabeth's twenty-second birthday, 29 September 1832, they arrived at their new home. It was a corner house of a row of nine new houses let at a rental of £32 a year.[12] William had secured possession of it in April immediately after his first visit to Knutsford when Elizabeth's engagement to him was confirmed. Dover Street, besides offering homes at reasonable rents, was close to the centres of William's activities: the eventual university buildings (as Owen's College would become) with which he would be closely associated as lecturer for many years, the Cross Street Chapel, Manchester Unitarian New College (on its return from York in 1840), the lower Mosley Street Sunday Schools, and his principal's home in Greenheys. Such as it was, the house in Dover Street would be Elizabeth's home for the next ten years.

The whole span of her Manchester life, which covered thirty-three years, would indeed be spent in the same, relatively rural, district of the city, the family's removal to Upper Rumford Street in 1842, and finally to Plymouth Grove in 1850, taking them only a few streets away but into pleasanter and greener surroundings, always a little beyond the smoke-barrier of the manufacturing areas of the town. The slums of Miles Platting and Ancoats, where the cotton operatives lived in the back-to-back terrace houses and courts so forcefully described in her Manchester tales—*Mary Barton, Lizzie Leigh, North and South,* 'The Three Eras of Libbie Marsh'—would be known to her because of her passionate concern with the lives of the people condemned to live there, and because she voluntarily crossed the barriers that divided her world from theirs. She could, had she so wished, and like many of her acquaintances in the pleasanter parts of the city, have lived out her days without penetrating into the courts and alleys where she found the young women, tender-hearted and hard-working, who appear in her stories. They lived in appalling poverty, in sub-human conditions, and the only hope of improving their lot, she realized, was by exposing it constantly to the public conscience.

How the city appeared to her fresh eyes she memorably described in *North and South*:

For several miles before they reached Milton [Manchester] they saw a deep lead-coloured cloud hanging over the horizon in the direction in which it lay. It was all the darker from contrast with the pale grey-blue of the wintry sky . . . Nearer to the town, the air had a faint taste and smell of smoke; perhaps, after all, more a loss of the fragrance of grass and herbage than any positive taste or smell. Quickly they were whirled over long, straight, hopeless streets of regularly-built

12 Chadwick, *Mrs. Gaskell*, p. 192.

houses, all small and of brick. Here and there a great oblong many-windowed
factory stood up, like a hen among her chickens, puffing out black 'unparlia-
mentary' smoke, and sufficiently accounting for the cloud which Margaret had
taken to foretell rain. As they drove through the larger and wider streets . . . they
had to stop constantly; great loaded lorries blocked up the not over-wide thorough-
fares.[13]

Already in that glimpse of the new life opening out before her, the
impression of unchecked speed, of the vitality and force of the machines
and of the men directing them, mitigated the first fearful response; there
was a grandeur in the very power of the combined forces of men and
machinery to which her intellect bowed, even if it shocked her sense of
beauty and of justice. One question haunted the heroine of *North and
South*, as it did Elizabeth Gaskell herself: was everything being done 'in
the triumph of the crowded procession' of the successful, of the prosper-
ing few who directed the gigantic operation, to prevent the helpless
being trampled on, of lifting them out of the roadway of the conqueror,
whom they had no power to accompany on his march? The answer, as
she soon found, was a resounding 'No'. The prosperity of Manchester
was a juggernaut whose very progress was a menace to the helpless
minority of the useless poor.[14] ? SOMEWHAT NARROW VIEW OF POVERTY ?

Elizabeth Gaskell had married a man burdened with a conscience like
herself, and she whole-heartedly fell in with whatever voluntary work he
took on in addition to his regular duties. In her first years of marriage,
she shared in his Sunday School work and evening classes for boys. In
those early days he was an educative influence in himself from whom she
learnt much. He was not only a fine classical scholar, but well read in
literature and history, and absorbed in the new scientific studies. Before
his leisure time was totally filled by lecturing at Manchester New College,
where he was appointed lecturer in English Literature, History, Logic,
and Composition, and by his evening sessions at the Mechanics' Institute
for Working-Class Men, he took private pupils to augment his income;
and it is clear that he was also a ready tutor to his wife.

In July 1833 she gave birth to her first child, a still-born girl, whose
loss she was long in getting over. It was the first of many griefs and cares
that darkened her early married life and which stirred a certain morbid
vein in her which threatened at times to upset the finely adjusted balance
of her nervous temperament. Visiting the child's grave on the third

[13] *North and South*, pp. 66–7.
[14] Ibid.

anniversary of its death, after the successful birth of a second child, she was moved to write the following sonnet:

On Visiting the Grave of my Stillborn Little Girl
Sunday, July 4th, 1836

I made a vow within my soul, O child,
When thou wert laid beside my weary heart,
With marks of death on every tender part,
That, if in time a living infant smiled,
Winning my ear with gentle sounds of love
In sunshine of such joy, I still would save
A green rest for thy memory, O Dove!
And oft times visit thy small, nameless grave.
Thee have I not forgot, my firstborn, thou
Whose eyes ne'er opened to my wistful gaze,
Whose sufferings stamped with pain thy little brow;
I think of thee in these far happier days,
And thou, my child, from thy bright heaven see
How well I keep my faithful vow to thee.[15]

The loss of her first child made her, understandably, more passionately attached to the second, Marianne, born on 12 September 1834. The existence of this healthy little girl absorbed much of her attention for the next two years, even after the birth of a third child, Margaret Emily, on 5 February 1837 ('Meta', who was to become her favourite daughter, as the diary she kept on her progress shows).

To her, motherhood was an exalting experience, a keen joy. Writing to Marianne on her twenty-third birthday she recalled the delight she had taken in her from birth: 'yesterday . . . I thought of *you* often my darling, and of twenty-three years ago, when you lay by my side such a pretty wee baby, and I was always uncovering you to look at you, and always getting scolded for giving you cold by the nurse.'[16] She never lost the sense of complete fulfilment that the birth of her children gave her. Long years after the last was in her teens, she wrote to her friend Charles Norton whose wife had just had a baby: '. . . tell her I think she has passed the acme of her life,—when all is over and the little first born darling lies nuzzling and cooing by one's side. I do rejoice with you dear friend on your new title of Father.'[17] She was wrapped up in her children

[15] Printed by A. W. Ward in the Biographical Introduction to the Knutsford edition, vol. 1, pp. xxvi–xxvii.

[16] GL 372, 13 and 14 Sept. 1857.

[17] GL 528, 28 July 1863.

over the next ten years; and, indeed, frankly declared that so long as they needed her constant care she would not consider becoming a writer. In 1862, writing to a prospective author, a young woman overburdened with domestic difficulties, she gave her candid advice on the conduct to be pursued:

When I had *little* children I do not think I could have written stories, because I should have become too much absorbed in my *fictitious* people to attend to my *real* ones. I think you would be sorry if you began to feel that your desire to earn money, even for so laudable an object as to help your husband, made you unable to give your tender sympathy to your little ones in their small joys and sorrows; and yet, don't you know how you,—how every one, who tries to write stories *must* become absorbed in them, (fictitious though they be,) if they are to interest their readers in them. Besides viewing the subject from a solely artistic point of view a good writer of fiction must have *lived* an active and sympathetic life if she wishes her books to have strength and vitality in them. When you are forty, and if you have a gift for being an authoress you will write ten times as good a novel as you could do now, just because you will have gone through so much more of the interests of a wife and a mother.[18]

The experience of motherhood, like the impact of her husband's powerful mind, was of the utmost importance in shaping the writer she became.

Though she might suppress the temptation to write while her children needed her, the strength of the imaginative urge within her was ceaselessly at work in plot-spinning, as in her childhood days, and she could not altogether forgo the satisfaction of writing. She was an abundant letter-writer, crowding into the long discursive news-sheets she sent her correspondents not only reports of the family's doings but narratives of her friends' lives, reports of conversations, thumb-nail sketches of new acquaintances, employing in these outpourings all the arts of the story-teller.

When Marianne was six months old she decided to keep a journal[19] of the child's development. It is a little mine of observation, penetration, and perception that is as revealing of the mother as of the child observed.

'MY DIARY', as she called it, was kept from 10 March 1835 to 28 October 1838. While the writer's intention was to observe and analyse every phase of her daughter's developing intelligence and character, the diary evolved into a strict self-examination of the mother, that allowed no complacency in the relating. The whole document is intensely religious in tone and often morbid in character. The sense of insecurity

---

[18] *GL* 515, 25 Sept. 1862.
[19] 'My Diary', privately printed by Clement Shorter (London, 1923).

quickened by the loss of her first child clouded her expectation of happiness in the living child. She frequently prays for resignation should God 'take what He has given', and fears loving her child too much, lest she should lose her. She makes a confession of rejoicing in the child's beauty, as though she reckoned it a fault in herself. 'With health, beauty has come; and I confess I think beauty a desirable thing . . . it is a high gift in the influence which may be used for such noble purposes.'

Opening the diary on a 'Tuesday Evening', she regrets the time already lost, and writes: 'The day after to-morrow Marianne will be six months old. I wish I had begun my little journal sooner.' Her descriptions of the child's distinctive ways are always objective: 'She takes great delight in motion just at present . . . shutting and opening the hand pleases her very much . . . I never leave her till she is asleep.'[20] In August she reproaches herself keenly for her neglect in keeping up the journal but finds it difficult to 'know when to begin or when to stop when talking, thinking or writing about her'. The child's face reflects the expressions on the faces of those about her and the mother fears 'her catching cross or angry expressions'.[21] So early in her experience of motherhood did she show that respect for the feelings of her children that later so remarkably characterized her attitude towards them. On 4 October she makes the resolution never to disappoint Marianne by making light promises.

. . . her sensibilities seem to me very acute. If she sees others laughing when she is grave and serious, or is not aware of the joke, she bursts into tears . . . unexpected pleasure has occasionally made her cry; seeing her Papa after an absence of a few days . . . She is in general very gentle, rather grave, especially with strangers, and remarkably observing, watching actions, things, etc., with such continued attention. She is very *feminine*, I think . . . She is extremely fond of her Papa, shouting out his name whenever she hears his footsteps . . . and dancing with delight when she hears the bell which is a signal for her to come in after dinner . . . She can say pretty plainly 'Papa' . . . leaving poor Mama in the background . . .[22]

Admitting to the hurt she felt at any sign of preference shown for others by Marianne, Elizabeth honestly judged the jealousy of her feelings.

William told me the other day I was not of a jealous disposition; I do not think he knows me. In general, Marianne prefers being with me, I hope and think; yet at times she shows a marked preference for Betsy, who has always been, as far as I can judge, a kind, judicious and tender nurse. To-night Marianne was

[20] Ibid., pp. 6–8.   [21] Ibid., p. 10.   [22] Ibid., pp. 15, 19.

sadly tired, and I would fain have caressed and soothed her while Betsy was performing various little offices for her on her knee, and M.A. absolutely pushed me away, fearing I should take her. This was hard to bear; but I am almost sure I have never shown this feeling to anyone; for I believe Betsy fully deserves and returns her love.[23]

From the 'Diary' can be learnt the details of the early years at Manchester. The greater part of the summer of 1836 was spent at Knutsford, Warrington (with Mr. Gaskell's mother, Mrs. Dimock, a fond grandmother as Mrs. Lumb was a devoted aunt), or at the seaside. As a matter of course Dr. Samuel Gaskell, William's brother, assumed the medical care of the Gaskell babies, and his first recommendation was to take Marianne to Grange-over-Sands on Morecambe Bay, a place with which the whole family eventually became intimate.

Few records of the Gaskell family life reflect greater happiness and more complete harmony with her surroundings than Elizabeth's letter written from Sandlebridge during her visit to Knutsford that summer. Staying at her grandparents' old home, long since passed to the old aunts and uncles of the Holland connection, she made Eliza Gaskell the confidante of her joy. She was there with Marianne, rediscovering the happy haunts of her childhood and feeling their effect anew in the fresh delight of her little girl. This was her spiritual home, and the place that would recur in memory the most often and the most vividly when she needed to escape from the pressures of life.

I wish I could paint my present situation to you. Fancy me sitting in an old-fashioned parlour, 'doors and windows opened wide', with casement window opening into a sunny court all filled with flowers which scent the air with their fragrance—in the very depth of the country—5 miles from the least approach to a town—the song of birds, the hum of insects the lowing of cattle the only sounds—and such pretty fields and woods all round—Here are Baby, Betsy, Mama, and Bessy Holland [a cousin]—and indeed at this present moment here is Sue [Dr. Peter Holland's daughter] who has ridden over, to bring us news of the civilized world—in the shape of letters, etc., etc. One from Aunt Lumb [from Knutsford] enclosing yours . . . I do so wish you were here to revel in flowers, and such thorough country. We are up with the birds, and sitting out on the old flag steps in the very middle of fragrance—'far from the busy hum of men', but *not* from the busy hum of bees. Here is a sort of little standard library kept—Spenser, Shakespeare, Wordsworth, and a few foreign books, and we sit and read and dream our time away—except at meals when we *don't* dream over cream that your spoon stands upright in . . . Baby is at the very tip-top of bliss; and gives a happy prospect of what she will be at your Aunt Holbrook. There are chickens,

and little childish pigs, and cows and calves and horses, and *baby horses*, and fish
in the pond, and ducks in the lane, and the mill and the smithy, and sheep and
baby sheep, and flowers—Oh! you would laugh to see her going about, with
a great big nosegay in each hand, and wanting to be *bathed* in the golden bushes
of wall-flowers . . .

Reporting on a ride with her husband and a visit to friends to whom they
were invited again, she added: 'but I longed to see the old familiar place.
The house and walls are over-run with roses, honeysuckles and vines—
not quite in flower *but all but.*'[24]

   She was already then co-operating in a project of her husband's to
bring the poets within reach of the working classes, and helping him
prepare a series of lectures on the English poets.

I have brought Coleridge with me, and am *doing* him and Wordsworth—*fit place
for the latter*! I sat in a shady corner of a field gay with bright spring flowers—
daisies, primroses, wild anemones, and the 'lesser celandine', and with lambs
all around me—and the air so full of sweet sounds, and wrote my first chapr. of
W. yesterday in pencil—and today I'm going to finish him—and my heart feels
so full of him I only don't know how to express my fullness without being too
diffuse . . . I have done all my *composition* of Ld B[yron], and done Crabbe outright since you left and got up Dryden and Pope—so now I'm all clear and
straight before me . . . If I don't get much writing done here, I get a great many
thoughts on the subject—for one can't think any thing but poetry and happiness.
. . . Oh! that Life would make a stand-still in this happy place?[25]

   The year 1837, auspiciously begun with the birth of Meta Gaskell
on 5 February, was to bring a further great sorrow to Elizabeth with the
last illness and death of her beloved aunt Lumb. The close ties between
aunt and niece had not been broken by the latter's marriage; Mrs. Lumb
stayed frequently in Manchester as Elizabeth stayed at Knutsford, and
throughout January she stayed in Dover Street to relieve Elizabeth of
the care of Marianne, already an active child. On her return to Knutsford she took Marianne with her 'to stay with her over the time of my
approaching confinement', as Elizabeth recorded in the 'Diary'. On
8 March, barely a month after Meta's birth, Mrs. Lumb suffered a first
stroke and two days later Elizabeth hurried over to Knutsford with her
month-old baby, still weak from her recent confinement. Her aunt
lingered on for eight weeks, Elizabeth and the children and 'our dear
servant Betsy'[26] staying in lodgings next-door to Heathside 'so that
whenever Baby needs nursing I am in in a minute'.[27] She felt for her

[24] *GL* 4, 12 May 1836.   [25] Ibid.
[26] 'My Diary', p. 28.   [27] *GL* 5, 18 Mar. 1837.

aunt all the force of filial love that she had never known for a mother. She confided to Eliza:

When I see her almost intolerable sufferings, which are in no way relieved by any efforts of those around her I almost feel as if I could give her up, so that she could 'enter into her *rest*'—Then again, as now, when she is gently and calmly asleep I hope against hope that my uncle [Dr. Holland] may be wrong and that we may yet have her once again among us with her gentle loving voice and deep tender interest in those around her—Oh there never will be one like her.[28]

Mrs. Lumb died on 1 May 1837. 'It was such a beautiful spring morning, that 1st of May, when Aunt Lumb died,' she wrote in her 'Diary', 'such a contrast to the dreary weather before',[29] and such a painful contrast, too, to the May Day celebrations when the little town was gay, with every doorstep 'sanded' and the house fronts hung with fresh boughs and flowering shrubs gathered overnight in the woods.

The death of Mrs. Lumb brought to an end the first period of Elizabeth's married life. While she always remained in contact with Knutsford and her Holland relatives, especially with her uncle Peter and his daughters—Mary and Lucy the children of his first marriage, and Susan and Catherine the children of his second—her visits were no longer made to her old home, Heathside. That was left by Mrs. Lumb to her sister Abigail (a woman with a highly uncertain temper), and Elizabeth would go to her uncle's home, Church House, instead.

True to her word, Mrs. Lumb left Elizabeth an annuity of £80, with the reversion at the death of Abigail Holland of the further half of her estate. The legacy marked the beginning of Elizabeth Gaskell's financial independence.

[28] *GL* 5, 18 Mar. 1837.   [29] 'My Diary', p. 30.

CHAPTER VII

DISCOVERING A VOCATION

THE death of her aunt left Elizabeth severely shocked, already weakened as she was by her recent confinement. 'I had very bad health till my dear little Meta was born,' she wrote in her diary, 'and I had hardly recovered my strength when (March 10th) I received a summons to Knutsford . . . on May 1st I lost my best friend . . . After that I was much out of health for some time.' Her husband took her away to Wales for three weeks in the hope of reviving her spirits, the little girls with their nurse being left in the care of their Gaskell grandmother and Gaskell aunt Anne at Warrington.[1]

It was the first of those recurring breakdowns that marked the great emotional crises of her life—the price she had to pay when her nervous temperament could no longer sustain her normally soaring spirits. So long as her husband had time to take her away to fresh scenes she quickly revived. As his own commitments increased, however, and Elizabeth was left more often on her own she began, despite her absorption in her children, to suffer from low spirits and loneliness. It was then that, as she explained to her favourite correspondent, her sister-in-law Eliza, that she felt the void left by her aunt. During one of William's absences in August 1838, Elizabeth wrote to Eliza, 'Wm goes to Buxton to-morrow and comes back Monday . . . I do hope my dear Willie will have fine weather—I shall be so lonely.'[2] And two days later:

. . . I heartily wish you were here, with your sweet comforting face, and I would listen, and talk, and talk, and listen. I feel lonely from comparing this absence of Willm's to those old absences when I had dear Aunt Lumb to care about, and open my heart to—Times that can never come again! However I hope I am not complaining, for I *am* very happy.[3]

She was very proud of William's social work, and immersed herself in it as much as her own commitment to the care of two young children allowed.

---

[1] 'My Diary', p. 28.   [2] *GL* 11, 17 Aug. 1838.   [3] *GL* 13, 19 Aug. 1838.

My husband has lately been giving four lectures to the very poorest of the weavers in the very poorest district of Manchester, Miles Platting, on 'The Poets and Poetry of Humble Life'. You cannot think how well they have been attended, or how interested people have seemed. And the day before yesterday two deputations of respectable-looking men waited on him to ask him to repeat these lectures in two different parts of the town. He is going on with four more in the winter, and meanwhile we are *picking up* all the 'Poets of Humble Life' we can think of.[4]

Further deputations, she explained in another letter to Eliza, were from the 'Teachers of the Sunday School and Senior Scholars—the other from Salford Mechanic's institution. Neither of them pay, whilk is a pity—but *if* the Manchester M[echanics'] Institution come—shan't they pay for all.'[5]

The lectures were the outcome of her own and William's joint work on the poets begun two years before; their success fired her to pursue the subject further. 'As for the Poetry of Humble Life,' she told Mary Howitt, 'that, even in a town, is met with on every hand. We have such a district, and we constantly meet with examples of the beautiful truth of that passage of "The Cumberland Beggar".

> "Man is dear to man; the poorest poor
> Long for some moments in a weary life
> When they can know and feel that they have been,
> Themselves, the fathers and the dealers out
> Of some small blessings; have been kind to such
> As needed kindness, for this simple cause,
> That we have all of us a human heart."[6]

Already, though as yet unconsciously, Elizabeth was finding the subject of her own future work—work that would be distinct from her husband's educational programme for introducing beauty and poetry into the lives of the working poor. What Elizabeth was discovering in her as yet early contacts with the sad lives of the operatives she passed in the streets, at midday as they hurried to their homes, or sat on the walls of the factories to eat their meagre meal, was that beauty and poetry were already there in their lives; this revelation stirred her profoundly. While she and her husband had much to teach *them*, their endurance, courage, and kindness to one another revealed truths of which she had never dreamt: 'the beauty and poetry of many of the common things and daily events of life in its humblest aspect does not seem to me sufficiently appreciated', she told

---

[4] *GL* 12, to Mary Howitt, 18 Aug. 1838.   [5] *GL* 11, 17 Aug. 1838.
[6] *GL* 12, 18 Aug. 1838.

Mary Howitt.[7] All this she set herself, eventually, like a prose Wordsworth, to glorify in her stories of humble life. 'The Three Eras of Libbie
Marsh', *Mary Barton*, and many others proclaim that the lesson to be
learnt comes not from the author, but from the suffering and charitable
poor. Her first approach to Mary Howitt, already an established writer,
in May 1838, was in itself a significant gesture, prompted by her growing
need to exercise her own gifts. William and Mary Howitt were a husband
and wife team whose articles were then beginning to appear in the literary
journals. Their 'charming descriptions of natural scenery and the
thoughts and feelings arising from the happy circumstances of rural life',[8]
as Elizabeth expressed it, moved her to write her thanks for the pleasure
their works had given her. She also found their humanitarian outlook
very much in harmony with her own.

The Howitts had just announced their plan for publishing a work of
topographical and historic interest—directed principally at working-
class readers as were all their productions at the time—to be called
Visits to Remarkable Places. This appealed particularly to Elizabeth
Gaskell, who wrote to applaud the project, and to beg that they include
in their sketches some places that she had known in her Warwickshire
schooldays that they might have overlooked—Old Clopton Hall at
Stratford-upon-Avon, in particular, 'a fine old seat' fit for Mr. Howitt's
interest. She followed by giving her personal description of the place.
Years later Mary Howitt recalled in her *Autobiography* the letter written
to her husband: 'It described in so powerful and graphic a manner the
writer's visit as a schoolgirl to the mansion and its inmates, that, in
replying, he urged his correspondent to use her pen for the public
benefit.'[9]

It was a recommendation that reached Elizabeth at a most auspicious
time. It released a flood of stored memories, of abandoned intentions,
of confidences shared with no one but her husband. Rather sadly she
replied to Mary Howitt:

We once thought of *trying* to write sketches among the poor, *rather* in the manner
of Crabbe (now don't think this presumptuous), but in a more seeing-beauty
spirit; and one—the only one—was published in *Blackwood*, January 1837. But
I suppose we spoke of our plan near a dog-rose, for it never went further.

In the same letter, relating several of the 'country customs' still preserved
in her old home, she had explained the superstition about the dog-rose.

[7] Ibid.   [8] *GL* 8, 1838.
[9] Mary Howitt, *An Autobiography* (London, 1889), ii. 28.

'The dog-rose, that pretty libertine of the hedges . . . is unlucky. Never form any plan while sitting near one, for it will never answer.'[10]

Reading the Howitts' descriptions of rural beauty spots stirred Elizabeth to nostalgic memories of the sights and scenes of her girl-hood and made her all the more acutely conscious of her present sur-roundings.

> I was brought up in a country town, and my lot is now to live in or rather on the borders of a great manufacturing town, but when spring days first come . . . I feel a stirring instinct and long to be off into the deep grassy solitudes of the country, just like a bird wakens up from its content at the change of the seasons and tends its way to some well-known but till then forgotten land. But as I happen to be a woman instead of a bird, as I have ties and duties to perform . . . why I must stay at home and content myself with recalling the happy scenes which your books bring up before me.[11]

In her case the nostalgia was not a destructive, nor even a sterile emotion—as with so many of her unfortunate contemporary fellow women—but the incentive to future creative work.

William Howitt included her account of Clopton Hall almost verbatim in his volume *Visits to Remarkable Places; Old Halls, Battle Fields, Scenes Illustrative of Striking Passages in English History and Poetry*, series one, published in 1840, and sent her a copy with the dedication: 'I have at length the pleasure to send you a copy of Visits to Remarkable Places, in which I hope you will find something to your mind. You will find that I have made great and various use of your suggestions.' It was proof enough that she had impressed him. The Howitts knew as yet nothing about their unknown Manchester correspondent, except what she was moved to tell them.

Her description of Clopton Hall in the letter to William Howitt shows that it was no great step from her habitual style of expressing herself in her letters, her descriptions of people and places freshly observed, to inventive writing. Her letters demanded to be written, just as her fictions did later: she needed to communicate, and such a need is not to be con-fused with the craving for self-expression experienced by so many frustrated writers.

Such change of scene and company as came her way in the weekly round of her Manchester duties found her keenly alert, observant, and responsive, and ready with her pen to record everything in detail for her

[10] *GL* 12, 18 Aug. 1838.
[11] *GL* 8, May 1838.

'dear Eliza'. She wrote on 17 July 1838 with the same breathless haste that had marked the visit she reported:

Friday after breakfast D. Darbishire[12] called, and arranged that Marianne and I should go to Rivington (where Mrs. D D. and all the little D D's are staying) that afternoon and Wm who has to preach at Cockey Moor on Sunday should join us on Monday. So such a bustle . . . and at 5 MA and I were off in the Bolton railway, and thence on in D D's gig to Rivington. A walk and a heavy thunderstorm that night. The next morning a most charming drive . . . We were not home till ½ past 8 having been on our legs since 4. Sunday to chapel in the morning two walks in the afternoon—Oh Rivington is such a very pretty place, and so thoroughly country. Yesterday morning I sketched and Wm came; in the afternoon we both rode on horseback up and down the country—then a walk after tea. This morning we were off at half past 8 for Bolton, home per rail road . . . MA's cough is much better thank you. This Rivington air has done wonders; and made me so strong and so hungry. Good air for ever![13]

The year 1840 brought with it fresh appointments for Mr. Gaskell, reducing yet further his leisure hours at home. The Unitarian College at York where he had himself been trained, and which had already twice been moved since its foundation at Manchester, was once again trans-ferred back to Manchester, and William was given the post of Secretary to the College Committee, and successively the lectureships in English Literature, History, and Composition. While the new appointments were a welcome addition to the family budget, they also added con-siderably to his labours. Work never daunted him; and he was a natural teacher, equipped with the right mental and physical qualities to make him a successful lecturer. His voice was remarkably good, as a former student of his remembered. 'Mr. Gaskell showed a marked preference for a fine word, and I remember how he used to gloat over Gray's use of *redolent* and how similar words had great fascination for him. He was a beautiful reader.' Whether he was lecturing to his college students or to the mill hands who crowded his Mechanics' Institutes' lectures at night, his sense of dedication was complete and he always gave of his best. 'Mr. Gaskell was a master of literature,' remembered one of the latter. 'I thought at the time, that he was the most beautiful reader I had ever heard. Prose or Poetry seemed to acquire more lustre and elegance when he read it. Our literary evenings under Mr. Gaskell were ambrosial evenings indeed.'[14]

Inevitably relations between husband and wife were affected. Like

---

[12] Samuel Dukinfield Darbishire, solicitor, of Greenheys, Manchester and Rivington.
[13] *GL* 9, 17 July 1838.   [14] Chadwick, *Mrs. Gaskell*, pp. 209-10.

any other intensely busy man constantly called away from home, Mr. Gaskell defended his dwindling leisure from sterile interruptions: he became less and less socially available to his wife. She reported with humour on his defections. While she went off to 'a stupid dinner at the Darbishires . . . Wm went off to finish his lectures in the shape of one on Burns. He was famously clapped, bless him.' 'Wm is at a ministers' meeting tonight—and tomorrow dines with a world of professors and college people at Mark Philips.'[15] The letters are punctuated by such reports of William's activities and absences from home. He was approached at about the same time also to give private coaching in Greek—to the young Winkworths among other students—who in due course added their enthusiastic tributes to the general chorus of praise of his exceptional gifts. He was, as his wife more than once deplored, 'Oh, so *very* busy'.

But after six years of marriage Elizabeth was still, despite the difficulties, very much in favour of the institution. Eliza Gaskell was hesitating about accepting the proposal made to her in the summer of 1838 by Elizabeth's cousin, Charles Holland, the eldest son of Sam Holland of Plas Penrhyn, and a lively exchange of letters between the sisters-in-law followed. Charles was head of a Liverpool firm exporting to South America and there were no material obstacles in the way of the match. He was extremely in love and made his cousin his confidante; Eliza did the same, but was chary of committing herself. It was Elizabeth's role—not without much exercise of patience and humour—to bring Eliza to 'name the day', and to pacify Charles. She pronounced herself against long engagements, except 'where the circumstances render it imprudent . . . Better to suffer a little poverty than to have the *wearing* anxiety of an engagement . . . And what reason of *this kind* have you to wait for, I cannot tell', she wrote to Eliza on 19 August.[16] 'The circumstances are favourable, and you are each arrived at years of discretion.' From the vantage-point of her six years of marriage, Elizabeth delivered a message on the state of the union that speaks well for her own experience:

You may depend upon it when I say you will gain more real knowledge of his tastes and habits in a week living in the house with him, or in a day married to him, than by years of these pop visits, where the joy of seeing you swallows up as it were any individual peculiarity of character. In another person's house too how could he express wishes or feelings or tastes about many little things . . . I do not think a long engagement a bit desirable for you. . . .[17]

[15] *GL* 16, 23 Dec. 1841.   [16] *GL* 13, 19 Aug. 1838.
[17] Ibid.

The wedding of Eliza Gaskell and Charles Holland took place in the late autumn of 1838 and on 2 December, the day before the honeymoon couple returned to take possession of their home in Liverpool, Elizabeth wrote to Eliza:

I wish I could have given my dear dear Lizzie a welcome to her new home by word of mouth rather than by word of pen, but as that cannot be, you must take my very warmest wishes dearest Lizzie for many many happy years, not exactly in that house, but in your husband's home, 'his dear delight to make' wherever you are. I do think you have every chance for happiness, but of course there will be joys and sorrows to vary every life, (like the pretty sunlight and shade which keep chasing each other over the lawn I see as I write,) and you must try and make yourself as trustful as possible, not that I don't think you are very trusting;— you must trust in your husband, and even more trust that God from 'seeming evil still educeth good'. Oh it is such a beautiful morning—I hope it will be like this to-morrow when you are carried over the threshold, alias up that long flight of steps.[18]

Eliza's marriage interrupted the flow of correspondence between the sisters-in-law, though nothing ever diminished their fondness. As Eliza became absorbed in her own growing family—there were eight children of the marriage—Elizabeth lost her closest confidante and most frequent correspondent. This was not without its effect on the future occupation of her time. With William's evenings often fully engaged with his classes for working men, Elizabeth found herself with long stretches of hours to fill till his return. Significantly, she stopped keeping the 'Diary' of her children's progress in October 1838; not that she was any less absorbed in them, but because in all probability she was trying her hand at writing of another sort. She did not become a story-teller overnight, nor merely because William Howitt had given her encouragement; she had been writing since her teens, as the sketch of *Captain Barton*, commended by her brother, shows. The number and variety of short stories she had available for publication when at last she came to the notice of Dickens— who needed just such material—also indicate clearly enough that she had been busy writing for some considerable time. And she still kept in touch with the Howitts.

It is not clear to what extent the Gaskells' trip up the Rhine and their stay at Heidelberg in the summer of 1841 was instigated by the Howitts, but the fact remains that the Howitts went to Heidelberg in 1840, after the publication of the first series of *Visits to Remarkable Places*, for prac-tical purposes: for William to collect material for a book on German

[18] *GL* 14, 2 Dec. 1838.

student life, and for Mary to study Swedish with a view to translating the novels of the fashionable Swedish novelist, Frederika Bremer. Taking their large family with them, they settled in Heidelberg for what proved to be a three-year absence from home. That the Gaskells' first holiday abroad should take them fortuitously to Heidelberg is improbable, and Elizabeth's letter to Eliza Holland (as she now was) describing their meeting with Mary Howitt suggests that it was expected and previously planned. This proved to be of importance to Elizabeth when she finally attempted publication.

That such a trip was financially possible for the Gaskells was some indication of William's improved income. Foreign travel became not only one of the major delights of Elizabeth's life, but one of its shaping influences. Her response on this first journey to the impact of the Flemish cathedrals is strangely reminiscent of that of Charlotte Brontë in the same year, 1841. As yet unknown to each other, the two women were alike in their passionate response to noble and elevating scenery and great forms of art; both in that year were enjoying a new aesthetic experience. For Charlotte Brontë it had been enough even to read a description in a friend's letter of the Flemish cathedrals for her to yearn to see them:

Mary's letter spoke of some of the pictures and cathedrals she had seen—pictures the most exquisite—and cathedrals the most venerable—I hardly know what swelled to my throat as I read her letter—such a vehement impatience of restraint and steady work. Such a strong wish for wings . . .[19]

Elizabeth Gaskell, writing some weeks after the event to Eliza, was still wondering at what she had seen:

I know it's dull work talking about cathedrals, but I must just say, no human being who has not seen them can conceive the sublime beauty of the cathedrals in the grand old cities in Flanders. The architects, (so unknown by name to us) must have been the noblest poets, for I never saw such practical poetry—I enjoyed Bruges Ghent and Antwerp—more than I can tell . . . If ever you go—don't miss these towns on any account . . .[20]

Her account of the holiday, contained in a monumental letter to Eliza, is shot through with her humorous reactions to the German way of life, her enjoyment of the long rambling walks with William and their hosts on the banks of the Neckar, of the nocturnal alfresco meals and concerts in the woods, of the diverting insistence by newly ennobled Germans on being addressed by their full titles; of the 'gaffes' she committed in taking

[19] See Gérin, *Charlotte Brontë* (Oxford, 1967), p. 174.
[20] *GL* 15 (p. 41), Aug. 1841.

her dancing-partner's arm and her recall to propriety by her hostess whispering in her ear:

'Don't be offended with me, Mrs. G.—but I forgot to tell you no one takes a gentleman's arm and I have heard English ladies so much remarked upon for this,' so I very properly stood holding and being held by the tips of my fingers in the most decorous manner, thinking of the funniness of morality which in one place makes it immoral to be taken by the waist, in another to be taken by the arm. I had a glorious share of dancing every dance till I was worn out and when the end of the evening came I had danced every dance but one, the great mistake of the evening. William said I was sadly tired and very dizzy when a very ugly man asked me to dance—I told him I was too much tired when lo and behold he turned out to be Wolfgang von Goethe, grandson of the illustrious Wolfgang—and Wm said I should have danced with the *name* . . .[21]

As it turned out, William Howitt had gone to London on a visit to his publisher (to see the second series of his *Visits to Remarkable Places* through the press), and the Gaskells found only Mary Howitt and a daughter on their arrival at Heidelberg. They had not, of course, met before. The Gaskells stayed as paying guests with a sister of their Manchester acquaintance Mrs. Schwabe (who was married to a German), a Frau von Pickford, who was a widow with three daughters.

The house is out of Heidelberg, with a splendid view from the windows, gardens and fountains on each side . . . We got there the first evening at tea-time unexpected as to the day, though they were aware of our coming. Mrs P. told us they were all planning to go with Mrs and Miss Howitt to a festival at the Wolf's brunnen about 2 miles off—would we like to go. To be sure we were up to anything—and hardly staid to enquire what and where but flew to put on our things and on returning to the drawing room found Mrs and Miss Howitt and every body ready. Our first glimpse at 'Mary' as we called her in joke to each other till I was afraid we should slip it out before her was in the dusk, and I could only see instead of the simple Quaker I had pictured to myself, a lady in a gay-coloured satin, black satin scarf and leghorn bonnet with a plume drooping white feathers. It was such a funny feeling of astonishment, and Miss Howitt was equally unquakerish— so we sallied forth with very dancing spirits along the picturesque road overhung with walnut trees and winding by the side of the Neckar, the moon rising over the hill-tops.[22]

Recalling the crowded social life of that German holiday, and the frequent contacts with the Howitts, Elizabeth told Eliza:

We never drank tea alone I think. Sometimes some of the students when we had music dancing and all manner of games; sometimes the Howitts—when we all

[21] Ibid. (p. 821).   [22] Ibid. (pp. 42–3).

told the most frightening and wild stories we had ever heard,—some *such* fearful ones—all true—then we drank tea out at the Howitts,—looking over all the portfolios of splendid engravings, casts etc. they had collected—(My word! authorship brings them in a pretty penny).[23]

Elizabeth could not conceal her surprise, and this first contact of the uninitiated amateur with the successful professional made perhaps a deeper impression at the time than Elizabeth liked to tell her sister-in-law. Even the telling of gruesome tales, which became a habit with them and inspired some of her own short stories, shows the Howitt influence at work, and they themselves were a model of success and enterprise that helped to prompt her own literary ambitions.

[23] *GL* 15 (p. 44).

CHAPTER VIII

THE 'NEVER-ENDING SORROW'

THE time, however, was not yet for those literary beginnings. The winter found her as totally absorbed in her family as ever. The children were ill—Marianne quite alarmingly so—and she was pregnant again. The high spirits engendered by Heidelberg had given way to a corresponding depression. As she wrote to her sister-in-law, Anne Robson, late in the evening of 23 December 1841, she saw everything in a morbid light.

My dearest Nancy, I am sitting all alone, and not feeling over and above well; and it would be such a comfort to have you here to open my mind to—but that not being among the possibilities, I am going to write to you a long private letter; unburdening my mind a bit. And yet it is nothing, so don't prepare yourself for any wonderful mystery . . . I am so glad to say MA is better . . . though I fear she is not strong. . . . We have Mr Partington of course and he was very encouraging this morning and she certainly *is* better—but one can't help having 'Mother's fears' . . .[1]

For the first time in the whole range of her correspondence—of her preserved letters, at least—she was critical of her husband. It was a complaint that she would often repeat in years to come—when the basic differences of their temperaments would be ever more defined, her expansive nature needing the constant reassurance that his reserved character found it hard to give. 'Wm', as she now wrote to Anne, 'I dare say kindly, won't allow me ever to talk to him about anxieties, while it would be SUCH A RELIEF often. So don't allude too much to what I've been saying in your answer.' William, as Elizabeth was to discover even after thirty years of marriage, 'does rather hate *facing* anxiety; he is so *very* anxious when he *is* anxious'.[2] It was a characteristic that puzzled her, as did his apparent self-sufficiency. She could not make him adapt to her swift changes of mood or penetrate his defensive guard. She had reached the stage in their relationship of realizing that she did not wholly understand him. In her morbid state this left her fearful for the future; in the case of her death, how would the children fare at his hands?

[1] *GL* 16, 23 Dec. 1841.   [2] *GL* 570, May 1865.

I have of course had MA more with me during this delicacy of hers, and I am more and more anxious about her—not exactly her health; but I see hers is a peculiar character—*very* dependent on those around her—almost as much so as Meta is *in*dependent . . . I am more and more convinced that love and sympathy are very *very* much required by MA. The want of them would make MA an unhappy character, probably sullen and deceitful—while the sunshine of love and tenderness would do everything for her. She is very conscientious, and very tender-hearted—Now Anne, will you remember this? It is difficult to have the right trust in God almost, when thinking about one's children—and you know I have no sister or near relation whom I could entreat to watch over any peculiarity in their disposition. Now you know that dear William feeling most kindly towards his children, is yet most reserved in *expressions* of either affection or sympathy— and in case of my death, we all know the probability of widowers marrying again,— would you promise, dearest Anne to remember MA's peculiarity of character, and as much as circumstances would permit, watch over and cherish her. The feeling, the conviction that you were aware of my wishes and would act upon them would be *such* a comfort to me.[3]

Memories of her own motherless childhood lay no doubt behind these fears for her children's happiness; memories of her *own* stepmother's failure to supply a mother's love. Such morbid imaginings were, it has to be remembered, as much a part of her highly strung constitution as that other side of it reflected in the popular image of her as the sunny-tempered author of *Cranford*. Both aspects were equally true, and both equally affected her writings.

As it happened, events proved her to be doubly wrong; she did not die, but gave birth to a third daughter, Florence Elizabeth—'Flossy' as she was known—on 7 October 1842, and her husband had so little intention of replacing her that he lived in terror, he humorously told her, of a pupil called Susannah Winkworth, who had obvious designs on him. 'She snubs me so, and makes such love to William,' wrote Elizabeth in great spirits to a friend in later years, 'he says "my life is the only protection he has—else he *knows* she would marry him." I wish you could hear him speaking thus in a meek fatalist kind of way, and I believe she *would* too. *Can't* you marry her to Mr Forster; then I *cd* die in peace feeling that my husband was in safety.'[4]

Before the birth of Flossy in October 1842, the Gaskells moved into a larger house. Mr. Gaskell's improved situation, and the new domestic requirements of an increasing family of three children (there is evidence of three domestics a couple of years later) made the move a necessity.

[3] *GL* 16.   [4] *GL* 124, May 1852.

It was only into the next street—Upper Rumford Street. Their house was at No. 121, still in the relatively green and pleasant part of Manchester: 'our home is a mile and a half from the *very* middle of Manchester', Elizabeth wrote later to Eliza Fox; 'the last house countrywards of an interminably long street, the other end of which touches the town, while we look into fields from some of our windows; not very pretty or rural fields it must be owned, but in which the children can see cows milked and hay made in summer time.'[5] The family lived there for eight years, and Elizabeth loved it with a stronger feeling than for any of her other homes, because it was there she experienced both the greatest happiness of her life and its profoundest sorrow.

Little more than two years after Flossy's birth the Gaskell family was at last completed by the birth of a son, called William after his father. He was born on 23 October 1844. The only son, not only because he was sole and singular and so long awaited, but because he was of an easy, jovial temperament, and exceptionally responsive to the adoration of his family, brought Elizabeth untold delight. She could not half express the fulness of her joy while she possessed it nor record its short duration when it was gone. In this happy healthy child she found herself perfectly fulfilled. There were none of the forebodings that attended the childhood of Marianne or Meta, and he was perhaps the only one of her children to give her unalloyed delight.

Her settled sense of peace, her enjoyment of every moment of his day, is conveyed in the long letter she wrote her sister-in-law Eliza in the summer following his birth, the summer of 1845. His place in her life is indicated even in the heading of her letter:

Sunday Morning, Willie asleep everyone else out.

My dearest Lizzie,

I have just received your letter and if one does not answer a letter directly when the impulse is on one there is no knowing how long one may wait for 'a convenient season'. So here goes though I've nothing to say very particular except that I want your mother to come and wonder I don't hear; could make her so comfortable and children long for her and William's holidays begin end of next week . . . My laddie is grunting so I must make haste . . .

In telegraphic style she proceeded to give Eliza a lightning sketch of the current family routine, apologizing for her abbreviations and omissions: 'articles and pronouns very useless part of speech to mothers with large families aren't they?' The passage is interesting as mentioning for the

5 *GL* 48, 29 May 1849.

first time the presence of Hearn, the children's nurse who, after bringing them all up, remained with the family to complete forty years service.

I have Florence and Willie in my room which is also nursery, call Hearn at six, ½p 6 she is dressed, comes in, dresses Flora, gives her breakfast the first; ½p. 7 I get up, 8 Flora goes down to her sisters and Daddy, and Hearn to her breakfast. While I in my dressing gown dress Willie. ½p. 8 I go to breakfast with parlour people, Florence being with us and Willie (ought to be) in his cot; Hearn makes beds etc in nursery only. 9 she takes F. and I read chapter and have prayers first with household and then with children. ½p. 9 Florence and Willie come in drawing room for an hour while bedroom and nursery windows are open; ½p. 10 go in kitchen, cellars and order dinner. Write letters; 1/4p. 11 put on things; ½p. 11 take Florence out. 1 come in, nurse W. and get ready for dinner; ½p. 1 dinner; ½p. 2 children, two little ones, come down during servants' dinner half hour open windows upstairs; 3 p.m. go up again and I have two hours to kick my heels in (to be elegant and explicit). 5 Marianne and Meta from lessons and Florence from upstairs and Papa when he can comes in drawing room to 'Lilly a hornpipe', i.e. dance while Mama plays, and make all the noise they can. Daddy reads, writes or does what he likes in dining room. ½p. 5 Margaret (nursemaid) brings Florence's supper, which Marianne gives her, being answerable for slops, dirty pinafores and untidy misbehaviours while Meta goes up stairs to get ready and fold up Willie's basket of clothes while he is undressed (this by way of feminine and family duties). Meta is so neat and so knowing, only, handles wet napkins very gingerly. 6 I carry Florence upstairs, nurse Willie; while she is tubbed and put to bed. ½ past 6 I come down dressed leaving (hitherto) both asleep and Will and Meta dressed (between 6 and ½p.) and Miss F. with tea quite ready. After tea read to M.A. and Meta till bedtime while they sew, knit or worsted work. From 8 till 10 gape. We are so desperately punctual that now you may know what we are doing every hour.

Willie comes on grandly and so does his red hair. He has dimples just like *your* Willie—is very good and *very* hungry . . .

Marianne and Meta were invited to stay with their aunt Eliza at Liverpool, and their mother hoped

they will give no trouble or anxiety and I am sure they intend not to do so and ought not. This visit is *such* a pleasure in store and the *not* going such a Damocles' sword. . . . All the directions about them I have to give are please let Meta's feet be warm in bed (a hot bottle she has here by Dr. H' direction) and *please* (though not likely at all) don't let them ever come in contact with Martineau children . . . I have many more oddments to say but W. wakes.[6]

In the second half of July the Gaskells snatched a holiday in Wales. Willie had necessarily to go with them and they took Marianne, nearly

[6] *GL* 16a, summer 1845.

eleven and already, as her mother's last letter described, capable of being helpful with the little ones. They stayed at the inn at Festiniog, where they had been on their honeymoon, a place of concentrated beauty set in a circle of hills, where every view from the inn windows was already familiar to Elizabeth, and yet so fresh in the endless shift of light as to rivet her gaze and to become indelibly imprinted on her memory. Fully seven years later she made of it the setting for dramatic scenes in her novel *Ruth*, both because of its beauty, and because of the sorrow associated with it.

The valleys around were filled with thick, cold mist, which had crept up the hill-sides till the hamlet itself was folded in its white, dense curtain, and from the inn-windows nothing was seen of the beautiful scenery around . . . He led the way into a large bow-windowed room, which looked gloomy enough that after-noon, but which I have seen bright and buoyant with youth and hope within, and sunny lights creeping down the purple mountain slope, and stealing over the green, soft meadows, till they reached the little garden, full of roses and lavender-bushes, lying close under the window. I have seen—but I shall see no more.[7]

They had not been there many days when Marianne caught scarlet fever. Strangely enough, and despite her mother's early fears for her health, she took the illness lightly and after ten days was out of danger. To flee the infection, which Willie appeared to have escaped, they moved on to Portmadoc for Marianne to recuperate in the sea air. They were hardly settled in when Willie caught the disease. He was only ten months old and had no chance against such an illness. He died on 10 August. They had taken rooms with a Mrs. Hughes, and her kindness during the tragedy was something Mrs. Gaskell never forgot. Totally unforeseen as the disaster was, they had little time in which to make arrangements for the funeral. There was no burial-ground to the Cross Street Chapel, and as the Gaskells were a Warrington family it seemed not unsuitable at the time for the grave to be made there, in the Cairo Street Unitarian Chapel ground. When poor Mrs. Gaskell saw the place, however, she took a horror of it.[8]

Her sorrow crushed her. What she wrote to her correspondents at the time has carefully been destroyed; no account of Willie's illness and death remains from her pen. Only gradually could she speak of him as the memories came flooding back. Nearly three years later she wrote of his loss to a new friend, Anne Shaen:

I have just been up to our room. There is a fire in it, and a smell of baking, and

7 *Ruth*, ch. 5, pp. 61–3.   8 *GL* 25a, Apr. 1848.

oddly enough the feelings and recollections of 3 years ago came over me so strongly —when I used to sit up in the room so often in the evenings reading by the fire, and watching my darling *darling* Willie, who now sleeps sounder still in the dull, dreary chapel-yard at Warrington. That wound will never heal on earth, although hardly any one knows how it has changed me. I wish you had seen my little fellow, dearest dear Annie. I can give you no idea what a darling he was—so affectionate and *reasonable* a baby I never saw.[9]

In 1850 when a further move was in preparation and the last weeks in the Rumford Street house were arrived, she wrote to Tottie Fox:

I want to get associations about that house; *here* there is the precious perfume lingering of my darling's short presence in this life—I wish I were with him in that 'light, where we shall all see light', for I am often sorely puzzled here—but however I must not waste my strength or my time about the never ending sorrow; but which hallows this house. I think that is one evil of this bustling life that one has never time calmly and bravely to face a great grief, and to view it on every side as to bring the harmony out of it.—Well! I meant to write a merry letter.[10]

The healing effect of great sorrow was a subject that dominated her thinking, and her writing, for several years. It was at the heart of her first novel, *Mary Barton*, and the very substance of *Ruth* too, a tale of motherhood into which she put so much of her suffering and the memories of that time.

While she deplored the 'evil of this bustling life', that prevents the sufferer remaining undisturbed with his grief, what saved her at the time were the claims of her family. Though she said that 'hardly any one knows how it has changed me', her husband for one knew her well enough to dread the effect of such deep depression. He made a practical, and quite surprising suggestion. He urged her to write a book—a work of some length 'to turn her thoughts from the subject of her grief'.[11]

That she acted on the suggestion, then and there, appears from her Preface to *Mary Barton*, dated October 1848, in which she said: 'Three years ago I became anxious (from circumstances that need not be more fully alluded to) to employ myself in writing a work of fiction', placing the inception of Mary Barton in 1845, the year of Willie's death.

She made a further and revealing statement in a letter of 1849 after the completion of *Mary Barton* in which she told her correspondent:

The tale was formed, and the greater part of the first volume was written when I was obliged to lie down constantly on the sofa, and when I took refuge in the

[9] *GL* 25a, Apr. 1848.   [10] *GL* 70, 26 Apr. 1850.
[11] A. W. Ward, Biographical Introduction to the Knutsford edition, vol. 1, pp. xxvii-xxviii.

invention to exclude the memory of painful scenes which would force themselves upon my remembrance. It is no wonder then that the whole book seems to be written in the minor key . . . I acknowledge the fault of there being too heavy a shadow over the book; but I doubt if the story could have been deeply realized without these shadows.[12]

The need to lose herself in the life of others, to fill the blank of the empty evenings when she no longer had Willie to watch over, was so urgent at the time that her tale took immediate hold of her, like a new life taking shape within her. At the same time she became pregnant again. Almost exactly a year after Willie's death, on 3 September 1846, her last child, a girl, Julia, was born. Though intended no doubt to replace the lost son, Julia proved no disappointment, but early took her place as the most enchanting of the Gaskell girls—the one who succeeded in captivating the sad heart of Charlotte Brontë.

Mr. Gaskell's suggestion to his wife to write a full-length novel shows two things: firstly that he knew his wife wanted to write and was capable of writing; and secondly that he knew that she had already written short pieces, some to help him with his classes, and others with no other purpose than because she loved story-telling—stories that had been laid aside as soon as written and perhaps forgotten. His encouragement to her to undertake a long work showed that he had faith in her powers, and knew how absorbed she could become once her subject was found.

[12] *GL* 42, early 1849.

CHAPTER IX

MARY BARTON

ON New Year's Day 1847 the Howitts launched a new literary weekly, which they called *Howitt's Journal*, and sold at a shilling a copy. In the course of the year Elizabeth Gaskell contributed to it three stories, the first, 'The Three Eras of Libbie Marsh', running to three parts subtitled 'St. Valentine's Day', 'Whitsuntide', and 'Michaelmas', which appeared respectively on 5, 12, and 19 June; the second called 'The Sexton's Hero', published 4 September; and the third a belated Christmas contribution, called 'Christmas Storms and Sunshine', which came out on New Year's Day 1848. All her tales appeared under the pseudonym of 'Cotton Mather Mills', after the New England preacher Cotton Mather, to whose name she added what appeared to her an appropriate surname for a Manchester writer. 'The Three Eras of Libbie Marsh', was, indeed, subtitled, 'Life in Manchester'.

Elizabeth was already deeply immersed in the writing of her full-length novel, *Mary Barton*, which leaves little doubt that these stories were written some time before; to judge by interior evidence, they were written before Willie's death in 1845. Their distinct character and moods would suggest that they had been written over a period of time, laid aside, and brought out afresh when the Howitts applied to her for a contribution to their new venture. What they all had in common and what made them peculiarly suitable to the Howitts' purpose was the humanitarian approach apparent in each.

Published weekly, handsomely produced, and attractively illustrated, *Howitt's Journal* was no business proposition; it gave too much for too little in return. The working-class public at which it was aimed was not yet ready to receive what was offered: improving literature, instructive information, educational material. The poor were for the most part too deprived as yet of the essentials of living to be concerned with its ornaments. What they would have liked, and what the editors learned too late, was light-hearted entertainment. The *Journal* failed after a year and the editors had to face bankruptcy. WHAT A DILEMMA! FOR WRITE & THE POOR!

It was not from this enterprise that the newly launched author could look for any financial benefit. Elizabeth received no payment for her tales (they were ultimately sold to Chapman and Hall for £12), but like the Howitts she placed the humanitarian purpose first and self-interest last. The stories' appearance under a pseudonym did nothing, furthermore, to bring her name to the fore as a writer; such an ambition was as yet far removed from her. Writing was an end in itself, and, as she found after her great sorrow, an effective solace.

The tales clearly demonstrated that Elizabeth Gaskell was a born writer, with a natural style that flowed as effortlessly in the telling of a tale as in communication with a correspondent, a style which created among other impressions one of total authenticity. There was nothing to differentiate the opening of 'Libbie Marsh', for example, from the beginning of one of Elizabeth's own letters:

Last November but one, there was a flitting in our neighbourhood; hardly a flitting, after all, for it was only a single person changing her place of abode from one lodging to another . . . Dixon's house was the last on the left-hand side of the court. A high dead brick wall connected it with its opposite neighbour. All the dwellings were of the same monotonous pattern, and one side of the court looked at its exact likeness opposite, as if it were seeing itself in a looking-glass.[1]

The scene, the typical back-to-back terraced houses hurriedly run up in Manchester with the population influx at the beginning of the century, was one with which Elizabeth Gaskell was not only familiar from her visiting among the poor; it had indelibly impressed itself on her mind as the symbol of the sort of human misery she was determined to expose. It is the same scene she evokes in the beginning of *Mary Barton*, every detail observed with photographic precision. She has brought her characters home from their Sunday walk in the adjacent woods and pastures of the Greenheys district:

They turned out of one of these innumerable streets into a little paved court, having the backs of houses at the end opposite to the opening, and a gutter running through the middle to carry off household slops, washing suds, etc. The women who lived in the court were busy taking in strings of caps, frocks, and various articles of linen, which hung from side to side, dangling so low, that if our friends had been a few minutes sooner, they would have had to stoop very much, or else the half-wet clothes would have flapped in their faces.[2]

In both stories, the relative prosperity of the characters when in good

---

[1] Knutsford edn., vol. 1, pp. 459-60.   [2] *Mary Barton*, ch. 2, pp. 11-12.

work is marked by their prodigious meals: the Wilsons entertain the Bartons to tea in *Mary Barton*, with the addition of rum, as the landlord's family entertain Libbie Marsh on her arrival with ham and fresh bread and butter and eggs to thicken the cream, luxuries that the author explains were made possible by the fact that the hosts 'were fine spinners, in the receipt of good wages; and confined all day in an atmosphere ranging from seventy-five to eighty degrees. They had lost all natural healthy appetite for simple food, and, having no higher tastes, found their greatest enjoyment in their luxurious meals.'[3]

The comment, made in no moralizing spirit, is merely the result of observation. What made Elizabeth Gaskell's stories of Manchester working-class life so impressive was the fairness of the evidence she advanced. She might be pleading for better living and working conditions for an inarticulate population, but she never pretended they were angels.

Her unique achievement, both as a woman and an author, was that she got to know them, from without and within, by the sheer sincerity of her sympathy and receptivity. How different the women and girls of Manchester were from those with whom she had grown up at Knutsford—the labourers' daughters who became the little maid-servants of the ladies of Cranford, polite, frightened, ignorant—she soon learnt in her first contacts in the streets. It was, incidentally, to her advantage as a writer that she was a poor clergyman's wife obliged to walk to and from her engagements, unlike her social acquaintances among the wealthy mill-owners, who drove out in their carriages. The aspects of the city slums that most struck her were not merely the dwellings of the poor, and their conditions of employment, but their independent spirit, their cheerfulness, their mutual kindness and generosity, and their persistent love, despite the hideousness of their homes, of the countryside.

The story of 'Libbie Marsh' is built upon just such observations of a lonely little seamstress who wishes to give some small pleasure to a crippled boy who lives in the same court as herself. She saves up her wages to give him first a canary, then to send him a Valentine, and finally to take him for a day's outing into the country during the 'Feast-week' when the whole town is on holiday. Since he was crippled, this meant hiring a coach to take him and his mother down to the canal from where the pleasure-boats operated. From then on the crowds of happy holiday-makers take charge of Franky. 'The driver lifted him out with the

[handwritten margin note: NOTE CHANGE FROM POOR TO WORKING CLASS]

[3] 'Libbie Marsh', pp. 461-2.

3 (a). Mrs. Lumb

3 (b). Dr. Peter Holland

4 (*a*). Lodge Gates, Tatton Park, Knutsford

(*b*). Brook Street Unitarian Chapel, Knutsford

tenderness of strength, and bore him carefully down to the boat; the people then made way, and gave him the best seat in their power.'

The object of the annual outing is Dunham Woods, where

every conveyance, both by land and water, is in requisition in Whitsun-week, to give the hard-worked crowds the opportunity of enjoying the charms of the country. Even every standing-place in the canal packets was occupied, and, as they glided along, the banks were lined with people, who seemed to find it object to watch the boats go by, packed close and full with happy beings brimming with anticipations of a day's pleasure.

For years has Dunham Park been the favourite resort of the Manchester work-people . . . Its scenery . . . presents such a complete contrast to the whirl and turmoil of Manchester: so thoroughly woodland, with its ancestral trees (here and there lightning-blanched); its 'verdurous walls'; its grassy walks leading far away into some glade, where you start at the rabbit rustling among the last year's fern, and where the wood-pigeon's call seems the only fitting and accordant sound. Depend upon it, this complete sylvan repose, this accessible quiet, this lapping the soul in green images of the country, forms the most complete con-trast to a town's-person, and consequently has over such the greatest power of charm.

This was the subject ever nearest to her heart, brought up as she had been in the country, and forced on her attention in the early years in Manchester by the sheer contrast of life in a manufacturing town with those former sights. Her belief in the purifying influence of the beauty of natural surroundings is eloquently present both in 'Libbie Marsh' and in *Mary Barton* (another point of resemblance between the two works). Describing the return at the day's end of the holiday-makers 'all abounding in happiness, all full of the day's adventures', she sees in their altered looks something of the beneficent influence of the place.

Long-cherished quarrels had been forgotten, new friendships formed. Fresh tastes and higher delights had been imparted that day. We have all of us our look, now and then, called up by some noble or loving thought (our highest on earth), which will be our likeness in heaven. I can catch the glance on many a face, the glancing light of the cloud of glory from heaven, 'which is our home'. That look was present on many a hard-worked, wrinkled countenance, as they turned back-wards to catch a longing, lingering look at Dunham woods, fast deepening into the blackness of night, but whose memory was to haunt, . . . many a loom, and workshop, and factory, with images of peace and beauty.[4]

In *Mary Barton* this same gospel of the healing and purifying effects

[4] Ibid., pp. 472–4, 478.

D

of the contact with nature forms the subject of the opening chapter in the words already quoted:

There are some fields near Manchester, well known to the inhabitants as 'Green Heys Fields', through which runs a public footpath to a little village about two miles distant. . . . in spite of the want of wood . . . there is a charm about them which strikes even the inhabitant of a mountainous district, who sees and feels the effect of contrast in these commonplace but thoroughly rural fields, with the busy, bustling manufacturing town he left but half-an-hour ago . . . Here in their seasons may be seen the country business of haymaking, ploughing, etc., which are such pleasant mysteries for townspeople to watch: and here the artisan, deafened with noise of tongues and engines, may come to listen awhile to the delicious sounds of rural life: the lowing of cattle, the milkmaid's call, the clatter and cackle of poultry in the old farmyards. You cannot wonder, then, that these fields are popular places of resort at every holiday time.[5]

In 'Libbie Marsh' are contained, already, both the best and the worst features of Elizabeth Gaskell's ultimate style: the lively dialogue, in the regional dialect as she so accurately rendered it, the keen observation of types, the humour, and the sheer narrative interest were already of her best.

For Libbie was very plain, as she had known so long that the consciousness of it had ceased to mortify her. You can hardly live in Manchester without having some idea of your personal appearance; the factory lads and lasses take good care of that; and if you meet them at the hours when they are pouring out of the mills, you are sure to hear a good number of truths, some of them combined with such a spirit of impudent fun that you can scarcely keep from laughing, even at the joke against yourself.[6]

The loud personal remarks of the operatives in the streets were a feature of Manchester life that young Margaret Hale in *North and South*, freshly arrived from the south of England, found hardest to face; as had doubtless young Mrs. Gaskell in her first encounters with her fellow Mancunians, till her sense of humour prevailed.

Side by side with the saving humour, in these early tales, appeared the defects of her narrative style: the morbid streak; the prevalence of death-bed scenes (so frequent in *Mary Barton* as to be sharply objected to by the book's first critics); the tendency to point a moral; the too-frequent personal commentary. Remembering that the intention of *Howitt's Journal* was to improve and inform their unlettered readers, such characteristics are the more excusable in the tales contributed to its numbers; they are less excusable and more artistically damaging in such

[5] *Mary Barton*, ch. 1, pp. 1-2.   [6] 'Libbie Marsh', p. 461.

a work as *Mary Barton*, where every form of propaganda only weakens the central case and would have been better avoided.   *S H A M E !*

The deathbeds and the incident of the sick boy in 'Libbie Marsh' raise the question of the date of the tale's composition, whether before or after Willie Gaskell's death. Accepting Mrs. Gaskell's own timing for the composition of *Mary Barton* as following that event, and the relative speed with which it was written—it is a long book of 400 pages—there would seem to have been no time to write 'Libbie Marsh' concurrently. The morbid element apparent in the early tales, which became more conspicuous over the years, has to be accepted as an integral part of Elizabeth's emotional make-up—the other side to her usually buoyant and ebullient spirits, as the dark side to the comic view of life—equally present after all in her great contemporary Dickens.

It shows itself again in the delightful and Dickensian story 'Christmas Storms and Sunshine' published in the 1848 New Year number of *Howitt's Journal*, where the moral is somewhat heavily underlined with the reconciliation over the Christmas dinner of the rival newspaper editors and their quarrelsome wives. It seems hardly likely that the author would choose to describe a child in the throes of croup if she had recently lost her own only son. The terrible frequency of infant mortality from croup was a subject with which she had had lifelong familiarity from her Knutsford girlhood, when her uncle was called out at all hours to combat the menace.

The plot of 'The Sexton's Hero' can also be traced to experiences reaching back over the years, and was probably not of recent composition. The subject of quicksands had fascinated Elizabeth ever since her first visit to Wales in 1827 when she wrote to her brother about the narrow escape of a girl—probably their cousin Kate Holland—from the quicksands about Portmadoc. Since then, she had had further report of their danger, when the same cousin Kate was to be married and, together with all her wedding outfit, was to 'ford across the Tratte, a most dangerous place by the way full of quick sands' for the wedding breakfast to be held 'at the beautiful little inn near there', before taking the stage for London and on to Paris.[7] This was described by Elizabeth in a letter written in March 1838, nine years before the story was published.

In the summer of 1836, when Marianne was a delicate baby and Dr. Sam Gaskell advised sea air, her mother took her on his recommendation to Grange-over-Sands.[8] There she witnessed the kind of scenes she

[7] *GL* 7, 1838. 'Tratte', i.e. 'Traethe', the local word for estuary tides.
[8] 'My Diary', p. 26.

described in 'The Sexton's Hero', the guides leading parties across the treacherous sands. The drama she relates in 'The Sexton's Hero' was dependent on 'the last safe crossing-time' of the sands that the narrator, his wife, and child, missed by setting out late for home. There were, as the author knew from personal experience, 'two channels to cross, let alone holes and quicksands. At the second channel from us the guide waits, all during crossing-time from sunrise to sunset; but for the three hours on each side high-water he's not there, in course. He stays after sunset if he's forespoken, not else.' The travellers, being late in setting out and caught in the hollows on the shore ('for all the sands look so flat, there's many a hollow in them where you lose all sight of the shore'), miss the last crossing with the guide at night and are overtaken by the incoming tide 'and when the wind blows up the bay it comes swifter than a galloping horse.'[9] Their destruction is certain, but for the action of a former rival of the husband—and lover of the wife—who rides out to meet them, exchanges his fresh horse for their forspent one, and, while they are saved, is himself drowned. His action earns him, in the little community where they lived, the respect due to a hero—hence the title of the tale.

By publishing Elizabeth Gaskell's first tales in their journal, the Howitts had become her literary sponsors, and it is natural that she should confide in them her intention of writing a full-scale novel, and when the time came, submit the manuscript to them for their opinion. The *Autobiography* of Mary Howitt shows that, on the completion of the first volume of the novel Elizabeth sent it up to William Howitt, and that it was warmly received by him. Both William and Mary were, as she remembered, 'delighted with it',[10] and urged her to complete the work. While this was in progress, Howitt showed the manuscript in his possession to John Forster, reader for the publishers Chapman and Hall, and on his favourable recommendation submitted it for publication to the firm. On 17 November 1847 Howitt wrote to Elizabeth of his progress in negotiating an agreement with Edward Chapman, the firm's director, which shows that he had been her intermediary throughout, her identity being as yet undisclosed. He wrote to her from 107 Strand, London, on 17 November 1847:

It gives us great satisfaction that you are so much pleased with the arrangement regarding your work. I shall take great care that Messrs Chapman and Hall do not imagine that you would have been satisfied with less. Of course, I took the proposal quite coolly and as a matter of business.

[9] Knutsford edn., vol. 1, p. 497.   [10] *Autobiography*, ii. 28–9.

What is to be done in drawing the agreement? It should be done in your own name, and in that case it must be confided to them in strict confidence. If you have any objection to that we must see whether they will be satisfied to have it made in the name of Cotton Mather Mills.

But it seems to me that as you will write (I trust many) other works, it would be as well for them to be known as the works of a lady. I think they would be more popular; and in that case the question still arises what will you do? Pray let me know.[11]

The price agreed for the copyright of *Mary Barton* (which to William Howitt appeared so advantageous, considering the author was unknown) was £100.[12] So far from bargaining for better conditions, the author, together with her husband, hurried up to London towards mid-December, taking the complete manuscript of the book to the Howitts, with whom they were to stay at their home in north London pending the completion of the negotiations with Chapman. An echo of the enjoyment of that expedition, taken in company with her husband and bound on such a hopeful errand, can be found in the long letter she wrote her elder girls, left in charge of their grandmother and aunt Anne at Warrington.

My dearest girls, here we are, safe and sound so far! And very anxiously looking forward to a letter from you, darlings, at Crix. I want to hear how you, Marianne are; don't over-tire yourself, and be wise and ready to go to bed at night in good time, for on Monday night I thought you looked rather pale. Well! We had time to get a comfortable breakfast, and sit awhile with the little ones [Flossy and Julia left at home in charge of Hearn], (who are still confined to the nursery with colds,) before setting off to go to the Station. We left Manchester at 26 minutes to 10, and from that time till we got here last night, we never stirred out of the Railway carriage. . . . Then when we got to London we took a cab and went driving through wide lighted streets—Papa said very much like Oldham Road in Manchester, but I thought much handsomer. They sell geese here with their necks hanging down at full length, instead of being tidily tucked up like Lancashire geese,—and the shops are full of them against Xmas, and you can't think how funny they look. Well after a five miles drive we got to Mr. Howitts—Aunt Anne can describe the house having been here, but I don't think she can describe the room we had,—such a blazing fire—such a crimson carpet—such an easy chair—such white dimity curtains—such a pretty vase of winter flowers before the looking glass. Then we came down into an equally comfortable dining-room, where was a dinner-tea to which we did ample justice I can assure you. Then Mr. and Mrs. and Miss and Master Howitt, and we went on talking till 12 o'clock.

[11] R. D. Waller (ed.), *Letters Addressed to Mrs. Gaskell from Famous Contemporaries* (Manchester, 1935), pp. 5-6.   [12] *GL* 34, 7 Dec. 1848.

What do you think of *that*? And now I am sitting writing in such a pretty dining-room, looking into a garden with a rockery, and a green-house, and all sorts of pretty plants, arbutus, and ever-greens—There are so many pretty casts here that you would like so much to see. The isis out of a flower that Selina Winkworth copied is on the stair-case—And a Venus picking up a shell, that is so beautiful—I wish you could see it. . . . Tell Aunt Anne to send a message *by the electric telegraph*, if you are both drowned, or burnt, etc.—My best love to her and Grandmama; to you two darlings—write very soon to yr very affec.

E. C. Gaskell[13]

While the purpose of the journey was kept from the girls, and indeed from all the Gaskells' acquaintances, they prolonged their stay over Christmas—which they spent at Crix, the Essex home of their friends the Shaens—to be back in London early in January to meet Chapman. The published correspondence of Elizabeth Gaskell and Chapman shows that she understood on that occasion that publication would follow in three months—immediately after the next title on his list, Geraldine Jewsbury's new novel—and its eventual delay for nearly ten months caused her considerable anxiety.[14] Her letters to him throughout March and April show that a suspicion had entered her mind that the book might have proved too topical in its implications, coinciding as it did in that spring of 1848 with the uprisings in Poland, Italy, and France, and that publication was being deferred on that account. She was astute enough to recognize the appeal of the book's subject in that revolutionary summer, and pointed out to Chapman that as the book 'would bear directly upon the present circumstances', it was most likely to do well. However, in a subsequent exchange of 10 July following a request from him to write an 'explanatory Preface' to the book, she disclaimed all intention of cashing-in on the continental labour troubles. 'I hardly know what you mean by an "explanatory Preface"', she told him in reply. 'The only thing I should like to make clear is that it is no catch-penny run up since the events on the Continent have directed public attention to the consideration of the state of affairs between the Employers, and their work-people.'[15] Her book, as she repeatedly affirmed after its publication, had been the result of a purely personal reaction to the labour conditions obtaining in her town, and was written from a humanitarian, not from a political standpoint.

What led Elizabeth Gaskell to choose such a subject at all for her first

[13] *GL* 18, Dec. 1847.
[14] See her letters to Edward Chapman of 21 Mar., 2, 13, 17 Apr., 10 July, 19 Oct., 13 Nov., 5, 7 Dec. 1848. *GL* 22, 23, 24, 25, 26, 28, 33, 34.
[15] *GL* 24, 13 Apr. 1848; 26, 10 July 1848.

novel is plainly set out in the Preface to *Mary Barton* where she confessed to having wished to write a tale of country life, for which she 'had a deep relish', removed from the present day by a hundred years. What had deterred her even after she had well begun such a tale was the impact of the life around her, the appeal of a dumb human misery to which she felt she could and ought to give a voice. What had begun as a piece of escapist poetry set in the romantic Past was transformed into a drama of topical life, far more compelling by reason of the immediacy of its appeal.

I bethought me how deep might be the romance in the lives of some of those who elbowed me daily in the busy streets of the town in which I resided. I had always felt a deep sympathy with the care-worn men, who looked as if doomed to struggle through their lives in strange alternations between work and want; tossed to and fro by circumstances, apparently in even greater degree than other men.[16]

Deliberately, she set her tale back into the 1830s, when the Great Depression began, and the Chartists organized their march on London to bear their Petition—signed by 1,200,000 workers—to the House of Commons. Her treatment of the whole incident was dramatic, not political: what concerned her was the effect on John Barton of the Government's rejection of the people's plea, not its theoretical or social implications. She brought the heart-break of the situation home to her readers by no grand analysis of the causes at stake, but by homely touches, such as the return home of Barton from his fruitless errand on 'a night of warm, pattering, incessant rain . . . Drenched and way-worn, there he stood! He came in with no word . . . He sat down by the fire in his wet things, unheeding.' When at last he spoke it was to say to his daughter: 'Mary, we mun speak to our God to hear us, for man will not hearken; no, not now, when we weep tears of blood.'[17]

The theme of *Mary Barton* is the breakdown in human communications; the total incomprehension of each other's point of view in the labour relations existing between masters and men; the ruthlessness of the former in their self-interest, the deep resentment of the men when, in hard times for all, they are turned away with no legal redress, no rights of appeal, starvation their only prospect. In *Mary Barton* Mrs. Gaskell fairly and squarely took the side of the men, not because she had any political axe to grind, but from humanity, and pity for their plight. She put the case into the mouth of her 'hero' John Barton, the chief sufferer and also the chief instrument of the tragedy to follow. With the eloquence learnt not from teachers or from books, but from his own suffering, he

---

[16] Preface to *Mary Barton*.   [17] *Mary Barton*, ch. 9, p. 111.

sees the causes of their misery clearly defined: his wife has died of sheer
destitution and he looks to the future of his daughter, Mary, as promising
little better. HOW THIS SIMPLIFYS A COMPLEX
ECONOMIC SYSTEM

'When I lie on my deathbed, and Mary (bless her!) stands fretting, as I know she
will fret, . . . will a rich lady come and take her to her own home if need be, till
she can look around, and see what best to do? No, I tell you, it's the poor, and the
poor only, as does such things for the poor. Don't think to come over me with
th' old tale, that the rich know nothing of the trials of the poor; I say, if they
don't know, they ought to know. We're their slaves as long as we can work; we
pile up their fortunes with the sweat of our brows, and yet we are to live as
separate as if we were in two worlds; ay, as separate as Dives and Lazarus, with
a great gulf betwixt us; but I know who was best off then,' and he wound up his
speech with a low chuckle that had no mirth in it.[18]

Unaware that Disraeli was using the same image at that very time to
symbolize the division between rich and poor—the Two Nations as he
saw them—Mrs. Gaskell showed something more than political flair,
a deep understanding of human nature and an acceptance of the bad
with the good in every man. In that 'low chuckle' of John Barton's that
'had no mirth in it' is the alarm-signal for the violence to come, the
ineluctable fate that makes of him a murderer, the instrument of the
workers' vengeance, drawn by lots to strike down the mill-owner's dandy
son who had scoffed at their sufferings.

How personal the book was to her own experience, and how little
influenced by contemporary writing, is best realized by comparison with
the almost exactly contemporary novels of Disraeli, *Coningsby*, published
in 1844, and *Sybil*, published in 1845, which Elizabeth seems not to have
known.[19] To define what *Mary Barton* was and was *not*—fiction used
as a forum for political debate—no better foil exists. In Disraeli the
arguments are put into the mouths of law-givers and privileged men,
perfectly competent to assess the problems of labour from a national
viewpoint. What Elizabeth Gaskell did was to make the inarticulate
workers speak for themselves in their own dialect. The novelty of the
book lay in the fact that the characters were all working-class, with no
admixture from the middle or upper strata of society. Even the wealthy
mill-owner, Carson, is correctly shown as having risen from the ranks
of the operatives, and his wife, as so often happened at the time, as having

[18] *Mary Barton*, ch. 1, p. 8.
[19] A. T. Quiller-Couch quotes Professor Ward as testifying that Mrs. Gaskell was quite
unacquainted with either *Sybil* or *Coningsby*, *Charles Dickens, and other Victorians* (Cambridge, 1925), p. 208.

been a former mill-girl. The setting for the tale is, unrelievedly, Manchester. Dickens was so impressed with the daring innovation that he set *Hard Times* in similar surroundings. Except to the commercial travellers of England, Manchester was virtually unknown in the south, as Elizabeth Gaskell found when planning her novel *North and South*. Her descriptions of the back-to-back insanitary dwellings of her dramatis personae, of the stationary pall of smoke polluting the air, well removed though the mills were from the residential areas where the prosperous cotton-spinners and calico-printers lived, had in themselves the power to shock.

Elizabeth Gaskell's first-hand knowledge of her characters is seen not only in the tragic scenes of their lives but in her recognition of the indomitable spirit to be found among the younger men and women. As a teacher in her husband's Sunday school she got to know the typical Lancashire lassies whom neither hardship nor the monotony of their lives succeeded in crushing. Characteristic of all her Manchester girls are the cheeky, witty, happy-go-lucky impulsive types challenging Libbie Marsh and Margaret Hale in the streets with their laughter, their curiosity, their triumphant spirits. They also had their code of morals, as Elizabeth reported to a correspondent in a letter of 26 November 1849:

I must tell you about some of the Sunday school girls, one of the teachers had been teaching them what dancing mistresses call calisthenic exercises, thinking that as they worked so much in factories, this exercise (which she called doing their arms), would be good for them; but one day two or three refused to do it, looking grave and conscientious, but very resolute; so she asked why, and they said it was forbidden in the Bible,—She asked where and they showed her 'Do not thy alms before men', thats truth and happened this week.[20]

It was through such girls among her pupils that Elizabeth came into contact with the men of their families, the care-worn workers only glimpsed in the streets, and with one in particular who, as she distinctly declared, was the prototype of John Barton.

Replying to questions about the authenticity of her characters in the novel, she confided to her friend Tottie Fox: 'Nobody and nothing was real (I am sorry for you, but I must tell the truth) in M. Barton, but the character of John Barton; the circumstances are different, but the character and some of the speeches, are exactly a poor man I know.'[21]

She had originally intended to call the book *John Barton*[22] and it was only under pressure from her publisher that she was brought, unwillingly,

[20] *GL* 54.   [21] *GL* 48, 29 May 1849.   [22] *GL* 42, early 1849.

to change the title to *Mary Barton*. Her whole intention in planning the book had grown out of her knowledge of this man: 'An ignorant thought-ful man of strong power of sympathy dwelling in a town so full of striking contrasts as this is . . . the victim of the excessive wealth of one fraction of the community at the cost of the labour of the vast majority.'[23] Where the fault lay, as Elizabeth clearly understood, was primarily a matter of economics, with which she did not attempt to meddle; but the fault was also, as she eloquently pleaded, in the want of communication between the 'two worlds'. A MEN

How little she intended the book for political propaganda appears from her own early view of it as a 'tragic poem'[24] in the Wordsworthian acceptance of the term; but no one, in the event, judged the book as that. Writing to Mary Ewart, she complained of the want of understanding in the public of her purpose: nothing had been further from her thoughts than to stir up strife. 'No one can feel more deeply than I how *wicked* it is to do anything to excite class against class.'[25] IT NEEDS NO STIRRING.

The whole tale grew up in my mind as imperceptibly as a seed germinates in the earth [she wrote early in 1849]. . . . I can remember now that the prevailing thought in my mind at the time when the tale was silently forming itself and impressing me with the force of reality, was the seeming injustice of the inequalities of fortune. Now, if they appeared unjust to the more fortunate, they must bewilder an ignorant man full of rude, illogical thought, and full also of sympathy for suffering . . . Round the character of John Barton all the others formed them-selves; he was my hero, *the* person with whom all my sympathies went, with whom I tried to identify myself at the time, because I believed from personal observation that such men were not uncommon, and would well reward such sympathy and love as should throw light down upon their groping search after the causes of suffering.[26]

The grandeur in the conception of the character—the nobility of mind that raises John Barton to the stature of an epic figure fit for 'the tragic poem' of the author's first intention—is best brought out in his end. There was no need for the justices to condemn him to a felon's death, for it was his own breaking heart that passed judgement on his crime. He was not made to be a murderer, and could not survive his act. With the creation of the character of John Barton, Mrs. Gaskell stepped straight into the front rank of the novelists of her time.

The effect of the book was electric. Not for the last time in her life,

---

[23] *GL* 39, 5 Jan. 1849.
[24] See her comments *GL* 37, 1 Jan. 1849, and 39, 5 Jan. 1849.
[25] *GL* 36, late 1848.   [26] *GL* 42.

she shocked her public by taking the side she did: the Manchester mill-owners and the London Tory press were vociferous in their condemnation of the book. 'My poor Mary Barton is stirring up all sorts of angry feelings against me in Manchester', she wrote to her cousin Edward Holland on 13 January 1849, 'but those best acquainted with the way of thinking and feeling among the poor acknowledge its *truth*; which is the acknowledgment I most of all desire, because evils being once recognized are half way on towards their remedy.'[27]

Of her husband's support, however, she could be quite sure. The whole bent of his working life had been to bring enlightenment and encouragement to such men as John Barton who crowded his evening lecture-rooms at the Mechanics' Institute and Owen's College. He was proud of his wife's achievement and contributed the Explanatory Notes to the first edition on the Lancashire dialect used.[28] A keen collector and propagator of dialect himself, he eventually gave two lectures on the dialect used in the book, which were reprinted in the fifth edition of *Mary Barton* in 1854.

The first praise from the outside world to reach Elizabeth came from Carlyle, whose understanding compensated for every disappointment: 'In the midst of all my deep and great annoyance, Mr Carlyle's letter has been most valuable,' she wrote to Chapman on 5 December 1848, 'and has given me almost the only unmixed pleasure I have yet received.'[29]

Despite the anonymity, Carlyle had penetrated the disguise to the extent of realizing that the author of *Mary Barton* was a woman. He wrote to her on 8 November 1848 from Chelsea:

Dear Madam, (For I catch the treble of that fine melodious voice very well)—we have read your book here, my wife first and then I: both of us with real pleasure. A beautiful, cheerfully pious, social, clear and observant character is everywhere recognisable in the writer, which sense is the welcomist sight any writer can show in his books; your field is moreover new, important, full of rich material (which as is usual, required a soul of true opulence to recognise them as such). The result is a Book deserving to take its place far above the ordinary garbage of Novels—a book which every intelligent person may read with entertainment; and which it will do every one good to read. I gratefully accept it as a real contribution (about the first real one) towards developing a huge subject, which has lain dumb too long, and really ought to speak for itself, and tell us its meaning a little, if there be any voice in it at all. Speech or literature (which is, or should be, select speech) could hardly find a more rational function, I think, at present. You will probably give us other books on the same matter; and 'Mary

[27] *GL* 39a.   [28] *GL* 25, 17 Apr. 1848.   [29] *GL* 33.

Barton', according to my auguries of its reception here, is likely to procure you sufficient invitation. May you do it well and ever better! Your writing is already very beautiful, soft, clear and natural. On the side of veracity, of devout earnestness of mind, I find you already strong. May you live long to write good books.

T. Carlyle.[30]

Mary Barton was published anonymously, with the sub-title *A Tale of Manchester Life*, in two volumes, by Chapman and Hall on 25 October 1848. The author herself was not previously notified of the date, and wrote to Chapman as late as 19 October to make a final suggestion about her pseudonym: 'Shall you have any objection', she wrote, 'to the name of "Stephen Berwick" as that of the author of "Mary Barton"?'[31] (Berwick-on-Tweed was, it may be remembered, her father's birthplace.) Her letter was written from her uncle Samuel Holland's house at Portmadoc, where, in anticipation of the event, she had fled.

On each successive publication of her works she took refuge in flight, a gesture that appears surprising in a woman of her apparent strength of character, but deeply revealing of her nervous temperament. She dreaded notoriety to a morbid degree. 'I can scarcely yet understand how people can reconcile it to their consciences to try and discover what it is evident the writer wishes to conceal. I have been made very unhappy by my own self-reproaches for the deceit I have practised, and into which I have almost been forced by impertinent enquiry',[32] she wrote to her publisher in December after public curiosity had reached its height. 'I do think praise to one's face is a greater impertinence than blame; and either with reference to a book published anonymously a most under-bred thing.'[33]

Utterly unforeseen by her, and whether she liked it or not, the publication of *Mary Barton* revolutionized her life. It forced her into the ranks of professional writers; it brought her the acquaintance of an ever-widening circle of celebrities whose demands on her were the measure of her success; and it brought her a wealth of personal friends whose importance to her emotional life cannot be reckoned.

[30] R. D. Waller, *Letters Addressed to Mrs. Gaskell.*
[31] *GL* 28, 19 Oct. 1848.
[32] *GL* 34, 7 Dec. 1848.   [33] *GL* 40, 8 Mar. 1849.

CHAPTER X

THE LITERARY SCENE

ELIZABETH GASKELL had not only intensely maternal feelings but a great capacity for friendship. Apart from her sisters-in-law, whom she loved instantly on first acquaintance, her Manchester circle did not afford her the kind of intellectual or emotional stimulus her nature needed. It was made up in the main of her husband's professional colleagues and parishioners: the Robberds, the Potter brothers— Edmund and Sidney—with whom he had been at Glasgow University, and who had remained his close friends, different as were their avocations. They were wealthy calico-printers with fine houses out of town and factories employing large numbers of workers. (Edmund's son, Rupert, became the father of Beatrix Potter, born 1866, whose recollections of Mr. Gaskell in old age are a tribute to the lasting sweetness and charm of his character.) There were the Alcocks, Mr. Alcock being chairman of the Cross Street Unitarian Chapel; the Dukinfield Darbishires; the Schwabes—Adolf and Salis, calico-printers like the Potters, members of the large German colony operating in Manchester, whose acquaintance enlarged Elizabeth's experience by the continental atmosphere of their homes and their connections abroad. Other Unitarians were the American-born Bradfords whom Elizabeth liked so much as to call her last daughter Julia Bradford, after Mrs. Julia Bradford.

While all these acquaintances gave Elizabeth insights into the commercial and professional life of Manchester, indispensable to her as a novelist of contemporary life, they were not people with whom she could share her intellectual tastes, or confide the secret of her authorship. Sheltering behind anonymity in publishing her novel, she believed herself secure from recognition. In the event, the character of the book she wrote forced the issue, and brought her face to face with Manchester opinion on the vexed question of employment and labour. She suffered some very hostile comment from local opinion. 'Some people here are very angry and say the book will do harm; and for a time I have been shaken and sorry', she wrote early in January 1849.[1] 'Half the masters here are bitterly angry with me—half (and the best half) are buying it to give to their work-people's libraries . . . I had no idea it would have proved such a fire brand',[2] she told Chapman at the same time. 'Mr Edmund Potter thinks the book so true he is going to buy it for his men', she reported to a new friend, Catherine Winkworth, on 23 December 1848.[3] Deeply upset as she was by the strong and often openly hostile reaction to her book in her immediate Manchester circle, the timely friendship of Catherine Winkworth and her sisters brought her the double compensation of understanding for her work and the emotional outlet she needed.

She had made the acquaintance of the Winkworth girls shortly before the publication of *Mary Barton*. They were students of her husband's, who began attending his evening classes in English Literature, Composition, and Chemistry in 1841. Their father was a London silk-merchant who had moved to Manchester in 1828 and, belatedly and half-heartedly, set about providing a higher education for his children.

The Winkworth household was intensely religious, and the young people, five girls and two boys, were narrowly brought up. The girls—Susanna, Emily, Selina, Catherine, Alice—were in their early twenties when Mrs. Gaskell met them, and the boys, William and Stephen, in their teens. The death of their mother and their father's remarriage in 1845 had made home life as unhappy for the girls as it had been for Elizabeth Stevenson in comparable circumstances. To escape from home some of them went to Dresden to study German and art in the hope of qualifying themselves for some sort of independence; and on their return to Manchester in 1846 they had asked Mr. Gaskell to add Greek to their other coachings. They attended James Martineau's lectures on logic, and for both their teachers they had boundless admiration and enthusiasm, which manifested itself at times in a way that was rather too much for Mr. Gaskell's modesty. They declared themselves deeply indebted to his 'rich and varied culture, rare critical power, and exquisite refinement of taste'.[4]

They were convinced that he would have been capable of original work of his own had he not sacrificed all his time to the 'unselfish and lifelong devotion to religious and benevolent labours for others'.[5] While Mr. Gaskell shielded himself as best he could from the Miss Winkworths' *schwärmerei*, their earnestness in study and their unhappiness at home

---

[1] *GL* 39.   [2] *GL* 37.   [3] *GL* 35.
[4] M. Shaen, *Memorials of Two Sisters* (London, 1908), p. 23.   [5] Ibid.

gained them the sympathy and kindness of Mr. Gaskell's wife, and late in 1847 they made her acquaintance. Susanna memorably recorded their first impressions of her:

When we first knew Mrs. Gaskell she had not yet become celebrated, but from the earliest days of our intercourse with her we were struck with her genius, and used to say to each other that we were sure she could write books, or do anything else in the world that she liked. And the more we knew of her the more we admired her. She was a noble-looking woman, with a queenly presence, and her high, broad, serene brow, and finely-cut mobile features, were lighted up by a constantly-varying play of expression as she poured forth her wonderful talk. It was like the gleaming ripple and rush of a clear deep stream in sunshine. Though one of the most brilliant persons I ever saw, she had none of the restlessness and eagerness that spoils so much of our conversation nowadays. There was no hurry or high-pressure about her, but she seemed always surrounded by an atmosphere of ease, leisure, and playful geniality, that drew out the best side of everyone who was in her company. When you were with her, you felt as if you had twice the life in you that you had at ordinary times.[6]

Almost immediately Mrs. Gaskell's sympathy and interest were aroused, and her friendship transformed their rather joyless lives. They were evidently captivated by her vital presence, and as they were in need of encouragement and sympathy she set about helping them to cultivate their talents. They were keen German scholars and Susanna was soon putting her knowledge of the language to translating German works for the English press; Catherine and Selina were gifted artists and studied drawing; all of them were dedicated social workers and eager to help Mrs. Gaskell with her classes for working girls. They were young women after her own heart, and she welcomed their friendship.

In the autumn of 1848, just before the publication of *Mary Barton*, Catherine Winkworth, then aged 20, was ordered to the coast for her health (there was some anxiety on the score of her lungs) and she was sent first to Southport and later to the milder climate of the Isle of Wight. While she was at Southport from September to November 1848, Mrs. Gaskell visited her twice, a kindness that bound Catherine to her for life.

Southport has a halo of glory round it in my eyes now, because of Mrs. Gaskell's visit to us [Catherine wrote from there on 27 October 1848]. It *was* so delightful having her here all to ourselves, and we got so intimate together. Everything I see of her makes me admire and love her more. She is so full of information on such various subjects, has seen so many clever and curious people, so much life altogether;—and then she is so thoroughly good. Her thoughtful kindness and

[6] Ibid., pp. 23-4.

gentleness to me, because I was ill, was as great as if I were one of her own children. Well! she certainly is as near perfection as any one I know, . . .[7]

Mrs. Gaskell's own sparkling letters to Catherine show how much attuned were their minds, despite the difference in their ages. By 11 November she was writing to Catherine: 'Do call me Lily, and never mind respect to your elders. *Ils sont passés ces beaux jours là* . . . I wish I had five sisters, who were bound to love me by their parents' marriage certificate; but as I have not, I mean to take you for sisters and daughters at once.'[8]

On her flight to Wales to hide from the publicity attending the publication of *Mary Barton*, Elizabeth took Emily Winkworth with her. Within the year Emily was to become engaged to the son of the Gaskells' friends, the Shaens of Crix, and settle in London. It is from the correspondence of Emily with her sisters during the visit to Portmadoc that the details of Mrs. Gaskell's reactions to the publication of *Mary Barton* are known.

What do you think? [Emily wrote to Catherine on 3 November 1848]. I'm positive 'Mary Barton, a Story of Manchester Life', is by Mrs. Gaskell! I got hold of it last night going to bed, and knew by the first few words it was hers—about Green Heys Fields and the stile she was describing to Kate and me the other day;—but we haven't talked a word about it yet . . . The folks here [the Hollands] know it I am sure—they all turned so silent when I began to talk about it at breakfast time, and Mrs. Gaskell suddenly popped down under the table to look for something which I am sure wasn't there. It is *exquisitely* written, makes one cry rather too much, that is all; the little bits of description perfect; the dialogue, too, extremely clever, humorous here and there. It was finished a year ago, the preface says, and begun three years ago—no doubt to help her to take her thoughts off her poor lost baby.[9]

Writing to Catherine by the same post (under cover of Emily's letter) Mrs. Gaskell herself made no reference whatever to the subject. This was how she wanted it; and the perfectly relaxed tone of her letter shows how much she could enjoy authorship—on her own terms. Back in the Hollands' lovely home, where she had spent part of her honeymoon, she felt herself secure. She wrote:

I don't know how it is our days go away in doing so little. We breakfast nominally at half-past 8, only it is always 9; sit an hour over it talking; come into the drawing-room, and stand over the fire talking, and looking at the lovely view through the window . . . suddenly remember the post comes in and whisks out again any time

[7] Shaen, *Memorials*, pp. 29–30.   [8] *GL* 30, 11 Nov. 1848.
[9] Shaen, *Memorials*, p. 31.

between 12 and 2, so hurry away to write letters for the bag; are urged to go out and not lose the beautiful weather by Fanny [Fanny Holland 1800-83, her cousin], but do contrive to hang about . . . till the bag comes in; tumble over each other in our haste to get our letters; speak crossly to anyone who speaks to us till we've read, and if possible answered, our letters—then comes a calm in which we can draw deep breaths, for the event of the day is over—the bag is gone off again. Then walk till dinner (4 to 5). Uncle Sam always comes in to dinner and we talk to him; he is charmed with Emily and they carry on a regular flirtation. . . . Emily will come back brimful of Welsh stories I think; for Sam pours them into her not unwilling ears. Give my best love to Süschen, the prettiest abbreviation I have seen for Susanna yet. And believe me, dearest Kate-Bettina (for somehow you two are inextricably blended, with a touch of Selina over both), your very affectionate E. C. G.[10]

The pleasant acquisition of £100 of her own (which if not *legally* hers at the time, was in her pocket), and some encouragement from the Howitts and her publisher to visit London, tempted her to take a trip there in the spring. Already in February she wrote to engage lodgings, and as the plan took shape in her mind, she consulted Chapman on ways and means of procuring 'Orders' for concerts, theatres, and exhibitions she especially wanted to attend. While welcoming her plan and showing himself most helpful in getting her Orders, Chapman warned her of what she must expect if she appeared in the capital: the lionizing inseparable from success. Her complete surprise at such an eventuality is the measure of her whole attitude to her work: that it was a private thing that had no connection with her social life. Thanking Chapman in a letter of 8 March for warning her against being 'lionized', she added: 'I am truly grateful to you for it. I hardly understand *what* is meant by the term.' That Chapman had hinted at the ill effects on authors' characters of an excess of publicity and praise is evident from her reply:

. . . nor do I *think* anything could alter me from my own self; but I will be on my guard. . . . it would ill become me to say I might not be materially altered for the worse by this mysterious process of 'lionizing'. How am I to help it? . . . Oh dear! I wish poor Mary Barton could be annihilated this next month; and then I might go where I liked, and do and see what I liked naturally and simply.

There were people she wanted to see, as well as things, she told Chapman, and among these, besides the Howitts and her friends the Shaens, it may be supposed were Forster, to whose recommendation she owed the publication of *Mary Barton*, and Carlyle, the most illustrious as well as one of the most genuine of her early admirers. His praise had truly pleased her.

> I do indeed value Mr Carlyle's note, it bears the stamp of honesty and truth; in the discriminate praise; and shows that he thinks me worthy of being told of my faults . . . I have seen enough of the way in which authors in general *flummery* each other up with insincere and overdone praise to be disgusted with flattery for ever.[11]

It was unthinkable for a married lady to go up to London alone, and as Mr. Gaskell could evidently not leave his duties at that time of the year, she invited her cousin Anne Holland (daughter of her uncle Sam of Plas Penrhyn) to 'chaperone' her. When reassuring Chapman of her ability to stand up to the threat of 'lionizing' in London, she told him: 'Luckily for me Miss Holland possesses excellent sense, and a very fair proportion of satirical power, which she is not at all unwilling to exert; and I shall tell her not to spare me in the least.'

Coinciding with her visit, Emily Winkworth was also in London, staying with relatives at Islington, so as to see something of her fiancé, William Shaen. Mrs. Gaskell frequently invited her to join in her visits to interesting people and places, which Emily usefully reported in her letters home; thus affording an eye-witness account of many of the events of that first London visit of the 'Author of Mary Barton'.

The landlady having at last replied to her letters, they went up to London, presumably on 14 March as planned, and settled in lodgings recommended by their friends the Darbishires in Panton Square, Bloomsbury—'dear charming, dingy dirty Panton Square', as she spoke of it afterwards, with its 'little dusty noisy lodgings'. But later still it became 'my dear old dreamy Panton Square',[12] and whatever the drawbacks the lodgings were to be her London headquarters on subsequent visits.

The early part of her stay in London has left few records, in contrast to the fully documented reports of the later days. She succeeded in preserving her independence of movement, in escaping notoriety (except for calls on her publisher and on Carlyle), and in keeping to her original programme of seeing places of interest in preference to people. She visited the Academy several times, attended lectures at the Athenaeum, went to the opera and also to Sadler's Wells. She made a new and wholly congenial friendship with the portrait painter, Eliza Fox, with whom acquaintance ripened overnight into the easiest and most stimulating intimacy.

---

[11] *GL* 40.   [12] *GL* 48, 47, 69.

'Tottie' Fox, as Mrs. Gaskell was to call her, was the daughter of William Johnson Fox, a man of many parts not unlike her own father, whose successive professions—preacher in the Unitarian Church, journalist, and parliamentarian—brought him a vast circle of acquaintances in almost every sphere of public life, chief and foremost among them being Charles Dickens. Mrs. Gaskell's acquaintance with Tottie could therefore have originated with any one of the Fox connections, religious or literary. As a practising Unitarian she would attend either one or other of the two London chapels—that in Essex Street, Strand, of which the minister was Thomas Madge, or that in Little Portland Street (nearer her lodgings) of which Edward Tagart was the minister. With both these ministers and with William Fox, Mr. Gaskell had had previous contacts.

The eloquence of William Fox as a preacher had earned him the nickname of 'the golden-tongued apostle of untaxed bread', whilst his reformist views had earned him the friendship of Charles Dickens, who had long counted him among his intimates and who, on the foundation of his liberal paper *The Daily News*, had appointed him his principal leader writer. Fox had contributed a sensational leader to the opening number of the paper on 21 January 1845 demanding the repeal of the Corn Laws.[13]

Eliza Fox's young girlhood had been made difficult by the separation of her parents, but in the Bohemian ambience of her father's home, where writers, artists, politicians came and went as in an open forum, she had developed pronounced tastes and an emancipated character that craved independence and a career. She had early wanted to go on the stage, and her father had consulted his friend Macready, who had advised against it. Eliza was very small and perhaps had not the physique for so exacting a profession; she took up art instead, training as a portrait painter, a profession she was successfully pursuing in her Charlotte Street studio when Mrs. Gaskell first met her.[14]

The 'lionizing' process with which Chapman had threatened Mrs. Gaskell appears to have built up steadily. By the end of April and early May, from which time her London letters describing this visit survive, her acquaintance and her engagements with celebrities of the day are already considerable. Her first extant note to Eliza Fox, dated 5 May, gives the measure of these: from her original circle comprising the Howitts, Edward Chapman, and the Unitarian preachers, she was, as

[13] Edgar Johnson, *Charles Dickens* (London, 1953), i. 465, 531, 577–81.
[14] The records of the Royal Academy show that Eliza Fox exhibited in the Summer Exhibition from 1848 onwards.

she expressed it, 'so whirled about . . . that I hardly know what I write',[15] having by then been drawn into the innermost circle surrounding Dickens.

Dickens had expressed his admiration of *Mary Barton* from the moment of publication—reading it in one of his favourite working retreats, Brighton, from where he sent a copy to Samuel Rogers on 18 February with ardent commendations. If he had not succeeded in contacting the author before her London visit, the reason lay with his complete absorption in planning his new book, *David Copperfield*, with whose opening chapters, even its title, he was wrestling up to the very time of serial publication, on 1 May 1849. The overwhelming success of this opening number exceeded all his previous records, and he and his friends and vast circle of admirers were basking in the sunshine of popular acclaim at the very moment Mrs. Gaskell was writing her letter to Tottie Fox. Tottie, as one of the inner Dickens circle, had immediately sent Mrs. Gaskell a copy of the opening number. Writing to her at half-past eleven at night on 5 May, Mrs. Gaskell said:

I think I have behaved most abominably in never taking any notice of your great kindness in sending me David Copperfield, *and* your note. Oh dear! I have been so whirled about since I saw you last that I hardly know what I write. I do so like D. Copperfield; and it was a charming liberty you took in sending it. I don't know if you did *finally* ask us to dinner at five on Wednesday; but the Fates (in the shape of Mr. Forster,) seem to have determined it for us, whether you will or no, my dear! And we mean to Sadlers-Wells it afterwards, as you proposed. May we?

Mentioning that she had changed lodgings to 27 Woburn Square, and enumerating her next day's engagements, which included a musical evening at the music critic Henry Chorley's, she concluded: 'I am intoxicated with sparkling conversation heard tonight at Mrs. Proctor's. I keep smiling to myself and trying to remember things—all to no purpose,—the foam has faded from the Champagne.'[16] The 'lionizing' that afforded such ambrosial feasts was obviously proving an unqualified delight and exactly suited to her quicksilver temperament.

The programme of her next few days' engagements reads like a Court Circular: after the dinner at Eliza Fox's—with Sadlers Wells to follow— she breakfasted with Richard Monckton Milnes, in company with the Revd. Frederick Maurice, for whom she was to conceive a great and lasting admiration; followed the next day by that crowning honour for

---

[15] *GL* 44a, 5 May 1849.   [16] Ibid.

all successful authors, breakfast at Samuel Rogers's (where she met the Macreadys and was moved and charmed with the conversation of Mrs. Macready); followed the next day by dinner at Forster's, at his famous Lincoln's Inn chambers, under the allegorical painted ceiling to be immortalized in *Bleak House*; which in turn led up to the climax of her London visit, the dinner given by Dickens on 12 May to celebrate the publication of *David Copperfield*.

Characteristically, and generously, Elizabeth Gaskell wrote her mint-fresh impression of this memorable evening to her old friends the Greens, the Unitarian minister's family at Knutsford, with whom Marianne and Meta had been left in charge, and where such splendours were most likely to give pleasure.

The day had been crammed with engagements up to the very time of dressing for the dinner. It began with breakfast at Richard Monckton Milnes's (when the entire House of Lords was there, according to her cousin Anne Holland), and they were 'very merry and it was a very short two hours which every one had said was the proper number of hours to stay at breakfast'. This was followed by a visit to 'the Exhibition' (Burlington House) and 'thence to Stafford House, the Duke of Sutherlands'', where they saw 'the most beautiful picture-gallery, statues, and furniture and flowers I ever could have fancied, and in the most perfect taste'. Looking up at the pictures and the gilding tired her not a little, 'and [I] was very glad to come out and proceed leisurely home', dress and go to dine at Mr. Dickens's, 'making what Annie calls "a rich day"'.[17]

In all her varied and detailed account of the personalities present, it is significant that she omitted all description of Dickens himself, or of her impression of him. This was unlike her, fired as she usually was in the presence of genius. Seated between him and Douglas Jerrold at dinner, in the place of honour, it is striking that it was Jerrold's wit that impressed her. With Dickens she would have close business connections over the next few years, but it may be doubted whether, with all her admiration of his work, she ever liked him as a man.

We were shown [she wrote to Annie Green] into Mr. Dickens' study; this is the part, dear Annie, I thought you would like to hear about.

It is the study where he writes all his works; and has a bow-window, is about the size of Uncle Holland's drawing-room. There are books all round, up to the ceiling, and down to the ground; a standing-desk at which he writes; and all manner of comfortable easy chairs. There were numbers of people in the room. Mr. Rogers (the old poet, who is 86, and looked very unfit to be in such a large

[17] *GL* 45a, 13 May 1849.

party,) Douglas Jerrold, Mr and Mrs Carlyle, Hablot Browne, who illustrated Dickens' works, Mr Forster, Mr and Mrs Tagart, a Mr Kenyon. We waited dinner a long time for Lady Dufferin . . . but she did not come till after dinner. Anne [Holland] sat between Carlyle and Rogers,—I between Dickens and Douglas Jerrold. Anne heard the most sense, and I the most wit; I never heard any one so witty as Douglas Jerrold, who is a very little almost deformed man with grey flowing hair, and very fine eyes. He made so many bon-mots, that at the time I thought I could remember; but which now have quite slipped out of my head. After dinner when we went upstairs I sat next to Mrs Carlyle, who amused me very much with her account of their only servant who comes from Annandale in Scotland, and had never been accustomed to announce titles . . . In the evening, quantities of other people came in . . . I kept trying to learn people's faces off by heart, that I might remember them; but it was rather confusing there were so *very* many. There were some nice little Dickens' children in the room,—who were so polite, and well-trained. We came away at last feeling we had seen so many people and things that day that we were quite confused; only that we should be glad to remember we had *done* it.[18]

How Mrs. Carlyle, who had so well entertained Mrs. Gaskell before the gentlemen's return to the drawing-room, reacted to the night's guest of honour, appears in her own piquant account of the occasion. Writing as usual to her aunt Jeannie Welsh on 17 May, she said:

I have been to several parties—a dinner at Dickens's last Saturday where I never went before . . . Such getting up of the steam is unbecoming to a literary man who *ought* to have his basis elsewhere than on what the old Annandale woman called 'Ornament and grander'. The dinner was served up in the new fashion—not placed on the table at all—but handed round—only the dessert on the table and quantities of *artificial* flowers—but such an overloaded dessert! pyramids of figs raisins oranges—ach! At the Ashburton dinner served on those principles there were just *four cowslips* in china pots—four silver shells containing sweets, and a silver filigree temple in the middle! but here the very candles rose each out of an artificial rose! Good God! Mrs. Gaskell the Authoress of *Mary Barton* was there—I had already seen her at my own house, a natural unassuming woman whom they have been doing their best to spoil by making a lioness of her.[19]

Both Mrs. Gaskell and Mrs. Carlyle mentioned the presence of old Samuel Rogers at the dinner, their respective comments affording illuminating insights into their own natures. Mrs. Gaskell wrote of his looking 'very unfit to be in such a large party', while Mrs. Carlyle, as fully equal as ever old Rogers could be to answer spite with spite, com-

[18] *GL* 45a.
[19] Jane Welsh Carlyle, *Letters to her Family*, ed. L. Huxley (London, 1924), p. 326.

mented: '. . . old Rogers, who ought to have been buried long ago, so old and ill-natured he is grown.'

In the further crowd of celebrities that arrived after dinner, including Thackeray, artists, ladies of title, and musicians, what patently pleased Mrs. Gaskell most was hearing 'some beautiful music'; and seeing some of the little Dickens children. Small wonder that, despite her efforts 'to learn people's faces off by heart', she came away feeling confused, only 'glad to remember we had *done* it', a comment that suggests she had emerged unscathed—and immensely stimulated—from the lionizing ordeal.

She was not yet out of the wood. The Howitts claimed her to breakfast again the next day, Sunday; then they took her to church to hear the Revd. Frederick Maurice preach ('whom I like very much indeed').[20] She made farewell calls on the Carlyles at their request, on the Monday, and on Samuel Rogers on the Tuesday, when she was invited again to breakfast and was enthralled by his collection of Etruscan wares; and finally made her escape from London on Wednesday, 16 May, after exchanging Christian names with Eliza Fox. From then on, Eliza Fox became one of her most constant and intimate correspondents, and the one to whom she was most self-revealing.

Her London initiation, whether she recognized it or not, had been a personal triumph for her. The Dickens dinner marked her admittance into the inner circle of London literary society; from then on, she ceased to be an anonymous provincial writer, and became a much courted one, whose work was eagerly sought by the inventive and restless promoter of all reputations, Dickens himself. Not content with his sensational triumphs as a novelist, he had founded first a daily paper (*The Daily News*) into which he absorbed the talents of all his friends, and within the year set about launching a weekly journal as well, *Household Words*, the first number of which, published on 30 March 1850, carried a contribution from Mrs. Gaskell. It was as a direct result of Dickens's highly flattering invitation to her to contribute regularly to his journal that she achieved her most lasting fame with the *Cranford* sketches, which she contributed serially and irregularly over the next three years.

[20] *GL* 47.

CHAPTER XI

THE 'HIDDEN WORLD OF ART'

IN spite of the lionizing, which appeared to have had no ill effects but had inevitably built up her self-confidence, Elizabeth did not consider herself 'her own woman' as yet, free of her time and of all other obligations than those of creative work. She loved her children too much ever to put them second to other interests, and was completely absorbed in them, enjoying every phase of their growth with amused and patient sympathy. She had suffered too much herself for want of a mother ever to neglect the innumerable claims they made on her.

Flossy and Julia were as yet very young—seven and three years old respectively—at the time of her return from London in the summer of 1849; while Marianne and Meta were fourteen and twelve respectively. She herself was the most educative influence in their childhood, not only directing their studies but stimulating their feelings for the finer things of life. Though their father loved them intensely, he was, as his wife said, of so anxious a disposition as to fear rather than enjoy even the care-free hours when she planned changes of scene and holidays for them—often taken riskily in his view.

The girls had a governess at home, Miss Rosa Mitchell, who taught them with the help of visiting masters for many years until they reached their teens, when each was sent in turn to boarding-schools of their own choice. Miss Mitchell was so much a member of the family as to be called 'Rosa' by Mrs. Gaskell, and greatly loved. She had previously run her own school in Manchester and was competent to take the girls in all subjects, including Italian.

As the mother of four girls, with as yet no great financial resources to provide for them, there was never a day when the claims of domesticity did not come thick and fast. 'I've scarcely seen anyone yet,' Elizabeth wrote after her return to Catherine Winkworth; 'but then I've made four flannel petticoats, and I don't know how many preserves and pickles, which are so good and successful I am sure it is my vocation to be a house-keeper; not an economical one, but a jolly extravagant one.'[1]

[1] GL 49, 21 Aug. 1849.

Do you know what an American 'Bee' is [she further asked Catherine, who was still on the south coast for her health]? You know it's the sort of pic-nic they get up in the back-woods, when they want to build a house or a bridge, etc., in a hurry. Well; I'm going to have a 'Bee' here next week, and I wish you and Emily could come to it. There are 192 tucks to be run in my children's garments all at once! so I am going to have a 'Bee' . . . The refreshments are a puzzle to me. I find that in America, toasted cheese spread with honey is *the* thing at 'Bees'; but I am afraid my guests would not appreciate it. What do you suggest?[2]

The family's summer holidays were always planned to get them as far away from Manchester as finances allowed; to the coast or the country—either to the shores of Morecambe Bay or to Wales—no matter how primitive the accommodation, so long as it was close to beautiful surroundings. In the late summer of 1849 they stayed at a farmhouse in the Lakes, at Skelwith near Ambleside. It was during this holiday that the Gaskells made the acquaintance of Edward Quillinan, the widower of Dora Wordsworth, who lived at Lesketh How at Ambleside, and through him had the opportunity of a meeting with Wordsworth, who died the following April (1850). For Elizabeth Gaskell, who had loved his poetry all her life, it was a moving occasion, which he marked by writing in her album: 'He that feels contempt / For any living Thing, hath faculties Which he hath never used. Lesketh How. 20th July 1849.'[3] Quillinan wrote to Crabb Robinson on the occasion: 'Mrs. Gaskell . . . is a *charming* person—She is coming to us (to tea) with her two daughters and a friend on Wednesday', and later, 'She is a very pleasing interesting person.'[4]

While Skelwith drew them back in later summers, the place that had already taken hold of their imaginations as the perfect holiday-retreat was Silverdale on Morecambe Bay, where they were to take root the following summer (1850). This is no idle term as applied to a place that brought such a flowering; affecting as it did not only the growing years of her children, but the best part of Mrs. Gaskell's own working life.

Back in Manchester for the autumn and winter and settled down 'into soberness', Elizabeth urged her new friend Eliza Fox to visit them.

Are you prepared for a garret [she wrote to her in November], rather like Campbell's rainbow, 'a happy spirit to delight mid way twixt earth and heaven'; with *no* fireplace, only a great cistern, which however we lock up for fear of our friends committing suicide. Are you prepared for a cold clammy atmosphere, a town with

---

[2] Ibid.

[3] Shaen, *Memorials.*

[4] *The Correspondence of Henry Crabb Robinson with the Wordsworth Circle*, ed. Morley (Oxford, 1927), ii. 700, 705.

no grace or beauty in it, a house full of cold draughts, and mysterious puffs of icy air? Are you prepared for four girls in and out continually, interrupting the most interesting conversation with enquiries respecting lessons work, etc:— If these delights thy mind can move, come live with me and be my love. I like the house very much, though I acknowledge we have out grown it; you shall have a bottle of hot water in bed, and blankets ad libitum, and we keep glorious fires. The girls *are* very nice ones though I say it that should not say it, and I do think you will like them all in their separate ways, so please write soon and fix your time for coming.[5]

The visit was made, at the beginning of December, when Eliza completed the conquest of the entire Gaskell family. Few were the friends to whom Elizabeth was emboldened to send her husband's 'best love', as she did subsequently to Eliza Fox,[6] or of whom he was 'pleased to say', as his wife laughingly reported, 'that it is not often I make such a "sensible" friendship as the one with you, which I rather resent; for I am sure all my friends *are* sensible.'[7]

The visit of Eliza Fox in December coincided with a new and absorbing concern of Elizabeth's, with which Eliza was able to be of help. Over and above the rival claims on her time between her family and her writing, Elizabeth had a strong compulsion towards social service, as her involvement in the real-life case of John Barton had already shown; and she had lately become deeply interested in the case of a young prostitute imprisoned for theft whom she hoped to rescue. She heard (probably through Eliza Fox) of the rescue work sponsored by Angela Burdett-Coutts, largely administered by Dickens himself, and applied to him directly for advice and information on their emigration scheme.

The interest of the letter, apart from its revelation of her deeply charitable nature, lies in the sketch it contains—a pale outline sketch as yet—of the plot of the book that would grow out of this particular experience, *Ruth*. The incident affords tangible proof, if any were needed, of the close relation between art and life exemplified in Mrs. Gaskell's work. Hers was a spontaneous, unforced talent that took its inspiration direct from daily life.

She wrote to Dickens on 8 January 1850:

I am just now very much interested in a young girl, who is in our New Bayley prison . . . when she was about 14, she was apprenticed to an Irish dress-maker here, of very great reputation for fashion. Last September but one this dress-maker failed, and had to dismiss all her apprentices; she placed this girl with a woman who occasionally worked for her, and who has since succeeded to her

---

[5] *GL* 51, Nov. 1849.   [6] *GL* 63, Jan. 1850; 69, Apr. 1850.   [7] *GL* 69, Apr. 1850.

business; this woman was very profligate and connived at the girl's seduction by a surgeon in the neighbourhood who was called in when the poor creature was ill. Then she was in despair, and wrote to her mother (*who had never corresponded with her all the time she was at school and an apprentice;*) and while waiting the answer went into the penitentiary; she wrote 3 times but no answer came, and in desperation she listened to a woman, who had obtained admittance to the penitentiary solely as it turned out to decoy girls into her mode of life, and left with her; and for four months she has led the most miserable life! in the hopes, as she tells me, of killing herself, for 'no one had ever cared for her in this world,' — she drank, 'wishing it might be poison', pawned every article of clothing — and at last stole. I have been to see her in prison at Mr Wright's request, and she looks quite a young child (she is but 16,) with a wild wistful look in her eyes, as if searching for the kindness she has never known, — and she pines to redeem herself . . . and what I want you to tell me is, how Miss Coutts sends out *her* protegees? . . . and might she be included among them? I want her to go out with as free and unbranded a character as she can; if possible, the very fact of having been in prison etc to be unknown on her landing. I will try and procure her friends when she arrives; only how am I to manage about the voyage? and how soon will a *creditable* ship sail; for she comes out of prison on Wednesday, and there are two of the worst women in the town who have been in prison with her, intending to way-lay her, and I want to keep her out of all temptation, and even chance of recognition. Please will you help me? . . . I can manage all except the voyage . . . and we can pay all her expenses etc. Pray don't say you can't help me . . . She is such a pretty sweet looking girl. I am sure she will do well if we can but get her out in a *good* ship.[8]

Dickens's reply was not only helpful but prompt; it put her in immediate touch with the persons concerned with the emigration scheme in London, and enabled her to ship her protégée out in safe company to the Cape. Her share of activity in achieving these ends was not slight; she visited the girl three times a week in prison 'to keep up and nurse her hopes and good resolutions', applied to the Ragged School master to accompany her on her journey to London and to take charge of her there till the ship sailed; and above all, found a man and his wife going to the Cape 'who will take loving care of her'.[9]

The girl sailed on 4 March, with a complete outfit furnished by Mrs. Gaskell and Eliza Fox. Despite the satisfactory outcome, the incident left Mrs. Gaskell unhappy and disturbed, haunted by the near-destruction of a young and helpless creature. The emotions then roused were never quietened until she had voiced her great appeal in *Ruth*.

Immediately after her letter to Dickens, Elizabeth received another

[8] *GL* 61, 8 Jan. 1850.   [9] *GL* 62, 12 Jan.; 63, 24 Jan. 1850.

one from him. He wrote on 31 January 1850 to invite her to contribute to his new periodical *Household Words*. The very flattering terms of his letter must have convinced her, there and then, of her potential as a professional writer—had conscience and modesty permitted. As it was, she still resolutely put family claims first, while the temptation to write came in a good second.

You may perhaps have seen an announcement in the papers of my intention [Dickens wrote] to start a new cheap weekly journal of general literature.

I do not know what your literary vows of temperance or abstinence may be, but as I do honestly know that there is no living English writer whose aid I would desire to enlist in preference to the authoress of Mary Barton (a book that most profoundly affected and impressed me), I venture to ask you whether you can give me any hope that you will write a short tale, or any number of tales, for the projected pages. . . . I should set a value on your help which your modesty can hardly imagine.

He explained that all contributions would remain anonymous, and outlined the general objectives of the paper as humanitarian—'the raising up of those that are down, and the general improvement of our social condition'[10]—objectives very close to Mrs. Gaskell's heart as he knew, not only from *Mary Barton* but from their recent correspondence over the emigration scheme. Dickens showed how genuine his desire for her collaboration was by offering to go to Manchester for a few hours to discuss the project with her. He did not have to do so. Mrs. Gaskell accepted his invitation and sent him a story which appeared in the opening number of *Household Words*, on 30 March 1850, and in the two following issues.

The story she sent Dickens was 'Lizzie Leigh', a Manchester tale strongly reminiscent in atmosphere and sub-plot of *Mary Barton*, and depending again on types of character and rural and city descriptions for its strongest effects. The theme, the seduction of an innocent country girl employed in Manchester, while it appears to look back to the story of Esther in *Mary Barton*—it may in fact have been a first draft of that story—looks forward also to the total treatment of the subject in *Ruth*. Whatever the chronology of the respective tales, it is certain that Mrs. Gaskell was preoccupied at the time with the subject of prostitution, to which her experiences as a social worker were introducing her. The pathos of Lizzie Leigh's story, in which she is shown as an innocent victim of betrayal, is balanced by the real-life story of the little seamstress with

---

[10] *The Letters of Charles Dickens*, ed. W. Dexter (London, 1938), ii. 202.

whom Mrs. Gaskell had been so absorbed at the time. As in *Mary Barton*, the descriptive passages evoking the country home scenes of the ruined girl are used to heighten the sense of lost innocence and to point the contrast with the misery of city life; its wretched housing conditions, sad streets, noxious climate. The human element is again used to dramatic and emotional effect, the love and compassion of Lizzie's mother being held up as a beacon in the surrounding darkness; and the pathos of the death of the little child—Lizzie's little bastard—used to achieve her redemption. Here, as in *Mary Barton*, and as Elizabeth Gaskell would repeat in almost all her tragic tales, redemption is reached through suffering. It was a doctrine she clung to passionately and used, sometimes, to morbid effect.

There is very little sunshine in 'Lizzie Leigh' but, barring some passages of intolerable melodrama, it is a freshly written tale, full of sensitive observation and humane feeling.

Dickens was delighted with it, although already the editor in him was at work to modify the author's original intentions; the story had been planned to end with Lizzie's death, but he objected. As late as 14 March (the tale appeared on the 30th) he wrote to her:

I am strongly of opinion that as Lizzie is not to die, she ought to put that child in Susan's own arms, and not lay it down at the door. Observe!—The more forcibly and strongly and affectingly, you exhibit her mother's love for her, the more cruel you will make this crime of desertion in her. The same sentiment which animates the mother, will have been done violence to by the daughter; and you cannot set up the one without pulling down the other.[11]

The editorial comments of Dickens, then and thereafter, show the degree of his involvement even in fiction that was not his own; so all-pervasive was his creativity.

How little Mrs. Gaskell estimated her own market value as yet is humorously seen by her astonishment at the payment of £20 for 'Lizzie Leigh'. 'Do you know', she wrote to Tottie Fox,[12] 'they sent me 20£ for Lizzie Leigh? I stared, and wondered if I was swindling them but I suppose I am not.' Such compunction rather corroborates the view that the story was not a new one. 'William', she went on, 'has composedly buttoned it up in his pocket. He has promised I may have some for the Refuge.' William's action, which was perfectly in accordance with the usage of the time before the introduction of the Married Women's Property Act, has often been cited in evidence against him and as proof

[11] Ibid. 210.   [12] *GL* 70, Apr. 1850.

that his wife could not keep her earnings. The facts are quite different. Mrs. Gaskell amassed considerable sums by her writings, made free use of them herself on foreign travel, and ultimately bought a house without her husband's knowledge. Payments by cheque to Mrs. Gaskell would necessarily have to go through William's account before being cashed.

Dickens was so delighted with 'Lizzie Leigh' that he was impatient for further contributions. 'This is a brief letter,' he wrote on 3 July, 'but if you only knew it!—a very touching one in its earnestness. Can't you—won't you—don't you—ever mean to write me another story?'[13] He wrote again on 7 August when Elizabeth was intensely preoccupied with moving house and with the family holidays at Silverdale. That she had no more manuscripts laid by would appear from her delay in supplying the material he wanted; she kept him waiting for both her further contributions of that year, 'The Well of Pen Morfa', which did not appear in *Household Words* until 16 and 23 November, and 'The Heart of John Middleton', which did not appear until the closing issue of the year, on 28 December.

The fact was that she had scruples in devoting too much of her time to writing, lucrative as she was finding it. To her friend Eliza Fox, a fellow artist, she could confide the nature of her dilemma, at the very time Dickens was first soliciting her for contributions: the strong compulsion to write had to be set against the claims of domesticity.

Eliza had just written to her to discuss a plan to go to Munich for six months of art-training. Her relative freedom of movement prompted Elizabeth Gaskell to review her own very different situation.

And now I could say so much about the Munich plan; and what follows in your letter about home duties and individual life; it is just my puzzle . . . if you were here we could talk about it so well. Oh! that you were here! I don't like the idea of your being a whole six months away from call; but that is selfish and not to be taken into consideration. One thing is pretty clear, *Women*, must give up living an artist's life, if home duties are to be paramount. It is different with men . . . However we are talking of women. I am sure it is healthy for them to have the refuge of the hidden world of Art to shelter themselves in when too much pressed upon by daily small Lilliputian arrows of peddling cares; it keeps them from being morbid as you say; and takes them into the land where King Arthur lies hidden, and soothes them with its peace. I have felt this in writing, I see others feel it in music, you in painting, so assuredly a blending of the two is desirable . . . I do believe we have all some appointed work to do, which no one else can do so well;

[13] *Letters*, ii. 220.

Which is *our* work; what *we* have to do in advancing the Kingdom of God; and that first we must find out what we are sent into the world to do, and define it and make it clear to ourselves, (that's *the* hard part) and then forget ourselves in our work. . . .[14]

What that appointed work was, she had still to decide.

The housing problem, brought to the fore by Eliza Fox's visit, was acute at the moment, with the Gaskells facing the necessity of finding a new home by midsummer. The lease of the Rumford Street house would expire by then and they must move and be settled in to their new home by September, when Mr. Gaskell's lectures started up again.

When the new house was found, in April 1850, Elizabeth faced the same moral conflict as in her joy in writing: she had to reconcile it to her conscience. To Tottie Fox she wrote:

And we've got a house. Yes! we *really* have. And if I had neither conscience nor prudence I should be delighted, for it certainly *is* a beauty . . . You *must* come and see us in it, dearest Tottie, and try and make me see 'the wrong the better cause', and that it is right to spend so much ourselves on *so* purely selfish a thing as a house is, while so many are wanting—thats the haunting thought to me; at least to one of my 'Mes', for I have a great number . . . One of my mes is, I do believe, a true Christian—(only people call her socialist and communist), another of my mes is a wife and mother, and highly delighted at the delight of everyone else in the house . . . Then again I've another self with a full taste for beauty and convenience which is pleased on its own account. How am I to reconcile all these warring members? . . . Well! I must try and make the house give as much pleasure to others as I can and make it as little a selfish thing as I can. My dear! its 150 a year, and I dare say we shall be ruined . . . We have a greenhouse . . . which delights the girls . . . *When* will you come and see us—in August if you don't go to Munich. . . . Your room will be over the drawing-room, our's over the dining-room—the girls over their schoolroom, Nursery over Hearn's bedroom—What's your opinion about gas? Healthy or not . . . Dearest little Tottie, we all send love and shall want you to 'handsel' our house . . .[15]

In a very self-revealing aside in the same letter Elizabeth wrote: 'My idea of Heaven just now is, a place where we shan't have any consciences, —and Hell vice versa.'

The house whose acquisition gave her such qualms of conscience was in Plymouth Grove, quite near their former home, and still in the academic area of Manchester. From the outset, 42 Plymouth Grove (as it then was) acquired a character for civilized living that has outlasted the family who brought it fame. Mrs. Gaskell made of it all that her

[14] *GL* 68, Feb. 1850.   [15] *GL* 69, Apr. 1850.

conscience dictated, a place of pleasure and refreshment for countless people—not only celebrities—as well as a home for those she loved. It was a house of generous proportions, in keeping with the character of the family who inhabited it, with seven bedrooms, two attics, and three living-rooms; a handsome square house with pillared portico and surrounding garden, standing on a corner that gave it an appearance of even greater spaciousness and isolation than it actually owned. The greenhouse and the garden even today shed a fresh and verdant air around the house, and that in the Gaskells' day was its chief attraction.

Do you know [Elizabeth wrote to Tottie Fox], I believe the garden will be a great delight in our new house. Clay soil it *will* be, and there is no help for it, but it will be gay and bright with common flowers; and is quite shut in,—and one may get out without bonnet, which is a blessing, I always want my head cool, and stray about in the odd five minutes. You should see Baby and Florence! their delight is most pretty to see every day they go there; and every flower (plant) that peeps up is a treasure.[16]

The move took place, as required, at midsummer, but not without a pang at parting from the old home which held for Elizabeth such poignant memories of her lost boy.[17]

By the end of June the family were gone to the coast, to Silverdale for their annual holiday, while the furnishing and redecorations of the new house were completed. They stayed five weeks in a farmhouse at Silverdale, their first long experience of the place. What it gave them all can be felt by the report of it Mrs. Gaskell sent to a new acquaintance of that summer, Lady Kay-Shuttleworth: speaking of 'our annual migration to the sea-side', she added: 'Silverdale can hardly be called the sea-side, as it is a little dale running down to Morecambe Bay, with grey limestone rocks on all sides, which in the sun or moonlight, glisten like silver. And we are keeping holiday in most rural farm-house lodgings, so that our children learn country interests, and ways of living and thinking.'[18] The importance of Silverdale for her children's education in natural beauty was fully matched by the refreshing influence it exercised on Mrs. Gaskell herself. It combined an amplitude of shore and sky that appealed peculiarly to her sea-loving nature, with wooded hills and rocky promontories, rustic simplicity of life, country fare, and customs that recalled her childhood; a place never lacking in grandeur, either, with the crests of the

16 *GL* 70, 26 Apr. 1850.   17 See p. 74.
18 *GL* 72a, 16 July 1850.

5 (*a*). Barford House, Warwicks

5 (*b*). Avonbank, Stratford-upon-Avon

6. Elizabeth Cleghorn Stevenson, miniature by W. J. Thomson, 1832

Cumbrian hills soaring above the bay to the north. It was a view on whose daily—and nightly—presence Elizabeth Gaskell came to depend more and more for her future writings.

The summer of 1850 was an altogether stimulating and eventful time for her, not only on account of the move to Plymouth Grove and the first close contact with Silverdale, but for the meeting it was to afford her with Charlotte Brontë.

In the course of a visit to her Knutsford friend, Mrs. Davenport, at Capesthorne earlier that summer, she had met Lady Kay-Shuttleworth, of Gawthorpe Hall, Burnley, whose husband—the former Dr. Kay— had distinguished himself during the Manchester cholera epidemic of 1829, and in connection with Poor Law Reform during the 1830s. Married to the heiress of Gawthorpe and settled on his wife's estates as a landed and titled proprietor, Sir James's chief hobby was literary lion-hunting, and he instantly took up the successful authoress of *Mary Barton*. After *Shirley* had been published in October 1849, confirming the reputation of the author of *Jane Eyre*, the Shuttleworths sought out the retiring Charlotte Brontë, and in August 1850 succeeded in obtaining her unwilling consent to visit them at their summer villa on Windermere, Briery Close. An invitation was immediately dispatched to Mrs. Gaskell and her husband to join the party. To his subsequent regret, Mr. Gaskell excused himself on the grounds of sermons to prepare for an impending visit to Birmingham, but Mrs. Gaskell jumped at the opportunity. She had already told Lady Shuttleworth how interested she was in Currer Bell. She had to confess that she did not care much 'for a good deal of the plot of *Shirley*',[19] but was much impressed with the 'expression of her own thoughts' which she found 'so true and brave' that, altogether, 'I greatly admire her'. Mrs. Gaskell travelled to Windermere on Tuesday, 20 August and stayed at Briery Close for three days.

She wrote several accounts to different friends afterwards of that first meeting with Charlotte Brontë, which vary in detail but are constant in essentials. Their importance lies in their ultimate effect on the biography she would come to write of her new acquaintance. Here, in the first rapid sketches of the character and circumstances of Charlotte, can be traced all the errors of the finished portrait. She had been ill informed by the Shuttleworths in the first place of the nature of the Brontë household. They had paid one short courtesy visit to Charlotte and her father the previous March, and depicted the place as destitute of even basic

[19] *GL* 72, 14 May 1850.

E

comforts. Mrs. Gaskell was roused to pity and anger for the victim, as she believed it, of a 'strange, half mad' father, who had 'denied' his daughters all medical care, and would again so deny Charlotte. Mrs. Gaskell was already convinced that Charlotte herself was 'tainted with consumption'.[20] Few subjects could more passionately have stirred the generous and maternal feelings of Elizabeth Gaskell than such a surfeit of misfortunes befalling one defenceless girl—and she the gifted Currer Bell! If there were things in Currer Bell's novels—'coarseness', for example—that she herself and many others did not like, was the explanation not to be found in the unbelievable circumstances of such a home? 'I have never heard of so hard, and dreary a life!'[21] Mrs. Gaskell exclaimed after hearing all the Shuttleworths could relate of it; and did not hesitate even to report widely that Currer Bell had been refused all education by her father and was entirely self-taught.

These initial impressions that figured so largely in her first reports of Currer Bell are all to be found in the biography—except the allegation that she had been denied an education, which would have been difficult to sustain after meeting the Brontës' schoolmistress, Miss Wooler. None the less, the overdramatized portrait was allowed to remain the basis of the finished work, founded almost wholly upon irresponsible hearsay.

The source of her information, as she told Catherine Winkworth in her first letter about Charlotte Brontë, was Lady Kay-Shuttleworth quoting 'an old woman at Burnley'.[22] This woman happened to be the nurse of Mrs. Brontë's last illness, who had been dismissed by Mr. Brontë, and who had been taking her revenge over the years by telling colourful and malicious tales.[23] In these reports, guaranteed as Mrs. Gaskell believed by the character of her informant, were to be found all the accretions to the authentic Brontë story—'All this Lady KS told me'. Here can be found already the sawing-up of the family chairs, the children's partial starvation, even the neglect of their education—'Their father never taught the girls anything.' The myth that he also refused medical care for the dying girls also begins here.[24]

Small wonder that Mrs. Gaskell looked on Charlotte Brontë with amazement and anger, and saw in her an object for unqualified compassion.

Miss Brontë's actual story was sad enough without need of invention: she had within the previous year lost her two very much loved younger sisters and her only brother from galloping consumption, and had only

[20] GL 75, 25 Aug. 1850.   [21] GL 78, 25 Aug. 1850.   [22] GL 75.
[23] F. A. Leyland, The Brontë Family (London, 1886), i. 47.   [24] GL 75.

her old half-blind father for companion. Mr. Brontë was 'wayward, eccentric and wild' at times, as Mrs. Gaskell reported him,[25] for he had more than a dash of genius himself, but he was neither heartless nor ungenerous, as the repeated witness of his parishioners and servants attest, and he was passionately fond and proud of his children. To accuse him of refusing his daughters an education was carrying malice to ludicrous lengths, for he was as much obsessed by their education as he was by concern for his children's health. As the remaining letters of Charlotte show, he was so watchful of the least fluctuation in her health at this very time as quite to harry her with his precautions.

In Charlotte's life Elizabeth Gaskell perceived elements of drama that appealed peculiarly to her as a novelist; and already then, when she first became absorbed in the personality of her new friend, the book she would ultimately write was taking shape in a form far nearer to great fiction than to strict biography. As with Mary Barton, Lizzie Leigh, Libbie Marsh, and the heroines to come, the problems oppressing Charlotte Brontë were taking hold of her imagination, while she sought a solution to them, just as though the real-life heroine were as capable of manipulation as the invented ones. From then on, few months would pass without Mrs. Gaskell attempting to ameliorate the lot of her friend by invitations to her home, or by engaging those of her friends, like the Shaens or the Winkworths, with comfortable and hospitable homes of their own, to invite her to the milder climate of the south for the benefit of her health.

The reticence of Charlotte herself, the shyness ('She is said to be frightfully shy, and almost cries at the thought of going amongst strangers')[26] were, it has to be remembered, among the contributing causes for the continued withholding of essential information about herself and her life. That life, as her published writings reveal, was lived far more on a subjective and visionary level than Mrs. Gaskell ever divined, or Charlotte herself ever wished to be known. How little of her true thoughts she admitted even to her oldest and closest friend, Ellen Nussey, the correspondence is there to prove. So, though she liked and trusted Mrs. Gaskell from that first meeting, she hid the inner flame of genius by which she really lived even from *her* kindness. To Ellen, writing of that visit to Windermere, Charlotte merely reported the presence as fellow guest, of 'Mrs. Gaskell, the authoress of *Mary Barton*, who came to the

[25] *GL* 78.
[26] *GL* 77, 25 Aug. 1850.

Briery the day after me. I was truly glad of her companionship. She is a woman of the most genuine talent, of cheerful, pleasing, and cordial manners, and, I believe, of a kind and good heart.'[27]

The friendship then formed proved to be one of exceptional surrender —and softness—on Charlotte's part, and of ever-increasing liking and respect on Mrs. Gaskell's. Their correspondence, opened immediately on their return to their respective homes, was marked by constant small kindnesses on Mrs. Gaskell's part—enclosing flowers from her garden which Charlotte Brontë was so little spoilt as to cherish inordinately; the exchange of books (their own or those of favourite authors like Tennyson or Wordsworth); the discussion of future work-plans; the prospect of further meetings; all of which brought unaccustomed happiness to Charlotte Brontë. Her letters to Mrs. Gaskell are markedly different in tone from those to her other correspondents, responding to the soothing effect of her new friend's considerate kindness. 'I have a thousand things to be thankful for,' she wrote to Mrs. Gaskell on the return from Windermere, 'and, amongst the rest, that this morning I received a letter from you, and that this evening I have the privilege of answering it.'[28] Thanking her for an invitation to stay at Crix in Essex with Mrs. Gaskell later in the autumn, which she was unable to accept, she wrote, 'Meantime the *mere thought* of it does me good.' 'Kind, pleasant and cordial is your little note, and you are thanked for it', she wrote on 25 March 1851.

In return Charlotte Brontë gave her new friend that encouragement and perceptive appreciation of her writing that she was singularly equipped to give. She was a most penetrating critic and a most honest one. Her slightly longer experience of publishing and dealings with publishers was of use to Mrs. Gaskell, then only at the beginning of her professional career.

At Windermere, where the fellow authors had been thrown so much together, Mrs. Gaskell had confided in Charlotte Brontë her problems as a prospective writer and the degree of her literary commitments to date. While her home duties prevented her engaging in another full-scale work in succession to *Mary Barton*, she was writing and publishing —although anonymously as yet—short stories in the periodical press. Just before leaving home for Windermere, she had finished a commission for Chapman who had asked her for a Christmas story—eventually published as 'The Moorland Cottage'. The terms of publication were

[27] C. K. Shorter, *The Brontës, Life and Letters* (London, 1908), ii, letter 462.
[28] Ibid., letter 463.

so unsatisfactory and Chapman's cavalier conduct in changing the title so disagreeable as greatly to incense her.

Her annoyance was heightened by Chapman's conduct over the successive editions of *Mary Barton*, which had by that summer gone into its fourth edition without notification to the author—or supplementary royalties. She had, as she later explained to Lady Kay-Shuttleworth, received a down payment of £100 for *Mary Barton* and had retained no further hold on succeeding editions. 'I only know from the public papers *when* a new edition is published; I am never consulted.' About the new story she told Lady Kay-Shuttleworth:

I am almost sorry you know I am going to publish another because I don't think you will like it. Mr. Chapman asked me to write a Xmas Story, 'recommending benevolence, charity, etc', to which I agreed, why I cannot think now, for it was very foolish indeed. However, I could not write about virtues to order, so it is simply a little country love-story called Rosemary, which will I suppose be published somewhere in November, and not be worth reading then; it is bad to make a bargain beforehand as to time or subject; though the latter I have rejected.[29]

Her dissatisfaction with Chapman made her all the readier to listen to the advice of Charlotte Brontë who warmly recommended her own publisher, George Smith, of the firm of Smith, Elder & Co.

When the work, entitled 'The Moorland Cottage', appeared in December and Charlotte received a copy from the author, she wrote in acknowledgement: 'My dear Mrs. Gaskell, You are twice thanked. First for the real treat afforded by the "Moorland Cottage". I told you that the book opened like a daisy; I now tell you that it finishes like a herb—a balsamic herb with healing in its leaves.'[30] From then on, the paths of the two authors ran along parallel courses, and their friendship had a mutually inspiring quality that was to survive the death of Charlotte Brontë.

Despite the new house, the new friendships, the fresh incentives to work—perhaps because of all these—Mrs. Gaskell's health broke down in the autumn and she was ordered from Manchester for a complete change of air. As yet her complaint was not recognized for what it was, a heart condition, but was diagnosed by the family doctor as 'spinal irritation'[31] that gave rise to violent headaches and nervous lassitude. 'Manchester was undoing all the good I had received in the country', she told Lady Kay-Shuttleworth from Warwick in November. By then it

[29] *GL* 81, 25 Sept. 1850.
[30] Letter dated 22 Jan. 1851, Manchester University Library.   [31] *GL* 81.

was becoming clear to them all that Manchester was not good for her health; every return to country life, whether Knutsford, Silverdale, Wales, or Warwickshire, proved it. 'I am a different creature to what I am in Manchester', she told Lady Kay-Shuttleworth again, writing from Worcester a month later.[32] It was her husband who determined she should stay away through the worst weather: 'my dear husband determined that I should again set off on my travels and spend these two months, (usually so damp in Manchester,) in a warmer and drier place.' In Manchester 'there was thick fog till ten or eleven, beginning again at four. The worst is my husband's duties prevent his joining me, (even for a few days,) at present.'[33]

Urged by her friends to consider leaving Manchester for good, however, she was the first to recognize that 'the work appointed both for my husband and me lies in Manchester . . .',[34] and she had no intention of shirking her work. Meanwhile, she was too ill to return home and remained in the country (mainly in Warwickshire with 'dear cousins from whom I have been separated nearly eighteen years'),[35] with Marianne for companion.

Marianne was now fifteen, and, as her mother admitted, not very talented for anything, except for music. By the end of the year her parents had come to the decision to send her to school in London for a year, where she could have the best teachers. 'We want her to view this gift rightly and use it well',[36] her mother wrote in November 1850. Much as she had been away from home that year, it was obvious that Mrs. Gaskell must accompany Marianne up to London to find a suitable school and settle her in. 'You know Wm's anxiety about his girls', Elizabeth wrote to Tottie Fox, thanking her for proffered hospitality.[37] Mother and daughter set off in mid December, therefore, to investigate the recommended schools (Queen's College among them) and spend Christmas in London, where Mr. Gaskell was to join them with Meta. 'As the two sisters have never been separated so long before', Elizabeth wrote, explaining her plans to Lady Kay-Shuttleworth, 'and have neither of them ever been in London I fancy they will have a very merry pleasant week, if—they come.'[38] In the event, it was Eliza Fox who found the school at Hampstead, kept by Mrs. Lalor, wife of John Lalor, editor of the Unitarian paper *The Inquirer*. There Marianne remained for the next eighteen months, except for the two annual holidays. From then on, she became her mother's chief correspondent and the repository of all the family news; though strange to say, the mother confided little as yet to her about her literary work.

CHAPTER XII

THE SERIALIZATION OF *CRANFORD*

AFTER 'The Moorland Cottage' was out of the way, Elizabeth submitted her two stories for Dickens's *Household Words*, 'The Well of Pen Morfa', and 'The Heart of John Middleton', which appeared towards the end of 1850. Their plots, which depend heavily on accident, are unrelievedly morbid; redemption by suffering is still their theme. In the first tale a young Welsh beauty, deeply in love and shortly to be married, falls on ice while carrying water from the well, and is crippled for life. Her lover abandons her and she becomes an embittered recluse. Only by the death of her mother who had patiently nursed her through her trials is her heart touched and her repentance achieved. She adopts an idiot girl to save her from institutional life, and assures her own salvation in so doing. The tale is relieved only by some very finely observed descriptions of the country around Portmadoc.

The plot of 'John Middleton' is equally contrived and morbid, though more powerful in execution. Middleton is a victim of persecution in the mill where he works, but endures all for the love of a young girl, Nelly, who is crippled for life by a stone thrown by his enemy and meant for him. Though Middleton marries her (unlike the lover in 'Pen Morfa') Nelly is a total invalid and eventually dies. Middleton lives only for the revenge he plans against the enemy who struck her; but when chance puts his enemy in his power, he is moved to spare him, for Nelly's sake, and thus achieves his redemption.

Dickens had a surprisingly high opinion of this tale; writing to Wills, his sub-editor on *Household Words*, on 12 December 1850, he said: 'The story is very clever—I think the best thing of hers I have seen, not excepting Mary Barton—and if it had ended happily (which is the whole meaning of it) would have been a great success.' Despite this surprising opinion, Dickens saw the ludicrous element in Mrs. Gaskell's accident-ridden plots: 'As it is, it had better go into the next No., but will not do much, and will link itself painfully, with the girl who fell down at the Well, and the child who tumbled downstairs.[1] I wish to Heaven her people would keep a little firmer on their legs!'[2]

Comparison between these tales and Elizabeth's contributions to periodical literature in the following year shows a very considerable advance in technique, selectivity, and above all, in wit. The change of style between such a story as 'John Middleton' and *Cranford*, which began to appear exactly a year later in the December 1851 issue of *Household Words*, is like the change of voice in a singer who has consistently misplaced her powers and suddenly finds she is no contralto but a soaring soprano.

The change is first apparent in a story called 'Mr. Harrison's Confessions', which she did not give to Dickens, but which appeared in a relatively new feminine periodical *The Ladies' Companion*, with which Mary Howitt was closely connected. It came out in monthly numbers in February, March, and April 1851. The story concerns the misadventures of a young doctor in his first practice in a small country town (unmistakably Knutsford) where the disengaged females of the locality are determined to entangle him. The humorous situation is exploited with great zest, fine perception of character, and lively incident; it was a situation that would not have been unfamiliar to Elizabeth Gaskell with a doctor uncle, who lodged his apprentices and steered his junior partners through their novitiates. The introduction of such familiar landmarks as Old Tabley Hall, and the Miss Tomlinsons—early sketches of Deborah and Matty Jenkyns—links the tale with *Cranford* and looks forward to the incidents and individuals of her crowning work, *Wives and Daughters*.

Elizabeth Gaskell was finding her true style—the style natural to her lively observation, love of people, eye for comical situations—such as she had for years past made her own in her letters, and which had little to do with pointing a moral. No work of hers would be entirely devoid of a moral to point (it is present in *Cranford*) but the situations would be freshly observed, the characters no longer typecast but individualized, subject to the real and imperfect laws governing human conduct. She was, in fact, emerging as an artist who sees a new world to create. It was an immense step forward.

Dickens very early perceived what was in her, and eagerly tried to engage her talent for his new journal. His patient angling over the next couple of years did not, perhaps, meet with the full return it merited. Elizabeth Gaskell was patently one of those independent, wayward

[1] See 'Lizzie Leigh'.
[2] *Letters*, ii. 250.

spirits who did not like being caught, and she made the operation as difficult for Dickens as she could. The relationship between the two was a curious upside-down affair, difficult to define, and more difficult still to resolve. While Dickens, whose reputation at the time stood at its highest and who had everything to offer her, was cast in the role of suppliant, she, who had everything to gain from the connection, showed unwilling. Despite the initial success of *Mary Barton*, she was not yet an established author, and the chance he gave her of publishing short, serialized pieces, suited to her limited opportunities for writing, appeared on the face of it ideal. He paid well for her contributions and generously left her her copyrights. Nevertheless, she invariably kept him waiting for a reply to his invitations, and even when she accepted them kept him waiting for copy. She resented any editorial decisions he might have to take, though they were usually wise ones. Dickens's correspondence with her is punctuated with appeals, with reminders, with every courteous consideration for her delays—and with unshaken enthusiasm for her work; but to very little avail. She remained an unwilling collaborator.

It was, one must suppose, a question of incompatibility—not of temperament, because they had much in common, but of standards. Mrs. Gaskell was a scrupulously sincere and truthful person, disliking more than anything else insincerity and flattery; and she suspected Dickens, justly or unjustly, of both. From the very outset of their relations, when he hailed *Mary Barton* with high-sounding words, she doubted his praise and rated it as 'soft sawder'. There was nothing in his ebullient personality, when she met him at last, to dispel this impression; and though she loved and admired his work, she hesitated to succumb to his charm. He was, perhaps, too different from the ascetic scholarly sort of men among whom her life had been spent wholly to please her. In time, after repeated transactions, Dickens became aware of her sentiments, and treated her, as she perhaps deserved, with teasing gallantry. 'If you were not the most suspicious of women, always looking for soft sawder in the purest metal of praise, I should call your paper delightful, and touched in the tenderest and most delicate manner. Being what you are I confine myself to the observation that I have called it A Love Affair at Cranford, and sent it off to the printer.'[3] The 'paper' in question was the first instalment of the serial that would ultimately appear as *Cranford*.

Had Elizabeth read his comment to Wills about the inability of her characters 'to keep a little firmer on their legs', she might have felt herself justified in the reserve with which she received his praise, fully justified

[3] *Letters*, ii. 364, 21 Dec. 1851.

as *he* was in his opinion. It is notable too, that when the separation from his wife occurred, Mrs. Gaskell wholly sided with Mrs. Dickens.

Complicated though their relationship was, there can be no doubt that Dickens made a professional writer of her and established her name. Though her work with him was published anonymously, it brought her within the circle of his friends, eminent and influential critics like Forster, and through them reached a wide reading public.

After repeated solicitation, Dickens gained his point with her in the summer of 1851 when at the end of May she voluntarily offered him a story for *Household Words*, which appeared in the issue of 7 June under the title 'Disappearances'. He was delighted with it and wrote to her by return on 27 May: 'I can't help writing to you to thank you for it at once. It is exactly suited to us.'[4] 'Disappearances' was yet another collection of tales with a recognizably Knutsford setting that characterized her work of that year—beginning with 'Mr. Harrison's Confessions' and reaching their climax with the triumphant *Cranford*.

What it was that so suddenly sparked off Elizabeth's 'Knutsford vein' —as one might call it—remains unclear. Knutsford had been with her since her childhood, and despite her immersion in the tide of Manchester life had been accessible both as a material and spiritual refuge ever since her marriage. The very contrast it afforded to the thrusting innovations of life in the great city could have made it a suitable theme for fiction before now. One is tempted to wonder whether the death in 1848 of Miss Abigail Holland—'Aunt Ab' to Elizabeth Gaskell—did not kindle the flame of memory and reanimate the past with a new understanding of its quality.

Abigail Holland (1773-1848) had lived with Mrs. Lumb in the old home at Heathside. She had inherited her sister's property and was bound by the terms of her will to leave half of it to Elizabeth Gaskell—the rest to be shared among the Holland relations. Thus the death of Miss Holland brought a substantial sum to her niece while it lost her the old family home. The Knutsford relatives were fast thinning out and the old homes passing into strangers' hands. Dr. Holland—uncle Peter—was going blind, and Elizabeth's visits to him and his daughters at the old Church House were no longer happy occasions, but acts of charity intended to ease the burden laid on the old cousins. Uncle Peter's son, the successful physician Sir Henry Holland, the inheritor of Sandlebridge, was fixed in London—it would be almost true to say at Court, where he was the Queen's and the Prince Consort's personal physician. Knutsford was no longer what it had been, nor the Knutsford circle so solidly entrenched

[4] Copy in Shorter Collection, Brotherton Library, Leeds.

in its possessions. Mrs. Gaskell's visits there were increasingly made to the relatively young Revd. Henry Greene and his family, his daughters being the contemporaries of her daughters. The slow decay wrought by old age—even if not by change, in that stronghold of immutable custom—was taking its toll of the familiar landmarks. No more, perhaps, was needed to spur the writer to record, while memory was still fresh, the peculiar character of that small and closely bound community of which she had been a part.

The first piece of recognizably Knutsford inspiration, 'The Last Generation in England', was, significantly enough, not contributed to an English periodical, but to the American *Sartain's Union Magazine*, Philadelphia, through Mary Howitt as intermediary, for the July issue of 1849. The date would, indeed, appear to link the story with the death of Abigail Holland, and the author's introductory comments confirm her intentions 'to put upon record some of the details of country town life, either observed by her or handed down to her by older relatives'. 'The Last Generation in England' is not a story in the fictional sense, but a record of the social fabric of small-town life at the beginning of the century, for the authenticity of which the author pledges her faith. It is, as certain incidents betray, a first sketch for the setting of Cranford, without the immortal dramatis personae. *Cranford* itself, as the author clearly stated in the wake of its success, had not been intended as a story in serialized parts, but as a single paper describing a fast-disappearing way of life.

'Disappearances' was a collection of unrelated tales concerned with the over-all subject of mysterious and unexplained disappearances, the incidents of which were claimed by the author as being substantially true. The theme was one that understandably haunted her since her brother had disappeared without trace on his last voyage to India. To each story in the collection she gave an uncomfortable twist that without being positively macabre leaves the reader disturbed for want of a rational explanation. Mrs. Gaskell, it has to be remembered, believed in the supernatural, and even claimed to have seen a ghost. This was on the occasion of a visit to Shottery, in May 1849, when she wrote to Tottie Fox of long drives in the surrounding country, 'in one of which (to a place where I believed the Sleeping Beauty lived, it was so over-grown and hidden up by woods,) I SAW a ghost! Yes I did; though in such a matter of fact place as Charlotte Street [Tottie's home at the time] I should not wonder if you are sceptical.'[5] While such beliefs may be not

[5] *GL* 48.

wholly surprising in a woman of her strong imagination and Celtic origins, they do not strike us as altogether compatible with the author of such works as *Mary Barton* and *Cranford*—to speak of none of the rest—with their down-to-earth acceptance of the material world. But the gift—if such it can be called—has to be remembered and·recognized as forming a part of her complex temperament.[6] She was said by the Howitts to have excelled at telling ghost stories round the fire at night.

Owing to her exceptionally busy summer in 1851, a more than usually crowded programme of social engagements, a visit to the Great Exhibition in London with husband and children, and family commitments, nothing more was forthcoming from Elizabeth till the autumn, when Dickens wrote to her, on 25 October, appealing yet again for a contribution to his journal. It was the memorable letter beginning: 'My dear Scheherazade,—For I am sure your powers of narrative can never be exhausted in a single night, but must be good for at least a thousand nights and one . . .'[7]

His appeal came at a propitious time for his author, who was just then staying at Knutsford, where she had gone for a fortnight's rest, taking Meta with her. She was staying with Dr. Holland while his daughter, her cousin Mary, went away 'for relaxation'. Her visit was a characteristic act of love as well as a gesture of self-preservation: she was exhausted with housekeeping and entertaining and found refreshment in assuming her old cousin's duties. The flight to Knutsford, the quietness of Church House, the company of old friends, had their usual healing effect on her health and overstretched nerves, and apparently refreshed and revived her to such an extent that the scenes and sentiments of girlhood all came flooding back.

Knutsford memories had haunted her of late, as the tales published earlier that year showed, but the evidence of dates would indicate even more certainly that, but for that visit of recuperation to Knutsford in the autumn of 1851, *Cranford* might not have been written when it was. The publication in *Household Words* of the first two chapters (the total story as Elizabeth then thought) was on 13 December, barely six weeks after her visit.

The visit, besides its quiet round of reading aloud to uncle Holland, tea-drinking, 'casino Evenings',[8] and calls on a few old friends, had given

---

[6] In volume 7 of the Knutsford Edition are included two undated fragments of ghost stories, found among her papers after death, that illustrate both her taste for the subject and her skill in evoking the right atmosphere.

[7] *Letters*, ii. 359.   [8] *GL* 102a, 17 Oct. 1851.

Elizabeth time for some clear thinking, and insight into her own needs. 'I am so much better for Knutsford,' she wrote to Anne Shaen on her return home in November, 'partly air, partly quiet and partly being by myself a good piece of every day which is I am sure so essential to my health that I am going to persevere and enforce it here.' She was determined to cut down on all unnecessary social engagements. To avoid callers, she would take her daily walk with the children at the time when they usually came; she would get all her 'society duties' done by giving occasional large parties 'where many people always entertain each other', and keep letter writing for the hours when her daughters' visiting masters required her chaperonage. Though she denied the application of the new programme to 'writing anything like a book' and declared it was 'solely for my own health and mind',[9] the immediate result was the first instalment of two chapters of *Cranford*, written and published in six weeks, and the genesis of *Ruth*.

The euphoria induced by this new liberty is apparent on every page of the new tale written on her return from Knutsford. *Cranford* is not only the most sustainedly witty of Mrs. Gaskell's writings but the most relaxed in mood. It is a tale told without apparent effort in a style of intimate confidence, like gossip exchanged with a friend; no previous writing of hers had achieved it, and only once again, in her final masterpieces, *Cousin Phillis* and *Wives and Daughters*, would she rediscover the mood.

To speak of 'mood', or 'euphoria', in connection with *Cranford* is to emphasize only the author's state of mind while the work was in process of creation; with it she achieved an artistry of style that was new to her work. The pathos and penetration of *Mary Barton* had not depended on it; her writing there had not been controlled writing; she had written, diffusely at times, as she had felt. But with *Cranford* she achieved a conciseness of exact expression, a selectivity of detail, that sharpened the wit to a point that invites comparison with Jane Austen. Strangely enough, the style of *Cranford* resembles far more the style of her letters than any of her other fictions; because in her letters she was herself— and it must be remembered that she was an educated woman expressing herself with ease and humour when writing to her friends—and not concerned with pleasing the public. Similarly in *Cranford*, written under no professional or personal pressures, she was herself in holiday mood. The book was presented to the public as a gesture of largesse, as a memento of an occasion. It was as though Elizabeth Gaskell said:

[9] *GL* 106.

'Let me tell you about this dear delightful oddity of a place, practising idiotic but old world courtesies, because before long it won't exist any longer.' With all the resources of memory at her command, and the fresh vision supplied by her recent visit, she was able to do just that.

The importance of the interlude at Knutsford that autumn was, as Elizabeth Gaskell later said, that it gave her time to be alone with herself and to recognize, in the ideal conditions of the peace of mind achieved, what was wrong with her usual way of life, and to decide how to amend it.

How personally involved she always became in whatever she wrote can be seen again in her confusion of fact with fiction during the time she was writing *Cranford*. Writing to Tottie Fox in mid-December 1851 she fell into the trap:

My dearest Tottie, I've a deal to say more than mortal can get through in the 1/4 of an hour I have before me, and now it's Sunday and I've the comfort of sitting down to write to you in a new gown, and blue ribbons all spick and span for Xmas—and cheap in the bargain, 'Elegant economy' as *we* say in Cranford— There now I dare say you think I've gone crazy but I'm not; but I've written a couple of tales about Cranford in Household Words, so you must allow me to quote from myself . . .[10]

The first instalment of *Cranford*, consisting of chapters one and two of the book, appeared under the title 'Our Society at Cranford'. Dickens was justifiably pleased and wrote to Elizabeth: 'I was so delighted with it that I put it first in the number.'[11]

Only one small problem arose to cloud the perfect understanding of the moment. In chapter two of *Cranford* Captain Brown was described as so absorbed in reading the current number of *Pickwick* that he was unaware of the approach of the train running along the newly opened track at Cranford, and was knocked down and killed. Dickens, as editor, could not allow this piece of self-publicity to appear in his paper, and changed the offending title to *Hood's Poems*. Mrs. Gaskell was much incensed and lost no time in restoring the deleted title in the first edition of the republished text. Even on this occasion, when he clearly had had every right to do what he did, Dickens wrote in humble vein to her on 12 December: 'I would do anything rather than cause you a minute's vexation.'[12]

His enthusiasm for the serial did not cool off and it was certainly due to his insistence that Mrs. Gaskell supplied four more instalments in the New Year: chapters three and four which appeared on 3 January; chapters five and six, which followed on 13 March, and chapters seven

[10] *GL* 110, Dec. 1851.   [11] *Letters*, ii. 361.   [12] Ibid.

and eight that concluded the current series on 3 April. It was not without his repeated prodding of the author even then that he secured so many instalments. 'O what a lazy woman you are,' he wrote on 25 February, 'and where IS that article!'[13]

On receipt of it he wrote his delight to Forster on 7 March: 'Don't you think Mrs. Gaskell charming? with one ill-considered thing that looks like a want of natural perception, I think it masterly.'[14] Forster wrote of his own intense enjoyment of her work to the author on 13 March 1852: 'I cannot tell you what charm the whole quiet picture has for me, with those shadows from the past . . . I have read your Cranford papers with delight. The papers are universally liked. I hope if Peter is to die in India, he'll leave Maty [sic] really well off after all her troubles.'[15]

The golden shower came to an end with the instalment of 3 April; she had sent him all she had up to date. Neither coaxing nor wheedling nor driving nor scolding could get more out of her for the time. What Dickens did not as yet know was that she had lost interest in *Cranford* and was totally engrossed in her next long novel, *Ruth*. Not until *Ruth* was finished and published in January 1853 would she work for him again. Then, in rapid succession, she sent him the final numbers of *Cranford* between 15 January and 21 May 1853, when the series was brought to an end.

Only then began the uneasy partnership over the serial publication of her next long novel, *North and South*, during which her total disregard for the basic principles of serial publication, punctuality and regulation of length, often tried his patience beyond endurance.

It was, perhaps, only in her dealings with Dickens that this intractable side of her nature came to light. It is not apparent in her relations with other people, though there were certain subjects that roused all her combativeness: ill-bred familiarity where no encouragement had been extended, and all forms of prying and vulgar curiosity. These she knew how to fend off with caustic contempt.

Dickens admired her too much, however, not to humour her a little, even while she exasperated him; and, as her editor, never drew the leading-strings too tight. But at times her intractability made him wonder what she was like at home, and he exploded once to Wills: 'If I were Mr. G. Oh Heaven how I would beat her!'[16]

[13] *Letters*, ii. 380.   [14] Ibid. 382.
[15] Shorter Collection, Brotherton Library, Leeds.
[16] Quoted by A. B. Hopkins, *Elizabeth Gaskell: Her Life and Works* (London, 1952), p. 152.

CHAPTER XIII

RUTH

THE subject of *Ruth*, the long novel that absorbed Elizabeth Gaskell throughout 1852, was no sudden inspiration: it had haunted her ever since the winter of 1849/50 when, as has been said, she applied to Dickens for information about Miss Burdett-Coutts's emigration scheme for prostitutes. She had been deeply concerned in the case about which she wrote to him throughout the autumn of 1849 and had interested Eliza Fox in it during her Manchester visit. On 26 November 1849 she had written to Eliza:

Our girl (yours and mine) sails in the Royal Albert on March 4, and her outfit is ready all except the sheets, which I must see about today; but except that, all is ready and right; and I like the girl much, poor creature. I have been to see her twice a week, and Agnes Ewart says she does so brighten up at the sight of me and seems so affectionate to every one.[1]

The girl's case was far from being unique, and it was because of this, and because of the pathos—the helplessness of such young victims of their pharisaical society—that Mrs. Gaskell was so deeply stirred by it. Already in her letter to Eliza Fox she was searching after some means of reform. 'Well I suppose it won't do to pull this world to pieces and make up a better, but sometimes it seems the only way of effectually puryfying it.'

The purifying process, as she came to see it, did not consist in throwing stones at the 'woman taken in adultery', but in exposing the hypocrisy of the social system: the discriminating morality that condoned the male partner in 'sin' and condemned the female, the hypocritical teaching that affected the moral outlook of all educated strata of Victorian society and left the others, the untaught and often destitute poor, with no other recourse than to break both divine and man-made law.

Like *Mary Barton*, *Ruth* can be seen as a perfectly straightforward tale, or as a study of Woman in Relation to Society—of Woman as a

[1] *GL* 55.

Victim of the existing Social Order. Without offering any prescriptions for improving that order, Mrs. Gaskell set out so to inform and touch her readers as to arouse their social conscience and pity, knowing that these are the preliminaries to any effective movement of reform. She was no theorist and never thought or wrote in generalizations; she was intensely personal in her responses to situations, and identified herself completely with the people whose tragedies came to her knowledge. It was the individual case of the little seamstress imprisoned for theft that gave her the theme of the outcast girl who had 'lost her character', who could never hope to find honest work again, and must necessarily become a prostitute to earn her bread. The total injustice of such a situation shocked her inexpressibly, and moved her to write the book which was to be a plea for a different and workably Christian morality.

The girl she had befriended in Manchester jail was called Pasley. She had been seduced by the doctor who was called in to prescribe for her on the occasion of an illness. Mrs. Gaskell's heroine, Ruth, was seduced by a gentleman who noticed her attending to the dresses of the ladies at a county ball. Mrs. Gaskell was at great pains to emphasize Ruth's innocence, virtue, and sweetness. There is not a trace of Hetty Sorel in her: she abandons herself to her lover because she loves him; no other consideration of pride or profit enters into her action. Bellingham, the lover, has an easy run of it with so guileless a girl. He takes her to Wales, tires of her, and after a brain-fever when his mother is sent for to nurse him, dismisses Ruth with a £50 bonus. She is rescued from her intention to commit suicide by a dissenting minister, Thurston Benson, who is on holiday at the same Welsh village (recognizably Festiniog) and taken home by him to his remote northern parish—'Eccleston', the author's name for Newcastle. He lives with his sister Faith and a characterful old servant, Sally, whose forthright manners, northern dialect, and rough independent honesty are a creation of real genius.

With Ruth's arrival at the Bensons' home, the author is faced with her first hurdle: how were the Bensons to explain the presence of Ruth, a visibly pregnant young woman, in their very quiet Christian home? The decision to represent her as a young widowed relative of theirs—a Mrs. Denbigh—is used by the author not only as the charitable expedient it was, but as the turning point in the plot, which hinges on this falsehood. Ruth has her child in peace, studies with Thurston Benson, learns moral values from him, repents her past life, and becomes an integrated member of the family and the little community about it. Years pass, and as the boy, Leonard, grows out of childhood, Ruth is able to go out to work as a daily governess, and is employed by the family of Mr. Benson's chief parishioner, the pharisaical Mr. Bradshaw, who are very satisfied with her.

The story could have ended there if Mrs. Gaskell had been content with the physical rescue of Ruth; but she was not. Relying heavily thereafter on coincidence, melodrama, and contrivance to develop the plot, she brings back Bellingham, Ruth's former lover, into her life (by sheer coincidence he stands for Parliament for the very borough that represents Eccleston). He discovers the existence of Leonard, urges Ruth to live with him again, and when she refuses offers her marriage.

The degree of Ruth's evolution as a responsible human being—of her moral regeneration, as the first readers of the book were intended to see it—is seen in her rejection of Bellingham's proposal. The scene is memorably set on the sands at Abermouth and the conflict between the former lovers used to dramatic effect. Bellingham, who had been unmoved by his former passing fancy for an ignorant girl, is now deeply stirred by her matured beauty and bent on recapturing her. Setting before her all the obvious advantages to their son of such a union, he is nonplussed by her steady and repeated rejection of his offers. He is both incredulous and uncomprehending. 'Why! what on earth makes you say that?' he asks, irritated by the repetition of her words. That he should be so surprised by Ruth's rejection is admirably perceptive on the author's part; and that Ruth should feel so differently towards him finely imagined too. Ruth's only fault in youth was in her *naïveté*, in her ignorance; never in her truth. Her total honesty guides her in this crucial decision, when her own and her son's future are at stake. She rejects Bellingham for the only reason that she no longer loves him, and that to accept him now would simply be out of self-interest. 'I do not love you. I did once. Don't say I did not love you then! but I do not now. I could never love you again. All you have said and done since you came with Mr. Bradshaw to Abermouth first has only made me wonder how I ever could have loved you. We are very far apart.'[2]

The story could still have ended there, but Mrs. Gaskell's plan was to show the spiritual 'rehabilitation' of Ruth. This, in accordance with the morality of the time, had to be bought at the price of further suffering and self-sacrifice. The falsehood on which Ruth's new identity was built had to be exposed. The Bradshaws learn the truth about her past, and vent their outraged virtue both on her and on the good Mr. Benson, whose richest pew-holders they are. Ruth is dismissed by them with ignominy and Mr. Benson still further impoverished.

[2] *Ruth*, ch. 24, p. 299.

To modern readers, this whole episode is inconceivable, and is followed by worse, when Ruth judges that Leonard must be told the truth about his mother. He is nine or ten by then, and is described as crushed by the shame of his bastardy,[3] abandoning school, avoiding his playmates. Fortunately for him the family doctor is an enlightened man and offers Ruth to teach Leonard himself, to take him eventually as his apprentice, and if he shapes well to make him his partner. The boy's future is thus secure, and this frees Ruth at the very moment when the chance of achieving her salvation comes. The calculation is not hers, but Mrs. Gaskell's. Ruth is shown as totally uncalculating, even about the matter of her salvation. She has reached a degree of selflessness that makes any action undertaken on behalf of others a perfectly natural and unforced thing. The town is suddenly thrown into a major emergency by a cholera epidemic, and Ruth volunteers to nurse the cases crowding the hospital wards. Her conduct is outstanding, her devotion absolute. Doctors and patients alike sing her praises. The townsfolk marvel at her courage; people are overheard saying: 'They say she has been a great sinner, and that this is her penance.' For the Victorian reader to whom the book was addressed, this was its message. Mrs. Gaskell brings her poor little 'sinner' full cycle with the final episode in which Bellingham catches the infection and is nursed—and saved—by Ruth, who, however, dies of it herself.

So morally and artistically right, in Mrs. Gaskell's view, was such an ending that there is a sense of triumph in her very writing. Ruth dies in the Bensons' little home:

They stood around her bedside, not speaking, or sighing, or moaning; they were too much awed by the exquisite peacefulness of her look for that. Suddenly she opened wide her eyes, and gazed intently forwards, as if she saw some happy vision, which called out a lovely, rapturous, breathless smile . . . 'I see the Light coming,' said she.[4]

Thurston Benson, in his funeral sermon for the dead girl, pushed away the notes he had made and read only from the Bible: 'These are they which came out of great tribulation, and have washed their robes, and made them white in the blood of the Lamb.' He had always felt fully justified in what he had done, despite the white lie that cost her and him such a retribution.

Understandably, *Ruth* remains the least acceptable of Mrs. Gaskell's books to the modern reader; the deep religiosity of its tone is too emphatic

---

[3] G. H. Lewes in his review of *Ruth* took great exception to this incident, as both unnatural and untrue to contemporary thinking. 'Villette and Ruth', *Edinburgh Review*, Apr. 1853.

[4] *Ruth*, ch. 35, p. 444.

for modern taste. In the opinion of one great contemporary, George Eliot, this was the book's weakness; a judgement that has proved both sound and prophetic. In 1853 George Eliot had not, as yet, written any of her novels (*Scenes of Clerical Life* first appeared in 1857), but her editorial work on the *Westminster Review* was a training in itself. Writing to a friend on 1 February 1853, she said:

Of course you have read 'Ruth' by this time. Its style was a great refreshment to me, from its finish and fulness . . . *Ruth*, with all its merits, will not be an enduring or classical fiction—will it? Mrs. Gaskell seems to me to be constantly misled by a love of sharp contrasts—of 'dramatic effects'. She is not contented with the subdued colouring, the half-tones of real life. Hence she agitates one for the moment, but she does not secure one's lasting sympathy . . . But how pretty and graphic are the touches of description . . . Mrs. Gaskell has certainly a charming mind and one cannot help loving her as one reads her books.[5]

While George Eliot took exception to the book on aesthetic grounds, it has to be remembered that to the majority of its contemporary readers the book was shocking on account of its subject and for the laxity of its moral tone. Mrs. Gaskell knew from the outset that she was taking great personal risks; she might well be ostracized from the circle in which she lived in Manchester, and condemned by the press (both these things happened), but she was a woman of great enthusiasms and strong faith, and she acted on her conscience. An injustice so vast in its application, human misery so far-reaching in its effects, demanded an answer. She believed she could supply one, by exposing the facts, by bringing them into the open, by discussing publicly what was rarely even whispered in polite society—especially in the hearing of ladies like herself—and by awakening the conscience of the virtuous to their real duty of Samaritan charity.

She wrote Charlotte Brontë a sketch of the plot, already fully realized in her mind as early as April 1852, according to the editors of the Brontë Letters who date Charlotte's reply as 26 April:

The sketch you give of your work (respecting which I am, of course, dumb) seems to me very noble; and its purpose may be as useful in practical result as it is high and just in theoretical tendency. Such a book may restore hope and energy to many who thought they had forfeited their right to both, and open a clear course for honourable effort to some who deemed that they and all honour had parted company in this world.[6]

---

[5] G. Haight, *The George Eliot Letters* (London, 1954), ii. 86.
[6] *The Brontës, their Lives, Friendships and Correspondence*, ed. T. J. Wise and J. A. Symington (Oxford, 1932), iii. 332.

That the sketch of the plot already covered the book's ending can be judged by Charlotte's appeal against its rigour:

Yet—hear my protest! Why should she die? Why are we to shut up the book weeping? My heart fails me already at the thought of the pang it will have to undergo. And yet you must follow the impulse of your own inspiration. If *that* commands the slaying of the victim no bystander has a right to put out his hand to stay the sacrificial knife; but I hold you a stern priestess in these matters.

If the published date of this exchange is correct, it explains why Mrs. Gaskell suspended all further contributions to *Cranford* after the instalment of 3 April 1852, so as to devote herself to the writing of *Ruth*. At all events, what we know of the chronology of the writing of *Ruth* bears evidence to the extraordinary speed of its composition.

It would have been well-nigh impossible for Mrs. Gaskell to enlist sympathy for her subject had she made Ruth a regular prostitute. This, of course, she was not, as Esther in *Mary Barton* or Lizzie Leigh were prostitutes; that there was no vice in Ruth is the whole argument of the book. Mrs. Gaskell was asking her readers to consider what, without the action of the Bensons in sheltering Ruth, could have become of her, other than prostitution. For Mrs. Gaskell's concept of charity the opportunity Ruth was offered to lead a decent life and the shelter granted her in which to bring up her child were all-important: this is made apparent by the contrary recommendation of Bellingham's mother, that Ruth go to a 'penitentiary'.[7] Condemnation of such institutions is inherent in the presentation of the character of the woman who advocates them.

It was not enough to enlist sympathy for Ruth, by showing how poetic she was, how sensitive to the beauties of nature, how truthful, how kind, how tender-hearted towards dumb animals, and so on. A practical workable means had to be found for rescuing her. Ruth had to be saved from despair, from poverty, from the will to die. The human agent who could effect all this must be made credible if readers were to see him as an example; and it would seem that Mrs. Gaskell had in real life come in contact with just such a man during the time that Ruth was taking shape in her mind. He may very plausibly be identified as the Revd. William Turner of Newcastle, with whose family she had spent two winters in her girlhood, and with whom she had recently renewed contact.

Old Mr. Turner had retired from his ministry at Newcastle in 1843 and settled in Manchester to be near his married daughter, Mrs. Robberds, the wife of William Gaskell's senior minister. He lived with his

---

[7] *Ruth*, ch. 8, p. 91.

unmarried daughter Anne (Elizabeth Gaskell's girlhood companion) in the Greenheys district of the city. He was turned 90 when in 1850 Anne Turner died, leaving him desolate and nearly blind. Lodgings were found for him with the Gaskells' governess, Miss Mitchell, and Mrs. Gaskell began visiting him regularly to read to him. She wrote about this plan to Marianne on 15 March 1851: 'After tea to Miss Mitchell's to read to old Mr Turner which I mean to try and do very often both for his sake and Miss Mitchell's; as it sets her at liberty. I was well tired at night.'[8]

Successive commentators on *Ruth* have identified the character of Thurston Benson, the dissenting minister who gives Ruth a home, with Mr. Turner of Newcastle, because of the obvious similarities in character and conduct. Mr. Turner lived to read the book (published in January 1853) and recognize in the description of the Bensons' home his own old home at Newcastle.[9] Mrs. Gaskell's renewed contacts with him in Manchester at the very time she was planning *Ruth* would revive her impressions of him that went back more than twenty years.

Portraits of Mr. Turner exist and can be compared with the description of Mr. Benson in the novel. Obviously wishing to confuse the identity and obviate a comparison, Mrs. Gaskell made Mr. Benson a partial cripple, a circumstance that recalls her own much loved uncle Peter Holland, the Knutsford doctor, who had been crippled for life by being thrown from his dogcart. In describing Mr. Benson as Ruth first saw him she wrote: 'She was struck afresh with the mild beauty of the face . . . something more and beyond the pallor of habitual ill-health, something of a quick spiritual light in the deep-set eyes, a sensibility about the mouth; but altogether . . . it was a most attractive face.'[10] Trying to describe the man to her lover, Ruth could only say of him: 'His face was very singular; quite beautiful!'[11]

What kind of man Mr. Turner was can best be judged by his conduct upon the death of his daughter Anne. He had been allowed a retirement pension by his Newcastle congregation in 1843 of £30 a year but when he lost his daughter he wrote to them to say he would only accept half that sum in future, needing only so much for himself. He was a totally unworldly, humane, and generous man, who had spent his working life in helping the vast population of the poor in Newcastle, teaching pauper boys, sponsoring every form of educational plan, like the Literary and Philosophical Society lectures inaugurated for working men, and giving

[8] *GL* 91b, 17 Mar. 1851.   [9] Chadwick, *Mrs. Gaskell*, pp. 149, 151.
[10] *Ruth*, ch. 5, p. 67.   [11] Ibid., p. 69.

away what little money he himself earned to help the destitute. The views of such a man, increasingly revealed to Elizabeth Gaskell, in their homely contacts, can only have confirmed her in her own views and given her a basis on which to build the portrait of her 'Good Samaritan' Mr. Benson. If, in real life, men like Mr. Turner had acted as they had throughout a long career, why should fiction lag behind truth in portraying them? It was far more difficult to make her readers believe in the goodness of such a man as Mr. Benson, than in the frailty of such a poor girl as Ruth whose case was all too common.

To Mr. Turner, again, could well be traced the climax of the plot of *Ruth*—the cholera epidemic with which the book closes. Elizabeth Gaskell, it will be remembered, had been at Newcastle in the years 1831-2 when one of the worst epidemics in the town's records occurred; Mr. Turner had dispatched her with his daughter to Edinburgh to keep them out of the way, but had himself remained to organize relief. What Elizabeth had not known then, but what she now had the opportunity to hear from himself, were his personal memories of the methods adopted by the authorities during the emergency, of the inadequacy of the organized help, and of the dearth of nurses. These incidents figure so vividly in *Ruth* as to suggest eye-witness reports.

Cholera was admittedly an all-too frequent scourge in Victorian England and present in lesser or greater degrees every year in the great centres of overcrowding like Manchester, Liverpool, and London. But the writing of *Ruth* preceded by two years the major outbreak of 1854, during which Florence Nightingale, a future friend of Elizabeth Gaskell, found her vocation. It was not from her, therefore, that the author of *Ruth* derived her information on the earlier epidemic.

The influence of *place* was always paramount in deciding Mrs. Gaskell's choice of setting for her plots, and in *Ruth* the influence of three places was as essential to the progress of the tale as the human factor: the places were Wales, the valley of Festiniog in particular, where she had spent her honeymoon and lost her son; Newcastle (the Eccleston of the story with the Turners' home as its centre, as already seen); and Silverdale, where the Gaskells spent the six summer weeks of 1852, which merges with her memories of Aber to become Abermouth.

The arrangements for the family's summer holidays were made as early as 4 May that year when Mrs. Gaskell announced the plan to Marianne: 'We have fixed to go to the Tower house at Silverdale 3 windows being made to open wide viz., two little bedrooms and staircase.'[12] The

---

[12] *GL* 122a, 4 May 1852.

accommodation thus summarily described—because already known to Marianne—was in Lindeth Tower, stone-built and high as a church tower, that stood in the grounds of Lindeth farm where the Gaskells had spent previous holidays.

The farm buildings dated from the beginning of the century, while the tower was of a far more recent construction, built by a retired banker from Preston called A. P. Fleetwood—as much as a look-out as a 'Folly'— and incorrectly described by Mrs. Gaskell as a 'Peel' tower, a remnant of the Border towers,[13] which it patently was not. It was four storeys high, with a single large room on each landing, with windows now made to open commanding views inland and out to sea, and ideally situated on a rocky eminence overlooking the shore, sheltered by oak woods behind but rising straight off the sands in front. There was a kitchen on the ground floor, bedrooms on the first, and a sitting-room on the top which communicated by an iron staircase with the battlemented roof. For Mrs. Gaskell the acquisition of Lindeth Tower was a boon beyond price. It afforded her a retreat for her writing, of impregnable security and inspiring view. It could accommodate the whole family, even a visitor or two, while the servants lodged in the farm buildings spread around, and the topmost floor with its battlemented roof was left for Mrs. Gaskell's exclusive use.

The very prospect of the holiday made her spirits soar. Mr. Gaskell also, it seemed, liked the plan. 'Papa seems very well and bright and likes the notion of Silverdale evidently', Marianne was told in the same letter. The glimpses of Mr. Gaskell in holiday mood, perceived in this letter and in the memories of the Winkworth sisters, show another side of his character from the ascetic recluse generally seen in his wife's correspondence. Marianne was told that, regretfully, it would not be possible to invite her favourite teacher, Miss Banks, to Silverdale because

I find Papa does not like the idea of having a *stranger* in the house in holiday time when you know he likes to play pranks, go cockling etc. etc. and feel at liberty to say or do what he likes. I told him I did not think Miss Banks *was* so very particular, but he says it would make him uncomfortable, and so it must be given up darling.[14]

No exception was taken, however, to the company of Tottie Fox at Silverdale; she was a general favourite with the family and Elizabeth urged her in further letters of the same month to join them there.

[13] *GL* 394, 10 and 14 May 1858.
[14] *GL* 122a.

You don't know how *beautiful* Silverdale is [she wrote after a half-refusal from Tottie] and a tower of our own! think of that! it's a sort of country you never saw before. I'll answer for it. I dare say we shall never go there again—and I for one, don't expect to live till another summer, when you so coolly talk of coming— *Do* come—think of it! difficulties vanish in thinking with me . . . *Do* go, darling Tottie do go to Silverdale with us.[15]

Despite the strange allusion to her anticipation of death, to which her overwork sometimes prompted her, the anticipated delight in the holiday at Silverdale and the prospect of peace, not just to enjoy her friend's company but to write her new story, runs through all her letters of the time.

The holidays lasted from 29 June to mid August, and the long summer days combined to create the ideal ambience for such a writer as Mrs. Gaskell, who was made articulate by the presence of beauty. '. . . One is never disappointed in coming back to Silverdale', she was to write several years later to her friend Charles Norton. 'The secret is I think in the expanse of view,—something like what gives it's charm to the Campagna—such wide plains of golden sands with purple hill shadows,— or fainter wandering filmy cloud-shadows, and the great dome of sky.'[16] The flat roof of the tower was the perfect look-out post on tranquil nights for the growing girls to learn to read the skies. As she admitted later, they often sat on the roof all night.[17]

Two distinctive features of Silverdale, the silvery colour of the sands and rocks, and the black posts used by the local fishermen to mark the emplacements of their nets, figure in the descriptions of Abermouth in *Ruth*, and betray the origin of the locale chosen by Mrs. Gaskell for the dramatic meeting between Ruth and her former lover. Every detail of the accompanying description fits Silverdale. Running to keep the rendezvous with Bellingham, Ruth

was carried by the impetus of her descent far out on the level sands . . . Without looking to the right hand or to the left, where comers might be seen, she went forwards to the black posts, which, rising above the heaving waters, marked where the fishermen's nets were laid. She went straight towards this place, and hardly stinted her pace even where the wet sands were glittering with the receding waves. Once there, she turned round . . . She was perhaps half-a-mile or more from the grey, silvery rocks, which sloped away into brown moorland, interspersed with a field here and there of golden, waving corn. Behind were purple hills, with sharp clear outlines, touching the sky. A little on one side from where she stood she

---

[15] *GL* 124, May 1852.   [16] *GL* 401, 25 July 1858.
[17] Ibid.

saw the white cottages and houses which formed the village of Abermouth, scattered up and down; and, on a windy hill, about a mile inland, she saw the little grey church, where even now many were worshipping in peace.[18]

The farmer's family, living in the buildings surrounding the tower, and with whom the Gaskells had spent previous holidays, later recalled Elizabeth's habit of rising early and settling to her writing before the labourers set off to work; sometimes she was writing before the summer dawn.[19]

She must have worked at an exceptional pace, for immediately on her return to Manchester in mid August she was in a position to sign a Memorandum of Agreement with Chapman for the publication of the book that is dated 23 August.[20] The work, for which she was to receive £500 on the day of publication, was to be published one month after the completed manuscript was placed in the publisher's hands. By the end of October the first two volumes had been read and approved by Forster and forwarded to Chapman,[21] and the completed work was off her hands by 20 December 1852.[22]

It would have been much better for the quality of the book had she not written so fast, had she deleted many of the melodramatic and exaggerated passages that defeat their own purpose by irritating the reader instead of gaining his sympathies. It was, however, a novel with a declared purpose—a piece of propaganda—and when Mrs. Gaskell was carried away by a subject she lost the power of self-criticism.

Only when the end was in sight, after the breathless speed with which she had progressed, was she halted—both in the writing and in her intentions. Writing to Marianne on 15 November she declared that she would give no complimentary copies away, and sheltered herself behind the excuse that the book was 'not *written* yet . . . *when* or *if ever* I shall finish it I don't know. I hate publishing because of the talk people make, which I always feel a great impertinence, *if they address their remarks to me* in any way.'[23] The irritable, even panicky tone of these comments, made so late in the book's composition, betray her perturbation as publication approached and the judgement of her work had to be faced. It was a very different matter from the enthusiasm of the book's inception, when no considerations, other than those of its importance, were allowed to obscure her clear-cut purpose. She was losing her nerve when it was too late to turn back.

---

[18] *Ruth*, ch. 24, p. 292.   [19] Chadwick, *Mrs. Gaskell*, p. 329.
[20] Shorter Collection, Brotherton Library, Leeds.   [21] *GL* 137, Oct. 1852.
[22] *GL* 146.   [23] *GL* 140, 15 Nov. 1852.

The emotional and inspirational manner of her writing can be seen from her comments in a letter to Eliza Fox written in late October 1852 from the house of friends near Ambleside (Dr. Davy's house) during the writing of the last volume of *Ruth*. After reporting the printing of the first two volumes, she said: '. . . all complete news to me! But I set to on the trumpet sound thereof, and was writing away vigorously at Ruth when the Wedgwoods, etc. came: and I was sorry, *very* sorry to give it up my heart being so full of it, in a way which I can't bring back. That's that.'[24]

Ruth was published on 24 January 1853 by Chapman and Hall, and the author received a down payment for it of £500. By the courtesy of Charlotte Brontë, whose *Villette* was already announced, and who had asked her publishers to delay publication to allow Mrs. Gaskell's work a clear run with the critics if only for four days, *Ruth* was given precedence over the sister author's work, which followed on 28 January.

The expected storm broke with a unanimity of violence that surpassed Mrs. Gaskell's worst fears. She knew she was risking censure on moral grounds: and herself admitted in a letter written to her sister-in-law, Anne Robson, on 27 January, three days after the book's publication: 'Of course it is a prohibited book in *this*, as in many other households; not a book for young people . . . but I have spoken out my mind . . . and I have no doubt that what was felt so earnestly *must* do some good.'[25] After the broadsides fired into her from the entire press, she was shaken even out of that consoling belief, and shocked at the virulence of the personal attacks upon her.

'I am in a quiver of pain about it,' she continued, '. . . I had a terrible fit of crying all Saty night at the unkind things people were saying; but I have now promised Wm. I will think of it as little as ever I can help.' A few days later she wrote to Tottie Fox: 'I *have* been so ill; I do believe it has been a "Ruth" fever. The beginning of last week my own private opinion was that I should never get better. I was so utterly weak after it but I have picked up, and this cold weather braces me.' The physical and emotional effects of the long strain of writing the book, followed by so swift and deadly a condemnation of her work, were understandably crushing: 'Oh! I was so poorly!' she confided to Tottie Fox, 'and cd not get over the hard things people said of Ruth. I mean I was just in that feverish way when I could not get them out of my head by thinking of anything else but dreamt about them and all that. I think I must be an

[24] *GL* 137, Oct. 1852.
[25] *GL* 148, 27 Jan. 1853.

improper woman without knowing it, I do so manage to shock people.' What upset her most was the conduct of her Manchester acquaintances, some of whom actually burnt the book. 'Now *should* you have burnt the 1st vol. of Ruth as so *very* bad,' she asked her friend, 'even if you had been a very anxious father of a family? Yet *two* men have; and a third has forbidden his wife to read it; they sit next to us in Chapel and you can't think how "improper" I feel under their eyes. However some people like it—Mr J. W. Darbishire for one.'[26]

The recorded conduct of these zealous Christians, parishioners and erstwhile friends of the Gaskells, has to be reckoned with when judging the truth to life of Mrs. Gaskell's invented character, the pharisaical Mr. Bradshaw in the novel; modern readers recognize that, hard as it is to credit, she knew what she was writing about, and what it was that needed radical reform. She had herself to blame to some extent for the delay in receiving the first words of comfort, for in several instances she had forbidden her friends to communicate with her.

I have *forbidden* people to write [she told Anne Robson], for their expressions of disapproval (although I have known that the feeling would exist in them) would be very painful and stinging at the time. An 'unfit subject for fiction' is *the* thing to say about it; I knew all this before . . . 'Deep regret' is what my friends here (such as Miss Mitchell) feel and express. In short, the only comparison I can find for myself is to St Sebastian tied to a tree to be shot at with arrows.[27]

The image shows how even her sense of humour was deserting her.

She was far too sensitive to people's opinion, to blame or praise, not to be deeply bruised by the public nature of the book's condemnation; she was crushed by the news of Bell's Library withdrawing it from circulation, and by the personal tone of such reviews as the *Literary Gazette* which deplored her 'loss of reputation'. Two circumstances stand out in the event: her husband's support of her, and her own undefeated spirit. Despite the hurt to her feelings and the injury to her health, she reiterated her belief in what she had done. 'I shrink with more pain than I can tell you from what people are saying, though I wd do every jot of it over again to-morrow.'[28]

Within a month the letters of praise and encouragement came in and she began to take heart. Kingsley wrote to her, saying that in all his large acquaintance there was 'but one unanimous opinion as to the beauty and righteousness of the book . . . whatsoever the "Snobs" and the Bigots may think, English people in general have but one opinion of "Ruth",

[26] *GL* 150, early Feb. 1853.   [27] *GL* 148.   [28] Ibid.

and that is one of utter satisfaction.' The wife of Archdeacon Hare wrote to say that when her husband 'heard that your virtuous friends had burnt "*Ruth*",' his comment had been: 'Well, the Bible has been burnt, and many other precious books have met with the same fate, which yet have done their work.'[29]

Dean Stanley's mother wrote, Richard Monckton Milnes wrote, Dickens wrote, Forster wrote, Charlotte Brontë wrote. So too did Frederick Maurice and his glowing tribute was later published in his *Lectures on the Unity of the New Testament* (1854): 'I desire to thank a noble-hearted and pure-minded writer of our day for the courage with which she has illustrated the doctrine . . . I allude to the beautiful tale of "*Ruth*", which on this point and on all others is, I think, as true to human experience as it is to the divinest morality.'[30]

With the leaders of literature and religion justifying her work, the tide of opinion began to turn in Elizabeth's favour and in defence of *Ruth*, and encomiums flowed in from every quarter. Readers as different as her Unitarian friends, the Greens of Knutsford, and Mrs. Browning from Florence, wrote of their delight and admiration. 'Henry', wrote Mrs. Green of her husband, 'says he has not cried so much for many years and we all do so admire not only the substance but the style.'[31]

Mrs. Browning, who declared she 'hated Mrs. Grundy worse than the Czar',[32] wrote from Casa Guidi:

I have just finished 'Ruth' . . . Hear the 'echoes in the hills'! . . . I love and honour your books—especially 'Ruth' which is noble as well as beautiful, which contains truths purifying and purely put, yet treats of a subject scarcely ever boldly treated of except when taken up by unclean hands—I am grateful to you as a woman for having treated such a subject—Was it quite impossible but that your Ruth should *die*? I had that thought of regret in closing the book—Oh, I must confess to it— Pardon me for the tears' sake![33]

The regret was shared by Charlotte Brontë and others,[34] and is a measure of the readers' total involvement in Mrs. Gaskell's books.

Ruth brought its author a greater *succès d'estime*, perhaps, than any other of her novels. It was certainly the book in which she had attempted most, risked most, and suffered most. Her reputation, for the time being at least, was at its highest.

[29] A. W. Ward, Introduction to the Knutsford Edition, pp. xiii–xiv.
[30] Ibid., p. xiv.
[31] Copy in the Shorter Collection, Brotherton Library, Leeds.
[32] Waller, *Letters Addressed to Mrs. Gaskell*, p. 43.   [33] Ibid., p. 42.
[34] Shorter, *The Brontës, Life and Letters*, ii, letter 570.

By April, she had regained enough tranquillity to be able to discuss the subject objectively in a long letter to Lady Kay-Shuttleworth: '. . . from the very warmth with which people have discussed the tale I take heart of grace,' she wrote on 7 April; 'it has made them talk and think a little on a subject which is so painful that it requires all one's bravery not to hide one's head like an ostrich.'[35]

Once again, as in *Mary Barton*, Elizabeth Gaskell had exposed a social evil, not from any expert knowledge of its causes or facile theories for its remedy, but from the purely human standpoint of pity for an individual case. Her sincerity and sympathy, her gift of imagination and her powers of eloquence secured her a far wider public than the Report of a Royal Commission on the subject could ever hope to reach. Though today *Ruth* may be the least readable of Mrs. Gaskell's novels, it must not be forgotten that to have written with such sympathy of a 'fallen woman' was in her day and age an act of courage that even Dickens, with his shadowy flitting figures of prostitutes—Martha and Little Em'ly— was reluctant to emulate. It was and remains a notable attempt for any man or woman at the time to have made.

[35] *GL* 154, 7 Apr. 1853.

CHAPTER XIV

CONTRASTING SOCIETIES:
NORTH AND SOUTH

DICKENS was predictably one of *Ruth*'s earliest admirers. Writing to Elizabeth on 13 April 1853 he said: 'My dear friends Ruth and Mary Barton, I can put no limitations on. Their visits are too like those of angels.' He was forwarding the last instalments of *Cranford* to the printer and already looking ahead. 'As to future work . . . you cannot write too much for Household Words . . . I receive you, ever, (if Mr Gaskell will allow me to say so) with open arms.'[1]

Whether or not her recent chastisement by the press made her more receptive to Dickens's cordiality, his invitation had an immediate effect: she sent him the outline sketch for a new book which she was prepared to publish serially with him. He replied on 3 May warmly encouraging the project.

My dear Mrs. Gaskell,—The subject is certainly NOT too serious, so sensibly treated. I have no doubt that you may do a great deal of good by pursuing it in Household Words. I thoroughly agree in all you say in your note, have similar reasons for giving it some anxious consideration, and shall be greatly interested in it. Pray decide to do it. Send the papers, as you write them, to me. Meanwhile I will think of a name for them, and bring it to bear upon yours, if I think yours improvable. I am sure you may rely on being widely understood and sympathised with.

Forget that I called those two women my dear friends! Why, if I told you a fiftieth part of what I have thought about them, you would write me the most suspicious of notes, refusing to receive the fiftieth part of that. So I don't write, particularly as you laid your injunctions on me concerning Ruth. In revenge, I will now mention one word that I wish you would take out whenever you reprint that book. She would never—I am ready to make affidavit before any authority in the land—have called her seducer 'Sir', when they were living at that hotel in Wales. A girl pretending to be what she really was would have done it, but she—never![2]

---

[1] *Letters*, ii. 457.   [2] Ibid. 459-60.

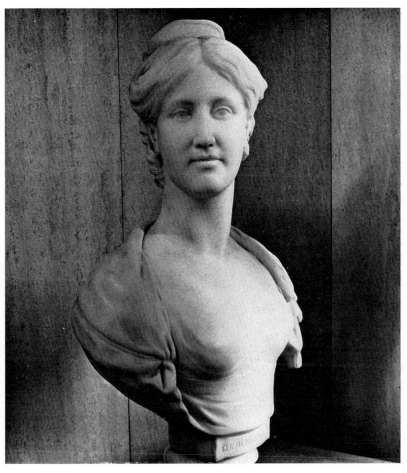

7. Elizabeth Stevenson, copy by Thorneycroft of marble bust by David Dunbar

8 (*a*). 'Plâs Penrhyn', Samuel Holland's house on Portmadoc estuary

8 (*b*). View of the Portmadoc estuary from the garden of 'Plâs Penrhyn'

The new work thus early projected, and left undeveloped for several months after, was the basis for her next novel *North and South*.

The year, as it turned out, did not prove conducive to consecutive work, though highly stimulating to observation and reflection because she was able to travel. Travelling always did her good and the perceptible rise in her spirits in her letters of April, as her pain over *Ruth* was subsiding, can be traced to the quite sudden prospect of a trip to Paris. This was made possible, it may be supposed, by the £500 payment on the publication of *Ruth*. From the gloom of her outlook in February when she wrote to Eliza Fox, 'I don't see any chance of my coming up to London this winter spring, or summer, though I should like very well to',[3] there is a total transformation in the excitement of her announcement to Lady Kay-Shuttleworth on 10 April that 'it is become "between a possibly and a probably" that we may go to Paris on May 12 or 13th!' (Whitsun that year). 'I have never been there,' she added; 'and we plan to take Marianne, our eldest girl, who is a most gentle and patient teacher of her two little sisters; Meta having taken her place at school.'[4]

Neither novel-writing, nor social injustice, nor concern for her friends ever filled Mrs. Gaskell's mind and heart to capacity, as her letters show. She was before all else the mother of four growing girls, ranging at this time from the eighteen-year-old Marianne to the nine-year-old Julia, each with her very different and distinct temperament and needs, and each demanding, and receiving, the exceptional understanding and attention of their mother.[5] The decision to send Meta to a boarding school in January 1853, in place of Marianne, was made financially possible by Marianne offering to teach her little sisters in succession to Miss Mitchell, their governess, who was leaving for a better-paid post as teacher in a girls' school. Meta, aged sixteen at the time, with an artistic bent that later earned her lessons from Ruskin, had decided for herself that she wished to go to school and made her own choice of Rachel Martineau's school at Liverpool where she was happy and did well.

Mrs. Gaskell stood back at times and viewed her daughters objectively; the very ability to do so being the effect of that fairness of mind that

---

[3] *GL* 151. [4] *GL* 154, 7-10 Apr. 1853.

[5] Edna Lyall reported Marianne, later Mrs. Holland, as saying of her mother: 'It was wonderful how her writing never interfered with her social or domestic duties. I think she was the best and most practical housekeeper I ever came across, and the brightest, most agreeable hostess, to say nothing of being everything as a mother and friend. She combined both, being my mother and greatest friend in a way you do not often, I think, find between mother and daughter.' 'Mrs. Gaskell', in *Women Novelists of Queen Victoria's Reign: A Book of Appreciations* (London, 1897), pp. 142-3.

F

allowed them such exceptional freedom to develop on their own lines—
the fairness that distinguishes not only her conduct as a mother, but as
a writer about young girls. 'Now about the children', she wrote to her
sister-in-law Anne Robson the previous autumn:

It is delightful to see what good it had done MA, sending her to school . . . She
is such a 'law unto herself' now, such a sense of duty, and *obeys* her sense. For
instance she invariably gave the little ones 2 hours of patient steady teaching in
the holidays . . . I wish you could hear MA sing. It is something *really* fine; only
at present she sings little but Italian and Latin Mass Music. It is so difficult to
meet with *good* English songs . . . Now to turn to Meta, who is a great darling in
another way. MA looks at nothing from an intellectual point of view; and will never
care for reading,—teaching music, and domestic activity, especially about
children will be her forte. Meta is untidy, dreamy, and absent; but so brim-full
of I don't know what to call it, for it is something deeper, and less showy than
talent . . . her drawings are equally thoughtful and good . . . She is *quite* able to
appreciate any book I am reading. Ruskin's Seven Lamps of Architecture for the
last instance. She talks very little except to people she knows well; is inclined to
be *over*-critical and fastidious with everybody and everything, so that I have to
clutch up her drawings before she burns them . . . Then she loses time terribly
. . . for she gets so absorbed in her own thoughts etc that she forgets everything.
Florence has no talents under the sun; and is very nervous, and anxious; she will
require so much strength to hold her up through life; everything is a terror to her;
but Marianne at any rate is aware of this, and is a capital confidante for all Florence's
anxieties . . . Julia is witty, and wild, and clever and droll, the pet of the house;
and I often admire Florence's utter absence of jealousy, and pride in Julia's doings
and sayings. These are my 4 children; for you must go on knowing them as they
are, not their mere outsides . . .[6]

The trip to Paris could but be short, ten days at most, till 23 May,
Elizabeth told Lady Kay-Shuttleworth, as 'Mr. Gaskell must come home
straight on account of his congregational duties, and Marianne must not
miss more of the music lessons she is having with Hallé. I don't know if
she or I are the most delighted with this sudden plan.'[7] The unexpected-
ness that so heightened the delight on this occasion characterized the
year's experiences as a whole. It was a year of rest after effort, refreshment after exhaustion, and frequent changes of scene. To the several
journeys both abroad and at home that Elizabeth Gaskell took in 1853
can be traced the development of *North and South*, the book that was to
become a study in contrasts between differing societies.

After a visit from Charlotte Brontë to Plymouth Grove from 22 to
29 April (when she was so captivated by the small Julia), the planned

[6] *GL* 101, 1 Sept. 1851.   [7] *GL* 154.

journey to Paris took place between 12 and 23 May. The Gaskells' only contact there as yet was with the Salis Schwabes, the brother and his wife of their Manchester friends, who lived there and with whom they stayed. The introduction to Mme Mohl, whose friendship was to make Mrs. Gaskell's future visits to Paris both possible and frequent, did not occur until the next visit in February 1854. The return to England, as planned in the last week of May, allowed Elizabeth to stay with Eliza Fox in London, with the Shaens at Crix in Essex and, while warding off many other invitations, to be caught up in multiple engagements, among which was the opportunity of visiting a reformatory school in Westminster and inquiring into newly founded hospitals and 'homes' for prostitutes.

On 9 June she was to have visited Charlotte Brontë at Haworth, but the visit had to be postponed owing to Charlotte developing a severe septic throat. After barely three weeks at home, Elizabeth was off on her travels again, this time with the two little girls, Florence and Julia, with Hearn in attendance, to stay with the Schwabes in their North Wales home, Glyn Garth, from 2 to 7 July. It was familiar territory to Elizabeth, within excursion distance of her favourite Anglesey beauty spots.

Meanwhile, another trip abroad had been planned for later that month with Mr. Gaskell, Marianne, and Meta, to visit Normandy. The girls were to join their parents in London, Mrs. Gaskell sending minute directions in advance to Marianne on 5 July from Wales: '*Unless you hear to the contrary from me* you must be at 36 Bloomsbury Square [their usual lodgings at Mrs. Dove's] *on Saturday morning next at* $\frac{1}{2}$ *past 11 o'clock*, with your boxes *directed Gaskell, W. Duckworth's Esq, Beechwood, near Southampton*. I have written to tell Meta this too.'[8] The family were to stay a few days at Beechwood with friends of Mr. Gaskell's before crossing over to France.

The closely interlocking timetables, planned with military exactitude by Mrs. Gaskell, together with the girls' requirements in clothes all listed in advance, reveal something of the intensity and responsibilities of family life that fell on her, even when she was not working; she was never really at rest.

The visit to Haworth, postponed from June, took place finally from 19 to 23 September. Mrs. Gaskell was lucky in her weather which allowed her to accompany Charlotte in long walks across the moors, and thus to see for herself the wide, free, untrammelled surroundings that had made

[8] *GL* 163.

the Brontë children what they were—poets of nature, introspective thinkers, keen observers of wild life. Mr. Brontë was immensely flattered at the visit of so celebrated a guest as Mrs. Gaskell, whose society he wished his daughter to cultivate, and received her with the maximum of attention. Mr. Brontë could at times be grandiloquent in language, outmoded in manners; he could also be witty and pawky, as his later letters to Mrs. Gaskell show. But of the man he had been in his prime, liberal-minded, generous, humane, ceaselessly educating himself, she saw nothing. She met him only late in life at the age of seventy-six when he was incapacitated by partial blindness and could no longer walk his parish bounds. The reduction in his activity and his practical confinement to the house gave Mrs. Gaskell no conception of the man he had been, though she heard something of it from others. She took a dislike to him on the spot that was to colour the whole of her subsequent account of the Brontës' home life, of Charlotte's in particular. Father and daughter were at that time in greater disaccord than they had ever been in their lives, because of the ill-received proposal of marriage to Charlotte made by Mr. Brontë's curate, Arthur Bell Nicholls, the previous December. In judging Mr. Brontë's violent dislike for the whole idea of such a marriage for his brilliant daughter, it has in all fairness to be remembered that Charlotte herself had at first rejected the proposal with almost as much distaste as her father could wish. She was not attracted to Mr. Nicholls in any way. There had been other proposals in her life, all of which she had rejected, and other men whom she would have given any-thing to be free to marry, but in so far as she had ever given Mr. Nicholls a thought he was only yet another of the obnoxious, High Church, narrow-minded curates whom she enjoyed pillorying in *Shirley*. That Mr. Nicholls was something far above this despised herd of uncouth ill-mannered young men with whom she suffered contact only in the Sunday School and the annual 'Feast' outing, she had to find out the hard way later. It was the violence and virulence of Mr. Brontë's rejec-tion of what he called the 'beggarly Irishman' (forgetting that he himself stemmed from an Irish cabin) that roused Charlotte's sense of justice, and that gradually brought her to think differently of the offer of marriage. Mr. Nicholls had, very wisely as it turned out, resigned his curacy at Haworth and departed, a visibly heart-broken man. His grief was so deep that Charlotte was moved. With nothing to look forward to but the death of her father, the loss of her home, and a lonely old age, she came to value the proffered love of this faithful man. By the time Mrs. Gaskell visited Haworth, Charlotte had fundamentally changed her original reaction to his proposal; she was inclined to accept it—though her lack of enthusiasm for the idea was painfully apparent to herself. It was, however, an objective worth fighting for, even if the opponent was her own violently prejudiced father. The tension between father and daughter on that visit was plainly visible to Mrs. Gaskell. Writing to John Forster afterwards she described the atmosphere:

He was very polite and agreeable to me, paying rather elaborate old-fashioned compliments, but I was sadly afraid of him in my inmost soul; for I caught a glare of his stern eyes over his spectacles at Miss Brontë once or twice which made me know my man; and he talked at her sometimes; he is very fearless; has taken the part of the men against the masters,—and vice versa just as he thought fit and right; and is consequently much respected and to be respected . . . There are little bits of picturesque affection about him—for his old dogs for instance . . .[9]

Mrs. Gaskell discussed the possibility of Charlotte's marriage with her in every light, and came away from Haworth convinced that it was the only solution to her problems, the foremost of which was her loneliness. Mr. Nicholls's poverty, however, presented an obstacle, and it is evident from the subsequent correspondence between Mrs. Gaskell and Monckton Milnes that she had broached the subject with Charlotte of obtaining for her a literary pension. Here she came up against Brontë pride and dislike of dependence on any one, and had to act with great discretion. A small pension for Mr. Nicholls would be the better proposition as it would give *him* some independence, and Mrs. Gaskell accordingly approached Monckton Milnes on the subject, and gained his support. Following up her first initiative she wrote to him again on 29 October:

My dear Sir,
            With skilful diplomacy, for which I admire myself extremely, I have obtained the address we want. The Revd. A. B. Nicholls, Kirksmeaton near Pontefract, Yorkshire . . . I felt sure you would keep the story secret,—if my well-meant treachery becomes known to her I shall lose her friendship, which I prize most highly. I have been thinking over little bits of the conversation we had relating to a pension. I do not think she would take it; and I am quite sure that *one* hundred a year given as acknowledgement of his merits, as a good faithful clergyman would give her ten times the pleasure that *two* hundred a year would do, if bestowed upon her in her capacity as a writer. I am sure he is a thoroughly good hard-working, self-denying curate . . . Her father's only reason for his violent and virulent opposition is Mr. Nicholls's utter want of money, or friends to help him to any professional advancement . . .[10]

[9] *GL* 166, Sept. 1853.   [10] *GL* 168.

Mrs. Gaskell's involvement in Charlotte Brontë's affairs did not stop there. By November she had persuaded Charlotte to take a trip to London, recommending her own old lodgings with Mrs. Dove in Bloomsbury Square, so that she should meet Mr. Nicholls. The trip had to be cancelled at the last moment, but Charlotte's determination to know more of Mr. Nicholls was now strong, and in January 1854 he was encouraged to stay with friends in the Haworth district to allow Charlotte to meet him several times. So far as her own feelings were concerned she was, by then, determined to have him and had only her father to convince. This took some doing, but by the beginning of April 1854, Charlotte could announce her engagement to Mrs. Gaskell, her only confidante in the matter. Monckton Milnes had personally seen Mr. Nicholls already and made the necessary applications for his pension. Mrs. Gaskell's pleasure in the event can be judged from her letter to him of 20 April 1854:

My dear Sir,
        I have grateful remembrance of your kind exertions; and I think that the enclosed letter [from Charlotte Brontë announcing her engagement] will give you true pleasure. May I beg you to consider it as confidential as all our previous communications on this subject, and to return it to me as soon as ever you can. I can't help fancying your kind words may have made him feel that he was not so friendless as he represented and believed himself to be at first: and might rouse his despondency up to a fresh effort. I like her letter; don't you?[11]

Charlotte had written to her on the 18th:

Things have progressed I don't know how. It is of no use going into detail. After various visits and as the result of perseverence in one quarter and a gradual change of feeling in others, I find myself what people called 'engaged'. Mr. Nicholls returns to Haworth. The people are very glad—especially the poor and old and very young—to all of whom he was kind . . . He is to become a resident in this house . . . The Rubicon once passed, papa seems cheerful and satisfied; he says he has been far too stern; he even admits that he was unjust—terribly unjust, he certainly was for a time, but now all this is effaced from memory—now that he is kind again and declares himself happy . . . I could almost cry sometimes that in this important action in my life I cannot better satisfy papa's perhaps natural pride . . . but Mr. Nicholls is conscientious, affectionate, pure in heart and life. He offers a most constant and tried attachment—I am grateful to him. I mean to try and make him happy, and papa too . . .[12]

Hard upon her letter Charlotte Brontë kept her promise to stay with Mrs. Gaskell for a few days at the beginning of May. Catherine Winkworth, who called twice at Plymouth Grove during the visit, has left a very full record of the mood of guest and hostess at this meeting which, all knew, would be their last before Charlotte's marriage the following month. For Elizabeth Gaskell as for Catherine Winkworth, there was a very real fear that this marriage with a High Church clergyman might sever Charlotte's connection with them as known Dissenters. They all dreaded to lose her friendship, which was very precious to them, and while they trusted to *her* fidelity they feared her husband's influence.

Charlotte Brontë's fears, on the other hand, were of another and more material nature: her husband should never make a bigot of her, she said, but she realized his intellectual limitations and, when reminded of his goodness and reliability, made the disconcerting remark: 'That is true . . . still, such a character would be far less amusing and interesting than a more impulsive and fickle one; it might be dull!'[13] For the sister of Branwell Brontë to have come to such a conclusion is illuminating. She was quite frank in expressing her own doubts and anxieties about her future happiness to her friends, and they rallied by commending marriage and husbands in general, and the husbands of their acquaintance in particular, and Mrs. Gaskell, Catherine reported, 'set off praising *her* husband for being a good sick nurse and so good to the children and how very winning that was to the mother'.[14] The meeting ended on a merry note. Summing up her impressions of Charlotte's mood on this eve of her marriage, Catherine Winkworth made the surprisingly perceptive comment:

If only he is not altogether far too narrow for her, one can fancy her much more really happy with such a man than with one who might have made her more in love, and I am sure she will be really good to him. But I *guess* the true love was Paul Emmanuel after all, and is dead; but I don't know, and don't think that Lily knows.

Charlotte Brontë left Plymouth Grove on 4 May to pay two other visits to old friends before her marriage on 29 June.

By then, after initial difficulties, *North and South* had been begun, as Elizabeth's correspondence of that spring attests, but by a curious stroke of fate the subject of her next book was even then being decided: the 'Life' of the friend from whom she had just taken an affectionate farewell, in the full confidence of future happy meetings. Nothing could have been further from Elizabeth's thoughts at the time than that the just-engaged Charlotte, aged thirty-eight, would be dead within the year.

---

[13] Shaen, *Memorials of Two Sisters*, p. 113, letter from Catherine Winkworth to Emma Shaen, 8 May 1854.   [14] Ibid., p. 114.

The beginnings of *North and South*, or rather *Margaret Hale*, as the author thought of the book at first after the name of its heroine, were unpropitious and constantly interrupted.

By the late autumn of 1853 she had still done nothing. Late in September she received via intermediaries an invitation from the publisher Bentley— of 'Miscellany' fame—to handle her next book. Losing no time in declining the offer, she made her current situation abundantly plain: 'I have not a line written of anything whatever', she wrote on 29 September (her forty-third birthday), and added the surprising denial: 'I do not at present look forward to ever writing again for publication, having literally nothing to write about. And if I did write, I do not think I should be justified in leaving Messrs Chapman and Hall, against whom I have no complaint to make; and who took the risk of Mary Barton, when Mr. Moxon refused it as a *gift*.'[15]

The statement, coming after her approach to Dickens the previous May with the sketch for an idea for a new book—which he warmly applauded—certainly comes as a surprise. Her declared loyalty to Chapman, after the overtures to Dickens, also comes as a surprise. But this can be explained to some extent by her own later statement to Anna Jameson, that she had not believed herself tied to Dickens, to whom she considered she had only 'made a half-promise . . . which he understood as a whole one'.[16] The uncertainty over commitment, and difficulties in the actual working-out of the plot, over which, as she confessed, she had 'often been in despair',[17] were not conducive to a happy creativity; and the book visibly suffers in impetus as a result.

In February (1854), whether or not the book were already begun, Mrs. Gaskell took time off again to go with Marianne to Paris, to stay as before with the Salis Schwabes. The visit was chiefly memorable for the acquaintance it afforded Elizabeth of three people who later became her very close friends: the American sculptor William Wetmore Story and his wife, who were wintering in Paris that year, and Mme Mohl, the famous *salonnière*.

Mme Mohl had as great a gift for friendship as Elizabeth herself, and the attraction was mutual and immediate. Elizabeth could not wish to go to Paris more often than Mme Mohl wanted her there. As from the next year, her famous apartment in the Rue du Bac became Elizabeth Gaskell's Paris headquarters from where all her subsequent journeys abroad began and ended.

<hr>

[15] *GL* 167a.   [16] *GL* 225, Jan. 1855.
[17] Ibid.

Work on *North and South* presumably began on Elizabeth's return to Manchester at the end of February 1854. By early April the first sections were sufficiently advanced to let Dickens, and one or two close confidantes like Emily Shaen, see them. By then she was much concerned to know whether Dickens intended having a strike of workers in his current novel, *Hard Times*, which he was then serializing in *Household Words*, and relieved to hear from him that he was not, since she planned to do so.[18] The subject of strikes is introduced in *North and South* in chapter seventeen and is used to dramatic effect in chapter twenty-two. As the whole book numbers fifty-two chapters, the strike theme was to occur half-way through. By 17 May, however, Elizabeth had only written seventy-six sheets,[19] and had complained to Forster only a few days previously that she dared not let him see them: she felt the book was 'flat and grey with no bright clear foreground as yet', and would not risk sending it to him till 'I have got something more distinct and telling' to show.[20]

She was perfectly right, of course; the opening chapters of *North and South* take no hold on the reader. The motivation behind Mr. Hale's conscientious scruples that drives him to resign his living in the Church and the affluent way of life he, his wife, and daughter have hitherto enjoyed, to retire to the grim northern town of Milton to earn a reduced living by teaching ambitious mill-owners, is not sufficiently clear or compelling. Though it was a situation personally known to Mrs. Gaskell through her father's quixotic conduct as a young man, it was not one that she could make convincing to her readers. The opening stages of the book failed either to interest or to persuade them.

The contrast in social standards between the North and South of England that had struck Mrs. Gaskell initially as a good basis for a plot, was not enough, she found, to carry her along. The idea had to be translated into terms of human drama, and her choice of contrasts was not dynamic enough. The Hales and the Thorntons are no true foils to each other. Mr. Hale's failure as a clergyman—a spiritual issue, a matter of conscience—is no adequate contrast to Thornton's striding sense of power as a mill-owner, that weights all the argument in his favour. The argument, to gain balance and interest, has to be brought back to the purely human one of every novel, of a conflict of love, and not until Mrs. Gaskell had firmly established the character of her heroine, Margaret Hale, the product of southern civilization, were the odds redressed. Margaret Hale represents as good a product of her cultural background

[18] *GL* 191, 23 Apr. 1854.   [19] *GL* 195, 17 May 1854.   [20] *GL* 192, ?8–14 May 1854.

as Thornton does of his purely material one. She is a queenly creature with whom Mrs. Gaskell is not a little in love. Margaret and Thornton are evenly matched. But from then on, the issues that divide them are the same human issues that divide lovers throughout English fiction: character and circumstances. That Margaret is repelled by the climate of the northern town to which her father's quixotry has banished her and her mother, that she is startled by the freedom of conduct among the workers in the streets, that she feels her superiority in taste and manners to Mrs. Thornton, are not essential to the concept of a divided England that Mrs. Gaskell first imagined. It is inherent in her character and circumstances; and the more her character is explored—and she marks an enormous stride forward in Mrs. Gaskell's perception of young womanhood—the more the book gains in interest. Which brings it back in line with her usual procedure of plot-building, based firmly upon a central feminine character. From the point of view of social history, *North and South* is but a poor successor to the realities of *Mary Barton*.

Only as the characters emerge, especially the colourful northern types, and establish their strong personalities by their racy dialect and their forceful deeds, does the setting begin to matter. It is not the incidents that interest, but the characters who provoke them. The clashes resulting from the inherent incomprehension dividing the two families from the North and South are the real issues at stake. Once they are established, Mrs. Gaskell can use her 'strike' and the attack on Thornton's mill to good effect, making it the theatre for her lovers' realization of their feelings—Thornton's life threatened by rioters and Margaret throwing herself in front of him to intercept the thrown stone. The compromising gesture, his obligation to propose, her proud rejection of him and the long severance of the lovers while Margaret fights every inch of her rear-guard action to capitulation, are the conventional stuff of which a multitude of novels have been made.

What was new by then in *North and South* was the wider implication concerned in Margaret's capitulation to the masterful Thornton. Though that would have been better done by a Brontë, what Mrs. Gaskell achieved was not merely to show the solution to an unpromising love-affair, but a possible solution to jarring cultures, standards, prejudices—in a truce between conflicting interests, in a victory for both sides in the conciliation of Masters and Men.   IMPOSSIBLE!

In the character of John Thornton, the hard-headed but just and high-minded mill-owner, Mrs. Gaskell made *amende honorable* to the mill-owners of Manchester who had taken such offence at her portrayal of them in *Mary Barton*. She gave the masters' point of view in *North and South* as well as the workers'; what interested her in this new approach towards labour relations was not the triumph of one or other side, but the real hope of a better mutual understanding. John Thornton is not so far removed from his workers' lives as was Mr. Carson in *Mary Barton*; it does not need much persuasion from Margaret for him to meet their needs.

North and South is a pacifying book despite some of the hard things said on either side. The worst of these, because the most unreasonable, are said by women: Mrs. Hale, the ignorant, narrow, effete, unteachable lady from the south, and Mrs. Thornton *mère*, the brilliantly realized mother of John Thornton, whose every word goes straight to the bull's-eye of any argument, hard, unrelenting, practical. She is as perfect a creation of a northern type, with her unused and unlovely drawing-room, as was Sally the maid in *Ruth*. After the utterances of the women, what the men in their greater wisdom say is of secondary account. There is a saving humour in *North and South* that marks an advance on *Mary Barton*.

Dickens announced the serialization of 'a NEW TALE by the author of Mary Barton' in the issue of 30 July 1854 of *Household Words*. It began on 2 September and ran weekly till 27 January 1855, not without friction between author and general editor.

Mrs. Gaskell's habitual style of writing had nothing of the 'script' quality required by serialization: she could not hurry on a development in the plot for the sake of creating a crisis—of suspense or fear—with each section. Her stories evolved from within with a slow and sometimes imperceptible growth; her effects were finely drawn; she relied much on description to convey the mood of her characters; her tales were not quick-moving. All this was little to the taste of the readers of *Household Words*—nor of its editor, whose job it was to content them. Dickens had many hard things to say to his assistant editor, Wills, as the instalments of *North and South* came in. They were generally late, over-long, and verbose.

By 14 October, after six weeks' serialization, the drop in sales of *Household Words* was dramatic. Dickens wrote to Wills from Boulogne:

I am sorry to hear of the Sale dropping, but I am not surprised. Mrs. Gaskell's story, so divided, is wearisome in the last degree. It would have scant attraction enough if the casting in Whitefriars had been correct; but thus wire-drawn it is a dreary business. Never mind! I am ready to come up to scratch on my return, and to shoulder the wheel.[21]

[21] *Letters*, ii. 596.

As Mrs. Gaskell found to her cost, writing for serial publication was a very different matter from publishing a finished work. Her labours were never ended; no sooner was one section dispatched to *Household Words* than she was struggling to meet the deadline for the next one. Her frequent journeys from home, to work in peace, during the summer and late autumn of 1854 when *North and South* was falling behind show the trouble she was in.

She found herself checked in her flow not only by her usual hindrances, 'headaches and dizziness' that kept her sometimes for days 'without writing one line of "Margaret"',[22] but by the sheer inability to write under compulsion. When the whole work was at last completed and published (the final number appeared in *Household Words* for 27 January 1855) and she received the reactions of her readers, she admitted to the trials and troubles the work had cost her. Writing to Anna Jameson in January 1855, she said:

You can't think what pleasure your kind note of appreciation gave, and gives me. I made a half-promise (as perhaps I told you) to Mr. Dickens, which he understood as a whole one; and though I had the plot and characters in my head long ago, I have often been in despair about the working of them out; because of course, in this way of publishing it, I had to write pretty hard without waiting for the happy leisure hours.[23]

With the end in sight she wrote to Tottie Fox on Christmas Eve (1854):

I believe I've been as nearly dazed and crazed with this c—, d—, be h— to it [cursed, damned, be hanged to it], story as can be. I've been sick of writing, and everything connected with literature and improvement of the mind; to say nothing of deep hatred to my species about whom I was obliged to write as if I loved 'em. Moreover I have had to write so hard that I have spoilt my hand, and forgotten all my spelling. Seriously it has been a terrible weight on me and has made me have some of the most felling headaches I ever had in my life . . . We are all well that's the first unspeakable comfort.[24]

In spite of the tribulations endured by both author and editor and of the occasional revolt attempted by the one and suppressed by the other, when *North and South* was finished Dickens wrote Elizabeth a congratulatory letter. She had not expected as much and answered him in mollified mood: 'I was very much gratified by your note the other day; *very* much indeed. I dare say I shall like my story, when I am a little further from it; at present I can only feel depressed about it, I meant it to have been so much better.'[25] Her own view of the book appears a fair one, even today.

As a natural reaction to the year's strain and worry, Elizabeth sought every excuse for a change of scene and company. She believed she could find peace of mind by frequently fleeing domestic cares (Marianne was by then a competent replacement in the care of the little ones), and she stayed with the Shaens in Bedford Row in June. In October she was offered the exclusive use of the Nightingales' country house, Lea Hurst, near Matlock, in their absence, with one servant to attend to her needs; it was 'my happy, happy pause of life' in retrospect. The burden of forced composition once lifted, her spirits picked up with the turn of the year 1854/5 and she sought further to restore them with more travel. There was the chance of a visit to Paris under exceptionally tempting circumstances. She received an invitation to stay with Mme Mohl, who, having failed to entice Mrs. Gaskell to Paris while she was working on *North and South*, now 'peremptorily' commanded her to come and bring Meta with her. They went over on 13 February and stayed a fortnight.

Mme Mohl was 'English in spite of her name', as Mrs. Gaskell tersely put it, and had the singular distinction of having lived in France throughout the revolutionary movements of the century. She was born Mary Anne Clarke of English parents in the City of Westminster in the year of the great revolution, 1793. When she was a young girl, she and her mother had been taken up by Juliette Récamier and lodged within her own famous apartments in the disestablished Abbaye aux Bois, where Juliette, the ageing Chateaubriand, and other survivors of the successive storms, lived out a posthumous existence of exquisite refinement directed by a protocol of almost regal punctilio. Mary Clarke, an Orleanist to the backbone, was as intelligent as she was captivating and had the good fortune to charm Chateaubriand as well as Mme Récamier. She was admitted to their inner circle and was adopted by their intimates. There was no one of note in art, letters, politics, who did not seek admittance to the Récamier salon, and in time, when ill-health and advancing age obliged Juliette to receive fewer visitors, the overflow sought comfort with Mary Clarke and her mother. In due course they moved into an apartment of their own in the Rue du Bac, while still maintaining the closest and tenderest links with Mme Récamier and Chateaubriand, and the salon of Mme Mohl took on all the characteristics of the former Récamier salon at l'Abbaye aux Bois. Mary Clarke made a belated marriage with a distinguished Orientalist, Julius Mohl, of German

[25] *GL* 220, Dec. 1854.

extraction, but more French than the French in his love of Paris. Their third-floor apartment at 120 Rue du Bac had a garden at the back over-looking the Invalides and the church of Ste Chlotilde. It became the rallying ground for distinguished English tourists, Mrs. Frances Trollope and her sons when *en route* for Italy, the whole Nightingale family, German scientists, Orientalists, and scholars from every uni-versity in Europe, and finally Mrs. Gaskell and her daughters.[26]

What drew them was the learning of their host and the singular character and charm of their hostess. She was a fearless woman, natural and frank in a predominantly formal society, outspoken to a fault, impulsive and generous. As she had no children she surrounded herself with the children of her friends, for whom her dancing parties were a regular feature of the Parisian season. She was attracted to children (because of their spontaneity) as much as she was bored by young girls, whose stupidity and ignorance she could not tolerate. She remained herself a childlike creature in appearance, with a piquant profile, and a head of close-cut curls, worn in the 'Roman' fashion of Napoleon's day, that caused Guizot to say that she went to the same *coiffeur* as his poodle. Emelyn Story, the wife of the sculptor, left a memorable vignette of Mme Mohl as they knew her during successive Paris seasons:

Mme Mohl used to drop out of an omnibus, often into a mud-puddle, at our door, and delight us with her originality and freshness. I can see her now, just arrived, her feet on the fender before the fire, her hair flying, and her general untidiness so marked as to be picturesque—since she showed a supreme indifference to the details of dress. Her talk was all her own; nobody was like her for a jumble of ideas and facts, which made her mind much like her clothes, topsy-turvily worn . . . She cared for nothing but what she was hearing or seeing, and her racy comments were always worth remembering . . . She was always at home on Friday evenings, which were occasions we so liked that we never, when in Paris, omitted one . . . She knew how to manage her clever people—it was what she was most remarkable for, putting them always on their strong points and effacing herself except for appreciation.[27]

Into this stimulating household Mrs. Gaskell and Meta arrived on 13 February 1855 and were immediately caught up in the maelstrom of Mohl hospitality. Mrs. Gaskell's and Meta's letters to Marianne, left in charge at home, provide glimpses of the tempo of life in the Rue du Bac.

[26] Data on Mme Mohl derived from the memoir of her published by her niece, M. C. Simpson, *Letters and Recollections of Julius and Mary Mohl* (London, 1887).
[27] Henry James, *William Wetmore Story and his Friends* (Edinburgh and London, 1903), i. 365-6.

There is going to be a dance here tonight [Meta reported in her first letter]—everything is in confusion—the great red cushions of the salon being beaten and shaken till the room is clouded with dust. They have been polishing the dining-room-floor, till I anticipate a *fall* in every waltz. It is so funny the way in wh. Mme Mohl has asked people to come in my name—Mrs. Hollond (whom I have never seen) was invited 'because it wd. give Miss Gaskell so much pleasure'—and Mlle Gaskell has a prominent part in most of the invitation-notes . . . We went to a magnificent party on Tuesday for grandeurs, titles and dresses [Mrs. Gaskell carried on]; but except for eyes, it was very dull, and prevented one going to Mme Hollond's to dinner to meet V. Cousin. Mrs. Hollond goes back to England on Monday. I mean her to carry my MS. tell Papa—*up to just* before Mr Bell's death. But I can finish it up in no time if desired . . .[28]

Work, and anxiety for news from home still haunted her, even on holiday. 'I am in a great fidget about Papa too. I shan't have any comfort till I hear again from you; and I'm writing standing, with my things on, just after reading yr letter because I do so want to hear.'[29]

Meta was reported to have danced the whole evening; in another letter 'the rooms were crowded, and I can't tell you half the people. No Tourghieneffs [*sic*] . . . A cotillon at the end. Quite new tours and some very pretty but too long to describe.'[30]

For Meta, the ardent art student just turned eighteen, the excitement of Paris lay chiefly in visiting the galleries and private collections, to which Mme Mohl could give her introductions, and in being admitted to the ateliers of the painters in vogue. This was such a 'swallower-up of time', as Mrs. Gaskell put it.[31] They were frequently admitted to the atelier of Ary Scheffer. Mrs. Gaskell wrote Marianne an account of their recent doings and of the long intervals between French meals:

Saturday Atelier and then a short walk along the Quai's; then to dinner at the Scheffers (such a good dinner!), Hollands, Pasteur, Vermeil, Mrs Schwabe, etc, etc. Thence to the Jardin des Plantes, a great soirée got up in my honour (no kissing) but cups of rich chocolate and cream cakes, which made Meta wish she could have kept either her good dinner, or her good tea to another day, for she is perpetually hungry. We hardly ever have more than twice to eat in the day. Breakfast, tea and bread and butter. *Then* 6 o'clock dinner, and *nothing* whatever after, not even when we go to the theatre.[32]

Of the theatre Mrs. Gaskell said that while Meta enjoyed it she could not, because 'of the air'.[33] The lack of fresh air constantly spoiled her

[28] *GL* 229, Feb. 1855. [29] Ibid.
[30] *GL* 230, Feb. 1855. [31] *GL* 229.
[32] *GL* 230. [33] Ibid.

pleasure at concerts, lectures, or any crowded gathering; it was a symptom of her condition.

One great delight of those Paris days was in renewing acquaintance with the young American sculptor, William Wetmore Story and his wife Emelyn, whom she had met the previous year, and to whom she wrote afterwards of her happy memories of that time: 'I like to think of *our* Sunday breakfasts in Paris, and your Sunday bunches of violets, and the dear little girl, and the magnificent baby, and the Italian nurse . . . and then of Mr. Story, high and far above all, with his — Island ghost-story and his puns. Oh, weren't we happy.'[34] It was like a foretaste of the joys to come at their next meeting, in Rome in 1857, which she spoke of later as marking the 'culmination' of her life.

She and Meta had to return to England on Monday, 26 February. Depending on the news she received, she would either return direct to Manchester or stay on in London to pay a number of promised visits. 'Do you think Papa wants me?' she asked Marianne before starting out; 'if so, I shd like to come home straight. If not, I should like to pay the promised visits in London; let me know particularly, and how he is.'[35]

She received Mr. Gaskell's blessing to stay on in London and remained there for over a month. She was staying at Prince's Terrace with Mr. and Mrs. Price, when on 4 April she received a letter forwarded from home and therefore delayed. It was from John Greenwood, the Haworth stationer, telling her that Charlotte Brontë was dead.

[34] *GL* 313, autumn 1856.
[35] *GL* 230.

CHAPTER XV

THE *LIFE OF CHARLOTTE BRONTË*

JOHN GREENWOOD had a small stationer's shop opposite to and just below the Black Bull at Haworth. It was, therefore, most conveniently placed for the family at the parsonage, at 'the top of Haworth' as it was locally spoken of, where the steep ascent of Main Street reaches the plateau of the village. Ever since 1843, as he later told Mrs. Gaskell, the Brontë family had bought from him all their writing materials—paper, pens, ink, wafers—and in such quantities at times as to arouse his suspicion. Though they did not confide in him he could not but suppose they went in for some form of writing—possibly for the literary reviews—and were so earnest in their requests for paper that, rather than disappoint them, he would at times walk the 8 miles to Halifax and back to buy in supplies. Not until the identity of 'Currer Bell' and the authorship of the Bell novels were revealed did he know for certain that they wrote. His vicarious pride in them was enormous, and he conceived a positive cult for Emily Brontë, watching her goings and comings like a lover. He kept a diary in which many incidents relating to the family were entered, and left on record a description of her that has not been equalled. He met her coming off the moors one day and noted how 'Her countenance was lit up with a divine light. Had she been holding converse with Angels, it would not have shone brighter. It appeared to me, holy, heavenly . . .'

Greenwood was, in the words of Mrs. Gaskell, 'a kind of genius in his way'; dabbling in poetry and painting himself, and turning his hand to various trades, house-mason, gardener, shopkeeper, to earn a living. He was a 'little deformed man', with acute sensibilities and, as the context of his letters to Mrs. Gaskell suggests, hypersensitive to imagined slights. Charlotte had shown him both personal and practical kindness ever since her successes, and obtained for him the representation in that district of Smith, Elder's publications. On the occasion of Mrs. Gaskell's visit to Haworth she had taken her to call on Greenwood and his wife, knowing what pleasure it would give him; and had begged for a kind message for him when last staying at Plymouth Grove: 'she turned back out of the carriage when she was going away', Mrs. Gaskell remembered, 'to say: "Do send a message to John Greenwood; he will so like it."' [1]

Deeply involved as he felt himself to be in the fortunes of the Brontë family, John Greenwood made himself the messenger of ill-news directly the passing bell of Haworth Church announced to the village the death of Charlotte. Mrs. Gaskell, very properly, at once addressed a letter of condolence to Mr. Brontë. She did not know Mr. Nicholls and had, ever since her friend's marriage, hesitated to make the first advances because of his reputed attitude towards Dissenters. The unhappy effect of this quite unnecessary reticence had been to leave her without recent news of Charlotte and in complete ignorance of her fatal illness. The greater was her shock on receiving the news:

My dear Sir [she wrote to Greenwood on the very day his letter reached her], I can not tell you how VERY sad your note has made me. My dear dear friend that I shall never see again on earth! I did not even know she was ill. I had heard nothing of her since the beginning of December when she wrote to a mutual friend saying that she was well, and happy . . . You may well say you have lost your best friend; strangers might know her by her great fame, but we loved her dearly for her goodness, truth, and kindness, and those lovely qualities she carried with her where she is gone.

I want to know EVERY particular. Has she been long ill? What was her illness? You would oblige me *extremely*, if you would . . . send me every detail . . . I loved her dearly, more than I think she knew. I shall never cease to be thankful that I knew her; or to mourn her loss. [2]

Charlotte Brontë was pregnant and died of a combination of pregnancy-sickness and the lung trouble which was the old curse taking its toll of the last member of the family, the only one to pass the age of thirty.

The death of Charlotte Brontë effaced almost all other interests for Mrs. Gaskell that spring. She entered into a regular correspondence with Greenwood, and kept recurring to it in all her other correspondence. She wanted very much to visit Mr. Brontë at the earliest appropriate moment, and she was shocked to learn that Thackeray, whom Charlotte so greatly admired, had not written to condole with him. 'I am surprised at Mr. Thackerays never writing to Mr. Brontë', she wrote to Greenwood on 5 May. 'I wrote myself to tell him of her death; I have never heard from him in acknowledgment, and I thought that he might not have received my note. But he must have learnt of her death through the public papers.' [3]

---

[1] *GL* 242, 4 June 1855.   [2] *GL* 232, 4 Apr. 1855.   [3] *GL* 239, 5 May 1855.

By the end of May an idea was taking shape in her mind that she would like to collect her memories of Charlotte and when 'no one is living whom such a publication would hurt, . . . publish what I know of her'. She made the suggestion to George Smith, Charlotte's publisher, on 31 May, introducing her suggestion with a query how to have a daguerreotype copy made for herself of Richmond's portrait of Charlotte that she had seen at Haworth. The portrait, originally given by George Smith, was of course no longer his property, but that of Charlotte's widower, whom instinctively she feared to approach. 'I cannot tell you how I honoured and loved her', she told George Smith. 'I did not know of her illness, or I would have gone straight to her. It seems to me that her death was as sad as her life.' The motive for writing a memoir of Charlotte was already present in this letter, as she confided to George Smith; it was to 'make the world (if I am but strong enough in expression,) honour the woman as much as they have admired the writer'.[4]

George Smith, both as a publisher and as a very humane and civilized man, could but applaud Mrs. Gaskell's sentiments, without as yet coming forward with any definite proposal of his own. Having entered into correspondence with him with her customary ease of manner, Mrs. Gaskell pursued it with verve. 'I think it is from finding that you are suffering from a somewhat similar regret (that of not having cultivated her intimacy more assiduously,) that makes me write so openly and so much at length to you. I wish you *would* ask for permission to have a copy of the portrait . . .'

Her plan to record her memories of Charlotte, of her 'happy visit to Haworth etc.' was taking increasing hold of her.

It was from finding how much names and dates which she then gave me in speaking of her past life had passed out of my memory, that I determined that in our country-leisure this summer I would put down every thing I remembered about this dear friend and noble woman, before its vividness had faded from my mind . . . I thought that I would simply write down my own personal recollections of her, from the time we first met at Sir J. K. Shuttleworth's, telling what was right and fitting of what she told me of her past life, and here and there copying out characteristic extracts from her letters . . .

The only impediment, as she conceived it, to such a plan would be the objection of Mr. Brontë. Of this she was firmly convinced. 'I *know* that Mr. Brontë and I *fear* that Mr. Nicholls, would not like this made public, even though the more she was known the more people would honour her as a woman.'[5]

[4] *GL* 241, 31 May 1855.   [5] *GL* 242, 4 June 1855.

How altogether wrong she had been in her estimate of Mr. Brontë was to appear almost immediately. To her immense surprise she received a letter from him, dated 16 June, in which he asked her to undertake the official biography of his daughter.

Finding that a great many scribblers . . . have published articles in newspapers and tracts—respecting my dear daughter Charlotte . . . and seeing that many things that have been stated are true, but more false . . . I can see no better plan under the circumstances than to apply to some established Author to write a brief account of her life—and to make some remarks on her works. You seem to me to be the best qualified for doing what I wish should be done. If, therefore, you will be so kind as to publish a long, or short, account of her life and works . . . Mr. Nicholls and I will give you such information as you may require . . . Mr. Nicholls approves of the step I have taken, and could my daughter speak from the tomb I feel certain she would laud our choice. Give my respectful regards to Mr. Gaskell and your family, and believe me, my dear Madam . . .[6]

Mrs. Gaskell might well have been forgiven had she believed some sort of telepathy had been at work to produce such a result. At the very time she was wishing to propose such a thing, she received a request to carry it out from the very person she expected to oppose it. Her eagerness is evident enough in her immediate letter to George Smith:

I have received (most unexpectedly) the enclosed letter from Mr. Brontë; I have taken some time to consider the request made in it, but I have consented to write it, *as well as I can*. Of course it becomes a more serious task than the one which, as you know, I was proposing to myself . . . Still I am very anxious to perform this grave duty laid upon me well and fully. Of course it strengthens my determination to go over to Haworth as now I *must* see Mr. Brontë; and you will extremely oblige me by confiding to me any information respecting her which you may possess, and not be unwilling to impart. Do you think that either you or I might venture to ask for a daguerrotype of the Richmond now. I think my wish to have a copy of it gains strength. I am so afraid of forgetting her face; and that was such a beautiful likeness.[7]

There can never have been any doubt in her mind, despite the time she said she had taken to consider it, that she would write the book. It had been fomenting in her imagination for weeks past, and no other subject could really have fired her to an equal fervour that summer. The family holiday plans taking shape fell in exactly with her mood and needs: it was already decided they were to go to Silverdale for six weeks (in the

---

[6] J. Lock and W. T. Dixon, *A Man of Sorrow: the Life, Letters and Times of the Rev. Patrick Brontë* (London, 1965), p. 493.

[7] *GL* 245, 18 June 1855.

event from 1 August to 6 September), where she was certain of seclusion in which to work.

She made her momentous visit to Haworth on Monday, 23 July in a blazing heatwave, taking Catherine Winkworth with her though she hardly knew in what capacity, whether ally or chaperone, given the mixed feelings of dread and daring with which she set out. The day was to be full of surprises, not the least being Mr. Nicholls, whom she found, contrary to all her expectations, very likeable. Even before meeting him she had begun to realize that she must not rely on Greenwood's emotional reports of anyone, and had written to George Smith in June: 'One can see that poor John Greenwood takes things according to the impulse of the moment, from the contradictory accounts of Mr. Nicholls that he sends—I enclose you two more of his letters.'[8] It was inevitably 'a most painful visit', as she told Marianne afterwards. 'Both Mr Brontë and Mr Nicholls cried sadly; I like Mr Nicholls. We left very late and got to Skipton that night, dead tired.'[9] There she spent the night at the inn.

Despite the emotions and fatigues of the day she came away fairly fired with her mission, and with Mr. Brontë's rousing words ringing in her ears: 'No quailing Mrs. Gaskell! no drawing back!'[10] Though Mr. Nicholls disliked publicity and shunned the exposure of the simple and austere lines of his wife's life to the curiosity of the world, he was over-ruled by Mr. Brontë's now 'impetuous wish' to make her life known. Both gentlemen promised her every help, and rather naïvely handed her some few family letters and mementoes as a basis for her work, utterly inexperienced as they were of the most elementary requirements for her task. But the goodwill was there. Elizabeth learnt in the course of the day that the initiative for approaching her had come from Charlotte's lifelong friend, Ellen Nussey, who had been outraged at the malicious and misinformed accounts coming from the press about the late Currer Bell, and had begged Mr. Brontë to put an end to them by authorizing an official biography of his daughter, recommending Mrs. Gaskell as the obvious choice.

What had brought the matter to a head had been the publication in the June issue of *Sharpe's London Magazine of Entertainment and Instruction* of an article on Currer Bell, 'A Few Words about Jane Eyre', a vulgar and facetious production abounding in errors. They had outraged Ellen

[8] *GL* 244.
[9] *GL* 259, 27 July 1855.
[10] *GL* 257, 24 July 1855.

Nussey who stigmatized them to Mr. Nicholls as 'a tissue of malign false-hoods'.[11] The article's only interest for the biographer of Mrs. Gaskell is in its curiously close adherence to the account of Charlotte Brontë first given her by the Kay-Shuttleworths on the occasion of her visit to Windermere, and which she reported in two letters written at the time (to Catherine Winkworth and to Froude), not knowing that the source of the grotesque allegations aimed particularly at Mr. Brontë was Mrs. Brontë's dismissed drunken nurse, now living in Burnley, where she had become known to the Shuttleworths. The similarity of the two accounts can leave little doubt that both were inspired from the same source, and even suggest the possibility of Sir James Kay-Shuttleworth being responsible for the article.[12]

Be that as it may, Mrs. Gaskell was charged by Charlotte's father and widower to refute these and all other falsehoods concerning the life of her dear friend and to publish the true facts about her. Ellen Nussey, she was told, would be the repository of more information about Charlotte than anyone living, having been her close friend since their schooldays. Without a day's delay, Mrs. Gaskell wrote to Ellen Nussey, to beg for her co-operation in the task before her, and suggesting calling upon her within the week.

Her eagerness to begin work was the effect of the normal creative urge in her when a new theme had taken possession of her imagination, but it was also, in the case of this particular book, the effect of her passionate desire to see justice done, as she believed, to a misjudged character. It has to be borne in mind that Mrs. Gaskell undertook the 'life of Charlotte Brontë' not merely as a record of the truth, but as an Apologia for an admired friend.

In the furtherance of this purpose Ellen Nussey was a great help, though her knowledge of Charlotte had never penetrated beyond the domestic, personal limits of an old school friendship: she had never probed into Charlotte's creative life. A good woman herself, narrowly Anglican in tenets, Ellen Nussey had seen, and evoked, nothing but resignation in her friend; she could speak for her devotion to duty, piety, and conscientiousness, but she had no understanding whatsoever of the rebel artist within, whose works had shocked as well as delighted the reading public. Currer Bell had been reckoned 'a naughty' writer (as

[11] Shorter, *The Brontës and their Circle* (London, 1914), p. 16.

[12] A suggestion put forward in the *TLS* 28 June 1963 by Richard Gilbertson that Mrs. Gaskell was the author of the *Sharpe's* article disregards all likelihood of character and style.

G. H. Lewes told the astounded Charlotte to her face) and had brought down on herself such virulent strictures as Elizabeth Rigby's in the *Quarterly Review*, who declared that if the anonymous author of *Jane Eyre* were a woman, then she was one who had forfeited the society of her own sex. Harriet Martineau had utterly condemned the 'prevalence of the one subject of the passion of love in *Villette*'[13] and had lost Charlotte's friendship by saying so. In setting out to rectify these distorted images of her friend, Mrs. Gaskell, briefed as she principally was by Ellen Nussey, erred just as much in the other direction by presenting a portrait of Charlotte deprived, not only of the acerbities of her character, but of that passionate temperament which had been present in her from a child. These had to be passed over in silence. The very qualities that had made the novels of Currer Bell open to the strictures of the godly—their profound analyses of the sufferings of love and the movements of the human heart which were as much a part of the author's nature as her rectitude and courage—had of necessity to be suppressed. The declared purpose in every application Mrs. Gaskell made to Charlotte's friends and acquaintances for details of her life was—to make 'the world honour the woman as much as they have admired the writer': such an approach sufficiently fixed the lines of the biography in advance. It did not allow for expansion or development—or even for a change of interpretation. It did not allow, above all, for any admission of Charlotte's great though unfulfilled love for a married man. The role of M. Heger in the biography must be reduced to that of mere teacher—though after her meeting with him in Brussels the following year, Mrs. Gaskell came as near knowing the truth as any one of Charlotte's contemporaries. The meeting with Ellen Nussey was decisive in laying the foundation of Mrs. Gaskell's subsequent attitude towards her subject. While Ellen knew more about the Brontë family than anyone else, it did not follow that she knew everything, and consequently she innocently deluded Mrs. Gaskell. Ellen was good and nice and loving, but since the days of their girlhood Charlotte had never confided her inner life to her. Charlotte herself made this perfectly plain:

When I first saw Ellen I did not care for her [she confided to W. S. Williams, in an attempt to explain the friendship]—we were schoolfellows—in the course of time we learnt each others faults and good points—we were contrasts—still we suited ... now—no new friend, however lofty or profound in intellect—not even Miss Martineau herself could be to me what Ellen is, yet she is no more than

---

[13] Review of *Villette* by Harriet Martineau in *Daily News*, 3 Feb. 1853.

a conscientious, observant, calm, well-bred Yorkshire girl. She is without romance—if she attempts to read poetry—or poetic prose aloud—I am irritated and deprive her of the book—if she talks it I stop my ears—but she is good—she is true—she is faithful and I love her.[14]

Ellen's exclusion from Charlotte's obsessive inner life, its frustrations and dreams, and the extensive juvenilia in which she expressed it, left Mrs. Gaskell without an important clue to her emotional life. Indeed, the revealing novelettes of her adolescent years, unknown to Ellen, were disregarded by Mrs. Gaskell, who paid scant attention to the minute manuscripts even when she held them in her hands.

Breaking her holiday at Silverdale, Elizabeth Gaskell travelled to Birstall to visit Ellen Nussey on Tuesday, 14 August, and thereafter kept up a continual correspondence with her over the following months.

From Ellen Nussey she would hear all she hoped for concerning Charlotte's dedication to duty, her goodness to her sisters, her courage under affliction. She would also see the district—Birstall and Gomersal, Hartshead and Roe Head—where Charlotte had spent her schooldays, and which she had subsequently described in her essentially regional novel, *Shirley*. All this was precious background material for the biographer. The Nusseys had been landowners in the parish of Birstall since the time of Edward IV, but already when Charlotte first knew them in the early 1830s their fortunes were declining. They were obliged to abandon their fine ancestral battlemented house, Rydings, the prototype for 'Thornfield', for the smaller Brookroyd. She stayed at both houses and knew most of the large Nussey family in her schooldays, even receiving an offer of marriage from Ellen's brother Henry Nussey (the supposed prototype for 'St. John Rivers' in *Jane Eyre*). For Mrs. Gaskell all this was valuable first-hand biographical material. Ellen lent her, furthermore, Charlotte's letters to her, some 350 of them. As yet, she did not hamper Mrs. Gaskell with restrictions on the use of proper names that made her task ultimately so difficult. From Ellen also she learnt of the identities of Charlotte's other friends—the Taylors of Gomersal, who had the distinction of figuring as the entire Yorke family in *Shirley*; Miss Wooler, the schoolmistress; the Wheelwright girls whom she had known at Brussels—all of whom she approached in due course and who supplied her with useful information. Ellen Nussey could give her, more-over, the names of the people who had employed Charlotte as governess; the Sidgwicks of Stonegappe, the Whites of Rawdon, and, more sig-

---

[14] Wise and Symington, *The Brontës*, iii. 63.

nificantly still for the fortunes of the book, she gave her the identity of Branwell Brontë's employers, the Robinsons of Thorp Green. It was from Ellen Nussey on the occasion of this first meeting that Mrs. Gaskell heard the story of Branwell Brontë's ill-fated love-affair with his employer's wife, which was to have such a disastrous bearing on her book. Assured of the truth of the facts communicated by Ellen Nussey, she never hesitated to make use of them, with the sole precaution of omitting the principals' names from the published work. The disgrace and ruin brought on Branwell by the Robinsons, which in turn laid such a heavy burden on his sister, was an argument exactly suited to Mrs. Gaskell's purpose of glorifying the character of Charlotte Brontë.

She let no time pass in following up the line of inquiry opened by Ellen Nussey, and wrote to an unknown correspondent particularly well informed on Yorkshire affairs (possibly Monckton Milnes) on 23 August for fuller details concerning, among other people, 'the Robinsons (she now Lady Scott) near York?'[15] The dramatic value of the ruin of Branwell Brontë to the story of his sister's life was apparent from the first to her biographer, who was, it must never be overlooked, before all else a novelist with a strong sense of drama and pathos. Neither then nor later did Mrs. Gaskell, the survivors of the Brontë family, or even, more surprisingly, her publisher George Smith, appear to consider the libellous character of such disclosures.

At Silverdale until 6 September, and throughout October at home, Elizabeth worked uninterruptedly in sifting the material supplied by Charlotte's circle of friends, and was in a position to write to George Smith by the end of the month: 'I almost fancy that I have material enough, or nearly enough, gathered together to enable me to make a vol: about the size of Carlyle's Life of Sterling, but of course I can not tell at present.'[16]

The only interruption to her work had been caused by a three-week visit to Glasgow in the latter part of September for a duty visit to her stepmother and stepsister, whom she had not seen for twenty-five years. Even so and in those unpropitious circumstances, she kept in touch with Ellen Nussey: 'I am staying here with my unknown half-sister [she wrote from Dunoon], whom it is 24 years, as I think I told you, since I met . . . and I believe we shall remain among our relations in Scotland until somewhere about the end of next week.'[17]

---

[15] GL 266.
[16] GL 271, late Oct. 1855.
[17] GL 267a, 25 Sept. 1855. Among those 'relations' were the Maxwells of Dumfries. See below, p. 210.

She paid a second visit to Ellen Nussey on 8 October, going on to visit Miss Wooler and to see some of the houses in the Roe Head district where Charlotte had visited. She was impatient to begin her work, but nothing is more revealing of her difficulties as a writer than the account of her domestic commitments that autumn: 'I wish I had more leisure [she told Ellen Nussey], but it is my busiest time of the year just now, and our house has been and is, almost fuller than it will hold of company, for whose amusement and entertainment I have to plan each day. I think with much pleasure of my two half-days with you.'[18]

It was not a time of year when she could put her work before her family and social commitments. 'My work . . . is getting on but slowly,' she told Miss Wooler on 12 November, 'owing to the pressure of business of other kinds that has been weighing upon me',[19] and Meta wrote to Ellen Nussey on her mother's behalf:

Mama is so terribly busy that she really cannot find time to write to you, but she has asked me to do so for her, as she cannot bear that you should remain any longer unthanked for your most interesting account of Miss Anne Brontë's death at Scarborough . . . which she hopes you will allow her to make use of in the Memoir. She is sadly afraid you will think her ungrateful . . . but she hopes you will understand that it is want of time which has prevented her . . . I am sure I can testify to the many calls which there have been upon her time for these last few weeks. First of all one of the servants was taken suddenly ill . . . so of course Mama had to pay her the greatest care . . . Ever since that there has been a succession of visitors staying in the house, which has quite prevented her from writing . . .[20]

As a postscript to Meta's letter, added 20 December, Mrs. Gaskell told Ellen Nussey: 'I have not yet written a line of the Memoir. I literally have had no time . . . The very first hours of leisure I shall have shall be given to this precious work.'[21] Not until the Christmas period was safely over could she write to Ellen on 9 January to say 'I believe now my engagements are clearing away, and that I shall soon be able to set to work in real earnest.'[22] By 22 February twenty pages of the 'Memoir' were written.[23]

News of the projected work was getting about and by early March she had received an offer for it from the American firm, Ticknor & Fields. She had already promised it, however, as she told them[24] to Messrs. Appleton & Co. of New York, who had offered her £75 for it—the

[18] *GL* 270a, 20 Oct. 1855.   [19] *GL* 272, 12 Nov. 1855.
[20] *GL* 275+, 17 Dec. 1855.   [21] *GL* 275a, 20 Dec. 1855.
[22] *GL* 276b.   [23] *GL* 280a.
[24] *GL* 282, 14 Mar. 1856.

American publication, obviously, to follow publication in the United Kingdom. From the start, it was self-evident that the English edition would come from Smith, Elder, as Currer Bell's publishers, and Mrs. Gaskell reported progress to George Smith as the year advanced. They had not yet met when she sent him the first sheets in April. His impression was good and hearing that she was in London he suggested a meeting. She was, however, on the eve of taking an important step in her research by a journey to Brussels, and wrote to him on 29 April:

I am in London, i.e. Chelsea, to show my two little girls London—in the true Country cousin sense of the expression,—and every day is planned cram-full . . . To-morrow we are off very early to Windsor Hampton Court and Kew . . . I am declining *all* invitations till my return, as I do not wish to separate myself from my children,—and consequently however great the temptation I could not accept your kind proposal to meet Mrs. Smith . . .[25]

Before sailing for Brussels she fitted in a visit to the Wheelwright family, however, who had known Charlotte Brontë at school there and who could give her some leads. She had already written to Mme Mohl asking her to recommend somewhere to stay, and had been put in touch with a Mme Haydon with whom she engaged rooms. She did not take either of her grown-up daughters (sensing perhaps the awkward situation with the Hegers into which her quest might lead her), but took a confidential maid, Eliza Thornborrow, who had been with the family off and on for years, and who joined her in London on the eve of sailing. Writing from the Victoria Hotel, Euston Square, on 'Tuesday morning' to Marianne she said:

My own dearest Polly, I must not leave England without a line or two to you darling child. We go to-night by the route you planned via Dover and Ostend. Eliza is here all safe and right; so far so good! But so many other things have gone wrong that I am in despair and can hardly keep from perpetually crying which is partly being so overtired . . .[26]

Her friend Lady Coltman was taking charge of Flossy and Julia for a further weekend's pleasures in London and then sending them home to 'Papa' on Monday's train.

The rooms she had engaged at Brussels were at 47 Avenue de la Toison d'Or, Avenue Louise, in the fashionable quarter of the town and also not far removed from the Rue d'Isabelle, where she must go to call on the Hegers. Of the outcome of that visit she later wrote to

[25] *GL* 284.   [26] *GL* 286a, 6 May 1856.

Ellen Nussey: 'Mme Héger, understanding that I was a friend of Miss Brontë's, refused to see me; but I made Mr. Heger's acquaintance, and very much indeed I both like and respect him.'[27]

The pirated French translation of *Villette*, published almost immediately after the death of Charlotte Brontë under the title *La Maîtresse d'Anglais, ou le Pensionnat de Bruxelles*, had by then reached the Hegers, the very thing that Charlotte had always done everything to prevent. She had made a special agreement with George Smith to preclude a French translation of *Villette* in her lifetime, but the pirates had forestalled her and the Hegers were by then in possession of the book.[28] The incriminating portrait of herself contained in it had irrevocably alienated Mme Heger; she was mortally and implacably offended. Years later, English pupils in the school were still forbidden to pronounce the name of Charlotte Brontë or, if they did, Madame visibly blanched.[29]

Whatever situation Mrs. Gaskell may have expected to find on reaching Brussels, the reality was so explosive as to need very careful handling. Mercifully, M. Heger came to her help. He not only saw her, but was frank with her. In a gesture of trust, he showed her the letters Charlotte had written to him after her return to England, the tragic letters that betrayed her love for him, and which remained unknown to the world till the Heger family donated them to the British Museum in 1913.

How greatly the revelation shook Mrs. Gaskell is evident from her instant decision to suppress all, even the slightest allusion to it in her work. Here was a situation that could never be explained to the readers of her biography. But even suppression had its problems. Since *Villette* remained as a permanent signpost to the passion that had inspired it, and Charlotte's school-years in Brussels could not altogether be omitted from an account of her life, some treatment of her relations with the Hegers must be attempted. It was decided then and there that M. Heger would furnish her with a few anodyne extracts from Charlotte's letters, dealing purely with her scholastic plans, and with a few of Charlotte's and Emily's French *Devoirs* written while at school, such as would fit suitably into the biography of M. Heger's one-time pupil. His letter to Mrs. Gaskell, dated 22 May 1856, written to her after her return to England, exists today in the keeping of Manchester University Library. It is the irre-

---

[27] *GL* 294, 9 July 1856.
[28] The present author was shown the actual copy of the book by the Hegers' grand-daughter, Mme Beckers-Heger.
[29] Frederika Macdonald, *The Secret of Charlotte Brontë* (London, 1914), p. 259.

futable proof of Mrs. Gaskell's knowledge of the compromising letters that her studied avoidance of the subject in the *Life* makes so revealing.[30] Translated into English, M. Heger's letter reads:

In compliance with your wishes I am sending you herewith some specimens of the work of the two sisters Emily and Charlotte. I also enclose a few extracts from the texts of the letters that Mlle Charlotte wrote me, and I will not delay in sending you as you requested, a summary of the teaching methods on the subject of style employed in my classes; but for lack of more time today I must confine myself to expressing anew, to you, dear Madame, my respectful regards   C. Heger.

The immediate effect of M. Heger's confidence in Mrs. Gaskell was to tie her hands completely about Charlotte's real experience in Brussels, the greatest single emotional experience of her life. To account for Charlotte's growing despair during her last year in Brussels and for her precipitate return to England in 1844, Mrs. Gaskell had deliberately to antedate the disaster overtaking the brother, Branwell, which in fact did not occur till eighteen months later. As a scapegoat Branwell Brontë did as well as another; and from that period in her story, she sought to heap on him the opprobrium for all the unavowable emotional stresses to which her heroine had succumbed. Pity for Charlotte made her unjust towards everyone else. M. Heger's understanding compassion for his unfortunate pupil only fortified Mrs. Gaskell in her intention. He had so far penetrated Charlotte's feelings as to judge her a sick woman—he spoke later of 'son pauvre coeur malade' (having first written 'son pauvre coeur blessé')[31]—and Mrs. Gaskell knew that with him Charlotte's secret was safe.

There remained, however, a further subject of great embarrassment for her on her return to England in the proposed posthumous publication of Charlotte's novel *The Professor*, the manuscript of which remained as yet in Mr. Nicholls's possession. George Smith was now eager to publish this remaining work of the dead Currer Bell and urged Mrs. Gaskell to get it out of Charlotte's widower.

This Mrs. Gaskell refused to do, dreading, as she later confesses, that *The Professor* might again implicate M. Heger, whose confidence she had sworn to keep.[32] Other people, however, were not so scrupulous and she found to her consternation that Sir James Kay-Shuttleworth was

---

[30] She further mentions her knowledge of the letters when writing to George Smith, 1 Aug. 1856, *GL* 299.
[31] Gérin, *Charlotte Brontë*, p. 247.
[32] See *GL* 299, 1 Aug., 301, 13 Aug., 308, 7–8 Sept. 1856.

resolved on browbeating Mr. Nicholls into relinquishing the manuscript. Sir James had plans for 'editing' the work himself, a possibility
that Mrs. Gaskell knew would have been wholly repugnant to the dead
Charlotte—who peculiarly disliked Sir James—and it decided her to
act in the matter herself. She therefore went over to Haworth in Sir
James's company on 23 July to act as mediator, if possible, between
Sir James, 'who is not prevented by the fear of giving pain from asking
in a peremptory manner for whatever he thinks desirable',[33] and the
bereaved gentlemen. They came away with the manuscript of *The Professor*, the first ten pages of Charlotte's last tale, 'Emma', and the great
mass of the juvenilia—

a packet about the size of a lady's travelling writing case, full of paper books of
different sizes . . . Mr. Gaskell says they would make more than 50 vols of print,—
but they are the wildest and most incoherent things, as far as we have examined
them, *all* purporting to be written, or addressed to some member of the Wellesley
family. They give one the idea of creative power carried to the verge of insanity.[34]

With this summary judgement of the literature of Angria, Mrs. Gaskell
dismissed one of the most potentially fruitful lines of research into the
creative processes of Charlotte Brontë.

The reading of the manuscript of *The Professor* brought her greater
satisfaction; she found, to her unspeakable relief, that it in no way
concerned M. Heger. She had had perforce to confide to a certain extent
in George Smith, and wrote to him on 1 August:

I can not tell you how I should deprecate anything leading to the publication of
those letters of M. Hégers.[35] I have not seen the 'Professor' as yet, you must
remember, so perhaps all my alarm as to the subject of it may be idle and groundless; but I am afraid it relates to M: Héger, even more distinctly and exclusively
than Villette does . . . I foresee, if Sir James has set his will upon it, *it is* to be
published whatever may be the consequences. He over-rides all wishes, feelings,
and delicacy. I saw that in his way of carrying everything before him at Haworth,
deaf to remonstrance and entreaty. But after all, it may not have so much reference
to M. Héger as I dread; yet ever so little, falling on a 'raw' in his, and his wife's
mind will be esteemed by them and their friends as such. I am sure from numerous
passages in her private letters that she would not have wished Sir James to edit
it . . . But also, I could not undertake the editing (which would to a certain degree
seem like my sanctioning it,) after receiving M. Hégers confidence, and hearing
her letter(s) if, as I fear,—it relates to him.[36]

33 *GL* 297, 25 July 1856.   34 Ibid.
35 *GL* 299.   36 Ibid.

In the event, her fears proved groundless; *The Professor* concerned neither Monsieur nor Madame Heger.

I dreaded lest the Prof: should involve anything with M. Heger [she wrote to Emily Shaen on 8 September]—I had heard her say it related to her Brussels life,—and I thought if he were again brought before the public, what would he think of me? I believed him to be too good to publish those letters—but I felt that his friends might really with some justice urge him to do so,—so I awaited the arrival of the Prof . . . with great anxiety.[37]

Quite evidently, from the context of these letters to George Smith and Emily Shaen, Mrs. Gaskell had confided her knowledge of Charlotte's letters to M. Heger to her intimates—though presumably *not* to Ellen Nussey—even while she intended resolutely to exclude all reference to the situation they betrayed from the Memoir. Her frequent allusion to 'those letters' shown her by M. Heger leaves no doubt whatever of her full knowledge of the facts. From then on, the difficulties in her passage seem cleared away.

Throughout August when she, Mr. Gaskell, and the girls stayed at the houses of various Holland cousins—at Dumbleton near Evesham, at Boughton near Worcester, and at Devizes, she gave herself no respite. Her self-imposed programme was arduous:

I wrote 120 new pages while we were absent on our holiday [she told Emily Shaen afterwards], which was no holiday to me. I used to go up at Dumbleton and Boughton to my own room, directly after 9 o'clock breakfast; and came down to lunch at $\frac{1}{2}$p 1, up again, and write without allowing any temptation to carry me off till 5—or past; having just a run of a walk before 7 o'clock dinner. I got through an immense deal; but I found head and health suffering—I could not sleep for thinking of it.[38]

She drove herself as usual beyond her capacity, with the inevitable effects, and by mid September had to suspend work. On 30 September she wrote to George Smith, in explanation of her 'ungrateful non-acknowledgement of your letters', that she

had a long fainting-fit one day ('quite promiscuous' as servants say,) consequent doctor, *consequent* illness, consequent ordering to sea side and prohibition of reading or writing, receiving or answering letters—I was to do nothing but eat and sleep and breathe fresh air—Now I'm home, not quite strong but pretty well; and I find I don't know how great an accumulation of letters.[39]

[37] *GL* 308.   [38] Ibid.   [39] *GL* 312, 30 Sept. 1856.

Her daughters, Marianne and Meta, relieved her whenever possible of routine inquiries in connection with the book, and of correspondence with Ellen Nussey, with whom she remained in close touch throughout its composition.

She was anxious to read the manuscript to Ellen at the earliest opportunity, but even there was faced with difficulties. She found, as she explained to George Smith, that

There is some little jealousy (the nearest word, but not the right one) of Miss Nussey on Mr Brontë's part, and he especially forbids my showing the MS of my biography to her. Now she is about the only person who would care to see it in MS, because she wants to know what extracts I have taken from all her letters; and she has a right to know this, if she wishes. So, after some consideration, I find I must *read* it to her . . . and today I have written to ask her to come here, and be read to about January 10th.[40]

Mr. Brontë's injunction, imposed on the author and auditor of the book alike, may explain why Ellen Nussey allowed the passages concerning the Brontës' childhood to stand: their deprivation of food, education, elementary care—all the malicious reports derived from the dismissed drunken nurse via the Kay-Shuttleworths that had eventually to be deleted from the third edition. In a later letter Mrs. Gaskell suggests that Ellen Nussey did actually read the manuscript herself, or parts of it, and it is true that Ellen had not known Charlotte in her early years and that there were many things that Charlotte had never confided in her. Even so, from what she knew of the Brontë household it is hard to believe that these damaging and untrue accounts, the effects of which on public opinion it took decades to efface, would have remained unquestioned and eventually published had Ellen Nussey read the manuscript in full. As it was, Mrs. Gaskell was unaware until too late of their untruth, and at the time was pleased with Ellen Nussey's commendations. Her visit to Plymouth Grove took place on 12 January 1857 and lasted several days. Mrs. Gaskell was able to report on it afterwards to W. S. Williams of Smith, Elder:

Miss Nussey was here last week reading the MS. I was gratified to hear her repeatedly say how completely the life at the Parsonage appeared to her reproduced. Much of this was owing to the remarkable extracts from letters; but she said several times how exactly and accurately I had written about the life and characters.[41]

[40] *GL* 322, 11 Dec. 1856.   [41] *GL* 335, 19 Jan. 1857.

9. Marianne, Meta, and Flossy Gaskell, pastel by C. A. Duval, 1845

10. Mrs. Gaskell by Richmond, 1851

Thus lulled into a false sense of security, Mrs. Gaskell worked on to the book's conclusion, all-too-little advised of the danger lying ahead, despite some few intimations from George Smith himself. In a highly flippant mood she had asked him, as early as 2 October, 'Do you mind the law of libel.—I have three people I want to libel—Lady Scott (that bad woman who corrupted Branwell Brontë) Mr. Newby, and Lady Eastlake, the first and last not to be named by name, the mean publisher to be gibbeted.'[42] A too unemphatic warning from George Smith went virtually unheeded.

First of all to the objection you raise [she wrote to him]. It is possible that it would be wiser not to 'indicate so clearly' (I was not aware that I had done so,) the lady concerned in Branwell's misdoing. I will see how this can be altered. What and where did you think pointed her out too distinctly.[43]

Branwell's Mrs. Robinson, widowed long since and remarried to an elderly titled relative, Sir Edward Dolman Scott, was the object of Mrs. Gaskell's keenest sense of retributive justice. 'I wished to show the contrast between her present life, and the life which others had led through her guilt; and for that reason I named the circumstances by which she is surrounded at present.'[44]

Defending herself for her strongly expressed feelings on the subject in a further letter to George Smith, she repeated to him the reports she had received at first hand about Lady Scott from sources quite removed from the Brontë family. Important and conclusive as these were from the point of view of historic truth, that they were dynamite in the hands of a biographer Mrs. Gaskell does not seem to have realized. She remained deaf to her publisher's warnings.

About Lady — (did I tell you the name?) I see you think me merciless,—but details of her life (past and present) which I heard from her own cousin when I was staying at Sir C. Trevelyans and which were confirmed by Lady Trevelyan (also a connection) showed her to have been a bad heartless woman for long and long,—and to think of her going about calling, and dining out etc etc—(her own relations have been obliged to drop her acquaintance,) while those poor Brontës suffered so—for bad as Branwell was,—he was not absolutely ruined for ever, till she got hold of him, and he was not the first, nor the last. However it is a horrid story, and I should not have told it but to show the life of prolonged suffering those Brontë girls had to endure; and what doubtless familiarized them to a certain degree with coarse expressions, such as have been complained of in W.H. [*Wuthering Heights*] and the Tenant of Wildfell Hall . . . you see *why* I wanted to contrast the two lives, don't you?[45]

[42] *GL* 314.   [43] *GL* 326, 26 Dec. 1856.
[44] Ibid.   [45] *GL* 328, 29 Dec. 1856.

G

Undertaking to omit from her veiled references to Lady Scott that she was a clergyman's wife or had a title, Mrs. Gaskell felt that she had sufficiently met George Smith's objections. Her last wish, as she told him, was to incur a libel action, either for him or for herself. But the main if still remote danger of such an action being brought came, in her view, from the shady publisher of *Wuthering Heights* and *The Tenant of Wildfell Hall*, Newby, and not from Lady Scott.

At the beginning of 1857 Mrs. Gaskell was hoping to have the book finished by the first week in February. She was working at high speed on the last sheets even while the first chapters were going to press and the proof-sheets reaching her throughout January. She was acutely anxious by then to have it finished and out and to turn her back on it by escaping abroad. As far back as October she had set her mind on avoiding the agitation of publication.

I am very sore about reviews [she confessed to George Smith]; I know it is a weakness, but unfavourable ones depress me very much . . . and I know I shall be doubly sore about this. More than doubly, for I shall feel as if I had done her an injury. So I plan getting out of England at the time of publication and, if possible, for us to go to Rome for a month ending up with the Holy Week— Easter being April 12th.[46]

The first idea of a visit to Rome had originated with her American friends, the Storys, who lived there and who had repeatedly urged her, since their meetings in Paris, to visit them. Such a prospect was further stimulated by the hope of a sufficiently high royalty on her book to pay the expenses. She had the courage to brave George Smith on the subject:

I have a great dislike to bargaining [she wrote to him after receiving his initial offer of £600 for the work], and I should not like to be (what the Lancashire people call) 'having'; but if I must deal frankly with you, as I wish, the terms proposed for the Biography are below what I thought I might reasonably expect. My way of reckoning was this—For 'North and South' I received 600£ (from H.W. [*Household Words*] and Mr. Chapman together) . . . Now the amount of labour bestowed on the Biography, (to say nothing of anxiety in various ways,) has been more than double at least what the novel cost me . . . I have also to take into account the expense which I have been at in journies to Brussels etc— and in collecting materials, which I can not set down at less than 100£ . . . I have put these points before you, in order that you may judge whether I am unreasonable or not in expecting some advance on your present offer.[47]

George Smith immediately offered her £800 and the copyright of the work, which she gladly accepted.

[46] *GL* 314, 2 Oct. 1856.   [47] *GL* 326.

Up to the very last minute, however, she was uncertain of her plans and what payment she might expect in advance royalties to defray her expenses. She planned to take Marianne and Meta with her, and as the time approached, her excitement at the prospect of the journey equalled, if it did not outweigh, her last anxieties for the book.

I wished very much to set out for Rome next week [she wrote to George Smith]; but I hardly know when you are intending to publish the Life, and if you meant to defer it long I would rather give up going abroad now, and go nearer to the time of publication. I suppose I have no right to expect any portion of the payment of the Memoir before the day of publication; but . . . it would be a very great convenience if you would kindly let me have 250£.[48]

She gave him directions for payment in Coutts's Bank, Circular Notes, to await her in London at Mr. Shaen's, 8 Bedford Row. She reckoned it would take them a week to reach Rome—and in order to economize they determined to make the journey from Manchester to London through to Calais in one day. By the 7th she could write to Laetitia Wheelwright, Charlotte's friend, to say she had finished the biography that very day and dispatched the last sheets to Smith, Elder in London. They planned to leave home on the 13th, expecting that by then the last exchanges with George Smith, relating to the plates for the frontispiece and all final corrections to the proofs, would have been attended to.

From the Storys she had received much useful information on Rome, addresses for accommodation, the cost of living, hints on climate, dress, and food, as well as a cordial invitation to stay with them at first until suitable lodgings were found. In a rising fever of excitement she wrote to them on 8 February:

We are really truly coming to Rome!!!!!! We are starting off on Friday next—the 13th—and if you don't want to have us on Saturday the 21st, will you write to us either to Paris, where we shall be on the 15th, 16th and 17th at the Hotel des Missions Etrangères, Rue de Bac, or to the Hotel de l'Orient, Marseilles, which we hope to reach on the afternoon of Wednesday 18th, and to leave by the direct (Thursday 19th) boat for Civita Vecchia—arriving there according to *promise* on 7 o'clock on Saturday morning, in time for the 10 o'clock diligence to Rome.

Will you really receive us for a few days? And are we really coming—and shall we truly see Rome? I don't believe it. It is a dream! I shall never believe it, and shall have to keep pinching myself![49]

With the last sheets of the biography only just dispatched to Smith, Elder, such precipitate flight out of the country would not have been

[48] *GL* 338, 4 Feb. 1857.   [49] *GL* 342.

possible but for the help of Mr. Gaskell. He undertook 'to complete all arrangements' with George Smith.[50] She was leaving him a heavier burden of responsibility than either of them could have suspected at the time. Her task completed, as she fully believed, exhausted as always after finishing a book by the long continuous strain, she was desperate to restore herself in fresh surroundings and thought only of weighing anchor and heading out to sea.

To George Smith on the eve of leaving England, she explained her peculiar feelings on finishing a book: they were strongly detached, surprisingly so in so maternal a woman. It was as if the very fact of her fulfilled maternity precluded her from feeling protective towards the creations of her mind. Thanking George Smith for all his 'kindness and obligingness', she went on to hope that the book would be published soon, adding:

And please to remember I am just the reverse of Miss Brontë; I never want to see or hear of any reviews; when I have done with a book I want to shake off the recollection thereof for ever . . . I hope it will sell well for your sake,—for I think you have behaved very liberally about it.[51]

[50] *GL* 344, 11 Feb. 1857.   [51] Ibid.

CHAPTER XVI

ROMAN CARNIVAL

THE boat from Marseilles was thirty hours out at sea when the boiler burst and they had laboriously to return to port,[1] the loss of time and the double crossing adding immeasurably to the fatigues of an already exhausting journey. Under normal conditions the crossing to Civita Vecchia took only forty hours. They were so far behind schedule that they did not reach Rome until late on 23 February. Driving through darkened streets to the Storys' house, the Casa Cabrale, at 43 Via San Isidoro, they could not really feel that they had arrived till the next morning when they awoke, transplanted as by magic into the full light and clamour of a Roman day.

They crowded out on to the Storys' balcony and gazed incredulous at the scene they had so often heard described: at the azure light flooding the dome of the sky, at the brown huddle of roofs spreading about the fabulous city with its cypresses and parasol pines guarding the landmarks; at the blossoming shrubs of mimosa and myrtle and wisteria pouring over the ancient walls. Only then did they realize that they were in Rome, and, though it was February elsewhere, that in Rome it was spring. It did not need the Carnival crowd already surging through the streets to make them feel on holiday. It was Shrove Tuesday, 24 February 1857.

The sheer novelty of the scene, the gaiety of the crowds disguised as figures of high romance with their 'Travestia' and masks, completed the spell cast by the spring morning. The Gaskells were intoxicated with the mere sight and sound of Roman life before ever they tasted it. It was like nothing they had experienced before and they were, mother and daughters alike, then and lastingly, profoundly affected by the place. Everything, indeed, conduced to make that morning magical.

To measure the importance for Mrs. Gaskell of the ensuing experience, of the long enchantment of her Roman holiday, of the strong words she later used to describe it, one has to remember of course that from her

[1] Shaen, *Memorials of Two Sisters*, p. 170.

young womanhood in Knutsford she had always been singularly sus-
ceptible to her environment. Her spirits had soared or sunk according
to whether she was surrounded by things of beauty or deprived of them.
Even her childish unhappiness in her father's house in Chelsea had been
mitigated by the sight of 'the beautiful, grand river'. It was the first
impact of Wales that had made a writer of her; and in recent years, she
had consciously fled to Silverdale whenever she needed to write. The
accumulative effects of years of bad weather, social problems, domestic
anxieties, and overwork, which were inseparable from her life in Manchester, had in the end injured her health and she was suffering from
constant and crippling headaches. Her flights from home were made
quite as much for her health's sake as for enjoyment, their object thera-
peutic. But only when her daughters were with her was she thoroughly
content.

The euphoria induced by Rome, therefore, had complex emotional
origins. It was enhanced by new and extremely agreeable human relationships, and by the exceptional surroundings that made those relationships
romantic beyond the analysis of reason.

The Storys had hired a balcony on the Corso from where to see the
Carnival processions and were settled there with their guests when
Charles Eliot Norton entered on the scene. Meta Gaskell recorded the
incident many years later.

I shall keep the anniversary of that Carnival Day when first we saw you [she wrote
to him] as a festa; for I can truly say that your friendship has been one of the
greatest pleasures of my life. It is sealed now, too, with deep gratitude to you for
your faithful affection to Mama, which she prized as highly as she returned it
truly. I can see your face and smile now (as distinctly as if I were only just turning
away from them) when you caught at some confetti that Mama was dangling on
a long stick from the balcony—and Mama said 'Oh look what a charming face!'
and Mr. Story (I think it was) said 'Oh, that's Charles Norton', and then there
was chorus of welcome and bidding you come up.[2]

Meta elsewhere set the scene in recollection:

The narrow street was filled with a boisterous crowd of Romans, half mad with
excitement at the confetti-throwing and horse-racing. Suddenly against this
turbulent background there stood out the figure of a young man just below the
balcony, smiling up at my mother, whom he knew he was to see there and whom
he easily distinguished from the others. It is fifty-three years since that day, and

----

[2] *Letters of Mrs. Gaskell and Charles Eliot Norton, 1855–1865*, ed. Jane Whitehill (London,
1932), Introduction, p. xix.

yet even now I can vividly recall the sweet, welcoming expression on the radiant face. He was brought on to the balcony, but how little he and my mother thought, as they greeted one another, that until her death they were to be most true and intimate friends.[3]

Charles Eliot Norton, aged just thirty at the time, was a fellow American and friend of the Storys, a student of art history of which he later became professor at Harvard, and was then on his second trip to Europe. Seven years before he had been introduced to Mrs. Gaskell during one of her London visits at the Proctors' house, and had retained a charmed memory of her. He was a sensitive and discriminating admirer of her books, and wrote to tell her, after his father's death in 1855, how *Cranford* read aloud had been one of his last pleasures on earth. Norton joined the Storys in Rome that spring and, advised by them of the expected arrival of Mrs. Gaskell, set out to renew the acquaintance.

It was a momentous meeting for him as for her. The middle-aged writer (she was now forty-six) and the young historian of art had so much in common, in temperament as well as taste, that the question of age seemed never to enter into their relationship. Her exceptional vitality compensated for his youth.

She is [he later told James Russell Lowell] like the best things in her books; full of generous and tender sympathies, of thoughtful kindness, of pleasant humour, of quick appreciation, of utmost simplicity and truthfulness, and uniting with peculiar delicacy and retirement a strength of principle and purpose and straightforwardness of action, such as few women possess.[4]

Such an appreciation, one of the most perceptive ever to have been made of Mrs. Gaskell, gives the measure of Norton's own rich nature, and sufficiently explains the instant sympathy that sprang up between these two. He was the perfect cicerone, she the ideal recipient for every beautiful scene or object he could bring to her notice. The intensity of her response to his guidance is apparent in all her recollections of the time; her deeply aroused emotions and the aesthetic experience merged indistinguishably into another one. That experience can perhaps best be described by the rather old-fashioned expression, Platonic Love. Given the total frankness of her nature, she abandoned herself to it without reservation or scruple, because nothing could conceivably be wrong with it. To Mrs. Gaskell it brought a fulfilment that nothing she had

[3] *Letters of Charles Eliot Norton*, ed. Sara Norton and M. A. DeWolfe Howe (London, 1913), i. 155.
[4] *Gaskell/Norton Letters*, p. xxiii.

known before—as she quite clearly perceived—had equalled. Her solemn words on the subject, written later to the Storys, must be accepted as the truth. On her return to England she wrote:

It was in those charming Roman days that my life, at any rate, culminated. I shall never be so happy again. I don't think I was ever so happy before. My eyes fill with tears when I think of those days, and it is the same with all of us. They were the tip-top point of our lives. The girls may see happier ones—I never shall.[5]

Had these words been intended to convey disloyalty to her husband, she would never have written them—certainly not to strangers. Her response to the young man, half maternal and half Platonic, seemed to be essentially an emanation of the place they were in; it could hardly have arisen to the same degree elsewhere. In subtlety it resembled the situation in a Jamesian novel that defies analysis. That it was also a composite, family infatuation, Meta Gaskell's recollections of the time make apparent: she wrote fifty years later about Norton to his daughter:

During the seven weeks that we were in Rome, we saw him constantly. He came to the famous breakfasts at the Casa Cabrale, where Manning and Aubrey de Vere were nearly always to be found. Every time he came he brought a beautiful bouquet of flowers, with the true American generosity and courtesy. He constantly joined us in our sight-seeing, and we learned from him, more vividly than any book on art could teach, all the deep principles of painting and sculpture.[6]

The Storys' apartment in the Via San Isidoro was in the same district as the Spanish Steps where Norton lodged, the traditional artists' quarter of the town to which visiting sculptors and painters like themselves naturally gravitated to seek each others' company and to find their models. These, for generations past, were to be found posing on the Steps, draped in togas or in Gladiatorial attire or as Renaissance Condottieri, waiting for hire. They were among the last sights to entertain the dying Keats from his rooms in the Piazza di Spagna at the bottom of the Spanish Steps. For the Gaskells no quarter of Rome could have been more picturesque or afforded a more constantly animated and evocative scene. From the windows of the Storys' apartment the view was open and facing towards the Vatican on the one side and to the Sabine hills on the other. It was a view to which Mrs. Gaskell was to become deeply and emotionally attached in her sojourn there. From the outset, the Storys made it clear that they would not consider allowing the Gaskells to move. Their apartment was too spacious for themselves and

[5] GL 375, Sept. 1857.
[6] Letters of Charles Eliot Norton, i. 155–6.

their two children and they had an adequate staff of servants—characters to whom the Gaskells became much attached—to cope with any number of visitors.

In retrospect there was an almost poignant emotion mixed with Elizabeth's memories of the place. She wrote to the Storys fully three years later:

I think Rome grows almost more vivid in recollection as the time recedes. Only the other night I dreamed of a breakfast—not a past breakfast, but some mysterious breakfast which neither had been nor, alas! would be—in the Via Sant' Isidoro dining-room, with the amber sunlight streaming on the gold-grey Roman roofs and the Sabine hills on the one side and the Vatican on the other. I sometimes think that I would almost rather never have been there than have this ache of yearning for the great witch who sits with you upon her seven hills.[7]

The Storys were relatively young people (still in their thirties at the time), with charming children—Edith, to whom Thackeray read 'The Rose and The Ring' (to cheer her during an illness), and Hans Christian Andersen the 'Ugly Duckling', and the little boy whose subsequent death brought the bereaved parents the lasting friendship of the Brownings and Thackeray's touching sympathy.[8] The news that the Storys had moved into a vast apartment in the Palazzo Barberini the next season really hurt Mrs. Gaskell, who pictured them framed for ever in the same setting she had known.

Oh, I so long for Italy and Albano that it makes me ill! [she wrote them the next summer]. I am glad Domenico is with you. It is bad enough your having changed your house; I don't like to think of your changing a single servant. Have you still Serafino? Our remembrances to Luigi and Clarke. Speak of us to Amante and Domenico. Have you still little birds for dinner, and the good 'dolci', the creams of which it was necessary to be forewarned, lest we should eat too much previously?[9]

After the long days sight-seeing, arduous sometimes, leisurely at others, the evenings would end either at Norton's rooms on the Spanish Steps, where he lodged on the 'ultimo piano'—the top floor—of his house, or sitting over a wood fire in the Story's apartment, 'knowing that the Vatican was in sight of the windows behind'.[10] There were the

---

[7] GL 482, ?1860.
[8] Henry James, *William Wetmore Story and His Friends*, i. 285-7.
[9] GL 402, July 1858.
[10] GL 498, 1861.

occasional grand evening outings to hear a Palestrina Mass, or to see a torchlight procession at the Vatican.[11]

Writing to James Russell Lowell in later years to thank him for the pleasure of his book *Fireside Travels*, Mrs. Gaskell told him how he was not unknown to her because of the echoes she had received of his Roman visit from his friends: '. . . my personal knowledge of you began in Rome 1857,' she wrote, 'when (did you know it?) you and one other went about with the dear Storys, and me and mine up and down Rome. "Here James and Anna lodged"—"Here we had such a happy day with the Lowells" etc etc etc. And our well-loved and highly-prized Mr. Norton used to say "I only know she came and went" to us in the happy evenings in the Piazza de Spagna.'[12]

Norton kept her very first note to him, concerning a drive he had planned to take the travellers.

Dear Sir, My headache is quite gone, and we shall like a drive very much indeed. I am afraid from what I saw of Miss Winkworth yesterday that she will not be well enough to accompany us—so pray don't trouble yourself to send her word. We are going to beg that François [Norton's courier] may take this note. Will you forgive me for taking the liberty? It is on the principle of 'Give an inch etc.'[13]

Norton's response to her was as sensible and spontaneous as hers to him; he wrote frequently of her in his letters home, of her

uncommon sweetness of voice and animation of expression . . . she is a wonderful story-teller, never exaggerating and always dramatic . . . The pleasantest incident of the winter to me (setting aside what belongs to Rome specially and by itself) has been the becoming acquainted with Mrs. Gaskell, who has been staying here for the last month. She is a very charming person, with all the qualities of heart that are best—such a person as her 'Cranford' and the best things in her other books would lead one to hope and expect she would be.[14]

A valuable tribute from an artist who saw the wholeness of Mrs. Gaskell's personality, the perfect fusion between her identities as woman and creative artist.

It was Norton who organized the programme of their Roman outings. Being an art historian, he was better qualified than most tourists to guide their steps and to help them appreciate what they saw. It was he, Meta recorded afterwards, who taught them to admire among the other masters at the Pamphili Doria gallery 'the sad Titian with his rosebuds and earrings'.[15]

[11] *Gaskell/Norton Letters*, p. xxii.   [12] *GL* 584, 8 Sept. 1865.   [13] *GL* 346.
[14] *Gaskell/Norton Letters*, p. xxii.   [15] Ibid.

For Mrs. Gaskell, however, the greatest appeal would always come from nature rather than from art, and her fondest recollections of the Doria Palace were not of the paintings hung in its galleries, but of the anemones she gathered in its gardens, and of 'the little green lizards' she watched while sitting there. She loved the gardens of the Villa Medici and, above all, lost her heart to Albano where, as the heat increased, they often fled. When she analysed her love for Silverdale afterwards it was, she reflected, because of 'the expanse of view,—something like what gives it's charm to the Campagna'.[16]

Her favourite reading during that Roman holiday was Edmond About's recently published novella of Roman life *Tolla*,[17] for which she felt a special tenderness, leaving her 'shabby copy' with the Storys to be bound in the 'pretty Roman vellum binding' which she thought alone worthy of its charm. The copy got mislaid and years later she was appealing to them to try to find it.[18] When asked by Eliza Fox who was on her honeymoon in Rome in 1859 what she would like brought back, she asked only for her lost copy of *Tolla*.[19]

The story seemed to have a special significance for her. It described the touching love of a young girl subject to too strict parental authority, and the tragic results of separating young lovers when the love on both sides was not equally strong. It was a subject, as would shortly appear, that was preoccupying Mrs. Gaskell at the time. The muted style in which it was written, the elegiac nature of the Roman landscapes described— especially the vineyards of Albano—were qualities to which Mrs. Gaskell fully responded. It seemed to epitomize her whole Roman experience.

The Gaskells had always planned to stay in Rome over Holy Week— Easter Sunday that year fell on 12 April—and after that they started on the leisurely journey home. By luck, Norton and another congenial American, the painter Hamilton Wild, were bent in the same direction, and they hired 'four horses and a good carriage that holds four people inside and two out' for the first lap of the journey—via Ronciglione, San Lorenzo, San Quirino, to Siena. After that they took the train to Florence, called on the Brownings, and went on through Bologna to their main objective, Venice, where they stayed until 10 May. In his letters home, Norton reported the failure of their visit to the Brownings and the reason. He wrote on 22 April: 'I went with Mrs. Gaskell this morning to see the Brownings,—but they could not receive us; Mrs. Browning was in great

---

[16] *GL* 401, July 1858.   [17] Published in Paris in 1856.
[18] *GL* 498, 1861.
[19] *GL* 421, 21 Mar. 1859.

grief, having just heard of the death of her father. I suppose she has not
seen him for years, and never has gained his forgiveness.'[20]

Norton, who had previously lived and studied in Venice, was the ideal
guide to the Tintorettos and the churches, and the mazes of waterways
through which to pursue the city's hidden treasures. For Mrs. Gaskell
Venice left two special memories: the first was of a beautiful Sunday
when Norton took them out through the islands in the Lagoon to Torcello, whose hold on her imagination she found it difficult to explain.
'Oh! that exquisite dreamy Torcello Sunday,—that still, sunny, sleepy
canal,—something like the Lady of Shalott,—tho' how, why, and wherefore I can't tell.'[21] A full year after the visit there, she wrote to Norton
on the anniversary of the day:

And do you suppose *we* forgot the Torcello Sunday? No! not to the material fact
of our hunger and cold when we came in! *Our* sky *here* was so like the sky over the
Lagoons on that day, and the lovely Stars of Bethlehem, and the stones, all carved,
and square cut below the water level of the Canal Banks; and the Cathedral—
oh happy lovely day . . .[22]

Norton wrote his mother his own painter's recollection of the day at
Torcello: 'Service was going on in the Cathedral . . . and a little red-
haired boy sat on the steps of the altar like one of John Bologna's singing
angels, chanting the responses as if he had long been used to doing so and
was rather tired of the work.'[23]

The other memorable incident connected with Venice for Mrs. Gaskell
was her first sight of a copy of her *Life of Charlotte Brontë*, in the Tauch-
nitz edition. The English edition had appeared on 25 March. Norton
spotted it in a booksellers, and bought it for Mrs. Gaskell who, after
glancing through it, gave it back to him with a dedication. Norton's
reaction to the work is contained in a letter to James Russell Lowell:

You have read the life of Miss Brontë, which is almost as much an exhibition of
Mrs. Gaskell's character as of Miss Brontë's—and you know what a lovely and
admirable character she has. Seeing her as intimately as one sees a companion
on a journey, I learned ever day to feel towards her a deeper affection and respect.
She is like the best things in her books.[24]

The only echo of her book to have reached her so far had been a letter
from Mr. Brontë, written on receipt of his presentation copy. Norton

[20] *Letters of Charles Eliot Norton*, i. 168.   [21] *GL* 384, 7 Dec. 1857.
[22] *GL* 394, 10 May 1858.
[23] *Letters of Charles Eliot Norton*, i. 169.
[24] Ibid. 171.

noted in his travel journal that Mrs. Gaskell had read it to him on their journey northwards, on 16 April:

Mrs. Gaskell read to me the letter Mr. Brontë wrote to her on receiving the volumes of her memoir of his daughter. It was a fine, strong, strange letter, quite characteristic of him . . . He speaks of the mingled pain and pleasure he had had in reading it,—not a word of what Mrs. Gaskell had said in it of himself, . . . and finds in the whole course of the work but one or two unimportant errors which may be easily corrected in a later edition.[25]

Mr. Brontë had written: 'You have not only given a picture of my Dear daughter Charlotte, but of my Dear wife, and all my Dear children, and such a picture too as is full of truth and life. The pictures of my brilliant and unhappy son, and his diabolical seducer, are masterpieces.'[26]

The commendation, the gratification of the father of her friend and the sponsor of the work, who repeated once again in that letter his original purpose—'I was fully determined that the Biography of my Daughter should, if possible, be written'—can have brought the author nothing but relief at the accomplishment of her task, and have left her with few fears for the book's general reception. Even Mr. Brontë's casual reference to the 'few trifling mistakes' to be corrected in due course, can have given her no inkling of what lay ahead.

The parting from Norton took place at Venice on 10 May. It was made less painful by the assurance that he was visiting England that summer, and would come to them at Manchester without fail.

Resuming their unhurried journey north via Verona, Milan, the Italian Lakes, Nice, and Marseilles, the travellers finally reached Paris late on 26 May, where at Mme Mohl's they found the accumulated correspondence of five weeks past,[27] containing among other matter the news, forwarded by Mr. Gaskell, that publication of the *Life of Charlotte Brontë* was suspended following a court order. A threatened libel action, brought by Lady Scott, could only be averted by a public retraction of all the 'offensive matter' in the book, to be published in the press. In concert with Smith, Elder, Mr. Gaskell was preparing such a statement to appear in the morrow's *Times*. William Shaen, Emily Winkworth's solicitor husband, was acting in the Gaskell's interest. Mrs. Gaskell's immediate return home was called for.

By a cruel irony she had wished to hear nothing about the book in her absence abroad, dreading the reviews, and had asked Mr. Gaskell not

[25] Ibid. 167–8.
[26] Lock and Dixon, *A Man of Sorrow*, p. 504.
[27] *GL* 351, 6 June 1857.

to mention it in his letters.[28] The result was that she had no warning of the disaster till she reached Paris and found his letters awaiting her. Barely resting a day in Paris, she travelled home without another break and reached Manchester late in the evening of Thursday 28 May.

[28] *GL* 350, 5 June 1857.

CHAPTER XVII

THE HORNETS' NEST

WHEN Charlotte Brontë's friend, Mary Taylor, who had emigrated to New Zealand in 1845, heard that a biography of her friend was being planned and that Mrs. Gaskell was being asked to write it, she had written to Ellen Nussey her informant: 'Mrs. Gaskell seems far too able a woman to put her head into such a wasp nest as she would raise about her speaking the truth of living people. How she will get through with it I can't imagine.'[1] The comment, reported by Ellen Nussey to Mrs. Gaskell, had in turn been repeated by her to George Smith. Instructing him on 11 February 1857 to send a copy of the published work to Miss Taylor she told him what had been written in the letter to Miss Nussey. 'Does Mrs. Gaskell know "what a nest of hornets she is pulling about her ears"'[2]—a paraphrase of the original metaphor preserved by subsequent editors.

Mary Taylor had heard all about the Robinson affair from Charlotte and thought her letters on the subject so dangerous that she burnt them. A strong 'feminist' and a declared enemy of parental authority, she had early considered Charlotte's 'selfish' father as the chief impediment to her success and happiness and had constantly urged her to leave home and make her own successful way in the world. She anticipated the trouble that would result from the publication of the facts of her friend's life, though it was from Mr. Brontë that she feared the worst. Mrs. Gaskell, knowing that she had his full support, met this with some amusement. But in the event, the trouble anticipated by Mary Taylor was multiplied beyond measure, and she was faced by multifarious and simultaneous attacks from all sides.

The *Life of Charlotte Brontë* was published on Wednesday, 25 March 1857 in 2 volumes, cloth, price 24 shillings, with a frontispiece portrait and an engraved view of Haworth. Owing to the General Election held that week, the reviews in the dailies were delayed until 4 April, with the result

---

[1] *Mary Taylor, Friend of Charlotte Brontë: Letters from New Zealand*, ed. Joan Stevens (Aukland, 1972), p. 126.   [2] *GL* 344, Feb. 1857, and 347a, 1 June 1857.

that the literary weeklies caught up with them in reviewing the book. From the outset there was a chorus of praise. The *Athenaeum* devoted eight and a half columns to its notice, concluding with the view that 'As a work of Art, we do not recollect a life of a woman by a woman so well executed'. *The Times* of the same date declared: 'We regard this record as a monument of courage and endurance, of suffering and triumph.' The *Daily News* reported: 'there is no feebleness of redundancy; every circumstance has a direct bearing on the main object of painting, vigorously and accurately, a real picture of the woman as she was.' In the *Spectator's* view 'The profound pathos, the tragic interest of this book lies in the terrible struggle that life was to a woman endowed with Charlotte Brontë's conscientiousness, affection for the family, and literary ambition . . . Its moral is, the unconquerable strength of genius and goodness.'

By such comments, dwelling even more upon the character of her heroine than upon her own art, Mrs. Gaskell might well have felt justified in her attempt to show her friend as 'a great and good woman'. For *The Globe*, however, her own achievement was paramount: it placed her on a level with the best biographers of any country. 'It is a truthful and beautiful book . . . No one can read it without feeling strengthened and purified.' Such a judgement, had Mrs. Gaskell read it in tranquillity, would have exceeded her highest hopes. As it was, she read nothing in tranquillity, only in total disarray.

Foreseeing an immediate rush on the book from its subscribers, Mudies had ordered 1,200 copies, promptly augmented to 1,500 copies. Smith, Elder, seeing the book's sensational reception, hurried through a cheap reprint of all Currer Bell's novels in an edition at 6 shillings; and announced a reissue even of the *Poems of Currer, Ellis and Acton Bell* in an edition at 4 shillings on 11 April. By 9 May sales of the *Life* were such that the publishers announced a second edition, and the advertisement, carrying laudatory excerpts from the reviews, appeared for successive days in *The Times* up until 16 May. Thus, until within ten days of Mrs. Gaskell's return home, the book's triumphant progress seemed assured.

The wide publicity, the rapid circulation, however, brought it also inevitably to the notice of those whose concern it had been, in the past years, to suppress some of the matter it contained. Lady Scott, the former Mrs. Robinson, was widowed again and living in Curzon Street, Mayfair, a well-known society hostess. The unmistakable references to the cause of Branwell Brontë's 'wreck and ruin', as *The Times* put it, represented a direct menace; it was, as *The Times* again put it, provoking 'gossip which for weeks past has been seething and circulating in the London coteries'.[3] Lady Scott no sooner became aware of what was going on than she instructed her family solicitors, Newton and Robinson of York, to threaten the author with a court case if the offending passages in the book were not immediately removed. In Mrs. Gaskell's absence, it was Mr. Gaskell who received the unwelcome communication, and who instantly acted upon it. There was no time to consult his wife, and he put her defence in the able hands of their friend William Shaen—the husband of Emily Winkworth.

He drew up the following statement, dated 26 May, which, together with Newton and Robinson's reply was, at their request, published concurrently in *The Times* and the *Athenaeum*—the papers that had given the greatest prominence to the *Life of Charlotte Brontë*—on 30 May. Mrs. Gaskell therefore reached home just in time to read the statements drafted in her name and on her behalf—and without her knowledge. Among the hundred letters awaiting her at home was one from Norton, to welcome her, and she answered it on 3 June: 'I found trouble enough awaiting me from the publication of my Life of C.B. or rather not "awaiting me", but settled without me; settled for the best, all things considered, I am sure . . .'

Under a large-type heading—ADVERTISEMENT 'The Life of Charlotte Bronte'—the correspondence appeared in the papers concerned, accompanied by a note from Newton and Robinson:

York, 27th May
1857

Sir, We shall feel obliged by your inserting the following correspondence. We are, Sir,

Your obedient servants,
Newton and Robinson.

This was followed by the official retraction drawn up by William Shaen on behalf of his client:

8, Bedford Row, London,
26 May 1857.

Dear Sirs, As Solicitor for and on behalf of the Rev. W. Gaskell and of Mrs. Gaskell his wife, the latter of whom is authoress of the *Life of Charlotte Brontë*, I am instructed to retract every statement contained in that work which imputes to a widowed lady, referred to, but not named therein, any breach of her conjugal,

[3] *The Times*, 6 June 1857.

her maternal, or of her social duties, and more especially of the statement contained in chapter 13 of the first volume, and in chapter 2 of the second volume, which imputes to the lady in question a guilty intercourse with the late Branwell Brontë. All those statements were made upon information which at the time Mrs. Gaskell believed to be well founded, but which, upon investigation, with the additional evidence furnished to me by you, I have ascertained not to be trustworthy. I am therefore authorised not only to retract the statements in question, but to express the deep regret of Mrs. Gaskell that she should have been led to make them.—I am, dear Sirs, yours truly,

William Shaen

Messrs Newton and Robinson, Solicitors, York.

The reply, notable for the moderation of its tone, followed immediately below:

York, 27 May 1857

Dear Sir, As Solicitors of the lady to whom your letter of the 26th inst refers, we, on her behalf, accept the apology therein contained, and we have to add that neither that lady nor ourselves ever entertained a doubt that the statements of Mrs. Gaskell were, as you say, made upon information which at the time Mrs. Gaskell believed to be well-founded. We are, dear Sir, Yours truly,

Newton and Robinson.

William Shaen, Esq.,
Bedford Row,
London.

The publicity thus given to the subject can only have increased the gossip, and the 'coteries' were given further grist to their mill by an Editorial published in the *Athenaeum* of 6 June, under the heading 'Our Weekly Gossip'.

We are sorry to be called upon to return to Mrs. Gaskell's 'Life of Charlotte Bronte'—but we must do so, since the book has gone forth with our recommendation. Praise, it is needless to point out, implied trust in the biographer as an accurate collector of facts. This, we regret to state, Mrs. Gaskell proves not to have been. To the gossip which for weeks past has been seething and circulating in the London coteries, we gave small heed; but the Athenaeum publishes a legal apology, made on behalf of Mrs. Gaskell, withdrawing the statements put forth on her book respecting the cause of Mr. Branwell Bronte's wreck and ruin. These, Mrs. Gaskell's lawyer is now fain to confess his client advanced on insufficient testimony. The telling of an episodical and gratuitous tale so dismal as concerns the dead, so damaging to the living, could only be excused by the story of sin being severely, strictly true; and every one will have cause to regret that due caution was not used to test representations not, it seems, to be justified. It is in the interest of letters that biographers should be deterred from rushing into print with mere impressions in place of proofs, however eager and sincere those impressions be. They *may* be slanders, and as such they may sting cruelly.—Meanwhile, the 'Life of Charlotte Bronte' we apprehend, must undergo modifications ere it can be further circulated.

For George Smith the disaster might have meant ruin. The second edition, already advertised and ready for publication, had to be withdrawn and, harder still for the publisher just beginning to reap the benefits of the book's success, the outstanding copies of the first edition had to be called in. A radically expurgated text had to be prepared for an eventual third edition, but even as Mrs. Gaskell faced the task of cutting the offending passages relating to Lady Scott, she received by every post fresh protests and demands from outraged persons appearing in or referred to in the book, threatening her with yet further legal actions if the passages referring to *them* were not either deleted or altered. On 16 June she wrote to Ellen Nussey:

I am in the Hornet's nest with a vengeance. I only hope you dear good little lady that nobody is worrying you in any way. We came home on *May 28th* and I never heard of the Letters in the Times till my return. I have much to tell you on this subject; but I am warned not to *write*; and must keep it till we meet.

Mr Carus Wilson threatens an action about the Cowan's Bridge School.

Mr Redhead's son-in-law writes to deny my account of the Haworth commotions . . .

Miss Martineau has written sheet upon sheet regarding the quarrel? misunderstanding? between her and Miss Brontë.

Two separate householders in London *each* declare that the *first* interview between Miss Brontë and Miss Martineau took place at *her* house . . .[4]

The triviality of some of the complaints crushed her even more than the major problem of preparing the third edition which she had to do, and which for her publisher's sake if not for her own had to do quickly. To a writer who never wished to consider a finished work again, her task was heart-breaking.

I am writing as if I were in famous spirits, and I think I *am* so *angry* that I am almost merry in my bitterness, if you know that state of feeling; but I have cried more since I came home that [*sic*] I ever did in the same space of time before; and never needed kind words so much,—and no one gives me them.[5]

Had the disaster not made her unjust to all concerned, she might have reckoned among her blessings of the hour, the gentlemanly and generous

[4] *GL* 352, 16 June 1857.   [5] Ibid.

conduct of George Smith, who never uttered one word of reproach for
her disregard of his warnings. Only later did she fully appreciate his
forbearance. For the moment she was only concerned with practical
questions on how the corrections were to be made and the additional
material inserted.

Of the absolute truth of what she had written she never doubted. As
she told Ellen Nussey:

I *did so try* to *tell the truth*, and I believe *now* I hit as near the truth as any one
could do. And I weighed every line with all my whole power and heart, so that
every line should go to it's great purpose of making *her* known and valued, as one
who had gone through such a terrible life with a brave and faithful heart.[6]

Her purpose, as we have seen, had been to present an Apologia for
the character of Charlotte Brontë and of her writings which in their time
had scandalized the censorious. The need still to whitewash her friend's
memory entered not a little into her comments to such a former severe
critic as Kingsley. Thanking him now for his appreciative letter after
reading the *Life* and telling him of the trouble into which the book had
run, she said:

I can only say Respect and value the memory of Charlotte Brontë as she deserves.
No one can know all she had to go through, but those who knew her well . . .
I tried hard to write the truth. I think I can stand it all patiently. Only do think
of her, on, through all. *You do not know what she had to bear; and what she had
to hear.*[7]

—a clear reference still to the scapegoat Branwell.

Much that had been found shocking in the writings of Currer, Ellis,
and Acton Bell—the 'coarse language', the violent conduct, the unlady-
like knowledge of dissolute men—had inevitably to be blamed on
Branwell. On him too Mrs. Gaskell had found it necessary to heap the
blame for his sister's unhappiness at Brussels, so as to suppress the fact
of her passion for her Belgian schoolmaster. How useful, therefore, had
been the evidence, received from Charlotte and from Mr. Brontë alike,
of his liaison with his employer's wife, and of its deady consequences in
wrecking his life and in ruining the happiness of his home. Here was
sufficient cause to explain all that appeared reprehensible in the Brontës'
writings and all that was 'unsociable' in Miss Brontë's way of life. To
expose the family skeleton had seemed to the devoted biographer of
Charlotte Brontë the fairest way to defend the memory of her friend.

[6] *GL* 352, 16 June 1857.   [7] *GL* 351, 6 June 1857.

That it blackened the character of the living Lady Scott, as well as of the dead Branwell, had not weighed with her; she had prejudged the case and believed that Lady Scott fully deserved what came to her. She was, as Mrs. Gaskell was already fully aware, the object of private family ostracism. To have to destroy the balance of her book for the sake of Lady Scott's blemished reputation, was hard for Mrs. Gaskell to bear. Had the matter rested there, the task before her would not have been so crushing. But, as every day brought in fresh complaints from readers, it became more and more daunting.

The one person who might, justifiably, have protested at some of her unverified and highly coloured reports concerning him, Mr. Brontë, proved to be the one who brought her the most comfort in the end. With great moderation and humour he pointed out to her some of the most glaring misstatements concerning himself and requested their deletion in the forthcoming edition. 'I do not deny', he wrote her later that summer (30 July)

that I am somewhat eccentrick. Had I been numbered amongst the calm, sedate, concentric men of the world, I should not have been as I now am, and I should in all probability never have had such children as mine have been. I have no objection whatever to your representing me as a little eccentric, since you and other learned friends will have it so—only don't set me on in my fury to burning hearthrugs, sawing the backs of chairs, and tearing my wife's silk gowns—With respect to tearing my wife's silk gown, my dear little daughter must have been misinformed—This you will be convinced of when I assure you that it was my repeated advice to my wife and children, to wear gowns and outward garments made *only of silk or wool*, as these were less inflammable than cotton or linen . . .

I am much pleased with reading the opinions of those in your letters, and other eminent characters, respecting the 'Memoir'. Before I knew theirs, I had formed my own opinion, from which you know I am not easily shaken. And my opinion, and the reading World's opinion of the 'Memoir', is that it is every way worthy of what one Great Woman should have written of Another, and that it ought to stand, and will stand, in the first rank of Biographies till the end of time . . .[8]

From this view Mr. Brontë never deviated. He early spotted, moreover, the passages that would cause most lasting damage to his reputation, and told Mrs. Gaskell of them. 'Some slips there have been but they may be remedied. It is dangerous to give credence hastily to informants', he wrote to her on 30 July. 'I think I have already stated to Miss Marianne Gaskell, that I never forbade my wife or children, or servants, the use of animal food. The error committed on this head was unfortunate, as

8 Lock and Dixon, *A Man of Sorrow*, pp. 508-9.

Mr. Carus Wilson and his party, most uncharitably, turned it to the advantage of their hollow cause. . . .'[9] As he points out, this was seized on to account for the decline and early deaths of his daughters Maria and Elizabeth at the Clergy Daughters' School, and to serve to exonerate the regimen of Wilson.

While Mr. Brontë was left to bear the stigma of this tragedy, it was from him notwithstanding that Mrs. Gaskell received her most constant support that 'terrible summer'—as she came to speak of it afterwards. 'I am not the least offended', he wrote in conclusion, 'at your telling me that I have faults—I have many—and, being a Daughter of Eve, I doubt not that you also have some. Let us both try to be wiser and better as Time recedes and Eternity advances.'[10]

Reflecting on the venom released by her unfortunate book, from Carus Wilson's family in particular, and the petty-mindedness shown by so many whose part in the book was insignificant, she wrote to George Smith on 23 August 'I only hope Mr. Brontë won't be over-worried. Hitherto he has acted like a "brick". (I hope you understand slang?)'[11] To Maria Martineau (Harriet's niece) she also wrote of letters just received from him, 'evidently meaning *very* kindly; and he really has been so steady in his way to me all along, that I would rather let them all go on attacking me, than drag him into any squabble either with me, or the public or any one'.[12]

It is a pity that none of Mrs. Gaskell's personal views about Mr. Brontë were added to the third edition of the book, if only in justice to him, for after the lapse of the required fifty years when the original text was reissued, all the old accusations reappeared without correction of text and without reference to her later findings.

It is significant that one of Mrs. Gaskell's first acts of reinvestigation into the evidence published in the first edition was to go to Gawthorp in Burnley[13] and to question anew the dismissed nurse who had made the chief allegations against Mr. Brontë. When all the tattle was sifted and weighed against the witness of the faithful parsonage servants, parishioners, and such educated people as the Bradford schoolmaster, William Dearden, who took her severely to task for publishing such rubbish, she saw how she had been gulled. It was hard to admit, and she sought what comfort she could in the thought that the same tales had been told Ellen Nussey and Miss Wooler (and perhaps equally believed

[9] Lock and Dixon, *A Man of Sorrow*, pp. 508–9. [10] Ibid.
[11] GL 369. [12] GL 358, 23 Aug. 1857.
[13] GL 352, 16 June 1857.

by them?).[14] Though she appears not to have apologized to Mr. Brontë, she was deeply grateful to him for his forbearance and support.

By any measure the troubles overtaking her in consequence of her book would have been enough to overwhelm her that summer. But they were far from being the only ones. Within a month of her return from abroad she was suddenly confronted with a domestic problem of considerable importance. Her beloved Meta wished to enter into a lightning engagement and marry almost out of hand so as to follow her husband to India. The flirtation, begun two years before when Meta danced the night through with the same partner,[15] a Captain Charles Hill of the Madras Engineers, appears to have flared up afresh the moment the young people met again. He was a widower with one child. Mrs. Gaskell admitted that she liked him very much but the situation took on an alarming aspect when news of the Mutiny at Cawnpore was received, all leave was cancelled, and Captain Hill was ordered back to India. He urged the Gaskells to consent to an immediate marriage so that Meta might accompany him. Despite their great and justified concern over such a prospect, her parents did not stand in the way of what she considered her happiness.

In view of Mrs. Gaskell's subsequent admission of the misery into which that decision plunged her and Mr. Gaskell, it is a measure of the real freedom they allowed their children that they did nothing to oppose it. Of all their daughters, Meta may be said to have been the favourite of both parents, and the prospect of losing her for a minimum period of five years, to a strange country in the throes of racial violence, was a terrible one.

Mrs. Gaskell's loving kindness and understanding for her daughters in all contingencies of life was a constant feature of their relationship. In the present instance, however, when Meta's security might have justified peculiar caution, her mother's selflessness in permitting the marriage can only be interpreted as a desire at all costs not to seem to stand in her way. It may not be too fanciful to see in her conduct the reflection of the feelings aroused by her reading of About's story *Tolla* that had so moved her at Rome, with its theme of the tragic consequences of separating lovers. She was essentially a woman of impulse and as likely to be influenced by the appeal of art as by any rational arguments.

The first effect of the sudden engagement was to decide her to delegate the work of revising the *Life of Charlotte Brontë* to someone else: she instructed George Smith to that effect in late July,[16] only to countermand the decision a fortnight later. 'An immediate marriage has been

<hr/>

[14] *GL* 368.   [15] *GL* 250, 8 July 1855.   [16] *GL* 363, 28 July 1857.

in contemplation,' she wrote on 28 July, 'but after many preparations were made in a tremendous hurry, absorbing *all* my time, and making me very very anxious and unhappy this plan has been given up: and she does not go till next year, when he meets her in Egypt if all goes well.' Under the changed circumstances, she was prepared to resume work on her 'weary and oppressive task'.[17]

Her heart, however, was never in the work and was, understandably, bound up with Meta's affairs. The fact that Smith, Elder had publishing and trade connections with India was intensely interesting to her. Learning that the firm published an Indian paper, she wrote eagerly to George Smith: 'Do you know India? How is it you publish an Indian newspaper?'[18] On receiving information from him, she wrote again, in early August:

Thank you very much for every word, every sign of sympathy about India. From the depths of ignorance, I am roused up to the most vivid and intense interest. This daughter of mine is a most dear friend, more like a sister to me than anything else; and I like Capt. Hill extremely; but the engagement is a most anxious one . . .[19]

Captain Hill stayed at Plymouth Grove for his final embarkation leave from 13 to 23 August. 'Capt Hill goes to-day,' Mrs. Gaskell wrote to George Smith on the latter date, 'and we are dreadfully in the dumps. Somebody is crying in every room.'[20] His departure, coming at the height of the Mutiny reports, could not have been worse timed for the feelings of the family. In this as in so much else, the sisters were united in their sympathy for Meta.

The scare of Meta's marriage and threatened departure had not only coincided with Mrs. Gaskell's troubles over her book, but with the widely acclaimed Exhibition of World Masters held at Manchester that year from May to October, which brought tourists to the city from all parts of the globe, and an almost uninterrupted flow of visitors to the Gaskells' home. Their hospitality was put to the furthest stretch not only of material but of nervous capacity. From early June when Ellen Nussey stayed five days ('You shall go to the Exhibition every day',[21] Mrs. Gaskell promised her) through July when Charles Norton came, playing Box and Cox with several other visitors, until August when Monsieur and Madame Mohl[22] and a German niece were expected for a fortnight, the flow of friends, relatives, and mere connections never ceased.

[17] *GL* 363, 28 July 1857.   [18] *GL* 364, 31 July 1857.
[19] *GL* 365, Aug. 1857.   [20] *GL* 369.
[21] *GL* 352.   [22] *GL* 367.

'We have two rooms and 19 people coming to occupy them before the Exhibition closes', Mrs. Gaskell wrote to Eliza Fox on 26 August. 'We are worn out with hospitality—but I should make no stranger of you dear, but gape in your face if I chose. Oh I *am* tired of it—X [the Exhibition] I mean,—I shd like it dearly if I weren't a hostess.'[23] 'Our house has been fuller than full, day and night', she wrote to Charles Norton on 28 September,

ever since you left, and this last fortnight it will be fuller than ever, as every one will want to see the Exhibition before it closes. I am *very* fond of all the people who are coming; but so worn-out that it is hard word [*sic*] to lash myself up into properly hospitable feelings. Marianne said yesterday 'Oh! are you not tired of being agreeable! I do so want leisure to sulk and be silent in;' and really after long hard hot days at the Exhibition showing the same great pictures over and over again to visitors, who have only time to look superficially at the whole collection, one *does* want to 'sulk and be silent' in the evenings.[24]

A glimpse of those gruelling days is afforded by her note to a London acquaintance, a Mrs. Clive, dated 1 October:

Thank you very much for proposing to call here; can you come and have a 'preliminary' cup of tea at five? or can you come before 11 in the morning,—I am afraid that the rest of the day, i.e. from 12 to 4, I shall be pledged to be at the Exhibition. But I will come at ½ past 1, and ½ past 2 to the green seat in the transept *outside* the Hertford Gallery, and will wear a lilac plaided silk; and a white bonnet,—just like a young lady answering a matrimonial advertisement—[25]

For Meta, showing enormous pluck in the separation from her lover (she was reported by her mother to be 'very bright and very cheerful, much less anxious, indeed, I think than any of us'), there was compensation in the presence of the world's masterpieces at her door. She obtained permission to go in to the Exhibition before opening time to copy specified works.[26]

At length the closing day arrived, 15 October, the last visitors left, and Mrs. Gaskell was free to relax from the long strain of the 'terrible summer'. It left her prostrate. 'I am inclined, either from laziness or depression', she wrote to Ellen Nussey in December

to refuse all invitations, and even to go out of the house as little as possible. I believe, however, this is reaction after all this last terrible summer. I kept thinking during that latter time of the Exhibition—Oh, in three weeks, in 3 days,

[23] *GL* 370a, *c.* 26 Aug. 1857.   [24] *GL* 374.
[25] *GL* 376.   [26] *GL* 373, 374.

in 3 hours I may give way to sorrowful thinking, the deadly feelings of fatigue. *Now* I must exert myself and live in the present, and I lashed myself up to being active, and talkative etc., when I really *could* hardly do it. Of course I must 'pay' for this, and it is well I have such a quiet time to 'right' myself in . . .[27]

In fact, she did not recover from the shocks of that year so soon. As a creative writer she was silenced for a long time to come and it was twelve months before she even began planning any new work.

Meanwhile, the current of life at Plymouth Grove resumed its normal course. The regular mail came in from India, and the family's worst fears on Captain Hill's account were calmed.

The revised third edition of the *Life of Charlotte Brontë* came out on 22 August when Smith, Elder advertised it widely in the Press. LIFE OF CHARLOTTE BRONTË JUST READY. NEW AND REVISED EDITION WITH EMENDATIONS AND ADDITIONS. The advertisement was repeated three times in September. Neither the Circulating Libraries nor the general public were confident enough to rush to buy as they had before. Mrs. Gaskell was resigned to the book's failure. On 9 November she wrote to Harriet Martineau:

I had however determined that should any future editions be required—(a *most* unlikely thing, as the success of this 3rd edition was problematical at the time of publication,—and it has sold very slowly indeed in fact) that I would have nothing more to do with preparing another edition for the press.[28]

She was much surprised therefore when in March 1858 she received a letter from George Smith containing a cheque for £200 in respect of sales of the book. 'I do not think I was ever more surprized than by the contents of your letter this morning', she wrote by return.

I had always felt that you had behaved to me most liberally in the first instance, and that in some respects, the book must have been a great source of annoyance and vexation to you . . . and now to receive a cheque for £200! I am most sincerely and heartily obliged to you for it. As *money* it is very acceptable just now, but I am even more touched by the kindness and liberality.[29]

It was a matter of incredulity to her that the book, which had cost her such pain, could ever be anything now but a failure. As edition after cheap edition came from the press over the following years, she expressed surprise, seldom satisfaction. It was not the book she had conceived. The revised text had lost for her, with all its errors, also some of its deepest truths. She *knew* she had been right about the Clergy Daughters'

---

[27] *GL* 385a, 30 Dec. 1857.   [28] *GL* 379.   [29] *GL* 387, 17 Mar. 1858.

School and about Mrs. Robinson, even if she had been wrong about Mr. Brontë.

It would have amazed her to know that the one just prognostic among the many hostile opinions expressed was that made at the very beginning by Mr. Brontë, when he said that the book 'ought to stand, and will stand, in the first rank of Biographies till the end of time'.

CHAPTER XVIII

WRITING *SYLVIA'S LOVERS*, 1859-1863

FOR Mrs. Gaskell the year 1858 brought no alleviation to the cares of the previous year and was as little conducive to sustained creative writing.

In April the engagement between Meta and Captain Hill was broken off on the initiative of Meta herself. While staying with friends in London in March[1] she received reports touching his character which, while not positively affecting his honour, were bad enough for her to take up with him and his family. He made no attempt to exonerate himself, despite her repeated appeals to him to do so, and his own people, a brother Captain Dudley Hill and two sisters, had regretfully to admit them to be true. Meta, probably the most intelligent and self-reliant of the Gaskell girls, acted without pressure from her parents in ending the engagement. We do not know what she had learnt about her fiancé, but it was enough to convince her that she would not be happy with him.[2]

What added immeasurably to Mrs. Gaskell's distress was not that Meta at the age of 20 should have been mistaken in a lover, but that she herself and all the family had been so taken in. They had all (perhaps with the exception of Mr. Gaskell who so dreaded the separation from his favourite daughter that he could never be brought even to pronounce Captain Hill's name)[3] liked him exceedingly. This was a sobering thought for a mother with four daughters to marry. Meta's ill luck and her own part in it—in so far as she had been too kind, too trusting perhaps, too unequal to saving her from such a wound—was a source of constant self-reproach and sorrow to her over the next couple of years. How deeply the subject troubled her mind can still be perceived in the theme of the first long novel she undertook after the event, *Sylvia's Lovers*, the plot of which is deeply and sustainedly concerned with the subject of the suffering and perils of ill-judged love. It is but another example of the

[1] *GL* 421a, 21 Mar. 1859.
[2] *GL* 394, 14 May 1858.
[3] *GL* 385a, 30 Dec. 1857.

way in which direct personal experience was at the source of her invention, as has already been noted with *Mary Barton* and *Ruth*. The fact that *Sylvia's Lovers* took so long to write—unusually long for her for it stretched over three interrupted years—indicates the difficulties of the subject and of the time needed for the author to probe it to the heart, with her usual scrupulous regard for truth.

Meanwhile, and long before she could take time off from her home duties for writing, she had to face practical considerations. 'Meta is *far* from well,' she confided to Charles Norton early in May,

more from disappointment in character, I think than from wounded affection; for she says, 'he is not in the least what she fancied he was'. All I do, is to wait to help her to hear much 'public-talking'—and possibly upbraiding from him; and to give her what strength and sympathy I can. I am sure she has done right, and with a pure and simple mind. It has been a most terrible anxiety to me.[4]

Her wish, if the money was forthcoming, was to take Meta abroad for some time 'out of the clatter of tongues', and to occupy her thoughts with fresh surroundings. Despite the £200 from George Smith, however, money was short. 'If I can muster up money', she confided in Norton,[5] '(but you see I am very poor, what with doctor's bills, half-got Indian outfit, inability to write, for want of health—) I would try and persuade Mr. Gaskell, to take us three abroad.' How greatly the strain of the previous year and the subsequent anxiety on Meta's account was affecting her health, to the almost total arrest of all creative work, can be judged by her admission to Norton: 'I am so far from strong that my only piece of work yesterday, (writing this letter) utterly knocked me up, and I have been quite unable to sleep.'[6]

The need to make money, and the inability to earn it because of ill health, was one of the preoccupations and frustrations of the year. It prompted her to look out, and in some instances to complete, the manuscripts of previously written tales with a view to quick periodical publication and payment, and to sell the copyright of tales that had previously appeared, like those in *Household Words*, for publication in book form. She was unfortunate in listening to the eager promptings of Sampson Low, Son & Co. (her 'rascally publisher' as she later called him) who offered her a good price for simultaneous American and English publication. To begin with, however, Harpers of New York, to whom Sampson Low had sent 'The Doom of the Griffiths', published without either referring to their London coadjutors or paying the author. It was a bad

---

[4] *GL* 394.   [5] Ibid.   [6] Ibid.

start, and one that made her doubly cautious in her future dealings with both Sampson Low and America.

The tale of 'The Doom of the Griffiths', as she told Norton in December 1857, was 'an old rubbishy one,—begun when Marianne was a baby,—the only merit whereof is that it is founded on fact',[7] but she had relied on payment for it, and the disappointment was real. She humorously related to Norton how she tried to defend her rights. In default of payment from Harpers, she sought to recover her manuscript from Low, who had never acknowledged receipt of it.

Very worldly, is it not? But really I had relied on the money . . . So don't give me up as a mercenary tricky woman, though I acknowledge I *should* like to out-dodge Mr. Sampson Lowe if ever our wits came in contact. Are you never as wicked as this? I am sure if I were a servant, and suspected and things locked up from me etc, I should not only be dishonest, but a very clever thief . . .[8]

'The Doom of the Griffiths' was published by Harpers in January 1858, without acknowledgement or fee. But despite this unpromising beginning she continued to deal with Sampson Low. She collected three previously published stories (serialized in *Household Words* during 1855–6), 'An Accursed Race', 'Half a Life-Time Ago', 'The Poor Clare', to which she felt entirely free to add 'The Doom of the Griffiths', and a new tale, 'The Half-Brothers', to make up the second half of the collection to which she eventually gave the generic title of *Round the Sofa*.[9] To link the tales, utterly unconnected as they were in subject and setting, she thought up the idea of a group of friends, regulars at the Edinburgh Monday evening drawing-room gatherings of an invalid lady called Margaret Dawson, round whose sofa they related them in turns.

She had, of recent years, made the acquaintance of the charming Mrs. Fletcher, widow of a former Advocate of the Court of Sessions of Edinburgh, a famous beauty and hostess in her time, on whose character and *salon* in Castle Street she modelled that of her protagonist Margaret Dawson—even to the extent of giving her Mrs. Fletcher's maiden name, which had been Dawson. To the Fletchers' *salon* had come all the intelligentsia of Edinburgh, the editorial staff of the *Edinburgh Review*, members of the University (amongst them Mrs. Gaskell's father), and the leaders of Whig society, including Lord Lauderdale, whose appointment of William Stevenson as his secretary in 1806 had been the cause of his move to London. Mrs. Fletcher had also known and befriended Mrs. Gaskell's cousin Henry Holland when he had been studying

---

[7] *GL* 384, 7 Dec. 1857.   [8] Ibid.   [9] See below, p. 206.

medicine in Edinburgh in 1816 and onwards and retained a lively affection for him. As a leading hostess in Edinburgh during that period she had distinguished herself by serving only light refreshments, followed by tea and coffee, a notable innovation in a society where heavy dinners had for long been the rule in entertainment. In Mrs. Gaskell's story the guests to Margaret Dawson's evening gatherings are advised that conversation and not food is the staple attraction.

The acquaintance between Mrs. Gaskell and Mrs. Fletcher when the latter was already eighty followed soon after the publication of *Mary Barton*. Mrs. Fletcher had made the first approach. Long ago widowed, she was living with a married daughter and son-in-law, Dr. and Mrs. Davy, at Lancrigg near Grasmere, and she begged Mrs. Gaskell to call on her when occasion permitted. This resulted in regular visits, on the first of which in 1850 she met Wordsworth.

Mrs. Gaskell always spoke of Mrs. Fletcher as that 'dear old lady', and entertained her and Mrs. Davy at Plymouth Grove in November 1851, when they all attended a meeting at the Free Trade Hall to hear Kossuth, the great Hungarian patriot, speak.[10] A further link between the two ladies was their mutual friendship with Madame Mohl, whom Mrs. Fletcher had known as Mary Anne Clarke in 1830. It may even be supposed that the long out of context narrative concerning an incident in the French Revolution inserted in *My Lady Ludlow* (Margaret Dawson's contribution to the tales in *Round the Sofa*) had its origin in memories confided to Mrs. Gaskell by Mrs. Fletcher. *My Lady Ludlow* was written during 1858, the year of Mrs. Fletcher's death, which must have revived in Mrs. Gaskell the many memories of their acquaintance.

The leisure and the partially restored peace of mind with which to do even so much work was made possible by a six-weeks' holiday at Silverdale where the whole family (except for Mr. Gaskell who went on a walking tour with his brother) went to stay from 17 June.

. . . there we shall remain [she told Norton] for six weeks, and all get as strong as horses, it is to be hoped. We live in a queer, pretty crampy house, at the back of a great farm house [accompanying her words with a sketch] . . . the house is covered with roses, and great white virgin-sceptred lilies, and sweetbriar bushes grow in the small flagged square court . . . In the garden, half flower half kitchen is an old Square Tower, or 'Peel'—a remnant of the Border towers. Think of the perils our legs of mutton undergo! First they are kept in the Larder, or lower story of the Tower. Rain or fair they have to be carried to the kitchen to be cooked. Rain or fair they have to be carried *hot* across the court. And to begin

---

[10] *Autobiography of Mrs. Fletcher*, p. 292.

with Silverdale is so wild a place we may be happy to get a leg of mutton at all. I have had to dine 15 people, as hungry as hounds, on shrimps and bread and butter,—and when they asked for more had to tell them there was no bread nearer than Milnthorpe 6 miles off, and they had to come down to oatcake, and be thankful![11]

She had obviously begun work on *My Lady Ludlow* before reaching Silverdale, since the first serialization of the tale appeared in *Household Words* for 19 June. From then on until 25 September the tale ran its not quite regular course in the periodical, giving Dickens cause for occasional alarm when he feared that copy would reach the office too late for that week's issue. 'I hope Mrs. Gaskell will not stop, for more than a week at all events', he wrote to Wills on 9 August.[12]

The speed of composition, her motive for writing it, and her uncertain health, all contributed to making *My Lady Ludlow* a very unequal production, lacking in most of the qualities that made her stories so attractive to the public. First serialized, as seen, in *Household Words*, it was published by Harpers of New York later in 1858, and issued in England in book form as the first volume of the two-volume collection *Round the Sofa* by Sampson Low in March 1859. While it could add nothing to Mrs. Gaskell's reputation, it served its immediate purpose which was to earn money to pay for the continental trip that was to restore Meta's spirits. She herself had no illusions about it. To her sister-in-law Annie Robson she wrote:

You will be seeing a book of mine advertized; but don't be diddled about it; it is only a REpublication of HW stories; I have a rascally publisher this time (Sampson Low, who publishes Mrs Stowe's books) and he is trying to pass it off as new. I sold the right of publication to him in a hurry to get 100£ to take Meta abroad out of the clatter of tongues consequent on her breaking off her engagement.[13]

Marianne and Flossy accompanied Mrs. Gaskell and Meta for the first part of the tour up the Rhine to Heidelberg which lasted, in the event, for three months. Heidelberg did all that was expected of it in occupying, delighting, and reviving Meta. She stuck to a regular programme of work, studying German and drawing every morning, and sight-seeing and visiting with her mother every afternoon. 'Meta is better, indeed quite well,' Mrs. Gaskell was able to write on 19 October to Marianne who had returned home after a month abroad, 'and that is the grand comfort.'[14] Of Flossy, aged 16, who remained abroad with her, she added, 'as for

[11] *GL* 394, 10 and 14 May 1858.   [12] *Letters*, iii. 36.
[13] *GL* 414, Feb. 1859.   [14] *GL* 405.

11. Drawing-room of the Gaskell's home, 42 Plymouth Grove, Manchester

12. The Revd. William Gaskell

Flossy I never saw so blooming a creature; rosy, merry, hungry, strong. She *says* she is growing and sadly wants to have her frocks lengthened.'[15]

As with each of the family trips abroad, the mother's absence from home was only made possible by the presence there of the invaluable Hearn, to whom Julia's happiness, as well as her well-being could be entrusted. But Julia was a genuinely delicate child, and Marianne's early return home was largely arranged on her account, as well as to relieve Mr. Gaskell who was always overanxious about the children's health.

Mrs. Gaskell herself was never idle, even during a pleasure trip like this. While at Heidelberg she worked at great speed to finish a couple of short stories for the Christmas Number of *Household Words*, so as to earn the ready money for the further trip to Dresden, where she longed to take the girls. In the event it did not materialize, but for the stories, written at top speed, Dickens generously paid her £40—more than they were worth, she confided to Charles Norton,[16] and in this opinion she was right. She was always at her most melodramatic when writing under pressure. 'Mme Gaskell écrit quelque chose pour le Christmas number des Household Words', reported young Ida Mohl from Heidelberg to her famous aunt in Paris on 4 November 1858. 'Je ne sais ce que c'est— Elle est très occupée—il faut que ce soit fini demain.'[17] One story, called 'The Manchester Marriage', published in the 7 December issue of *Household Words*, would not be remembered now but for the fact that its plot foreshadowed the theme eventually treated in full in *Sylvia's Lovers*: the return of a lost husband to find his wife remarried.[18]

Despite the disappointment over Dresden, the nine weeks spent in modest lodgings at Heidelberg were life-giving, as Mrs. Gaskell told Norton. She recalled

the most lovely, poetical *wintry* November; clear deep blue sky—white snow not very deep, except where it had drifted into glittering heaps,—icicles, a foot long, hanging on fountain and well,—trees encased in glittering ice,—and weighed down with their own beauty,—streets—walks—clear and clean—and the high peaked house tops so beautiful. But it was not weather for travelling, being 18 degrees below something in Reaumur ... the girls worked away at German; and we 'marketted' for ourselves; and dined at one,—and walked till the early November night came on; I hired a piano and music, and laughed harder than

---

[15] Ibid.

[16] *GL* 418, 9 Mar. 1859.

[17] Sharps, *Mrs. Gaskell's Observation and Invention*, p. 299.

[18] Both Mrs. Gaskell's stories on this subject, the short story and the long novel, published respectively in 1858 and 1863, preceded Tennyson's *Enoch Arden*, published 1864.

H

I ever laughed before or ever shall again, the air, clear delicious dry air, put one in such health and spirits.[19]

November in Manchester was never like that.

In Manchester, however, she had elected to live, and it was there that her deeply ingrained sense of duty found its fulfilment. In a sense she not only did not want to move but positively refused to. Early in 1859 Mr. Gaskell made a momentous decision. In March he was offered the most senior post in the Unitarian Church, that of minister to the London (Essex Street) Chapel, and he refused it. His wife entirely shared and supported him in his feelings. Though it would have brought a higher salary and meant living in London, where so many of her interests and much of her business lay, she unhesitatingly encouraged him in his refusal. He did so 'quite rightly', she commented to Norton, and his reasons seemed entirely valid. 'He has made his place here, and there must be a much stronger reason than mere increase in income before it can be right to pull up the roots of a man of his age.'[20] 'Mr. Gaskell was asked to succeed Mr. Madge,' she wrote to Eliza Fox on 21 March, 'and urged, and re-urged. But he declined and wisely and rightly I think. He could never get in London the influence and good he has here; and he is too old to be taken up by the roots and transplanted merely for an extra hundred or so a year. So he stays in Cross Street and the people are very much pleased.'[21]

The letter to Eliza Fox had been prompted, in the first place, by the startling news, announced in *The Times*, of Eliza's marriage in Rome on 9 March 1859 to the young landscape painter Frederick Lee Bridell (1833-63). The event was so romantic and so sudden that Mrs. Gaskell could not contain her curiosity, amazement, and delight. Characteristically, she ascribed it to the ambience of Rome.

We first saw it in the Times, and the news flew like wildfire in the house . . . But we knew no particulars; so I wrote off to Mr. Fox, and he gave us just a few. But after that came your letter. You are a good darling, for remembering to write to me, and tell me all about it. It *does* sound very nice. Fancy you meeting your *fate* at Rome. (I dreamt of you and your husband at Albano, in the gardens of the Villa Medici—think of me if you go there) I want to know a quantity more of course . . . Oh, and is not Rome above every place you imagined? . . . Oh, wretch, write! . . . I am *very* glad you are married my dearest little Tottie, and so are we all—Mr. Gaskell's love; and the girls send best love. I think you are a very fortunate person—which alludes especially to your being in Rome.[22]

[19] *GL* 418.	[20] Ibid.
[21] *GL* 421.	[22] Ibid.

Bridell had already established a reputation for landscape painting, in the style of Turner, and during the sadly short duration of the marriage— he died of consumption at the age of thirty in 1863—the couple exhibited regularly at the Royal Academy and at the Suffolk Street Galleries. In the summer of 1860, following their marriage in Rome, both husband and wife contributed romantically titled subjects to the Summer Exhibition: Bridell's picture was called *The Coliseum by Moonlight* and Eliza's *Amongst the Ruins—Rome*.[23] The couple settled in Eliza's old home in Charlotte Street where Mrs. Gaskell visited them whenever she was in London.

Mrs. Gaskell had been offered £1,000 for her next three-volume novel by the 'rascally publisher' Sampson Low.[24] Tempting as it was, she was uneasy and decided to confess all to George Smith. She wrote to him on 2 June 1859:

I must own, 1000£ does a little bit tempt me, it is such a great sum; but I do not like publishing with Messrs Lowe and moreover I *do* like publishing with you. But I know you have not the power of commanding a sale in America as they can do . . . But I would much rather have 800£ from you than 1000£ from them; so I have been weighing and balancing and never answering till the other day this letter came which I enclose and I suppose I must decide . . . Remember I mean literally what I say. I would far rather have 800£ from you than 1000£ from them . . .[25]

George Smith was ready enough to match the £1,000 and she concluded the agreement with him for her next novel. Her gratitude and heightened spirits radiate from her reply of 29 June: 'Oh! I will so try and write you a good novel,' she wrote from Auchencairn where the family were on holiday that year, 'as good as a great nosegay of honeysuckle just under my nose at present, which smells not only of honeysuckle, but of very good cake into the bargain.'[26] In this state of euphoria she conceived the story to which she later gave the title *Sylvia's Lovers*. Begun in a glow of gratitude to Mr. Smith (double gratitude when she remembered his forbearance over the disaster following her *Life of Charlotte Brontë*) the tale bore every trace of being a labour of love.

Among the many influences affecting the origins of *Sylvia's Lovers* the holiday at Auchencairn itself was not the least decisive. At the beginning of the summer the Gaskells' landlord had offered to redecorate Plymouth Grove throughout on condition the family absented itself.

---

[23] See *D.N.B.* and A. Graves, *The Royal Academy of Arts: A Complete Dictionary of Contributors . . . 1769-1904* (London, 1905).

[24] *GL* 414, Feb. 1859.   [25] *GL* 430.   [26] *GL* 434.

For Mr. Gaskell with his Manchester obligations this meant lodging with various friends in town; for Mrs. Gaskell and the girls, it meant a round of visits. At the beginning of June they went to London where they stayed three weeks in rooms, and on 27 June travelled direct to Scotland for a month's holiday in a place new to them, Auchencairn in Kirkcudbrightshire, 'a little village on a land-locked bay of the Solway', as Mrs. Gaskell described it to Norton.[27] The total seclusion of the place, 'far away from newspapers or railways or shops, or any sign of the world', exactly suited her needs. 'I mean to be so busy here', she assured George Smith, but at once had to confess that with the lure of rural life, and all the delights of high summer, 'I am, at present, continually tempted out of doors'.[28] He had, in accordance with the generous custom he had instituted with Charlotte Brontë, sent a parcel of his latest publication to the Gaskells for their holiday reading, which Mrs. Gaskell greeted with delight. 'You never no, *never*—sent a more acceptable present than Cousin Stella and The Fool of Quality,—and that irrespective of their several merits. But books are books here,—where potatoes have to be sent for from Castle Douglas, nine miles off.'[29]

At Auchencairn, where Mr. Gaskell joined them for part of his holiday, they lodged in an old house, 'larger than a farm-house, that had belonged to a smuggler, in the palmy days of smuggling, close to all the scenery of Guy Mannering, and within a mile of the Maxwells of Orchardston, an ancestor of whom was the lost heir'.[30] The proximity of Sir James and Lady Maxwell was to be of some importance in the evolution of *Sylvia's Lovers*.

This was not Mrs. Gaskell's first encounter with Sir James and Lady Maxwell. She had met them on her previous visit to Scotland, in the September of 1855 when she was staying with her 'unknown stepsister' at Dunoon, and had improved the acquaintance subsequently in London when the Maxwells had eagerly sought her out.[31] (The choice of Auchencairn itself for a summer holiday may indeed have been prompted by them.) When she first visited them at Orchardston in 1855 she was absorbed in the research for her *Life of Charlotte Brontë*, and had the good fortune to find Dr. Scoresby, a former Vicar of Bradford, staying there. Dr. Scoresby could tell her a lot about Haworth and, indeed, gave her a highly coloured picture of the 'unruly people' of the West Riding, which she duly incorporated in her work.[32] Mr. Brontë and Dr. Scoresby

---

[27] *GL* 444, 25 Oct. 1859.   [28] *GL* 434.   [29] Ibid.   [30] *GL* 444.
[31] She was, in a manner of speaking, connected with the Maxwells of Dumfries, through the marriage of Dr. Thomson (her stepmother's brother) with Christine Maxwell—his first wife. See above, p. 167.
[32] *Life of Charlotte Brontë*, Everyman edn., p. 18.

had crossed verbal swords on more than one occasion during the fiery
contest Mr. Brontë waged on his people's behalf against the levy of
Church Rates by Bradford. Though the subject was one of immediate
interest to Mrs. Gaskell, from the sequel it can be supposed that Dr.
Scoresby's conversation was not wholly concerned with his experiences
of Haworth, but spread to his far more dangerous and dramatic experiences
in early life as Captain of a Greenland whaler. A native of Whitby, he had
followed his father's calling and served in the whaling fisheries, adding
to the financial profit gained by his dangerous occupation a scientist's
acute observation of life in the arctic regions. In 1820 he published *An
Account of the Arctic Regions with a Description of the Northern Whale
Fisheries*. An abridgement of the work was republished in 1849. Mrs.
Gaskell no doubt heard of it when she first met him in 1855 but her
absorption in Charlotte Brontë's *Life* makes it unlikely that she would
have read it then. But the evidence of parallel incidents and descriptions
in Dr. Scoresby's work and *Sylvia's Lovers* makes it plain that at some
time she did so and was inspired by it.[33] Without it, she could not have
ventured on a tale the nautical background of which required so much
technical knowledge. It may be assumed that a copy was to be found in
Sir James Maxwell's library and that she read it during the summer at
Auchencairn. For Mrs. Gaskell, with her life-long love of the sea, the
attraction of such a book was irresistible. By the time she made her
decisive journey to Whitby in November she was primed with questions
on two essential aspects of her novel: the whalers and the press-gang.

At what exact moment she decided to incorporate both subjects in her
new novel cannot now be traced. That Dr. Scoresby's book was of tanta-
mount importance in deciding her to write about the whalers of Whitby
appears self-evident, and it was a subject quite naturally leading to the
action of the press-gang during the French wars, even without taking into
account Mrs. Gaskell's familiarity with Crabbe's poem 'Ruth', where
the subject was treated much as she would treat it in *Sylvia's Lovers*,
from the standpoint of broken lives and separated lovers. She had also,
as her unsatisfactory story 'The Manchester Marriage' showed, recently
been haunted afresh by the old theme of the lost sailor's return, and may
have planned her new novel on those lines and found in the enlarged
framework of the whalers' lives and the press-gang's activities the ideal
treatment for the subject.

From the moment that her choice of subject was made, she must also
have realized that it was a far more ambitious undertaking than any she

---

[33] See Sharps, *Mrs. Gaskell's Observation and Invention*, pp. 387-8.

had attempted so far, and one that would demand disciplined study and thorough research. She was the more resolved to take up the challenge because of her sense of obligation to George Smith. It was not a meaningless promise she had made him to 'write a good novel'. For this reason, irrespective of family commitments and uncertain health, *Sylvia's Lovers* took longer to write than any of her previous works.

By the end of October, when she wrote to Charles Norton about their holiday in Scotland and her contract with Smith, Elder for a new novel she told him 'Not a line of the book is written yet'. But she was gathering strength and the surroundings were ideal.

Our house at Auchencairn had a pretty field, or 'park' as the Scotch call it, between the front door and the road,—then two or three flat meadows, and then the bay, often dry alas! In this field which had a mossy bank on one side, with great beautiful trees, making armchairs of their roots, we sate and talked and lounged all through the hot summer's days, often thinking we were reading or sewing, but generally finding out at the end that it had all been a mistake on our parts. Behind the house was a beautiful rocky, heathery ferny glen, with little pools, and birch trees up which we might go to a deep inky purple mountain called Ben-Caèra.[34]

Writing from Auchencairn itself in July to an unknown correspondent she described the 'delicious' and 'invigorating air', and her plans for filling the 'delicious length of time before us; in which we mean to do everything from mending stockings up to writing novels . . . The honey suckles here smell so deliciously . . . But we have no candles, and have to go to bed by daylight in consequence.'[35]

Country air, as usual, worked its magic on her constitution, and she returned to Manchester at the beginning of August brimful of health and spirits.

At last we are at home [she wrote to George Smith], in a house oh! so clean, but smelling of paint to the last degree . . . Such a contrast to our delicious Auchencairn! I am sure I was made to breathe pure air, and let my brain lie fallow in agricultural dulness; for I am come home so strong, and so ignorant, I don't even know who we are at war with, but I am sure (from the income tax) that we are at war with somebody . . .[36]

Without 'a word of it written yet' in late October, she had, however, been so busy planning and reading for it and had it so well advanced in her mind as to warrant her sudden visit to Whitby at the beginning of November. Julia, aged 13 and out-growing her strength, was made the

[34] *GL* 444.   [35] *GL* 436.   [36] *GL* 438, 4 Aug. 1859.

excuse for this apparently uncalled for and unseasonal rush to the cold east coast in winter. Not even to George Smith did she give her true reason for the journey; she was keeping the plot and setting of her book a complete secret. Taking Meta (and Hearn) with her as well as Julia (not only as confidante but as illustrator of selected views) she left home on Monday, 31 October, stayed overnight at York (which the girls had not seen before) and reached Whitby the next day without having booked lodgings. They found rooms easily, however, at 1 Abbey Terrace, with a fine view of the sea and an admirable landlady, Mrs. Rose, who supplied all their needs, including recommendations and introductions to townsfolk likely to provide Mrs. Gaskell with local lore. They stayed for a fortnight. Though the weather, to judge from Mrs. Gaskell's letters, was consistently bad, they did 'nothing but go out',[37] as she reported to Marianne who was keeping house at home.

A fortnight, in the short days of November, was little enough time in which to gather the accurate and detailed descriptions of the town and surrounding countryside she was able to provide as the setting of her novel. All her work depended to a considerable degree on atmosphere, on the character of the places in which she set her dramas. There were the strongly etched streets and old houses of Ruth's native 'assize town' in the eastern counties (Ipswich); and the Welsh village and Lancashire shore in the same novel; the Greenhey Fields of *Mary Barton*; the smoke-laden sky of *North and South*—all of which had a vital symbolic part to play in their respective tales. It was to be even more so in *Sylvia's Lovers*. Whitby was the setting and its character had to be evoked first by observation and then by imposing her own vision on what she saw, by bringing out a certain grandeur in the place which was both literally and symbolically true of it. She had found an ideal setting in fact, and one that deeply moved her. Her descriptions of the high surrounding cliffs, holding up like a beacon to the ships at sea the noble ruined profile of the abbey, of the steep streets and cobbled lanes leading to the harbour, of the heathery grassy heights slashed by chines and dotted with sheep farms where the life of the rural community was centred, are fine spontaneous evocations. But not even the casual observer can overlook where the heart of Whitby beats, down at the little narrow harbour where the Esk frets its way out to sea, and the fishing fleets come and go. It was there in the days about which Mrs. Gaskell wished to write that the twice-yearly drama of the whalers' departure and return was played out. So impressive a spectacle, so momentous a yearly enterprise for the

[37] *GL* 447, Nov. 1859.

community that lived by the produce of the sea, could not be lost on a woman of her wide sympathies and passionate response to the sea and sea-faring folk. Here was everything to hand, danger, heroism, high drama, and tragedy, in the daily lives of these people. She was determined to see, hear, or read every traceable fact about the past of the place and its people. She worked indefatigably and missed little of the scene about her, noting the 'red and fluted tiles of the gabled houses of the town', the emplacement of the Butter Cross, the 'mists and sea-fogs' prevalent on that coast, the country sounds within earshot of the sea—the 'cackle of the geese blending with the tones of the great church bell'.[38] The book itself opens with a memorable passage on the whalers' return:

The narrow harbour at the mouth of the river was crowded with small vessels of all descriptions, making an intricate forest of masts. Beyond lay the sea, like a flat pavement of sapphire, scarcely a ripple varying its sunny surface, that stretched out leagues away till it blended with the softened azure of the sky. On this blue, trackless water floated scores of white-sailed fishing boats, apparently motionless, unless you measured their progress by some land-mark; but, still, and silent, and distant as they seemed, the consciousness that there were men on board, each going forth into the great deep, added unspeakably to the interest felt in watching them.[39]

Of the story which begins with an evocation of careless youth, self-assured manhood, high spirits, and healthy pursuits, she herself ulti-mately said it was the saddest she had ever written. The tragedy emerged from the varied material at her command, and the period she chose for her action—the anti-press gang riots that took place in the town in 1793 at the height of the French wars. Into that central and verifiable incident she wove the drama of Charlie Kinraid—the 'Specksioneer', as the chief harpooner on every whaler was called, who was loved by Sylvia and 'impressed' unknown to her. He is assumed lost at sea but returns to find her married most unwillingly to his rival Philip Hepburn. Here was the theme known to her from early womanhood when she was much influenced by Crabbe and the theme of his poem 'Ruth' which was published in 1819. At that time it was her ambition to write like him, as she confided to Mary Howitt.[40] It fitted perfectly into the framework of the Whitby riots provoked by the press-gang, and the whole drama of the arctic fisheries about which she had read in Dr. Scoresby's book. While at Whitby she took every opportunity for gathering first-hand accounts of those events from the old people who still remembered them.

---

[38] *Sylvia's Lovers*, pp. 19, 66, 72.   [39] Ibid., p. 15.   [40] *GL* 12, 18 Aug. 1838.

One old resident, George Corney, lent her a copy of Young's *History of Whitby* (published 1817), the standard work on the town, which she read in the evenings during her visit.[41] She made use of Mr. Corney's name in the book for the family of Sylvia's cousins. He was thanked for his pains, as Mrs. Chadwick relates,[42] by receiving an inscribed copy of *Sylvia's Lovers* on publication, which was treasured and handed down in the family.

Mrs. Gaskell's original contribution to the plot, the character and conduct of Philip Hepburn, has remained open to debate and criticism ever since the book appeared. As all readers of the tale remember, his treachery in hiding from Sylvia the fact of Kinraid's 'impressment', of which he was an eye-witness, and his consequent marriage to her is the pivot on which the whole plot turns. The battle of conscience that such an act provokes in a fundamentally honourable man makes heavy reading, and the long-drawn-out drama of the couple's marital relations and its final melodramatic solution appears far-fetched and contrived in contrast to the freshness and feeling for life of the opening chapters. Mrs. Gaskell's fine perception of the phases of young love between Sylvia and Kinraid are among the best in her work so far. Sylvia in love is described as being 'in a new strange state of happiness not to be reasoned about, or accounted for, but in a state of more exquisite feeling than she had ever experienced before'.[43] Mrs. Gaskell's recent experience of Meta's aborted love-affair may well have intensified her perception of such shades of feeling. Certainly, as her own daughters grew up, her preoccupation with girls in love in her books—*Cousin Phillis* following shortly upon Sylvia, and 'Molly Gibson' upon Phillis—becomes apparent.

That she should be more at her ease with young women's emotions than young men's is understandable, but with Philip Hepburn she attempted more than she could achieve. The character is subjectively presented throughout—in contrast to the extrovert Kinraid, whose rattling talk and easy manner with women is both entertaining and convincing, while most subtly conveying the hollow core within. Could his character have been based upon Captain Hill?

With Philip Hepburn she was on far more treacherous ground. He would have cost Emily Brontë no pains to portray, since he was motivated by genuine passion for Sylvia, but Mrs. Gaskell needed to moralize and excuse, and ultimately chasten him for his sins, and so lost herself finally

---

[41] See Sharps, *Mrs. Gaskell's Observation and Invention*, p. 375.
[42] Chadwick, *Mrs. Gaskell*, p. 364.   [43] *Sylvia's Lovers*, ch. 12, p. 159.

in metaphysics far more suited to the pen of a George Eliot. Yet Hepburn, the diffident, stooping, inarticulate young draper's assistant and later partner in the town's main store, was a necessary figure in the plot. He introduced that third force in the social structure of the town, of which Mrs. Gaskell would have been made aware during her visit to Whitby. Alongside the all-important fishing fleets and the farming community, there was the active trading interest pursued by the townsfolk, of which the Sanders brothers and their bank and main store in Church Street were notable examples. She clearly drew on them from first-hand reports, representing them in the characters of the Quaker Foster brothers of her tale, and she described their shop with the accuracy that only personal knowledge can give. It still stands today. The name 'J. Sanders', engraved in the glass fanlight, can be clearly read, a measure of the respect in which the brothers' memory is held. Bank notes issued by the firm are still on show in the local museum.

Mrs. Gaskell's visit to Whitby both kindled her historical imagination and provided the topographical and social bases for her plot, the focal points being the harbour, Haytersbank farm, and Foster's shop. The life of Whitby could not have been better epitomized.

Meta, whose original sketch of Haworth Church and Parsonage illustrated volume 2 of the *Life of Charlotte Brontë*, was useful to her mother once again in taking views of Whitby. Marianne was told on 8 November: 'Meta is going to sketch out of a house in the East Terrace to-day, where she fancies she shall have a pretty view—said house belonging to a friend of Mrs. Rose's.'[44] In due course the sketch, of the harbour, the parish church, and the abbey ruins on the cliffs above, was reproduced in *Sylvia's Lovers*.

On her return home Elizabeth Gaskell was so charged with the material she had collected and the visual impressions she had received that by Christmas she could give George Smith the title she had chosen for the tale—*The Specksioneer*—and tell him that though it was 'not far on' it was 'very clear in my head' and that she wanted to write it 'more than any thing'. Four days later she told him she hoped to have the book finished by September 1860.[45]

She did not begin consecutive work on it, however, till 8 April, a bad bout of influenza in February and March having incapacitated her, and the reading required for the research having proved considerable. She studied the Admiralty records, and the reports of the trials held at York Castle of the 1793 rioters, whose ringleader William Atkinson entered

    [44] *GL* 447b.   [45] *GL* 451a and 452, 23 and 27 Dec. 1859.

her story as Dan Robson, the father of her heroine, the former whaler turned farmer who proved to be one of her best rustic creations.

The simultaneous and prolonged absences from home of her two elder daughters (Meta on a sketching tour of the Pyrénées, Marianne to London), while the younger were still away at school, gave her the first complete leisure she had known for years in which to advance her book, and by early May she could announce to Marianne: 'I see nobody . . . I am getting on with my book; 117 pages done *of 570 at least*.'[46] The book faithfully reflects her early enthusiasm, in the breathless speed of the opening sequences, up to Kinraid's capture by the press-gang and Philip's opportune journey to London on his firm's behalf. But she had not the stamina to keep up the pace. 'It is hard work writing a novel all morning,' she confessed to Marianne in the same letter, 'spudding up dandelions all afternoon, and writing again at night. Moreover, I had a *dreadful* headache on Friday.' The initial impetus was over and, as with all her work, the time of pressure and uncertainty had set in. 'Oh! I am so tired of my story', she told Marianne before May was out. 'I dream about it. It is lovely hot weather, lovely for doing nothing I mean.'[47]

Writing to Charles Norton later in the summer she confessed how much she had missed the girls, 'and yet in the bustling life I too often lead, one has so little time for quiet thought . . . I got on splendidly too with my new book, that-is-to-be.'[48] She had just about finished the first volume—which would have meant that a third of the task had been accomplished—she told Norton, when on 6 June she was summoned to London in all haste on an alarm that Marianne had contracted smallpox. As it turned out it was only a severe attack of chicken-pox, but Marianne was never robust and the recovery was slow. The doctor ordered a convalescence in a reliably warm climate and so Mrs. Gaskell hurriedly arranged to take the girls and Hearn to Heidelberg. Marianne continued abroad for an extra month in the charge of Hearn, but the rest of the family returned home in mid-August.

The autumn brought further disruption to work with the usual influx of visitors, and since then, Mrs. Gaskell reported to Norton in her December letter:

we have never been alone; and I find two sitting rooms are rather small accomo-dation for *doing* anything [i.e. writing], when there are 4 daughters, and three or 4 visitors inhabiting them. So I seem to have read and written nothing, ever since

---

[46] *GL* 465, May 1860.
[47] *GL* 466.
[48] *GL* 476, 27 Aug. 1860.

we came back from Heidelberg. I *must* write though, and finish my book, about one quarter done.[49]

As 1860 drew to a close, the book, once rashly promised George Smith for September, was still only a quarter finished. It was not in fact finished for another two years, and the loss in brilliance and the want of unity that mar what promised to be her finest work to date may be explained by the difficulty she had in devoting to it her full and sustained attention.

The first half of 1861 was no better. There appeared to be no specific cause for her slow progress—neither illness, nor absence, nor influx of visitors, nor other problems. The everyday business of life with four fast-growing daughters in the house was occupation enough. In April 1861 she sent Norton one of her witty diary-like reports that sufficiently explains her position.

I am sitting here by myself in the dining room by the light of one candle—half disturbed and half-amused by the chatter of 'the children' in the next room—(Julia just come to wish me good-night, so it is 9 o'clock) where Meta Florence and Julia have been sitting till now, when Julia the chatter-box and perpetual singer having gone to bed, sudden silence succeeds. I suspect that Meta has taken up either the 5th vol. of Modern Painters, or Tyndall on Glaciers, both of which books she is reading now, and Florence is probably reading the 'Amber-Witch'. Mr. Gaskell is out, at a meeting of the Literary and Philosophical Society, making arrangements for the meeting of the British Association for the Advancement of Science, in Septr (4th to 10th) and Elliott (Elliott, Mary and Hearn are still with us) has just come in to ask me if Master would like some bread and milk when he comes home? So now you know the exact state of affairs on this Tuesday evening. Marianne has been nearly a fortnight at Buxton . . . being a bridesmaid at a friend's wedding . . . About the early middle of July we all . . . go to our dear old Silverdale on the borders of Morecambe Bay, to run wild there . . . for six weeks.[50]

Mr. Gaskell was given a month's holiday every year by the Unitarian Congregation of Manchester, which he usually spent partly with his family (if they remained in England) and partly on walking tours with friends. In 1861, however, he was given two months' leave of absence and a cheque for £50 to enable him to take a continental holiday, to mark his thirty-three years of 'faithful service' and also perhaps as a token of gratitude for his decision to stay with the Manchester Congregation. Mrs. Gaskell lost no time in contacting the Storys, who had given him a standing invitation to join them at any time in Rome, to help organize the ideal holiday for him. Humorously, and affectionately, she described

[49] *GL* 480, 10 Dec. 1860.   [50] *GL* 485, 16 Apr. 1861.

his dilemma: it was too hot for Rome, he was so tired that he was unequal to planning anything, too shy to approach strangers, and too fussed by his family to encumber himself with them. Where was he to go and with whom?

. . . altogether he was very 'low' about where he was to go, and what he was to do . . . until Friday at dinner; when on our suggesting that he should make his way to you in your summer retreat his face brightened immensely, and all he said was 'Oh they would think I was intruding . . .' So I took all the blame, promised, that if need were, you should hate *me* and not *him* for 'pushing himself in upon you',—and I sate down immediately to write the letter . . . I shall send him off viâ Marseilles to Genoa as soon as he will go . . . It is your bright charming *companionship* I want for him; so that if he has a lodging *near* you it is everything, and he is only too simple in his tastes and wants and wishes . . . Oh HOW I shall envy Mr. Gaskell if he does reach you. I feel so sure you will like each other.[51]

In one of her most revealing comments on her husband, revealing as much of herself and of her complete understanding as of his character, she described him:

He is very shy, but *very* merry when he is well, delights in puns and punning, is very fond of children, playing with them all the day long, not caring for them so much when they are grown up, *used* to speak Italian pretty well, but says he can't now, 6 foot high, grey hair and whiskers and otherwise very like Marianne in looks. You'll think him stiff till his shyness wears off, as I am sure it will directly with you.[52]

Mrs. Gaskell was rewarded for her confidence in all parties. Mr. Gaskell's holiday through northern Italy and Switzerland, where he joined up with the Storys—'liking Mr. Story *extremely* but saying little about the rest of the family, and never naming Edie to our great surprize'—was an unqualified success. He returned to England at the end of August, 'extremely well and happy and enjoying English food',[53] and full of zest for the opening of the British Association Meeting the next day, some of the delegates to which the Gaskells were entertaining in their home.

During his absence the family's six-week holiday at Silverdale had its usual restorative and inspiring effect. Mrs. Gaskell came back from there with her book half written and the resolve to get it done. She was, however, becoming uncertain of her title and told Norton, on the return from Silverdale on 28 August, that she thought of calling it *Philip's Idol*.[54]

[51] *GL* 490, 23 June 1861.   [52] Ibid.
[53] *GL* 493, 28 Aug. 1861.   [54] Ibid.

The change in title, away from the emphasis on the whalers implied in the original *The Specksioneer*, indicated her growing preoccupation with Philip's obsessive and self-destructive love for Sylvia.

Despite her good resolutions, she had only finished two out of the three volumes by the year's end, as she announced to George Smith on 9 December, and would not commit herself to a date for the finished work.[55] To Marianne she wrote on 26 December confessing to the need 'of a little *impetus* to set me off well with my writing'.[56]

Marianne had gone, rather suddenly, to Rome on 18 November for a five-month visit with a married friend, a Mrs. Dicey, who wintered regularly in Rome on account of an invalid son. Her offer to take Marianne had come at a moment of renewed anxiety for her health, never completely restored since the chicken pox the previous year. To spare her the rigours of a Manchester winter her parents had consented to the proposal, and Mrs. Gaskell had been rushed with preparations for her hurried journey and preoccupied with the problems of her settling in. Marianne's renewed contacts with the Storys and rapturous reports of her happiness there had in due course their inevitable effect on her mother. 'You may fancy the visions Meta and I build up of the possibility of our going to Rome to fetch her,' Mrs. Gaskell wrote to Norton in America on 31 December 1861, 'but if we went, Florence would have to go too; (Julia is at school) as she is too young and pretty to be left,— and then comes in the great question of money. But whenever a letter comes from Marianne we go in imagination to Rome.'[57]

As the new year began, and 'the impetus to set her off' with her writing did not come, she sent the manuscript of the first two finished volumes off to Smith, Elder in the hope of receiving from them 'just the fillip of encouragement' for her 'poor story' that she needed. There was no reply for a full month, and when at last a non-committal note came from Mr. Williams, the firm's reader, on 1 February it gave her no encouragement at all. She wrote in haste, and in confidence, to him rather than to Mr. Smith, to beg for his personal opinion and to confess to her inability to get on with the book.

In the first place, have you read my two vols of my new novel? If you have I am afraid you do not like them because you say nothing about them. . . . But if you have *not* read it I should be very glad if you would tell me so, as I cannot help feeling a little disheartened by the ambiguous sentence in your note to-day, which I cannot interpret either one way or the other as to your having read it or not. If somebody (out of my own family) would be truly interested in my poor story

[55] *GL* 495.   [56] *GL* 496.   [57] *GL* 497.

it would give me just the fillip of encouragement I want. I am sure you will understand this feeling, though you may think I ought to be too strong to have it. Mr.
Smith who has had it (the MSS. of the first two vols) for a month has never said
a word about it; which has made me fear he does not like it; and though I do not
imagine him to be any great judge of it from an artistic point of view, yet as our
bargain was made beforehand I should be sorry if he felt himself bound to take
it whether he liked it or no. I cannot help liking it myself, but that may be because
firstly I have taken great pains with it, and secondly, I know the end . . .[58]

There are two matters to surprise the modern reader in this letter:
Mrs. Gaskell's low estimation of George Smith's 'artistic' or literary
judgement, and her own estimation of the ending of *Sylvia's Lovers*. In
her view it would justify the whole work. Asking Mr. Williams if he has
read the first two volumes, she went on to say: 'If you *have*, I should like
to send you a sketch of the third vol: to make you see how everything in
the first two "works up" to the events and crisis in that.' The wish to
point a moral, and the ability to do so, were obviously at variance. Her
gift as a story-teller was for freshly observed scenes and characters, for
the fine shades of speech, for the comedy and tragedy of spontaneous
actions, of passionate unreflecting deeds; she was ill at ease when it came
to preaching sermons. It had been the stumbling-block in *Ruth*, and with
every melodramatic situation in the short stories; and though she aimed
at an apocalyptic end for her erring hero and heroine now, she was halted
in the attempt, obviously realizing at some level of her consciousness that
the contrived ending risked spoiling what she knew was a fine book so far.

Smith, Elder's delay in giving her the longed-for encouragement confirmed her fears, and brought the work to a standstill. It was not, in any
case, she told Mr. Williams in excuse, a propitious time of year for
writing: 'I have so many interruptions that it is difficult to abstract one-
self sufficiently from the day's business to write anything *entirely* out of
one's head.'[59]

At the same time, she had found another occupation and evidently
some relief in planning a series of short articles on French Society which,
she confessed to Mr. Williams, she had first intended for Dickens's new
periodical, *All the Year Round*. 'But I think my MSS. promises to be
very interesting, and I am rather unwilling to send it to 'All the Year
Round' to be broken up into bits.' Begun as a study of seventeenth-
century society, her sketches resolved themselves into 'Memoirs eluci-
datory of the Life and Times of Madame de Sevigné' (a life-long favourite
of hers) of which she gave Mr. Williams the outline, and frankly owned

[58] *GL* 499, 1 Feb. 1862.   [59] Ibid.

she would much rather not have dealings with *All the Year Round* but stick to Smith, Elder until *Sylvia's Lovers* was finished.[60] Then perhaps her Madame de Sevigné might be published with them in the *Cornhill*.

Though anxious to earn some quick money and therefore driven to think of serial publication, her disinclination to publish with *All the Year Round* was not merely aesthetic—a distaste for seeing her articles 'broken up into bits'—but a personal distaste for further dealings with Dickens, whose conduct towards his wife had greatly disgusted her. She was, all too evidently, in a very unsettled state of mind and could plan nothing definitely. Her last words to Mr. Williams sufficiently betray her perplexity: 'I hope you understand this rather confused letter, and will allow me to consult you as a friend on all these points.'[61]

Mr. Williams, one of whose first assignments as a young publisher had been to see the dying Keats off at the docks on his last voyage to Rome, and who had been the confidant of Charlotte Brontë's tribulations in finishing *Villette*, had a fund of sympathy in his nature that made itself unobtrusively felt by all who came into contact with him. He did not fail Mrs. Gaskell now; sensing how acutely anxious she was about the progress of her book, he sent her by return and with the utmost kindness of expression his not *quite* favourable judgement of it. 'I am truly obliged to you for your frank kind note, a note which I know gave you both more pain and more trouble to write than if your verdict had been more favourable', she replied on 6 February.[62] Any criticism, even if adverse, did her good in the state of mental lethargy into which she had fallen, and she responded to his comments on the title, which he did not like, by promptly suggesting her alternative, 'Philip's Idol'. Mr. Williams, meanwhile, got George Smith to read the manuscript, and by mid-March publisher and author were corresponding regularly again, Mr. Smith prepared to go ahead with setting the first two volumes in type, and Mrs. Gaskell concerned about the dispatch of the proofs to a prospective German translator—a Frau von Schmidt she had met on holiday—who needed to earn some money.[63]

At the very moment when confidence was reviving in her work, ill news from a quite unexpected quarter came to halt all progress again. She heard from Rome that Marianne was seriously thinking of joining the Roman Catholic Church. After a first warning from Mrs. Dicey (which Mrs. Gaskell dared not communicate to Mr. Gaskell until further confirmation) she received a most alarming letter from William

[60] *GL* 499, 1 Feb. 1862.   [61] Ibid.
[62] *GL* 499a.   [63] *GL* 501, 18 Mar. 1862.

Story who told her that Marianne had fallen under the persuasive influence of Dr. (later Cardinal) Manning. The Storys and Manning had been friends for years (Manning was a 'regular' at their Friday receptions) and Mrs. Gaskell herself had been charmed with him when they had met socially in Rome. The shock to both parents on receipt of Story's letter was overwhelming. To Mr. Gaskell, as a Unitarian minister, the whole fabric of Catholicism was abhorrent, and the arguments of their apologists 'utterly absurd', as his wife told Story.[64] The effect on Mrs. Gaskell was doubly wounding, both on religious grounds and as a fond mother who believed she had always had her children's confidence. She had taken such infinite pains with their religious and moral training. The injury to her feelings had the inevitable effect on her highly wrought nerves. She fell ill and had to go to bed.

For the first time in her relations with her cherished eldest daughter there entered recriminations. In the first heat of her anger she wrote off to Marianne and to the Storys letters which she later admitted regretting, and was glad to find that, in the event, the letter to Marianne was never sent. 'I am glad the letter did not go,' she wrote her when sufficiently recovered to be up for some hours each day,

as the quieter all is done and the less that is said the better. I leave all at your end to the decision of *you and Mrs Dicey* whatever you two think best had better be done; only do avoid Dr Manning. I concentrate all my wish on that for the present, till I know more . . . but oh! if I do but hear good accounts of you my child—good accounts in every way—that you are pretty strong, that you are not led off by excitement to go a few steps (as you think *only*) on a wrong and terrible way—that you are avoiding temptation and referring doubtful cases to Mrs Dicey who, you know love, is at present in the place of a parent to you, I shall get all right. Only tell me the truth. There is no news . . . compared with what I want to hear from you. *Don't go to the Storys' Friday afternoons* if it is there you meet Dr Manning because it will be awkward . . .

Very naturally, half Mrs. Gaskell's distress came from self-reproach: *why* had she consented to Marianne's going to Rome? 'Oh! I am so sorry I ever let you go to Rome—we have so missed you at home and if it is all to end this way, but I know it won't. Only you see I am not well and am so stupid and do so want your letter.'[65]

The incident caught her at a moment of weakness. She was harassed by long overwork and worry about her book, and felt her responsibility for what had happened more sharply than perhaps at a time of robust health, not alone towards Marianne but towards her husband. The event

[64] *GL* 507, 9 May 1862.   [65] *GL* 500a.

revealed her, to her super-sensitive conscience, as having failed both as a wife and mother. In her disarray, she quarrelled even with her beloved Storys—a temporary quarrel soon healed—and for the first time on record had some harsh things to say of Marianne herself. 'Marianne', she told the Storys, 'has all her life been influenced by people, *out of her own family*—and seldom by the members of it, in anything like the same degree, in all matters of opinion.'[66]

Once safely home, however, Marianne showed her usual amiable disposition, and agreed to study regularly with her Papa and to try hard to be convinced that the Unitarians were right. 'She is also trying to be so good and humble,' her mother wrote to Norton, 'that I feel as if the grace of God would be given her to perceive what to her may be saving truth.'[67] Soon the alarmed parents were pacified. Marianne was hardly equipped to argue on abstract principles; her strength, as her mother said, was essentially for practical things, and she was no match for her Papa, whose erudition was now marshalled in the service of his paternal love. Snatched away just in time from the reach of Dr. Manning (the spells of the enchanter were not so potent north of the Alps), Marianne settled down happily again in the bosom of her family, and was soon too busy falling in love to have much time for dogma.

There had been an unacknowledged attachment between her and her second cousin, Edward Thurstan Holland, eldest son of Mrs. Gaskell's cousin Edward Holland, since 1858, unacknowledged because of the Hollands' disapproval. Edward Holland was a very successful man. M.P. for Evesham, with a country house at Dumbleton between Evesham and Worcester and a large family to provide for, he was not inclined to countenance a poor match for his brilliant eldest son. The Gaskells for their part had seen two real objections to the match: the consanguinity of the lovers, and the possibility that if Mr. Holland cut his son off they would have no money to start life with. Thurstan, however, promised well to make his own way. Educated at Eton and Trinity College, Cambridge, he was training to be a barrister and was already in his third year. How Mrs. Gaskell regarded him appears from the letter of introduction she gave him for Charles Norton when he went for a six-month study course to the States in 1858. 'He is so good and intelligent that I am sure you will like him at once', she then wrote. 'I am sure he will do credit to any introductions you may be kind enough to give him . . . his father is my very dear cousin, and . . . he inherits—as well as individually owns—a great piece of my regard.'[68]

[66] *GL* 507.   [67] *GL* 504, 22 Apr. 1862.   [68] *GL* 389, 7 Apr. 1858.

On Marianne's return from Rome in 1862, however, Mr. Holland père was unsuspicious enough of the consequences to invite her once again on a visit to Dumbleton. The proximity to Worcester was excuse enough for the musical Marianne to be staying with her cousins for the concerts and a pleasurable round of engagements to revive her spirits, while her mother made a hurried and mainly business trip to Paris.

The purpose of the visit was to allow her to pursue her research into the projected book on Madame de Sevigné, for which she had George Smith's blessing, and with which she was much more engrossed than with finishing *Sylvia's Lovers*. It is a great loss that the book was never written, for no one was temperamentally better suited to the subject than Mrs. Gaskell. She was immensely attracted to the seventeenth-century 'grande dame', whose devotion to an only daughter inspired a correspondence that must rank among the finest in any literature. Madame de Sevigné's gift for spontaneous self-expression, for vivacious description, darting never pedantic, always witty but seldom malicious, and never less than entertaining comment could, at times, be equalled by Mrs. Gaskell herself. They were two of a kind, as Mrs. Gaskell obviously felt in wishing to introduce the French writer to the English public.

She certainly set about research for her subject in earnest. She went to Paris with Meta in early May and was back in London, where Marianne and Florence joined her, on 3 June.

Paris [she told Catherine Winkworth afterwards] altogether was abominable; noisy, hot, close, smelling of drains—*and*—perpetual cooking etc; and we were none of us well there. I however laid a good foundation for future work at Mme de Sévigné, saw M. Hachette about it, got all manner of introductions to the private part of public collections of MSS, books, portraits etc; went to every old house in Paris that she lived in, and got a list of books 'pour servir', and a splendid collection of all the portraits of herself, family and contemporaries. I could have done much more if I had not found that Meta was becoming absolutely *ill* with unappetizing food, noisy nights, close air . . .

She went to Chartres and even into Brittany to visit the Hotel de Sévigné —Les Rochers—at Vitré. 'No one has ever said half enough of its beauty',[69] she reported. Once again, she had found the natural setting of her subject as captivating as the subject itself.

In London, reunited with her daughters, except for Julia who was still at school, and staying in lodgings in Belgrave Road, she entered into a round of gaieties with the girls, escorted by Thurstan Holland's younger

[69] *GL* 509b, 23 July 1862.

brother Fred. Fred, who happened to be staying with a Canon Richson in Belgrave Square near his aunt's lodgings, came every morning to escort her and his cousins on their outings—'evidently most anxious to heal the old Thurstan breach' as Mrs. Gaskell told Catherine Winkworth, adding significantly 'you know Marianne *had* just been staying at Dumbleton'.[70] Hard upon Fred's heels followed Thurstan himself who evidently knew by then that his aunt was not implacably opposed to the match. He was allowed to escort them everywhere—including Eton, where they were joined by the youngest Holland, Scott, still at school there, for the river picnics and regattas of the Fourth. By the time Marianne left London, she and Thurstan had plighted their troth, though as yet no official engagement could be admitted.

Sylvia's Lovers was still unfinished. Early September brought fresh and increasingly urgent appeals from George Smith and Mr. Williams for *some* indication of the date for the delivery of the manuscript, but they received little comfort for their pains: Mrs. Gaskell could not, and would not, be hurried. Her time, she told Mr. Smith, was taken up with 'local causes' and she was 'so much occupied that I am unwilling to have any specified time'.[71]

Had she been more explicit then about the causes that absorbed her time, George Smith might have been mollified. Only later did she tell him how, throughout the autumn and winter of 1862-3, she and her daughters were caught up in the relief work, mainly organized by themselves, for the 'distressed cotton operatives' of Manchester thrown out of work as a result of the American Civil War.

Being the woman she was, Mrs. Gaskell could not enter lightly into such a commitment, but devoted all her time and energies to the organization of food kitchens, labour exchanges, and centres of training for women and girls setting up sewing-schools to teach them how to make saleable wares. In retrospect the period appeared as a nightmare to her. She described it to Charles Norton:

Last autumn and winter was *such* hard work—we were often off at nine,—not to come home till 7, or $\frac{1}{2}$ past, too worn out to eat or do anything but go to bed. The one thought ran through all our talk almost like a disease. Marianne worked quite as hard, if not harder, than Meta,—(tho' we all gave our lives to 'the Distress'—) but Marianne did not think so deeply about it all as Meta,—nothing like it. She decided quicker in individual cases; and shook them off sooner,— out of her mind I mean,—but Meta laboured day and night in weighing and planning and thinking,—and going out again, after a hard day if she thought one

[70] *GL* 509b, 23 July 1862.   [71] *GL* 512.

little scrap of duty or kindness or enquiry had been omitted. And Oh! I was so sorry to see her fade away under it all . . .[72]

Disappointment and disillusion with their protegés was the final trial they had to face.

. . . at the last we seemed to have done more harm than good, people who were good and hardworking before . . . were found paying a man 6d a week to answer to their name, and claim relief for them in different districts. Our charwoman . . . declined coming to wash here (which she had done for 7 years) because she could get more by *not* working, and applying to the Relief Board . . . One *local* Relief committee . . . were found to have supplied themselves with great-coats out of the Funds intrusted to them . . .[73]

Dispirited by the results after the enormous expenditure of effort and emotion, it is little wonder the family reached the point of forbidding the subject of the poor among themselves. In a cry from the heart Mrs. Gaskell told her publisher as the winter set in:

I wish North and South would make friends, and let us have cotton, and then our poor people would get work, and then you should have as many novels as you liked to take, and we should not be killed with 'Poor on the Brain', as I expect we shall before the winter is over. We were really glad before leaving home [for a short break to Eastbourne in September 1862] to check each other in talking of the one absorbing topic, which was literally haunting us in our sleep . . .[74]

Thanks to the escape to Eastbourne in September *Sylvia's Lovers* came within sight of the end, and the proof sheets of the third volume were put in hand. Even so, there was none of the elation at the end of her labours that had marked their beginning. Hers was a spontaneous gift, losing its strength as it consumed itself if no fresh fuel came to feed it. *Sylvia's Lovers* was but one of the many victims of the three-volume novel convention, dear to the Lending Libraries, which, like the frog in the fable, often distended a tale beyond its natural limits, with lethal results. While the atmosphere of *Sylvia's Lovers* is one of the most evocative in any Victorian novel, the contrivances to which the author resorted to keep her plot moving once the tale had run its natural term, with Kinraid's return and Sylvia's revulsion against Philip, only gave it a merely mechanical momentum. The events of the third volume are as far-fetched as any fairy-tale.

Here, as in her previous tales, it is in character and natural setting that she excels, not in plot. By its characters alone, however, the book shows

[72] *GL* 526, July 1863.   [73] Ibid.   [74] *GL* 517, Sept. 1862.

the hand of the mature novelist. She had reverted once again, as in *Mary Barton*, to a purely working-class community, with no leaven of intellectuals as in *North and South*, or social snobs as in *Ruth*; with the exception of the shopkeeper-bankers, the characters in *Sylvia's Lovers* are all rustics and fishermen, living by the land and the sea.

In the character of Daniel Robson, Sylvia's father, she added yet another memorable portrait to the gallery of North Country types, both men and women (one recalls the inimitable Sally in *Ruth*) in whose presentation she delighted and excelled. Boastful and loud-mouthed yet a nonentity at home, a racy talker and an ineffectual doer, full-blooded, warm-hearted, gullible, a butt for comedy yet the central actor in a grim tragedy, he represents a true and touching epitome of human frailty seen through the eyes of genius—for in portraying such people Mrs. Gaskell showed genius. She had a fine ear for catching the odd turns given by local dialects to language, that could endow the Dan Robsons of this world with the wisdom, as well as the ignorance, of the eternal rustic.

The truth of her observation is apparent even in such thumbnail sketches as those in which she brushed in the secondary characters: Farmer Corney for instance, Robson's neighbour and host for the evening at his young folks' New Year's Eve party:

Farmer Corney . . . had no notion of relinquishing his customary place for all the young people who ever came to the house . . . It was his household throne, and there he sat with no more idea of abdicating in favour of any comer than King George at St. James's. But he was glad to see his friends, and paid them the unwonted compliment of shaving on a week-day, and putting on his Sunday coat. The united efforts of his wife and children had failed to persuade him to make any farther change in his attire; to all their arguments on this head he had replied—

'Them as doesn't like t'see me i' my work-a-day wescut and breeches may bide away.'[75]

As the mother of four daughters Mrs. Gaskell had constantly under observation the workings of the adolescent female heart, but even such first-hand knowledge does not always carry with it sympathy; in her case the sympathy was universal and could breach every class barrier. She could make herself the spokeswoman for such wholly untaught girls as Mary Barton and Sylvia Robson, whose only dowry was in their wealth of feeling. She could register the fluctuations in a simple girl's feelings with the exactitude of a barometer. Her young women are a distinct

[75] *Sylvia's Lovers*, pp. 146–7.

innovation in the literature of her time when, except for her successor in the field, George Eliot, she was the only one to portray working-class girls from within. Her achievement was to show the middle-class readers of England how intense could be the emotional life of a slum-dweller in Manchester or of a country-bred girl. Without her Manchester and Knutsford background she would, doubtless, not have had these insights; and in this respect she can be regarded as a regional writer, in the tradition of Maria Edgeworth, Sir Walter Scott, and the Brontës.

Her own notable contribution to the genre was in the creation of sturdily true North Country types, fiercely individual men and women, such as she had known and loved—different in strength of character from the more amenable working classes of the south—and unaffected as yet by the levelling processes of general education. How wrong-headed they could be she demonstrated in the tragedies of John Barton and Daniel Robson, who both brought disaster on themselves, but such men were allowed an inherent stature, that cast them undeniably in the heroic mould.

Mrs. Gaskell's strength lay in comedy, but in *Sylvia's Lovers* her objective was not comedy. She set out to describe the havoc wrought by love, the deadening of once acute feelings, the failure of human relationships and, by implication, the precarious bond of marriage. Maybe it was to reassure him that, contrary to her custom, she dedicated the book in a loving tribute to her husband, when it appeared at last on 20 February 1863.

This Book
Is Dedicated to
MY DEAR HUSBAND
By Her
Who Best Knows His Value.

Sylvia's Lovers was little appreciated by the reviewers. For the *Athenaeum* of 28 February 1863 the fact that the story was 'laid in humble life and narrated chiefly in the broad vernacular Yorkshire dialect' was a 'drawback to the comfort of the reader and fatiguing to the eye'. Philip was found to be 'as wise, excellent and disagreeable a young man as can be well imagined. There is no fault to be found with him except that he is detestable . . . Mrs. Gaskell tries very hard to furnish him with redeeming traits of character and to make excuses . . . but quite in vain.' Of Daniel Robson's trial and conviction the critic found: 'This part is told vaguely and feebly; Mrs. Gaskell shrinks from this part of her narrative;

it is hastily huddled over.' The only commendation the book received at the critic's hands was for the part following the marriage of Sylvia and Philip where 'The real genius of the story now begins. Nothing can be more true and delicately indicated than the cold, disappointed married life of Philip.'

The *Saturday Review* of 4 April 1863 judged that in *Sylvia's Lovers* 'Mrs. Gaskell has fallen below her own standard', and faults the plot for lacking in 'unity and sequence'. As to the descriptive passages, which some readers might think the book's glory, the reviewer found them 'tedious reading'. Mrs. Gaskell's self-imposed embargo upon the reading of reviews appears the more justified in the light of such examples of their kind. She wisely spared herself much vexation.

After the long ordeal, the three years of constantly interrupted work, the wonder is not that she should be exhausted and in need of a complete change, but that she should re-emerge so soon with energies undiminished and sympathies widened and matured to produce in the short time still left to her the crowning works of her career, *Cousin Phillis* and *Wives and Daughters*, works to which George Sand's famous comment is peculiarly appropriate. 'Mrs. Gaskell', she said, 'has done what neither I nor other female authors in France can accomplish—she has written novels which excite the deepest interest in men of the world and yet which every girl will be the better for reading.'[76]

---

[76] Quoted by A. W. Ward in his Biographical Introduction to vol. i of the Knutsford edition, p. xlvii.

IF MRS G WAS "KNOCK UP" BY DOING RELIEF WORK; WHAT OF THE MILL GIRLS WITH YEARS OF MILL WORK AND LIFE IN MANCHESTER WITH NO CHANGE — BY GOING A BROAD FOR A TIME"?

CHAPTER XIX

KNUTSFORD REVISITED:
COUSIN PHILLIS

'WE were all so knocked up,' Mrs. Gaskell told a correspondent after a second winter of intensive relief work, 'that, as soon as the great strain of the Distress was lessened by the organization in the distribution of Relief, and by the increased amount of mill-work for our girls, we resolved to have some entire change before this next winter [i.e. 1863–4] by going abroad for a time.'[1] On 31 December (1862) the obliging George Smith had, on receipt of the completed manuscript of *Sylvia's Lovers*, paid Mrs. Gaskell the total copyright fee agreed, £1,000, and Mrs. Gaskell eagerly set about planning a continental holiday.

Her objective was Italy, Florence and Venice in particular, largely on Meta's account in order to give her the opportunity of seeing the Great Masters at home. Flossy and Julia were to be of the party, but for obvious reasons after her misadventure in Rome the previous year Marianne was not included in the Italian itinerary but was to join the travellers in Paris on their return journey. In any case Marianne was far too taken up with her own love-affair to wish to put any distance between herself and Thurstan Holland, her unofficial fiancé. She ostensibly kept house for her father and visited convenient friends during her mother's absence.

Early in March 1863 Mrs. Gaskell travelled as far as Paris, taking Julia with her, to stay a few days with Mme Mohl, where Meta and Flossy were to join them. The trip almost ended there for, while in Paris, the news reached her that Flossy had become engaged. It was a totally unexpected development and Mrs. Gaskell felt obliged to offer to return home. As she later told Charles Norton, she wrote at once to the young man, Charles Crompton, eldest son of Judge Crompton, a distant relation of the Gaskells, and to Flossy and Mr. Gaskell, to ask if she should still go on to Italy, 'and all three said yes,—so we went, and our little lassie was very happy and peaceful; and enjoyed everything very much; and was not anxious about letters or anything.'[2]

[1] *GL* 535a, 10 Oct. 1863.   [2] *GL* 526, 13 July 1863.

Flossy, of all her children, was the one Mrs. Gaskell was least expecting to see go. She was so young for her age, so clingingly childish still, so inexperienced. 'I have had to take a good while to reconcile myself to the parting from this dear child,' she told Norton, 'who still seems so much a child, and to want "mother's shelter" so much.'[3] The shock engagement, while Flossy and Meta were travelling through London to join their mother in Paris, was the result of a prolonged visit Flossy had paid the Cromptons the previous autumn. The young man himself was not known to the Gaskells other than by a first introduction when 'the pleasant straightforward look on his face' was about all that could be judged. He was ten years older than Flossy, a Fellow of Trinity, 4th Wrangler, and a promising barrister. The connection was unexceptionable and the marriage that followed was a total success. It took Mrs. Gaskell some time, however, not to fear for the consequences of so sudden an infatuation. Her daughters were rapidly growing up and she was too attached a mother not to feel acutely every alteration affecting their lives. As might be expected of her, however, the event found her selflessly active in promoting Flossy's happiness. The trip to Italy, as the young fiancé himself realized, was an advantage for Flossy that she would be very unlikely to enjoy once she was married to a man with his career to make.

Following the old route via Marseilles and ship to Civita Vecchia— where they arrived on 23 March—the Gaskells went on to Rome only for a limited stay, their main objective being Florence, where they stayed through April and part of May. Their chief social pleasure there was in the company of Thomas Trollope (Anthony's brother) who with his wife proved the most delightful of hosts. They 'completely won possession of our hearts in Florence,' Mrs. Gaskell later wrote to Catherine North, giving her a letter of introduction to the Trollopes, 'and I am so glad to think of any friends of mine succeeding to the pleasure of our intercourse at the Villino Trollope'.[4] Meta, as was to be expected, was reported by her mother as 'gobbling down pictures all day' and commensurably tired. The heat, in Florence, Mrs. Gaskell reported to Marianne on 20 May, was fearful, and they envied the Bishop of Siena, 'who made a gift to the Virgin of all his clothes'.[5]

At Julia's 'most earnest desire' they moved on to Venice for a week at the end of May. The journey north and homewards was begun on 6 June, via Verona, Milan, and up to Lucerne, to reach Paris by 11 June.

[3] *GL* 526, 13 July 1863.   [4] *GL* 527, 16 July 1863.
[5] *GL* 523a, 20 May 1863.

In Paris they were joined as planned by Marianne and Charlie Crompton. To face the considerable expense of entertaining so large a party in
town Mrs. Gaskell booked rooms at a Versailles Hotel, the Hotel du
Reservoir, from where they made daily incursions into Paris for the main
purpose of the visit, the choosing and confectioning of Florence's
trousseau. Nothing short of a Place Vendôme couturière, a Mme Lamy,
would satisfy the anxious mother, though it left her financially crippled
and her own wardrobe 'on its last legs'. The latter circumstance was the
more daunting since the entire party were invited to stay with the
Cromptons in their town house at Hyde Park Square for a fortnight on
their return from abroad. Mrs. Gaskell dreaded the prospect, as she
confessed to Marianne. 'I feel sure I shall never get on,—and I can never
play proper I am afraid and Florence is very shy of my going, I can see.
I think she thinks we shan't suit. However I shall do my best.'[6] Such
misgivings present a picture of Mrs. Gaskell from a quite novel angle.

The trousseau was made in time and the travellers returned, and the
visit to the Cromptons clearly passed off better than anticipated. Mrs.
Gaskell had the opportunity to judge her future son-in-law's character
and was satisfied by what she saw. 'His strong good, *un*sensitive character
is just what will, I trust, prove very grateful to her anxious, conscientious
little heart', she told Charles Norton afterwards.[7] An early marriage was
agreed upon and the date fixed. Florence was married on 8 September
at Brook Street Chapel, Manchester, by her father.

It was a very quiet wedding [Mrs. Gaskell told Norton later]; a very serious one
to me; for it was the first breaking up of a home; and the whole affair had appeared
to me so very sudden; only I believe it was not; and that it really was for my child's
happiness. I trust so. She had no doubts or fears; and she was in general an
undecided person.[8]

The marriage of Florence marked not only the 'first breaking up of
a home' as her mother put it, but the slackening of her life-long connections with Knutsford. While Florence had been at school there, from
January 1859 to midsummer 1860, these had been revived by the frequent
visits made to her by her mother and sisters. Mrs. Gaskell's closest surviving relatives by that time (her uncle Peter Holland having died in 1855)
were the two old maiden ladies, his daughters, her cousins Mary and
Lucy, who still lived on in the old Church House, but whose mode of
life was fast becoming a fossilized image of eighteenth-century decorum.
With them she found it increasingly difficult to stay, and during Flossy's

[6] *GL* 524, 1 June 1863.   [7] *GL* 526, 13 July 1863.
[8] *GL* 546, 1 Feb. 1864.

schooldays had preferred mostly her old friends the Greens, whose daughters' school Flossy attended.

These renewed contacts with Knutsford during Flossy's schooldays obviously revived Mrs. Gaskell's memories; they also afforded her a fresh image of the place undergoing even then its first major upheaval in centuries with the coming of the railways. She had been premature in portraying the effect on *Cranford* society of the event when writing about it in the 1850s, since in fact it only happened in the early 1860s, at the very time Flossy was at school there. The disruption brought to local life by the presence of imported labour, of the large construction sites, of the laying of the line and the building of the elegant little station —still standing today—were witnessed by Mrs. Gaskell as she came and went, noting the effect on the old rural community she had known so well of the advent of the thrusting modern inventive city types brought there for the construction of the line. It cannot have been by mere chance that the very next book she wrote, *Cousin Phillis*, serialized in the *Cornhill Magazine* during the winter and spring of 1863-4, dealt precisely with such a situation.[9] Knutsford railway station was officially opened on 12 May 1862.

In September 1863 George Smith appealed to Mrs. Gaskell for copy for a serial in the *Cornhill*, for which he had nothing in reserve. Answering him, just after Flossy's marriage, she said that, while she had 'ever so many things begun', she feared that *Cousin Phillis*, the one she had particularly in mind, would be 'too short for your purpose',[10] and, moreover, she had intended it to 'fill up and sell the copyright of a volume. So I don't know exactly what to do.' She was, once again, in pressing need of money and was hoping for a quick sale of the manuscripts she had available.

The fact that she did not offer to lengthen *Cousin Phillis* to suit George Smith's purposes of serialization would indicate that the story was already too far advanced to change. This is further evidenced by its inclusion in the November issue of the *Cornhill*. Pushed as he was for copy—even contemplating, to Mrs. Gaskell's great amusement, writing a story himself to fill the gap in his magazine—Smith immediately closed with her offer and bought the 'entire copyright' not only of *Cousin Phillis* but of her other previously published tales—'Six Weeks at Heppenheim', 'The Grey Woman', 'Curious but True'—for a total of £250, her receipt for which is dated 4 November 1863.[11] *Cousin Phillis* began

⁹ G. Payne, *Mrs. Gaskell and Knutsford* (Manchester, 1900), p. 12.
¹⁰ *GL* 532, 20 Sept. 1863.   ¹¹ Shorter Collection, Brotherton Library, Leeds.

at once to appear monthly in the *Cornhill*, beginning in the November issue and running until the February number, 1864.

The money was wanted by Mrs. Gaskell at the time for the realization of a plan she had at heart for Mr. Gaskell to have another Roman holiday. She was still hurriedly writing the last section of *Cousin Phillis* on 1 January 1864 when she wrote to George Smith asking by what deadline he needed copy for the final instalment.[12]

Cousin Phillis is a long short story of a mere hundred pages, immaculately constructed; the self-imposed limitation of length adding decisively to the classic proportions and the concentration of the plot. The setting, so familiar to the author, of the family farm outside Knutsford, the Sandlebridge of her grandparents, where her mother had grown up and where her father had first met her, was the perfect choice for the idyll she wanted to write. It was there, according to the evidence of Meta Gaskell, given later to Clement Shorter, that William Stevenson had come as an itinerant preacher when minister at Dobb Lane Unitarian Chapel, Manchester, sent out on Sundays to preach to rural congregations.[13] In the welcome given him by her grandparents and the love that sprang up between him and Elizabeth Holland, Mrs. Gaskell found the pattern for the similar situation in *Cousin Phillis*. In portraying Farmer Holman, his wife, and daughter Phillis, she called up all her memories of the old Hollands in their notable home (long since passed into the hands of Sir Henry Holland her cousin), the great rambling building dating back at least to 1718.

Once again in *Cousin Phillis*, as in *Cranford*, she dwelt lovingly on the approach to the house (once the holiday home of Clive of India), up a 'shady grassy lane' leading to the walled garden, called a court because there was a low wall, and 'two great gates, between pillars crowned with stone balls, for a state entrance to the flagged path leading up to the front door. It was not the habit of the place to go in either by these great gates or by the front door; ... I had to go round by a side-path, slightly worn, on a broad grassy way, which led past the court-wall, past a horse-mount, half covered with stone-crop, and a little wild yellow fumitory, to another door.'[14]

All round the house were acres of arable land, pastures for the splendid herds of cows, hedges, and bordering woods. Within such a framework, life is basically conditioned by the season's changes, and Mrs. Gaskell

[12] *GL* 545.
[13] Shorter Collection, Brotherton Library, Leeds.
[14] *Cousin Phillis*, p. 8.

uses all her skill and knowledge of rural life to make the revolving year convey the change in mood and fortunes of her characters. Never did she show herself more perceptive of the forces of nature at work in directing the lives of those who depend upon it, than in her memorable pictures of the patriarchal household of Holman, the preacher turned farmer. Like her grandfather Samuel Holland, and her own father William Stevenson, he too was a Dissenting minister who, like others of their contemporaries, tried to combine the ministry with agriculture, before scientific farming excluded such quixotic characters from attempting to make a living in the face of impossible odds.

The force of character needed to sustain such a way of life is seen in the person of Farmer Holman, an epitome, one senses, of all Mrs. Gaskell's admired forebears. It is Phillis who describes the day's time-table of work undertaken by her father. Asked by the newcomer why he gets up daily at three, and what he should have to do at that hour, she replies:

What has he not to do? He has his private exercise [prayer] in his own room; he always rings the great bell which calls the men to milking; he rouses up Betty, our maid; as often as not, he gives the horses their feed before the man is up . . . he looks at the calves, and the shoulders, heels, traces chaff, and corn, before the horses go a-field; he has often to whip-cord the plough-whips; he sees the hogs fed; he looks into the swill-tubs, and writes his orders for what is wanted for food for man and beast; yes, and for fuel, too. And then, if he has a bit of time to spare, he comes in and reads with me—but only English—we keep Latin for the evenings, that we may have time to enjoy it; and then he calls in the man to breakfast, and cuts the boys' bread and cheese, and sees their wooden bottles filled, and sends them off to their work—and by this time it is half-past six, and we have our breakfast.[15]

In appearance he was a labourer, yet educated enough to teach his daughter Latin.

Such a way of life is punctuated only by the recurrence of the seasonal operations—sowing, haymaking, harvesting, apple-picking—and receives its first shock of change by the arrival in the district of the work force engaged in laying the railway line. Here Mrs. Gaskell uses all her narrative skills to introduce into the pastoral, almost biblical, family life of the Holmans the go-ahead, efficient, travelled, and above all captivating head engineer in command of the works, Edward Holdsworth. He enters the age-old circle of the Holmans' home to steal the heart of Phillis and, without purpose or even intention, to proceed to break it.

[15] *Cousin Phillis*, p. 14.

It would have been easy to make Holdsworth a villain. Mrs. Gaskell did no such thing. She made him vividly alive and attractive, the better to account for Phillis's love. It was no drama of seduction and desertion she was writing; Phillis Holman is no Hetty Sorel, any more than Holdsworth is an Arthur Donnithorne. *Cousin Phillis* is something more subtle, an analysis of wounded feelings that only a woman of keen sensitivity and perception of others' feelings could have written; she shows a penetration rare even in her sympathetic studies of young girls' hearts. Without betrayal and without loss of reputation like poor Ruth, Phillis is convincingly shown as dying of grief. Mrs. Gaskell's advance as a novelist may be judged by her greater acceptance of everyday experience and less reliance on melodrama in developing the plot. Phillis Holman and Edward Holdsworth are shown as genuinely and mutually attracted. Holdsworth would have proposed and married her out of hand but for the sudden prospect of a superior and challenging post overseas that tempts him to postpone a decision. He goes to Canada without proposing to Phillis but fully intending to return. Once gone, the attraction of the new life of freedom and adventure, the allurements of fresh acquaintance, soon decide him to settle there. Within two years he is married to a French Canadian girl, satisfied in his own conscience that, since he never declared himself, he has nothing to reproach himself with; he had not tampered with Phillis's feelings. He is altogether too extrovert, too restless himself, to conceive of such feelings as hers.

Mrs. Gaskell used the simple but telling device of narrating her tale through the eyes of an onlooker, young Paul Manning—a relative of the Holmans and an articled engineer on the railway site under the orders of Holdsworth. It is through the innocent intervention of Paul, equally fond of his cousin and admiring of his principal, that Holdsworth is introduced into the Holman household; and a result of his naïve communication to Phillis of Holdsworth's unspoken love for her that the mischief is done.

The role of Paul Manning, just launched on his career, and living for the first time among strangers, may also have been suggested to Mrs. Gaskell by another circumstance of the time. A younger brother of Flossy's husband, Charlie Crompton, had at the very time she was writing *Cousin Phillis* been articled to an engineering works in Manchester and was living in lodgings in the city. Like Paul Manning, he was eighteen and conscientious in his work and in the study it entailed. A nephew of Mme Mohl's was recently arrived in England for a study-course in engineering plants, and Mrs. Gaskell referred him to young

Crompton to gain inside information on certain works in Manchester. 'His father took counsel with most of the principal engineers of the country,' Mrs. Gaskell told him, 'and followed their advice in sending him for a year, at least, to these works. He will give you his opinion of the work he has to go through in a very sensible way, I am sure. He is at home every *evening* (except Wednesdays and Fridays—) at work all day.'[16]

Once again, as in *Ruth*, *North and South*, and *Sylvia's Lovers*, a major role is assigned by Mrs. Gaskell to a country servant, a type she excelled in characterizing. It is Betty, the Holmans' farm servant, with her good sense and forthright language, who sees most clearly what ails Phillis and who helps her in the end to survive.

Now Phillis! . . . we ha' done a' we can for you, and th' doctors has done a' they can for you, and I think the Lord has done a' He can for you, and more than you deserve, too, if you don't do something for yourself. If I were you, I'd rise up and snuff the moon, sooner than break your father's and your mother's hearts wi' watching and waiting, till it pleases you to fight your own way back to cheerfulness. There, I never favoured long preachings, and I've said my say . . .[17]

With a life-long accumulation of love for the scenes of her childhood, Mrs. Gaskell evoked in passage after passage of this nostalgic tale the beauty and dignity of the work on the land. For her the bounty of the earth was a source of inspiration, and the communion with nature the surest way to find the poetry of life. It was haymaking-time at the Holmans' farm when Paul Manning returned there for a final visit.

Deep summer peace brooded over the place; the warm golden air was filled with the murmur of insects near at hand, the more distant sound of voices out in the fields, the clear far-away rumble of carts over the stone-paved lanes miles away. The heat was too great for the birds to be singing; only now and then one might hear the wood-pigeons in the trees beyond the ash-field. The cattle stood knee-deep in the pond, flicking their tails about to keep off the flies. The minister stood in the hay-field, without hat or cravat, coat or waistcoat, panting and smiling. Phillis had been leading the row of farm-servants, turning the swathes of fragrant hay with measured movement. She went to the end—to the hedge, and then, throwing down her rake, she came to me . . . So off I went, a willing labourer, following Phillis's lead; it was the primitive distinction of rank; the boy who frightened the sparrows off the fruit was the last in our rear. We did not leave off till the red sun was gone down behind the fir-trees bordering the common. Then we went home to supper—prayers—to bed; some bird singing far into the night, as I heard it through my open window, and the poultry beginning their clatter and cackle in the earliest morning.[18]

[16] *GL* 549, 9 Mar. 1864.   [17] p. 108.   [18] pp. 80-1.

13. Lindeth Tower, Silverdale, Lancs.

14. The Lawn, Holybourne, Alton, Hants.

Compared with the letters Mrs. Gaskell used to write from Knutsford, especially the letter written while at Sandlebridge in Marianne's first summer there,[19] the recollected scene has lost nothing by the passage of the years; it is, if anything, more deeply impressed on her memory, with all the scents and sounds that convey the living atmosphere, and refreshed by her recent visits. After more than thirty years of Manchester life, Knutsford was still her spiritual home, and in her desire to be a part of it again she almost at once started on her next book, *Wives and Daughters*, which, more completely than *Cousin Phillis* because of the far wider canvas, the more peopled scene, represents a tribute to the Knutsford of her youth.

[19] *GL* 4, May 1836.

CHAPTER XX

A WOMAN OF HER TIME

THE fact that Mrs. Gaskell reverted to the country setting of her beginnings for her last novels may have added to the impression created later—by the very excellence of the 'Knutsford' novels—that she was at heart a provincial woman spiritually at home in a backwater—and a backwater of past days at that. The increasing popularity of *Cranford* in the decades following her death, and the corresponding and inevitable eclipse of the once topical 'social' novels, tended to obscure yet further the extent to which she had evolved, and how completely she had become a woman of her time. It has needed the evidence of the letters to restore the original likeness of her as a woman living fully, actively, and influentially in the thick of contemporary life, during the most productive years of the Victorian expansion.

The long delays in the writing of *Sylvia's Lovers*—to the book's lasting loss—were, as has been seen, due in part to Mrs. Gaskell's complete involvement in relief work during the Manchester Cotton Famine of 1862-3; it was the most recent and typical instance of her setting aside her own interests in a public cause. Like her earlier involvements in the cause of the cotton operatives during the 'Hungry Forties', and in the rescue work among prostitutes, the Famine showed her adaptability to crises, her dedication to humanitarian causes, her practical sympathy.

In nothing do the letters demonstrate these qualities more completely than in the range and variety of her friendships with some of the most famous men and women of her day. To judge by the lack of intellectual men in her novels (clergy and Roger Hamley are the only exceptions) and the eschewal of aristocratic backgrounds (the exception again comes from *Wives and Daughters*) she might never have been on a footing of intimacy or ease with such people; and yet the letters show her acquaintance to have been with men in every walk of life—not alone with Manchester mill-owners or cotton operatives or even with fellow writers, publishers, and critics, large as these necessarily loomed in her life; but with academics and titled men and women, with churchmen (for a Unitarian minister's wife, she knew a surprising number of bishops); artists, Ruskin foremost among them; musicians like Hallé, whose concerts in Manchester even Mr. Gaskell made time to attend.

Mrs. Gaskell visited Oxford on several occasions, as the honoured guest of heads of colleges, and was rushed through the 'sights' by doctors in scarlet gowns ('with scarlet wings flying all abroad', as she reported it); was entertained to dinner by Jowett and by Mark Pattison, and dazzled by the manuscripts in the Bodleian. 'I saw so much, I have hardly yet arranged it in my mind', she told Norton after one such visit in October 1857. 'But I like dearly to call up pictures,—and thoughts suggested by so utterly different a life to Manchester. I believe I *am* Mediaeval—and *un* Manchester, and un American. I do like associations —they are like fragrance, which I value so in a flower.'[1]

Invitations to country-house parties became increasingly frequent as her reputation grew, and her presence was made the occasion for large gatherings of admirers. She stayed frequently with Richard Monckton Milnes (later Lord Houghton) and his wife in Yorkshire, with the Nightingale family in Derbyshire, and Lord and Lady Hatherton in Staffordshire. How uncontaminated she remained for all the flattery and fame, she herself best demonstrates: reporting to Norton on a visit to the Hathertons in October 1857, at which she met an American friend of his, a Mr. Sumner, she was wholly unimpressed.

... I don't think we 'got on' together much, in our three days of being under the same roof. I can hardly tell why. To be sure we only talked over 'stock' questions, —condition-of-working-classes (which *he* chose in compliment to the author of M.B.) which is too great a subject, and too much of a problem to be talked over with a stranger except as the vaguest philanthropic generality of a subject, and *then* one is apt to talk Cant, i.e. used-up forms of speech, with the life withered out of them. Then he talked Anti-Slavery,—of the ins and outs of which I know nothing,—so all I could say was that Slavery was a very bad thing, and the sooner it was done away with, and the better. So—don't you see,—we 'esteemed' each other exceedingly, and don't care if we never see each other again.[2]

When in London, every hour of her day was engaged, and she was sometimes so besieged as to have very little freedom at all. Staying there with Lady Coltman in May 1853 and invited to meet friends of Mazzini by Emily Shaen, she had regretfully to decline: 'I should so like to come, and above all things to know a little of Mazzini, but there is a great dinner-party here, made for me—Macaulay, Hallam, Sir Francis Palgrave, and

[1] *GL* 384, 7 Dec. 1857.　　[2] Ibid.

Lord Campbell [author of the fashionable *Lives of the Lord Chancellors of England*]—I don't *think* I can get away *before* 10, and then it is 3 miles to go—but I'll leave it a little open please, for all that.'[3]

Her own interests were by no means satisfied by contacts with the curious and the great. While in London she wished to see for herself the new institutions then going up, the hospitals, homes for 'Fallen Women', lodging-houses for working men, reformatories for delinquent boys. Her evenings might be spent at the opera, but her days had enlarged her sum of knowledge about the reforming work afoot. She was immensely drawn towards, and influenced by, the pioneers of 'Christian socialism': Francis Newman, '*our* own Mr. Newman', as she spoke of him, 'he is so high, and noble, and child-like';[4] F. D. Maurice whose sermons riveted her[5] (she, who was no lover of sermons); Kingsley, whom she called 'my hero'[6] and whose tracts on Christian socialism she circulated among Manchester working-men; and James Martineau, a lifelong friend and fellow lecturer of her husband's at Manchester New College; and, of course, Florence Nightingale, whose work combined every ideal she herself pursued.

Before Florence Nightingale was completely caught up, first in the cholera epidemic and then in the Crimean War, Mrs. Gaskell had an opportunity of meeting her during a fortnight's visit to the Nightingales' home at Lea Hurst, near Matlock, in October 1854. Writing to Catherine Winkworth then of her first impressions of her, she said:

Oh! Katie I wish you could *see* her outside only—. She is tall; very slight and willowy in figure; thick shortish rich brown hair very delicate pretty complexion, rather like Florence's, only more delicate colouring, grey eyes which are generally pensive and drooping, but when they choose can be the merriest eyes I ever saw; and perfect teeth making her smile the sweetest I ever saw. Put a long piece of soft net . . . round this beautiful shaped head, so as to form a soft white framework for the full oval of her face . . . and a black shawl on,—and you may get *near* an idea of her perfect grace and lovely appearance. She is like a saint.[7]

It needed a fortnight's propinquity, and Florence Nightingale's startling theories on the rearing of infants (the desirability of removing them early from the care of their parents and placing them in institutions) to modify somewhat Mrs. Gaskell's first rapturous impressions; where her maternal feelings were roused, not even a saintly spinster could convince her.

[3] *GL* 157, ?27 May 1853.   [4] See *GL* 52–5, Nov. 1849.
[5] See *GL* 47, 170, 172, 203.   [6] *GL* 55, 26 Nov. 1849.
[7] *GL* 211, 11–14 Oct. 1854.

There was, she found, a 'Jar' in Florence's character, a lack, best exemplified by the fact that she had—and sought—no friend.

She stands perfectly alone [Elizabeth confided to Emily Shaen]. . . . She is so excessively soft and gentle in voice, manner, and movement that one never feels the unbendableness of her character when one is near her . . . she and I had a grand quarrel one day. She is, I think, too much for institutions, sisterhoods and associations, and she said if she had influence enough not a mother should bring up a child herself; there would be crèches for the rich as well as the poor. If she had twenty children she would send them all to a crèche . . . That exactly tells of what seems to me *the* want.[8]

Strongly personal as were her judgements on people, Mrs. Gaskell was always curious to know what others thought of them. 'What would Miss Brontë say to Florence Nightingale?' she asked Catherine Winkworth. 'I can't imagine! for *there* is intellect such as I never came in contact with before in woman!—only two in men—great beauty, and of her holy goodness, who is fit to speak?'[9]

Mrs. Gaskell could be prejudiced, as she was over George Eliot's irregular ménage; she could be unappreciative, as she was of Thackeray (her admiration was 'malgré elle'), and she could, frankly, be mistaken; but her judgements were always her own, sharply perceptive, vividly alive, never indifferent.

To record the names of her personal acquaintance—assured friends as most of them became—among contemporary writers, is to list all great reputations of her day. No dull woman—*pace* Mrs. Carlyle—could have caught and held the interest, confidence, and friendship of such men and women. There were Carlyle himself, Dickens, Forster, Thackeray, Darwin, Froude, Kingsley, Charlotte Brontë, Harriet Martineau, Geraldine Jewsbury, Florence Nightingale. While her society was originally sought for her books, the growth and continuance of her friendships was entirely due to her own lively, original, and refreshing character, the quality of her mind, her charm of manner.

She met Harriet Beecher-Stowe on two occasions, and entertained her in Manchester. Stowe's reaction to her seems to have been typical of others: 'She has a very lovely, gentle face, and looks capable of all the pathos that her writings show.'[10]

---

[8] *GL* 217, 27 Oct. 1854.
[9] *GL* 223, 1 Jan. 1855.
[10] Chadwick, *Mrs. Gaskell*, p. 288, quoting Beecher-Stowe, *Sunny Memories of Foreign Lands.*

Of Harriet Beecher-Stowe Mrs. Gaskell herself left a sketch:

Oh! And I saw Mrs. Stowe after all; I saw her twice; but only once to have a good long talk to her; then I was 4 or 5 hours with her, and liked her very much indeed. She is short and American in her manner, but very true and simple and thoroughly unspoiled and unspoilable. She promised (almost *offered*) to stay with us the two days she is allowing herself in Manchester . . . but I don't know if she will, for she is not famous for keeping her engagements . . .[11]

The most notable, and to Mrs. Gaskell grievous, exception amongst her acquaintances was Tennyson, whose works she admired above all other poets of her time, and whom she came so near to meeting while at Windermere in August 1850. She regularly 'begged, borrowed or stealed' his new works as they came out, their expense seldom allowing her to buy a new copy for herself, though one of her characteristic actions was to obtain one for someone else, the Lancashire weaver-poet Samuel Bamford, a poor and proud man whom it was difficult to benefit without offending. Hearing of his devotion to Tennyson's poems, she wrote to Forster to beg his intervention with Tennyson to solicit an autographed copy; a machiavellian enterprise which, in the event, perfectly succeeded, and which afforded her the joy of hurrying herself to Bamford's cottage with the coveted copy. Shortly before her visit to the Shuttleworths on Lake Windermere in the summer of 1850 where she met Charlotte Brontë for the first time, she had been reading the newly published *In Memoriam*—from a copy borrowed from 'an innocent young man' who felt 'honoured' by the request, as she reported to Eliza Fox: 'oh *how* perfect some of them are—I can't leave them to go on to others, and yet I must send it back to-morrow. By dint of coaxing however, I've got Wm to promise he'll *give* it me, so I sing Te Deum.'[12]

Arrived at Windermere, she learnt from her host that Tennyson and his wife were summering on Coniston Water and was promised by Sir James that she should be taken to call on them. Writing to Catherine Winkworth afterwards, she said: 'After dinner we went a drive to Coniston to call on the Tennysons . . . Sir James on the box, Miss B[rontë] and I inside very cozy; but alas it began to rain so we had to turn back without our call being paid, which grieved me sorely and made me cross.'[13] To Eliza Fox she also complained: 'Do you know,' she wrote on 27 August, 'I was as near as possible seeing Tennyson. He and Mrs. are staying at Coniston, and Sir James, Miss B. and I were on the Lake

[11] *GL* 162, 19 June 1853.   [12] *GL* 73, ? July 1850.
[13] *GL* 75, 25 Aug. 1850.

there, when we heard it; and Sir James knows him, and said he would go and call; and then looked up at the sky, and thought it was going to rain, so he didn't. I held my peace, and bit my lips.'[14]

She did not find Charlotte Brontë shared her enthusiasm for Tennyson. What struck Mrs. Gaskell about Charlotte in that first meeting was, among other things, 'the way in which she makes language express her ideas' and 'the admirable use she makes of simple words', and the truth and sincerity of her pronouncements. 'She and I quarrelled and differed about almost everything—she calls me a democrat, and can not bear Tennyson—but we like each other heartily I think and I hope we shall ripen into friends.'[15] Reading *In Memoriam* on her return home to please Mrs. Gaskell, Charlotte wrote her impressions shortly afterwards:

I have read Tennyson's *In Memoriam*, or rather part of it; I closed the book when I had got about half-way. It is beautiful; it is mournful; it is monotonous. Many of the feelings expressed bear . . . the stamp of truth; yet, if Arthur Hallam had been . . . his brother instead of his friend—I should have distrusted this rhymed, and measured, and printed monument of grief. What change the lapse of years may work I do not know; but it seems to me that bitter sorrow, while recent, does not flow out in verse.[16]

Her friendship with Kingsley brought her the acquaintance of J. A. Froude, whose marriage with Mrs. Kingsley's sister, Charlotte Grenfell, caused a small sensation in its time. As the couple were to settle in Manchester, Mrs. Gaskell revelled in the gossip it provoked. 'We are all just now in a state of great curiosity about the Mrs Froude Mr F. is bringing home on Saturday; it is a very romantic story,' Eliza Fox was told in November 1849; 'she was going into a convent when he went away from Oxford . . . but instead of a nunnery she has chosen a marriage,—still she is a strict Puseyite, confesses to a priest, etc.' When seen, Mrs. Froude proved to be 'no heroine-of-romance-looking woman'. 'She is kind-hearted and hearty though, and that's a great deal in this cold world. But I don't know what her age is—and that was a blow.'[17]

Of Froude himself, who had been living in Manchester before his marriage, 'domesticated' with the Gaskells' friends the Darbishires, Mrs. Gaskell drew the following sketch:

If any one under the sun has a magical, magnetic, glamour-like influence, that man has. He's '*aut Mephistophiles aut nihil*', that's what he is. The D.D's all bend

[14] *GL* 79, 27 Aug. 1850.   [15] *GL* 78, 25 Aug. 1850.
[16] Shorter, *The Brontës, Life and Letters* (London, 1908), ii. 164.
[17] *GL* 51, 53, 54, Nov. 1849.

and bow to his will, like reeds before the wind, blow whichever way it listeth.
He smokes cigars constantly. Père Robert, Arthur, Vernon (nay, once even little
Francis), smoke constantly. He disbelieves, they disbelieve; he wears shabby garments, they wear shabby garments; in short, it's the most complete taking away
their own wills and informing them with his own that ever was . . . I stand just
without the circle of his influence; resisting with all my might, but feeling and
seeing the attraction.[18]

The Gaskells duly invited the Froudes on their return from their honeymoon in December 1849: 'My dear Mrs Froude,' wrote Elizabeth to her,
'It will give Mr. Gaskell and myself much pleasure if you and Mr Froude
will come and drink tea with us next Friday but one, (tomorrow week).
Pray get well, and come; though we have nothing to offer you but a very
quiet evening.'[19] The acquaintance once formed ripened into friendship
between the two ladies; Mrs. Froude helped Marianne with her music,
and Mrs. Gaskell was sure enough of Mrs. Froude's sympathy to discuss
with her Charlotte Brontë and her affairs.

The friendship that provided the greatest pleasure, instruction, and
benefit both to Mrs. Gaskell and to Meta, however, was that with Ruskin,
whose tickets for private views, exhibitions, lectures on art (held in Manchester during the Great Masters Exhibition of 1857), together with the
constant inspiration of his books, which Meta devoured with the understanding of an adult, her mother said, were a constant stimulus. The
friendship was not without its problems for Mrs. Gaskell, however,
who knew Ruskin in the first place through his wife, Effie Gray, who had
been a pupil at Miss Byerley's school, though years later than Elizabeth
Stevenson. When the marriage showed signs of breaking up, as it finally
did in 1855, a disagreeable situation arose for Mrs. Gaskell. First hints
of the couple's disagreements came from Eliza Fox as early as 1852. These
were followed by reports from the Nightingales who had been staying
in the same house in the Highlands with the Ruskins and Millais in the
summer of 1853, and who reported Ruskin 'very uneasy' at the conduct
of his wife.

The Nightingales knew the Ruskins [Elizabeth told Catherine Winkworth]—
were staying at some castle in the Highlands with them last year, with them and
Millais. She used to say about 11 am. 'Everett, come and walk with me', and they
were out till dinner time 7 o'clock, Ruskin very uneasy all the time. She used to
come down to *breakfast* with natural flowers in her hair, which he also objected
to but she continued the practice.[20]

[18] *GL* 49, 21 Aug. 1849.   [19] *GL* 58, 6 Dec. 1849.
[20] *GL* 211, 11–14 Oct. 1854.

When Forster finally broke the news of the rupture to Mrs. Gaskell laying the blame heavily on Ruskin, she was unwilling to admit it:

I don't believe one word of what you say about Mr Ruskin. It has given me *great* pain to have the idea, the diabolical idea suggested,—but I think I do know enough of them to assure myself it is not true . . . Now don't think me hard upon her if I tell you what I have *known* of her. She is very pretty very clever,—and very vain. As a girl . . . in Manchester her delight was to add to the list of her offers (27 I think she was *at*, then;) but she never cared for any one of them . . . I don't think she has any more serious faults than vanity and cold-heartedness . . . She really is very close to a charming character; if she had had the small pox she would have been so.

Knowing too much of Ruskin's 'kindness and tenderness and generosity' towards his wife (though admitting 'his bad temper which every body knows'), Mrs. Gaskell never faltered in her defence of his character. 'I can not bear to think of the dreadful hypocrisy if the man who wrote those books is a bad man', she concluded in her argument with Forster.[21]

She seldom missed public events of importance, and travelled up to London with her husband and Meta to visit the Great Exhibition in June 1851. She was uninfluenced, however, by the huge publicity surrounding the event. 'I went 3 times', she told Anne Robson, 'and should never care to go again; but then I'm *not* scientific nor mechanical. Meta and Wm went often, but not enough they say. That's difference of opinion.'[22]

George Smith invited her to see Wellington's funeral from his office windows, but she was prevented from going. Marianne, however, aged seventeen and at school in London, was taken, and with all the accumulated experience of her years, was wholly unimpressed by the spectacle.

. . . you sound tired! [her mother wrote to her after the event] I suppose that makes you so utilitarian and Joseph Humy as you are about the Funeral. You are the only person among all those whom we have heard, who have not felt that the solemn and impressive feelings of admiration excited in so many thousands is worth the money expended, even supposing it had not (as those well acquainted with the dead state of trade etc in London at this time of the year say it has,) given employment to thousands and thousands. As far as I can hear it was a far better way of expressing a nation's feelings than spending money on that great humbug of an Exhibition—a thing [from] which Manchester has not recovered yet.[23]

The meetings with her famous contemporaries were not wholly dependent on her London contacts. By the mid-century, Manchester

[21] *GL* 195, 17 May 1854.   [22] *GL* 101, 1 Sept. 1851.
[23] *GL* 141, 22 Nov. 1852.

was developing a strong cultural life of its own and able to entice north a succession of celebrities to lecture, perform, or exhibit, in the newly completed lecture halls, concert rooms, and theatres of the city. Thus Mrs. Gaskell saw Macready's *Lear*, heard Thackeray, Emerson, and Ruskin in their respective series of lectures; missed none of Dickens's theatrical productions, and lived in the thick of the exhibition of Great Masters of 1857, acting as hostess to a stream of visitors throughout the summer.

On 31 August 1852 the civic authorities gave a 'Banquet to the Guild of Literature and Art' to which all the celebrities were invited—Dickens of course (he flustered Mrs. Gaskell by calling with his wife and Miss Hogarth before 10 o'clock in the morning), Thackeray, Monckton Milnes, Mark Lemon, Charles Knight, etc., etc., as Mrs. Gaskell reported to Marianne in London.[24] Mr. Gaskell had a ticket for the banquet sent him at ten minutes' notice. Other events organized for the following days took place in the Free Library to which Mrs. Gaskell was invited into the seats reserved for Dickens and his party. The heat and want of air, in spite of the room's immense height and size, were, as usual, too much for Mrs. Gaskell and the speeches too long, so that she 'could not attend and wished myself at home many and many a time, my only comfort being seeing the caricatures Thackeray was drawing which were very funny. He and Mr. Monckton Milnes made plenty of fun, till poor Thackeray was called on to speak and broke down utterly, after which he drew no more caricatures.'[25]

Mrs. Gaskell's attitude towards Thackeray was mixed, made up of genuine admiration and fear. From the Storys, who were his close friends, she would never hear anything but good, especially of his genius with children; but she never felt at her ease with him. She herself described her relations with him as dogged by 'ill-luck'. 'Somehow or another,' she told George Smith, after ten years' acquaintance with him, 'my *luck* is against me in any intercourse with him, and being half-Scotch I have a right to be very superstitious; and I have my lucky and unlucky days, and lucky and unlucky people . . . Please to understand how much I admire him, and how I know that somewhere or another he has got a noble and warm self.'[26]

She first met Thackeray in Dickens's drawing room the night of the David Copperfield dinner, on 12 May 1849, and was inevitably thrown in his company on repeated subsequent occasions. In October 1852 he

[24] *GL* 131, 4 Sept. 1852.   [25] Ibid.
[26] *GL* 442, ?1 Oct. 1859.

was invited to give his series of lectures on the English Humourists
in Manchester. They were held in the Athenaeum Rooms on Tuesdays
and Thursdays for three consecutive weeks, and created the expected
stir among Mancunians. Mrs. Gaskell, wishing to give a treat to Annie
and Ellen Green, the Knutsford girls, daughters of her Unitarian
minister there, invited them to stay overnight and took them to the
lectures, for which the Gaskells themselves had season tickets. 'The
lectures are delightful', was Mrs. Gaskell's comment to Marianne.[27]
Thackeray was suitably lionized in Manchester, staying with the
Gaskells' friend, Dr. Scott, the first Principal of the new Owen's College,
where they dined in his company. After he had announced that he was
calling on Mrs. Gaskell in the afternoon of 1 October and failed to come
after all, Mrs. Gaskell declared to Marianne that she was not staying
in any longer to await him.[28] Directly after his visit to Manchester he
was off to America. On his return in the spring of 1853, Mrs. Gaskell,
staying in London, dined on two consecutive occasions in his company,
and was struck how 'gentle and kind and happy he is—he won't hear
a word, or a joke against the Americans: he says they never asked him an
impertinent question,—and are far less censorious and unkind than the
English,—he hopes to return there before long'.[29]

If Mrs. Gaskell was afraid of Thackeray, she was amused to know that
he declared himself to be afraid of Charlotte Brontë. Hearing some of
Charlotte's hottest assaults on his snobbery and love of titles, Mrs.
Gaskell told Forster: 'She gave Mr. Thackeray the benefit of some of
her piercingly keen observation. My word! he had reason when he said
he was afraid of her. But she was very angry indeed with that part of the
Examiner review of Esmond (I had forgotten it) which said his works
would not live.'[30]

Despite Charlotte's strictures—perhaps because of them—no one had
a greater admiration of Thackeray, and when she died Mrs. Gaskell took
it upon herself to write to Thackeray and ask him to condole with old
Mr. Brontë who, she knew, 'had so overbalancing a measure of pride in
his daughter's fame, that a letter of sympathy from T— wd do much
to comfort his grief. He never replied to either of these notes of mine,
nor did he ever write to Mr. Bronte.'[31] Mrs. Gaskell was rather hasty in
her conclusions on the subject, relying too completely on John Greenwood's information, as appears from the existence of a catalogue entry

[27] *GL* 135, 2 Oct. 1852.   [28] *GL* 134a, 1 Oct. 1852.
[29] *GL* 155.   [30] *GL* 161, ? June 1853.
[31] *GL* 442, ?1 Oct. 1859.

for a letter from Thackeray to Mr. Brontë once owned by the Brontë Parsonage Museum.

Mrs. Gaskell was unfortunate in angering Thackeray considerably by the freedom with which she quoted Charlotte Brontë's comments on him in the *Life*. He considered that she had no right to publicize opinions expressed in a private correspondence, and he made his feelings felt.[32] 'Why should his mocking tongue so perversely deny the better feelings of his better moods?' Charlotte had asked her friend; and deploring his 'indolence', declared 'Mr. Thackeray is easy and indolent, and seldom cares to do his best'.[33] What man in public life but would resent such comment?

Whether Mrs. Gaskell knew of his displeasure, or that she feared his sarcasm generally, she declined publishing under his editorship when George Smith invited her to contribute to his new periodical, the *Cornhill Magazine*, whose opening number appeared on 1 January 1860, and whose first editor was Thackeray. Replying to Smith's astonished query about her reasons, she wrote back: '. . . my only feeling about not doing any thing you ask me for the Magazine is because I don't think Thackeray would ever quite like it, and yet you know it would be under his supervision.'[34]

She reverted to the subject a little later when Smith brought it up again at the end of the year (December 1859). She admitted to having a story 'Begun and I *think* good; intended for C.M. [*Cornhill Magazine*]; but delayed because of extreme dislike to writing for Mr. T.'.[35] In the event, Smith was able to prevail upon her and her story, 'Curious If True', appeared in the second, February issue of the magazine; apparently without strictures from Thackeray.

Thackeray's daughter Anne, later Lady Ritchie, recalled a very pleasant evening in June 1862 when Mrs. Gaskell dined at her father's house in Kensington on the occasion of one of her visits to London, 'talking to him in the big dining-room at Palace Green, looking up laughing, inquiring, responding, gay, yet definite, such is the impression I have of her presence'.[36] Between the Gaskell girls and Thackeray's daughters a friendship, initiated during visits to Paris, ripened in time to a permanent relationship, dispelling any rumour, if it once existed,

---

[32] Gordon Ray, *The Letters and Private Papers of William Makepeace Thackeray* (London, 1945), vol. i, p. xciv n.

[33] *Life of Charlotte Brontë*, Everyman edn., pp. 304–5, 328, 335–6, 352–3, 376–7, 381.

[34] *GL* 442.   [35] *GL* 451a, 23 Dec. 1859.

[36] Chadwick, *Mrs. Gaskell*, pp. 402–3, quoting Lady Ritchie, *Chapters from Some Memoirs* (London, 1894).

of a coolness between the famous authors. There was nothing but generous sympathy in Mrs. Gaskell's feelings when news of the sudden death of Thackeray at Christmas 1863 reached her, and she wrote at once to George Smith: 'We were so glad to hear a word or two of the poor Miss Thackerays from your note to-day. How desolate they must be? What are their plans? or have they any yet?'[37]

While Mrs. Gaskell wrote unashamedly for money, it was never her first consideration. She had to write 'out of the fulness of the heart', or not at all. Sentiment dictated her motions, in private or professional life, and she deeply pitied other women writers, like her contemporary Dinah Mulock (Mrs. Craik) for the obligation to write for subsistence. 'I wish she had some other means of support besides writing', she said of her to a friend. 'I think it bad in it's effect upon her writing, which must be pumped up instead of bubbling out, and very bad for her health, poor girl.'[38] But once her own books had been conceived and produced, she thought it no shame to secure as good a price for them as possible. She was too much a North Country woman for that. Her exchanges with her publishers are there to show how forthright she could be on the subject of payment, and on the whole, she considered herself fairly dealt with. Only once, at the end of her career, when she was finding the serialization of *Wives and Daughters* for the *Cornhill* a longer and harder task than she had reckoned, and applied to Smith for a higher fee, was she dissatisfied. His refusal reached her at a peculiarly trying time of overwork and frustration in finding the house of her choice; but what envenomed the situation was her discovery that Smith, while refusing her request, had just agreed to pay Wilkie Collins £5,000 for a new story for *Cornhill* (the eventual *Armadale* that appeared during 1866). Mrs. Gaskell's reaction to this news raises the whole question of her earning powers as compared with those of her successful contemporaries. Wilkie Collins could command a higher price than she could, even after the great successes of her career, *Cranford* and the *Life of Charlotte Brontë*; and yet, compared even with Trollope (not so popular then as now) the prices she could command were uniformly high. Trollope kept minute records of his earnings, and while his career as a novelist covered thirty-odd years and his *total* earnings, including all reprints of his books, reached the respectable sum of nearly £70,000—a 'comfortable but not splendid' result as he himself viewed it—he did not command a price greatly superior to Mrs. Gaskell's £2,000 for *Wives and Daughters*. Only three

[37] *GL* 545, 1 Jan. 1864.   [38] *GL* 105, 29 Oct. 1851.

of the novels he had published by 1864 brought him £3,000 or more, and in his beginnings he had accepted even less than the £100 paid to the unknown author of *Mary Barton*; he received £20 in two payments for *The Warden*.[39] Setting aside the 'giants' of the day, Dickens and Thackeray, who could command £12,000 apiece for a new work, the only contemporary author who rapidly outstripped both Mrs. Gaskell and Trollope in the price-race was George Eliot, who quickly soared from £800 for *Adam Bede* in 1859, and £1,760 for *Silas Marner* in the first year of its publication, to £7,000 for *Romola* in 1862.[40] George Eliot's advantage over her sister novelist was in having Lewes as her business manager, who secured the best possible conditions for her, including the reservation of her copyrights.

With Trollope, Thackeray's successor as editor of the *Cornhill*, Mrs. Gaskell seems never to have made personal contact, despite opportunities and her enormous pleasure in his books. 'I wish Mr. Trollope would go on writing Framley Parsonage [then appearing in the *Cornhill*] for ever', she wrote to George Smith in March 1860. 'I don't see any reason why it should ever come to an end, and every one I know is always dreading the *last* number. I hope he will make the jilting of Griselda a long while a-doing.'[41]

With Trollope's brother, Thomas Adolphus, who had settled in Florence, she was more fortunate, and established a delightful holiday relationship with him and his wife in the course of her second Italian trip, in May/June 1863. 'Both he and his wife completely won possession of our hearts in Florence,' she told a correspondent to whom she gave a letter of introduction to Trollope, 'and I am so glad to think of any friends of mine succeeding to the pleasure of our intercourse at the Villino Trollope.'[42]

Disappointed of a first meeting with Mrs. Browning, on whom she had the ill luck to call in Florence on the very day news of her father's death reached her (22 April 1857),[43] Mrs. Gaskell certainly met her on a subsequent occasion—possibly in London on one of the Brownings' visits to England; at any rate, by March 1859, she could send them messages as to old acquaintances through Eliza Fox, whose marriage in Rome the Brownings had graced. 'How come the Brownings in Rome?' Mrs. Gaskell asked Eliza, 'Will you give my very kindest regards to her, and

[39] See Trollope's *Autobiography*, ch. 20.
[40] Gordon Haight, *George Eliot, A Biography* (Oxford, 1968), p. 341.
[41] *GL* 456, 1 Mar. 1860.   [42] *GL* 527, 16 July ?1863.
[43] *The Letters of* C. E. *Norton*, i. 168.

my kind regards to him. (I liked her better than him; perhaps for the reason that . . . he fell asleep while I was talking to him).'[44] Because of the Brownings' residence abroad, no very close contacts could be established; and Mrs. Browning's death in 1861 put an end to any further chance of meetings. To Norton, who had shared Mrs. Gaskell's abortive attempt to call, she wrote on receiving the news: 'Oh! *were* you not sorry about Mrs. Browning's death! I wrote to Mr Story to enquire all particulars and it seems he wrote me a full account; but the letter is lost so I know little more than the bare fact.'[45]

The biggest, and most regrettable, omission in Mrs. Gaskell's contacts with her fellow writers was with George Eliot, with whom she had most in common and from whose intellect she had most to gain. From the first anonymous appearance of George Eliot's works, Elizabeth Gaskell had expressed enthusiastic admiration for them. Captivated at once by the truth and pathos of *Scenes of Clerical Life*, appearing in *Blackwood's* during 1857, she wrote to Norton in delight: 'They are a discovery of my own, and I am so proud of them. *Do* read them.'[46] She instantly recognized the quality of *Adam Bede* when it appeared, still anonymously, two years later, and sought excuse for her own delay in beginning the new book promised George Smith (*Sylvia's Lovers*) in the discouragement provoked by such rival perfection: 'I think I have a feeling that it is not worth while trying to write, while there are such books as Adam Bede and Scenes from Clerical Life—I set "Janet's Repentence" above all, still', she wrote again to Norton.[47] Learning that she herself was suspected of being the unknown author of the books, she wrote a whimsical disclaimer to the true author in June 1859 who, she had mistakenly learned by then, sheltered behind the pseudonym 'Gilbert Elliot'.

Dear Mr. 'Gilbert Elliott',

Since I came up from Manchester to London I have had the greatest compliment paid me I ever had in my life, I have been suspected of having written 'Adam Bede'. I have hitherto denied it; but really I think, that as you want to keep your real name a secret, it would be very pleasant for me to blush acquiescence. Will you give me leave?

Well! if I had written Amos Barton, Janet's Repentence and Adam Bede I should neither be to have nor to hold with pride and delight in myself—so

[44] *GL* 421, 21 Mar. 1859.
[45] *GL* 493, 28 Aug. 1861.
[46] *GL* 384, 7 Dec. 1857.
[47] *GL* 444, 25 Oct. 1859.

I think it is very well I have not ... So, although to my friends I am known under the name of Mrs. Gaskell, to you I will confess that I *am* the author of Adam Bede, and remain very respectfully and gratefully,

Yours

Gilbert Elliott.[48]

Her unqualified admiration was tempered by regret when George Eliot's true identity began to leak out, and the books were ascribed to 'Miss Evans', whose liaison with Lewes had caused a sensation in its day, and which did, in the opinion of Mrs. Gaskell, 'so jar against the beautiful book'. Mrs. Gaskell could but hope that the report was not true. While maintaining that *Adam Bede* was 'a noble grand book, whoever wrote it', she pleaded with George Smith to deny the rumour. 'Oh, do say Miss Evans did not write it', she cried.[49]

Because of her dislike of the idea of Miss Evans's authorship, Mrs. Gaskell fell into the trap set by the partisans of the imposter Liggins, who claimed to have written both books, and had in the end to eat very humble pie in penance for her gullibility. *Adam Bede*, she had to accept at last, was the work of Marian Evans. What hurt and perplexed Elizabeth Gaskell was not just the fact that Marian Evans lived out of wedlock with a married man, whose record had not been of the most savoury, but with *such* a man as Lewes. '*How came she to like Mr. Lewes so much?* . . . so soiled for a woman like her to fancy', she asked George Smith outright.[50] When the fact could no longer be denied, she bowed her head to the inevitable, and with what philosophy—and charity—she might, answered Smith:

I was very much obliged to you for sending us so much about Mrs. Lewes? (what do people call her,—) Do you know I can't help liking her,—*because* she wrote those books. Yes I do! I *have* tried to be moral, and dislike her and dislike her books—but it won't do. There is not a wrong word, or a wrong thought in them, I do believe,—and though I should have been more 'comfortable' for some indefinable reason, if a *man* had written them instead of a *woman*, yet I think the author must be a noble creature; and I shut my eyes to the awkward blot in her life.[51]

Whatever Mrs. Gaskell's moral principles, they were not strong enough to prevail against her sense of beauty; she wrote to George Eliot herself a letter whose sincerity and frankness did not fail to touch the recipient and to elicit an answer equally frank and generous in return. The letter

[48] *GL* 431, 3 June 1859.   [49] *GL* 438, 4 Aug. 1859.
[50] *GL* 446, 2 Nov. 1859.   [51] *GL* 451, 30 Nov. 1859.

from Mrs. Gaskell was written from Whitby in November 1859 at the
time she was planning *Sylvia's Lovers*.

My dear Madam,
   Since I heard from authority, that you were the author of Scenes from 'Clerical
Life' and 'Adam Bede', I have read them again; and I must, once more, tell you
how earnestly fully, and humbly I admire them. I never read anything so complete, and beautiful in fiction, in my whole life before . . . Perhaps you may have
heard that I upheld Mr Liggins as the author for long,—I did it on evidence
. . . He is a regular rascal. But I never was such a goose as to believe that such
books as yours could be a mosaic of real and ideal. I should not be quite true in
my ending, if I did not say before I concluded that I wish you *were* Mrs. Lewes.
However that can't be helped, as far as I can see, and one must not judge others.
Once more, thanking you most gratefully for having written all—Janet's
Repentence perhaps most especially of all . . . Believe me to remain,
                                   Yours respectfully, E. C. Gaskell.[52]

   With admirable self-restraint George Eliot replied by return of post:

My dear Madam,
   . . . your letter, which has brought me the only sort of help I care to have—
an assurance of fellow-feeling, of thorough truthful recognition from one of the
minds which are capable of judging as well as of being moved . . . I shall always
love to think that one woman wrote another such sweet encouraging words—
still more to think that you were the writer and I the receiver.
   I had indulged the idea that if my books turned out to be worth much, you
would be among my willing readers; for I was conscious . . . that my feeling
towards Life and Art had some affinity with the feeling which had inspired
'Cranford' and the earlier chapters of 'Mary Barton' . . . [Describing how she
read *Mary Barton* during a trip up the Rhine to compensate for a spell of bad
weather, George Eliot concluded] I tell you these slight details because they will
prove to you that your letter must have a peculiar value for me . . .
                                   Yours with high regard, Marian Evans Lewes.[53]

   The same day George Eliot wrote to Mrs. Gaskell, she wrote to her
regular correspondent, Sara Hennell, to tell her of Mrs. Gaskell's letter,
and said: 'Very sweet and noble words they are that she has written me.
I wanted you to know that good of her.' The friends of George Eliot had
taken offence at Mrs. Gaskell's initial belief in the imposter Liggins.
   Despite the contact established, and the genuine regard for each other,
no attempt at a meeting seems to have been made between the two

women. Opportunities cannot have been lacking on the occasions of Mrs. Gaskell's journeys to London, and it must be supposed that 'the awkward blot' in Mrs. Lewes's life precluded the possibility of social intercourse. It was a form of ostracism to which George Eliot was well accustomed—none but men ever visited her—and she did not, apparently, judge Mrs. Gaskell any more harshly than the rest. The loss to both of them, however, can only be measured by the degree of their mutual appreciation. If, in her social dealings, Mrs. Gaskell outwardly subscribed to the prejudices of the day, it was not without inward rebellion; her words to Smith on the subject were not those of a Philistine, but of a writer for whom there were standards of value other than those of the Mosaic Law: 'I have tried to be moral,' she wrote, 'but I can't help liking her—because she wrote those books.'

As has been seen, Mrs. Gaskell travelled extensively abroad, visiting France, Germany, Switzerland, and Italy on repeated occasions. Through Norton she gained insights into the American way of life, on which she continually questioned him. When the Civil War broke out she became an ardent partisan of the North. Her on-the-spot comments on public events, like the death of the Prince Consort in November 1861, and the murder of Lincoln in 1865, remind us how caught up she was in the dramas of her day. 'Every one here is in *deep* mourning', she wrote to Marianne of the reaction in Manchester to the Prince Consort's death. 'Such sad national grief I never saw. No one wishes each other a *merry* Xmas this year—as if by one common consent every one says "the compliments of the season, and a happy new year".'[54] On reading of the President's murder, she wrote at once to Norton:

My heart burnt within me with indignation and grief,—we could think of nothing else,—but we *could* hardly talk of *that*—and all night long we had only snatches of sleep, wakening up perpetually to the sense of a great shock and grief. *Every* one is feeling the same. I never knew so universal a feeling. I hope you will hear of the deep national sympathy by this mail.[55]

In all Mrs. Gaskell's career no single achievement brought her the acknowledgement of her fellow writers so completely as did her *Life of Charlotte Brontë*, despite the troubles it provoked. With that work, in the opinion of her compeers, she reached the front rank among the writers of her age. Whether published in the press or voiced privately, there was only one opinion of the book's artistic excellence. If her objective had been to justify the author of *Jane Eyre*—a book that had

[54] *GL* 496, 26 Dec. 1861.   [55] *GL* 569, 28 Apr. 1865.

in its time been pilloried as 'lacking in a humble spirit', as showing
'a rebellious spirit', when not considered positively 'irreligious'—she
was rewarded by the complete change in outlook by such men as Kingsley,
who wrote to her after reading the *Life*:

Let me renew our long interrupted acquaintance by complimenting you on poor
Miss Bronte's *Life*. You have had a delicate and a great work to do, and you have
done it admirably . . . *Jane Eyre* I hardly looked into . . . *Shirley* disgusted me
at the opening, and I gave up the writer and her books with a notion that she was
a person who liked coarseness. How I misjudged her! and how thankful I am
that I never put a word of my misconceptions into print, or recorded my mis-
judgments of one who is a whole heaven above me. Well have you done your
work, and given us the picture of a valiant woman made perfect by suffering.
I shall now read carefully and lovingly every word she has written.[56]

Kingsley spoke for the virtuous in Victorian society. In the world of
letters no opinion bore more weight than that of Lewes—long noted for
his savagery and feared and deferred to by all for his critiques in the
Westminster Review—and when Mrs. Gaskell received a personal letter
from him of unqualified praise, she must indeed—irrespective of her
dislike, her avoidance of reviews, her natural modesty—have regarded
it as the consecration of her career. Lewes wrote her from the Scilly
Isles on 15 April 1857:

I have just finished your 'life of Charlotte Bronte'—which has afforded exquisite
delight to my evenings . . . If I had any public means of expressing my high sense
of the skill, delicacy and artistic power of your Biography, I should not trouble
you with this note. . . . The book will, I think, create a deep and permanent
impression; for it not only presents a vivid picture of a life noble and sad, full of
encouragement and healthy teaching, a lesson in duty and selfreliance, it also,
thanks to its artistic power, makes us familiar inmates of an interior so strange,
so original . . . so picturesque . . . that fiction has nothing more wild, touching
and heart-strengthening to place above it. The early part is a triumph for you;
the rest a monument for your friend.[57]

The book had brought her tribulation enough, but whether she realized
it fully or no, in the opinion of those best qualified to judge, she had,
in writing it, produced one of the masterpieces of the century.

[56] Shorter, *The Brontës, Life and Letters*, i. 10–11.
[57] Haight, *The George Eliot Letters*, ii. 315–16.

CHAPTER XXI

MR. GASKELL

MRS. GASKELL never left anyone, friends or readers, in any doubt that she considered motherhood to be woman's most enviable fulfilment; and in her own case, certainly, her most rewarding joy. To her, child-bearing was in itself an exalting experience. For her tragic heroines—Mary Barton, Ruth, Lizzie Leigh, Sylvia Robson—the ultimate consolation she could offer was in motherhood. For Ruth indeed motherhood was the way to redemption.

Few women have written more tenderly, whether in fiction or in letters, about young children, or with a closer sense of their physical presence. One recalls Ruth placing Miss Benson's finger in the 'little red fist' of her new-born child: 'That baby-touch called out her love; the doors of her heart were thrown open wide for the little infant to go in and take possession.'[1] One recalls, in the early letters, the description of Marianne aged eighteen months 'at the very tip-top of bliss' at Sandle-bridge, staggering about in the field 'with a great big nosegay in each hand and wanting to be *bathed* in the golden bushes of wallflowers'.[2]

Commensurate with the joy of giving life was the extremity of grief in losing a child. It happened to her twice, and was 'the enduring agony'.

Happily, with four children to bring up, she had no lack of objects for her love and, as they evolved, of companions to share in her active life. Her liberal views and benevolent training, at a time when repressive measures towards the young were generally recommended, deservedly won her the devotion and confidence of all her daughters. There built up between them a quite exceptional relationship of shared tastes and interests, enthusiasms and friendships, as appeared particularly in their common fondness for Charles Norton. It was to him that, in a little burst of feeling, she wrote in January 1860 when the youngest was already fourteen: 'My girls, my darlings, *are* such comforts—such happiness! Everyone so good and healthy and bright. I don't know what I should

[1] *Ruth*, 160.   [2] *GL* 4, May 1836.

do if any one of them married; and yet it is constantly a wonder to me that no one ever gives them a chance.'[3]

In speaking of marriage, her own or other people's, Mrs. Gaskell was noticeably more reticent. One recalls her words in relating the return from honeymoon of Charlotte Brontë and her husband: 'Henceforward the sacred doors of home are closed upon her married life. We, her loving friends standing outside, caught occasional glimpses of brightness, and pleasant peaceful murmurs of sound, telling of the gladness within.'[4] Physical love was not a subject of discussion for Victorian ladies, and Mrs. Gaskell's own great reticence and hatred of anything approaching indiscretion, precluded her from discussing her personal relationship with her husband, even with her closest friends. The result has been that because these relations are less well documented than those with her children, an element of doubt as to her happiness has crept in to the judgement of posterity, without there existing a shade of evidence to substantiate it. The marriage has been represented as a detached partnership between two very dissimilar people.

Since none of her letters to him has been preserved, and only one of his to her, it is almost impossible at this distance of time to determine the truth. The destruction of the letters, however, need not, of itself, denote anything to hide, but simply a reflection of the daughters' compliance with the mother's wish to thwart all prospective biographers. But if the words of husband and wife and their manner of speaking to each other are lost to us (he addressed her in the only extant letter, dating from 1860, as 'Dearest Lily') there remain the records of their actions, which appear eloquent enough of lasting love.

Different as they were by nature and training—he reflective and cautious, she impulsive and temperamental—and inevitable as the conflicts arising from such constitutional differences of outlook may have been, there is no trace in her many allusions to him of any fundamental disharmony. The frankness and humour with which she often, when writing to his sisters or her close friend Eliza Fox, commented on his oddities—the oddities of an anxious over-scrupulous, unworldly man— are the best indication that she had no greater cause for complaint.

Time inevitably works changes and emphasizes disparities of character, just as first love dispels them, and makes relationships complicated that appeared so simple in the early euphoria of the first exchanges. Both husband and wife were bound to experience this, like the majority of

---

[3] *GL* 453, 19 Jan. 1860.
[4] *Life of Charlotte Brontë*, Everyman edn., p. 395.

men and women. Mrs. Gaskell showed her personal knowledge of such changes and her acceptance of them in a passage in *Sylvia's Lovers* where, exceptionally for her, she discusses marriage:

> . . . it is an old story, an ascertained fact, that, even in the most tender and stable masculine natures, at the supremest seasons of their lives, there is room for other thoughts and passions than such as are connected with love. Even with the most domestic and affectionate men, their emotions seem to be kept in a cell, distinct and away from their actual lives.[5]

It may not be fortuitous that this book, written between 1860 and 1862, was the only one that Mrs. Gaskell dedicated to her husband.

That they started their married life deeply in love their honeymoon letters to their respective families sufficiently attest. Why should they not? They were both young, good-looking, and exceptionally gifted. They shared a love of natural beauty and an outdoor life; of poetry, music, and all the arts; and a common purpose of service to their fellow-men. They were convinced liberals, followers of John Bright. Both had genuinely sympathetic natures, as well as conscientious ones, and felt for the poor as well as wishing to improve them.

There is no evidence whatever to suggest that Mr. Gaskell under-estimated his wife's rich talents or sought to relegate her to the domestic domain before the birth of their children. On the contrary, it is evident that, despite his own superior learning and university training, he regarded her as his partner in preparing his lecture programmes for working men's classes, and in this respect he may be said to have dis-covered her talent and to have been the first to encourage her.

It was Mr. Gaskell, it has to be remembered, who urged her to write *Mary Barton* when grief for the loss of her baby son had brought her very low. It showed the truest insight into the needs of her romantic and imaginative nature that he realized how much her absorption in the charac-ters and incidents of her tale would divert her feelings from their present, and real source of sorrow. *Mary Barton* is a sad enough tale and she suffered in writing it, but it assuaged her personal sorrow. As will be remembered, when the tale had aroused the interest of William Howitt, Mr. Gaskell accompanied his wife to London at Christmas 1847 to support her during the negotiations for publication with Chapman, and both were perfectly satisfied by the £100 offered by Chapman for the copyright. There was no thought, as yet, of her writing as an additional source of income; she still regarded her gift for story-telling as a service

---

[5] *Sylvia's Lovers*, pp. 377–8.

to be rendered her fellow men. It was Dickens with his repeated requests to her for contributions to *Household Words* who put her work upon a professional footing. The steady rise in the prices she could command over the next fifteen years from the initial £100 for *Mary Barton* to £500 for *Ruth*, £800 for the *Life of Charlotte Brontë*, £1,000 agreed by George Smith for *Sylvia's Lovers* before even a word of the book had been written, to the £2,000 paid in advance by him for the seven-year copyright of *Wives and Daughters*, sufficiently shows her growing potential as an author and the financial independence that it secured her.

It was not 'independence', however, that she sought in the sense of a separate provision for herself. The money she earned was, on every occasion, used for the benefit of the family. While the girls were at school, it was to procure them first-class teachers for extra lessons: Italian singing-masters for Marianne, or drawing lessons with Ruskin for Meta. It provided the long summer holidays at Silverdale, or as they grew up trips abroad. Her earnings allowed her to dress well, to dress her daughters and develop their taste in dress, to accept invitations to country houses, to travel on business or pleasure to London or Edinburgh, the Lakes or Wales. None of these things could have been afforded on Mr. Gaskell's salary.

Much has been made by various biographers of Mrs. Gaskell's half-comic account of her husband's 'buttoning up' the cheque for £20 she received for 'Lizzie Leigh' in April 1850,[6] as though it were a regular habit of his. Such comments only show ignorance of the financial position of women at the time. As a married woman, Mrs. Gaskell could not open a bank account in her own name; any sums made payable to her, by money order or by cheques, had necessarily to be paid into her husband's account and he alone could withdraw them. That Mrs. Gaskell had the disposal of her earnings, particularly as they dramatically increased, is clear from the correspondence, where her arrangements with publishers, and her applications for advance royalties for specific purposes, such as holidays abroad, are fully recorded. Her request to George Smith to arrange for Circular Notes to be available for her Roman holiday was in fact met by Mr. Gaskell by arrangement with his bank.

Her independence in fact prompted a mock complaint from Mr. Gaskell to the M.P. William Fox, Eliza's father, when he begged him to introduce a Bill in Parliament 'to protect *husbands* against wives who will spend all their earnings'.[7] The sally was *à propos* of the petition then

---

[6] *GL* 70, Apr. 1850.
[7] *GL* 276, Jan. 1856.

in process of being drawn up for presentation to Parliament, to protect married women's property, to which all the women writers of the day subscribed. Mrs. Gaskell did not think the petition would do much good: 'I don't think it is very definite, and *pointed* . . . a husband can coax, wheedle, beat or tyrannize his wife out of something and no law whatever will help this that I see . . . so though I don't see the definite end proposed by these petitions I'll sign.'[8]

She was so little militant by nature as to wish sometimes that her own role in life was more clearly apparent to her. Even after the success of *Mary Barton* she was still questioning what she ought to do in life. 'I long (weakly) for the old times where right and wrong did not seem such complicated matters,' she confided to Tottie Fox; 'and I am sometimes coward enough to wish that we were back in the darkness where obedience was the only seen duty of women. Only even then I don't believe William would ever have *commanded* me.'[9] A very revealing comment, surely, on their mutual relations.

That Mr. Gaskell was 'canny' in the Scots sense of the word, is very probable; it was a part of his cautious character. His own Spartan and sober habits were well suited to his pocket. He had no expensive tastes, preferring a supper of bread and milk after a long evening's lecturing to a large dinner. But it is also plainly apparent that he was immensely generous of his intellectual endowments, never counting the cost in personal fatigue for his missionary and educational work. It is also evident that he did not impose his own ascetic tastes on his lively wife and daughters.

Apart from their love for their children, husband and wife were drawn together all through their married life by participation in each other's work. She participated in his social work, giving classes for working girls in her own home one Sunday in every month, visiting the poor of his parish, and when the emergency of the Cotton Famine arose, immersing herself totally in the organization of relief. His involvement in her work absorbed an increasing amount of his time, as her writing became a regular feature of their life. It was Mr. Gaskell who, in addition to acting as her agent and banker over the financial arrangements with her publishers, acted as proof-reader of her books[10] and magazine contributions as they went through the press, especially in the early days. Purist as he was, he frequently found as much to correct in her spelling as in the printers' errors. After the publication of *Mary Barton*, he gave

8 *GL* 276, Jan. 1856.   9 *GL* 69, Apr. 1850.
10 *GL* 235, 25 Apr. 1855.

a couple of lectures on the Lancashire dialect used in the book, wishing to make it better understood to readers outside Lancashire. The lectures were subsequently published. Sending Walter Savage Landor a complimentary copy, Mrs. Gaskell said:

May I venture to send you a copy of my husband's Lectures on The Lancashire Dialect? I am not sure if his modesty would sanction this act of mine if he were at home; but, once done, I know that he would feel gratified by the thought that you had read them.

He was, she later went on to explain, 'proud of his county, likes to consider these remnants of the old strong language as peculiar to Lancashire and the Yorkshire Dales'.[11] He was obviously pleased that his wife became so distinctly a regional writer, at home in the dialect of his adopted county. During the writing of *Sylvia's Lovers* and the indecision over the title—whether to call it *Philip's Idol*, *Monkshaven*, or *The Specksioneer*—she wrote in reply to George Smith's evident hesitation to accept the last because of its unpronounceability, 'Mr. Gaskell says if you will come and pay him a visit of a week he will undertake to teach you how to pronounce "Specksioneer" before the end of that time'.[12]

Mr. Gaskell played a major part in the threatened libel action following the publication of her *Life of Charlotte Brontë* in the spring of 1857. The entire onus of dealing with Lady Scott's solicitors and in engaging William Shaen to represent his wife's interests fell on him. On leaving home, suspecting no such eventuality but dreading the reviews, she had asked that no mention of her book be forwarded to her during her holiday. Keeping strictly to the letter of her instructions, Mr. Gaskell refrained from all communication on the subject, waiting for her expected arrival in Paris on the return journey to break the news to her. He had, on Shaen's advice, agreed to the total retraction of Mrs. Gaskell's statements regarding Lady Scott and Branwell Brontë. She accepted what he had done as right and unavoidable.

Where the differences in temperaments and tastes between husband and wife began to tell was with the alteration in style of living forced on her by her growing reputation. Inevitably, as she became widely known, and her charm and liveliness made her eagerly sought after, she had to accept invitations which he, increasingly, shunned. Except among those he loved—and he was devoted to his brothers and sisters, old college friends like James Martineau, the Potters, and some of his clerical

---

[11] *GL* 196 and 197, May 1854.
[12] *GL* 501, Mar. 1862.

colleagues—he was not sociable, preferring an evening at home among his books to accompanying his wife to parties.

Among the unavoidable sources of friction, like this growing unsociability which was partly due to fatigue, was the very nature of his work which occupied not only the regular hours common to all men but absorbed much of his leisure time too. When the number and variety of Mr. Gaskell's regular commitments are considered, it becomes plain how little of his time was left for his family. This was often hard for his wife to bear. The burden of his work inevitably affected his health and spirits and made him difficult at home. At such times she might well have felt that a less dedicated man would be easier to live with. Within a few years of their marriage, the number and nature of his appointments were trebled at the least, without a measurable increase of income. Despite his wife's goodness and charity, it is understandable and excusable if, on occasions, she resented the exploitation of his time and talents.[13]

His appointment in August 1828 at the age of twenty-three as assistant minister to Mr. Robberds at Cross Street Unitarian Chapel carried with it the normal routine as visiting preacher to outlying congregations, and as teacher in the Sunday Schools. To this was added in 1836 his quite voluntary work as lecturer to the working men's evening classes at the Mechanics' Institute,[14] which soon spread from Manchester to the outlying centres.[15] Meanwhile he contributed no fewer than seventy-nine hymns (many translated from the German) to Beard's *Collection of Hymns*, 1837. In 1840, when Manchester New College for the training of Unitarian ministers returned from York to Manchester, he was immediately appointed secretary to the Board of Governors, and concurrently appointed lecturer in English Literature, History, Composition, and Logic, while his principal, Mr. Robberds, was appointed lecturer in Hebrew, Syriac, and Chaldaic languages. A fellow minister of his who was later to be his own assistant, the Revd. James Drummond, was appointed professor in theology at the college.

While the Unitarians' strongest appeal was directed to the growing ranks of educated liberal-minded men, they could not as yet hope to reach the labouring illiterate masses. To supply this want the social reformer John Owens left his estate, at his death in 1846, for the foundation of a college affording educational facilities open to all—the foundation that came to be called Owen's College, opened in 1851. The appeal to Mr. Gaskell to contribute was instantly met, and he became one of the

---

[13] *GL* 570, May 1865.   [14] *GL* 9, 10, 11, July, Aug. 1838.
[15] *GL* 11, 12, Aug. 1838.

earliest lecturers. His opening address, as he was reminded at the commemoration celebration of his fifty years ministry in 1878, referred not only to Greek classical authors, but quoted texts in the original tongue. It was, as he soon learnt, a discourse somewhat above the heads of his audience.[16] He was not long in finding the right level, however, and he became one of the most liked and listened to of Manchester lecturers. As his students remembered, he was 'a master of literature, . . . Our literary evenings under Mr. Gaskell were ambrosial evenings indeed.'[17]

Several of Mr. Gaskell's and the Revd. James Martineau's sermons were collected into a volume for publication, which give an opportunity of seeing him at his clerical, as opposed to his academical, avocations. While he spoke with great care and feeling for words, there is none of the unction or pomposity so general at the time in the utterances of the clergy of the Establishment, and his message to his congregations was full of cheerfulness and hope. Typical of his own outlook is the tribute he paid to his friend, John Robberds, when he preached the latter's funeral sermon: speaking of his 'bright and cheerful mind', he said, 'Religion with him was not something to cover the earth with a cloud, but was "the light of life"'.[18]

In 1853 Manchester New College moved yet again,[19] this time to London, where it remained until 1870, when it moved finally to Oxford. To replace its work as a training centre for Dissenters in Manchester, the Unitarian Home Missionary Board was founded in 1854 by Mr. Gaskell's close friend, Dr. Beard. Mr. Gaskell was immediately appointed to its teaching staff as lecturer in English Literature and New Testament Greek. It was he who voiced the objective of the Board in an opening address, as aiming at 'the education of young men for the work of diffusing the Gospel among the poor, the untaught and neglected'.[20] In its beginnings the Board had no premises of its own and the work of the governing committee and the lectures were held at the lecturers' homes, Mr. Gaskell's students attending him at Plymouth Grove three days a week for four hours each time. The Board offered a three-year course, of two terms a year. Only in 1857 did the Board find premises of its own

---

[16] H. McLachlan, *The Unitarian Home Missionary College* (London and Manchester, 1915).

[17] Chadwick, *Mrs. Gaskell*, p. 210.

[18] *A Sermon on Occasion of the Death the Rev. John Gooch Robberds* (London, 1854; copy in a bound volume of 'Sermons and Addresses by James Martineau and William Gaskell' in the library of Manchester College, Oxford).

[19] See V. D. Davis, *A History of Manchester College* (London, 1932).

[20] H. McLachlan, op. cit., p. 29.

in very insanitary rooms at the top of a warehouse in Marsden Square. Eventually, in 1874, Mr. Gaskell succeeded Dr. Beard as the Board's Principal. He retired only a few months before his death in 1884. He had been tutor for thirty years, and Principal for ten.

In addition to his tutorial work with these various bodies, he was joint-editor, with two assistants, of the *Unitarian Herald*, a weekly paper published at one penny, to which he contributed regularly and supplied many of the book reviews.

His wife wrote of this accumulation of burdens and their effect on him to his sister Anne Robson, in the last year of her life. Clearly resigned by then to William's oddities as something that could not be changed and had to be accepted, she wrote

Everybody *here* wants him to take more holidays, and everybody *there* (away from home) wants him to come to them; but it is almost impossible to push, pull, or stir him from home . . . He has his 3 days (of 4 hours each,) at the Home Mission-Board,—and that is in a very close room which (*I* should say) added to the fatigue. However the Memorial Hall will be opened in August, where he will have a good-sized and well-ventilated room. Once a week he goes down to lecture at the Owen's College—for the six *winter and bad-weather* months of the year. That takes up two long hours; and on a Monday too which is often a hard day with committees etc, but you might as well ask St. Pauls to tumble down, as entreat him to give up this piece of work; which *does* interest him very much, and which no one could do so well certainly; only it comes at such an unlucky time. Then, there is the plaguing Unitarian Herald; which takes up six or seven hours a week, (*at the office*) and a great deal of odd time at home; and which we, his family, *wish* he would draw out of, and leave to be conducted by younger men. I think he really *likes* all these things; he meets with people he likes; and all the subjects he is engaged upon interest him very much. And when he *is* at home, we only see him at meal-times; so that it is not the giving-up of the *family* life to him, that it would be to many men. He seems very well, and very happy; and says he is never so well as in Manchester; but one wishes that at his age he could have a little more repose of mind . . . He keeps his study *terribly* hot; but then he likes it; and I sometimes fancy it is because he can't regulate the warmth of *other* houses that he dislikes so much leaving home.[21]

That Mr. Gaskell detested change as much as his wife needed it remained one of the unresolved problems between them. She could hardly credit how different her husband's tastes could be to her own, for whom the panacea for every ill was a change of air. 'The worst is that he dislikes change and travel so very much,' she wrote to Norton in March 1859;

[21] *GL* 570, May 1865.

'and if he gets a holiday I am afraid he will spend it in his study, out of which room by his own free will he would never stir.'[22]

After every major pleasure enjoyed by herself and the girls, Mrs. Gaskell could not rest until she had planned an equal pleasure for William—even though the planning had to be done behind his back. Thus, on her return from her first Roman holiday when she found him far from well, overworked and overtired, she longed to arrange an equally good holiday for him.

I wish Mr. Gaskell *looked* stronger [she wrote to Charles Norton in June 1857], he never complains, or will allow anything is the matter with him. I long for him to have the complete change of going from home. *I wish you could persuade him to go to America with you.* The congregation would gladly give him leave of absence—and I cd soon earn the passage and travelling money. He wants change, and yet hates leaving home. His flesh wants it, but his spirit abhors it, do you understand?[23]

It became a recurrent leitmotiv of her letters to try to provide him with an adequate holiday. Speaking of the departure of his colleague for London, in March 1859, she wrote to Norton:

And as he goes off directly Mr. Gaskell will have all the work to do for some time, which I am very sorry for as this is the time of the year when his digestion always gets wrong. I have been trying to put in the fine end of the wedge to get him a longer yearly holiday,—if only for once—after thirty one years of pretty hard work he should have it.[24]

It was not until the summer of 1861 that, having connived behind his back to procure him an extended leave of absence from the 'congregation' for the months of July and August ('not very long after 33 years of faithful service', as she commented to the Storys) and a £50 bonus 'to make a continental tour', she wrote to the Storys to arrange for him to join them, either in Siena or Spezzia, wherever it was that they were spending the hot months, 'to give my dear husband the welcome *there* you have so often and so kindly offered him in Rome'.

The urgency of her plea, to which the Storys cordially responded, was accompanied by a description of her husband which, written after thirty years of marriage, affords a clear indication of her feelings for him. It leaves no doubt whatever of her devotion, made up as it was of tolerance, humour, admiration, vexation, love:

. . . he can find no one to go with him, but the women of his family, and he says he feels so much the entire want of *change*, and the desirableness of having no

[22] GL 418, 9 Mar. 1859.   [23] GL 349, 3 June 1857.   [24] GL 418.

responsibility that he would rather not feel that he had any one dependant on him. And yet he would like society, if only to cheer him up a bit,—he is *so* over-worked —and I am sure you would like him—he is such a punster, and so merry when well, and so fond of children—after trying to tempt him to do what he *ought* by telling him of all manner of places, and planning all manner of tours he has, within the last 5 minutes, said that 'if it was not forcing himself on people, etc, etc'—and I have answered that I will take all blame of 'forwardness' 'intrusion' etc, etc,— and please, if you would like to have him, write *directly* back *here*.[25]

The great success of her 'lovely plan' in procuring Mr. Gaskell a foreign holiday, and his consequent revived health and spirits, only further determined Mrs. Gaskell in saving up for future continental holidays for all the family, including the reluctant Mr. Gaskell. After her own prolonged second visit to Italy in the spring of 1863 with Meta, Florence, and Julia, she set to work to organize a similar trip for him. Well aware by then of the prejudices and conscientious scruples that stood in the way of any enterprise designed simply to provide pleasure, that neither persuasion nor coercion could remove, she set about circumventing his every possible objection.

With all the inventiveness of the tried novelist, she plotted to secure a winter's leave of absence for him, in the autumn of 1863, when he once again showed signs of strain. She knew where to seek her allies, assured as she was of the respect in which Mr. Gaskell was held by his colleagues. She wrote to Dr. Beard, the Principal of the Unitarian Mission Board in September:

My dear Dr. Beard, I want you to enter into a conspiracy against Mr. Gaskell; and like all conspirators you must be so kind as to do your work quietly and silently.

The case is this. For years past Mr. and Mrs. Story (the American sculptor and his wife, he the son of Judge Story) who live at Rome have been urging Mr. Gaskell to pay them a visit there. Two years ago he met them in Switzerland, and he and Mr. Story became real friends. This year (in August) Mr. Story wrote to beg him to go to them at Siena,—saying (all that is very true,) that Mr. Gaskell would work the longer for having a complete holiday and change of scene. That was out of the question owing to our daughter's approaching marriage. Then came the question 'Could not Mr. Gaskell go to them in Rome in the winter?' This, we, his family, are exceedingly anxious that he should do. The congregation (as far as we can learn) are most willing. Six weeks would allow him *nearly* 5 weeks there. The Storys entreat him to come. He says 'It is too far off to plan for, but he does not see how he could go, because of the Home Mission.' Now could he not start *directly* after the January Examination; and would there not

[25] *GL* 489, 21 June 1861.

be some means, under the circumstances of prolonging his annual holiday from Home Mission work so as to allow him six weeks clear? He will (as you know) take no steps that can cause the slightest inconvenience to others, least of all to the Students; nor do I know what could be done . . . Is there no teacher in Manchester who could do something to keeping up the students to their work . . . I would willingly pay whatever might be required to secure the services of such a one . . . You know how Mr. Gaskell will dislike any 'fuss'—or asking any favour; but it does seem to me a pity he should miss this opportunity; for you know Rome is not visitable after May, or before November.[26]

Her appeal was not lost on Dr. Beard, to whom she wrote again on 24 September: 'Thank you *most truly* and heartily. With your help I feel confident that I shall win; and if I do, I shall not forget that I more than half owe my victory to you.'[27]

By mid-December Mr. Gaskell's visit to Rome was organized; the Storys, themselves greatly encumbered with American relatives, had secured 'a sleeping-room in the neighbourhood' and written to say 'that he must entirely *live* with them', Mrs. Gaskell herself now set to work with renewed vigour, and wrote to Dr. Beard of her husband's extreme fatigue.

May I therefore ask you to fix a time and place in town . . . when I can see you and ask your advice how to proceed. I do not believe that Mr. Gaskell *will make any requests for himself*; but I believe he will gladly accede to any arrangements *made for him*, to have a six week's holiday after the H.M.B. Examination is over.[28]

Eventually, her persistence was rewarded, and Mr. Gaskell was accorded a six-week holiday from 22 February 1864. She had, at one point, considered accompanying him, but decided in the end

to send him en garçon, for I dare say that he would feel more independent in an hotel without me, and with no tie to bring him back from his Forums, or the old book-stalls of the Piazza Navone, until the pangs of hunger remind him that there is such a thing as dinner.[29]

Mr. Gaskell's visit to Rome was a total success. He came home 'a different creature in consequence, showing the advantage of change and travel', as his wife jubilantly reported to Charles Norton.[30]

Already, at the beginning of 1865, Mrs. Gaskell was thinking of the approaching time when, with his sixtieth year impending, her husband might look to retirement and a shedding of his burdens. She might have

[26] *GL* 531, Sept. 1863.　　[27] *GL* 534.
[28] *GL* 543, 14 Dec. 1863.　　[29] *GL* 535, 2 Oct. 1863.
[30] *GL* 551, 4 July 1864.

known better. When he died, nearly twenty years later, he was still in harness. He resigned from none of his commitments, and indeed accepted others on a voluntary basis, such as his work for the Manchester Literary and Philosophical Society.

His ardour for educating the masses found its final expression in his foundation of a scholarship in 1879, to be called the Gaskell Scholarship, worth £70 a year as a benefaction for Owen's College. This was made possible by the gift of his congregation of £1,750 on the completion of his fifty years ministry at Cross Street Chapel.

At the ceremony held in the Town Hall of Manchester on 15 October 1878 to celebrate this occasion, in a succession of speeches made in his honour by the civic dignatories, the qualities in him that were most stressed were his 'generous spirit of religious charity', his 'work in the cause of education', his 'devotion to the principles of civil and religious freedom', and his 'kind and genial spirit of courtesy and charity'. In an address read out at the celebration, the Commemoration Committee and members of the Cross Street Congregation summed up his services to the community:

In the pulpit and through the press, your generous sympathies, your high attainments in scholarship and literature, your long and cultivated experience, have all been devoted to the promotion of the welfare and happiness of those amongst whom you have so long laboured.[31]

The person to whom these remarks would have brought the greatest pride and pleasure was no longer there to hear them; but the tribute, paid by his fellow townsmen after fifty years of public service, remains on record, as she would have wished, to show those who could not penetrate the exterior of this essentially shy man what sort of a husband Mrs. Gaskell had married.

She might, perhaps, at times have found a less crochety man easier to live with, or a more frivolous one better company; but none whom she could more completely rely on, or more deeply respect. For his part, he might have found a less mercurial wife more restful. So much—or so little—incompatibility was negligible in the long run, however, and could not undermine the solid fabric of mutual trust and love. The very personal terms in which she inscribed the copies of her works given to him over the years are worth recording: the first, *Mary Barton*, given him on 22 March 1849, read 'William Gaskell / With the dearest love / of his grateful and affectionate wife'; *Round the Sofa* of 1859, was inscribed

---

[31] *Commemoration of the Fifty Years' Ministry of the Rev. William Gaskell, M.A. . . . Report of the Proceedings at the Soirée Held in the Town Hall, October 15th, 1878*, p. 19.

15. Mrs. Gaskell, by Samuel Laurence, 1864

16. Marianne Gaskell, Mrs. Thurstan Holland, in old age

to 'William Gaskell / from his own beloved wife'; and the 1860 reprint of
contributions to *Household Words*, issued by Sampson, Low as *Right
at Last and Other Tales*, was inscribed on 29 April 1860 'To my dearest
husband from his affectionate and grateful wife, E. C. Gaskell'.[32] If
some admirers of Mrs. Gaskell tend to pity her for a detached, over-
scholarly and unworldly husband, they should remember that she herself
was possessed of a priceless gift of humour that could lend a sparkle to
the dullest surface. She was a woman of known good taste, who recognized genuine worth when she saw it.

Mr. Gaskell had a special rapport with children, and in the eyes of one
child he was beyond compare perfect. Beatrix Potter, who was very young
when he was very old, remembered the times when he stayed with her
parents in the Highlands and sought her company for his quiet morning
strolls. 'There has always been a deep child-like affection between him
and me', she wrote on hearing of his death in June 1884. 'Dear Old
Man . . . if ever any one led a blameless peaceful life, it was he.'[33]

[32] From the complete set of her mother's works, bound in morocco and preserved by
Marianne Gaskell; now in the possession of Mrs. Trevor-Jones.

[33] *The Journal of Beatrix Potter*, ed. L. Linder (London, 1966), pp. 90–1.

K

CHAPTER XXII

WIVES AND DAUGHTERS

THE last instalment of *Cousin Phillis* appeared in the February 1864 number of *Cornhill Magazine*. Mrs. Gaskell was still busy on it in January when she wrote to George Smith inquiring by what date he must have copy for the final issue. Yet, already by 3 May, she had a complete plan outlined for her next novel, showing a burst of creative energy rare with her after finishing a book. The tale which she could already estimate as a probable three-volume novel had taken such rapid hold of her imagination as quite to supplant a former project for a new work submitted to Smith.

I threw overboard the story of the 'Two Mothers' because I thought you did not seem to like it fully [she wrote to him then]—and I have made up a story in my mind,—of country-town life 40 years ago,—a widowed doctor has one daughter Molly,—when she is about sixteen he marries again—a widow with one girl Cynthia,—and these two girls—contrasted characters,—not sisters but living as sisters in the same house are unconscious rivals for the love of a young man, Roger Newton, the second son of a neighbouring squire or rather yeoman. He is taken by Cynthia, who does *not* care for him—while Molly does. His elder brother has formed a clandestine marriage at Cambridge—he was supposed to be clever before he went there—but was morally weak—and disappointed his father so much that the old gentleman refuses to send Roger, and almost denies him education—the eldest son lives at home, out of health, in debt, and not daring to acknowledge his marriage to his angry father; but Roger is his confidant, and gives him all the money he can for the support of his inferior (if not disreputable) wife and child. No one but Roger knows of this marriage—Roger is rough, and unpolished—but works out for himself a certain name in Natural Science,—is tempted by a large offer to go round the world (like Charles Darwin) as naturalist,—but stipulates to be paid *half* before he goes away for 3 years in order to help his brother. He goes off with a sort of fast and loose engagement to Cynthia,—while he is away his brother breaks a blood vessel, and dies—Cynthia's mother immediately makes fast the engagement and speaks about it to everyone, but Cynthia has taken a fancy for someone else and makes Molly her confidant.—You can see the kind of story . . .[1]

[1] *GL* 550.

This synopsis—evidence of Mrs. Gaskell's ability for sustained structural invention—is remarkably close to the finished tale, with its two-tier plot concerning the fortunes of the two interconnected families. It does not include, however, the Towers party, the Earl and Countess of Cumnor, their daughters, and aristocratic circle, who are introduced to hold the social balance and provide the irony latent in the social observances as practised in the provincial small-town life of Mrs. Gaskell's girlhood.

A more significant omission in the sketch of characters is that of Mrs. Gibson, barely mentioned in passing, the stepmother who is the book's pervading genius. The author can hardly have foreseen at the time the hold that she would take on her. Plots may be planned, but characters grow in a way that may be outside the author's control. Charlotte Brontë knew this, and submitted to the greater power that at times dictated to her. She once told G. H. Lewes of it in a letter which sufficiently impressed Mrs. Gaskell for her to include it in her life of Charlotte. Mrs. Gaskell was too self-effacing a biographer to say whether she had ever had the same experience herself; perhaps at the time of writing her friend's biography she had not. That is the whole difference in the quality of her early writing from that of her later work, and the difference that most generally strikes the reader between her own and the inspirational character of Charlotte Brontë's writing. To Lewes Charlotte wrote on 12 January 1848:

When authors write best, or at least, when they write most fluently, an influence seems to waken them, which becomes their master—which will have its own way—putting out of view all behests but its own, dictating certain words, and insisting on their being used, whether vehement or measured in their nature; new-moulding characters, giving un-thought of turns to incidents, rejecting carefully-elaborated old ideas, and suddenly creating and adopting new ones.

Is it not so? And should we try to counteract this influence? Can we indeed counteract it?[2]

Of Mrs. Gaskell herself Charlotte once asked, astounded at her capacity for detachment from the multiple pressures on her:

Do you, who have so many friends—so large a circle of acquaintance—find it easy, when you sit down to write, to isolate yourself from all those ties, and their sweet associations, so as to be quite *your own woman*, uninfluenced, unswayed by the consciousness of how your work may affect other minds; what blame, what sympathy it may call forth? Does no luminous cloud ever come between

[2] Quoted in the *Life of Charlotte Brontë*, Everyman edn., p. 240.

you and the severe Truth as you know it in your own secret and clear-seeing soul? In a word are you never tempted to make your characters more amiable than the Life, by the inclination to assimilate your thoughts to the thought of those who always *feel* kindly but sometimes fail to *see* justly? Don't answer the question it is not intended to be answered . . .[3]

The theme, the setting, and the characters for *Wives and Daughters*, were all to hand, and Mrs. Gaskell now had the experience and professional accomplishment, as well as the broad and humane tolerance of her nature, fully to realize her purpose. Mrs. Gaskell was most herself in this novel that reflects a life-time's vision of the scenes and characters that had animated her world. She could not, however, have written it earlier. The total experience would then have been lacking; and the processes of growth in the young—that constitutes its major charm—could not have then been observed with so experienced and sympathetic an eye.

Sylvia's Lovers may be said to have been written without a moral to teach and without a propaganda purpose; but a moral judgement is never far absent from the authorial comment. The beauty of *Wives and Daughters* lies in the absence of all authorial comment, in the severance of all visible ties between creator and created—with the cutting of the umbilical cord that alone gives a book total freedom from its parent. And this respect for the independent lives of her characters, not fully achieved in her early novels, gives *Wives and Daughters* the extra dimension of real life that makes it her crowning achievement. She was nearly fifty-four when she began it.

For those who seek the origins of inspiration, it could be said that there were special contributing factors at the time that determined her particular subject: the everyday, the apparently unremarkable subject of women in the home—of wives and daughters, with the emphasis notably on the latter.

In the previous twelve months all four Gaskell girls had reached decisive turning-points in their lives.

Florence, as has been seen, had suddenly become engaged at the age of twenty to a young barrister, Charles Crompton, whom she married on 8 September 1863. While no possible objections could be raised against so happy and suitable a match, which turned out well in all respects, the surprise, not to say shock, which Mrs. Gaskell felt on the marriage of so young, so inexperienced a girl—the most 'childish' of all her daughters— was not easily allayed; it left her long perplexed and anxious.

The course of Marianne's long-term love-affair with her second cousin,

[3] Wise and Symington, *The Brontës*, iv. 76–7.

Edward Thurstan Holland, had run far less smoothly in the six years since the lovers had first plighted troth. Both the fathers were against the match; Mr. Holland implacably so, on the grounds of consanguinity, lack of fortune, and Marianne's being slightly the older of the two. While Mr. Holland was a very rich man, he had a family of twelve children to provide for and could allow Edward little until he made his own way in his profession—a barrister also in Chancery law. By July 1864, however, after a good deal of worry, and when Marianne was already thirty, the young people made their engagement official with the sanction of Marianne's parents and in spite of the strong objections of Mr. Holland senior. The marriage had still to be postponed, but from then on Edward Holland became a part of the Gaskell family life in all its concerns.

In June 1864 Julia, aged seventeen, left school for good, 'full of promise', her mother said, 'the merriest grig, the most unselfish girl by *nature*, that I ever knew; with a deep sense of religion in her unusual, I think, at so early an age'.[4] Already, in keeping house together for their father in their mother's absence that summer Julia and Meta were showing the strong mutual affection that was a foretaste of the life-long friendship to come and that would last long after they were the last survivors in the home. Julia on return from school was soon 'the life of the house',[5] her mother noted with happiness. Julia, whose promise Charlotte Brontë had recognized, was a continual source of interest, surprise, and amusement to her mother, as the youngest and perhaps most witty—certainly the most outspoken—of her children.

Meta alone had been causing anxiety on the score of ill-health over the last two years, a condition diagnosed on the very faulty medical evidence of the time as 'nervous exhaustion and utter want of bracing',[6] with symptoms of headache and spinal trouble, attributed by her mother to overwork during the Cotton Famine, devotion to duty and refusal to give in. The evidence would suggest, however, that Meta's long illness was connected with the broken engagement to Captain Hill, bravely as she had borne herself at the time. It was a suppressed sorrow that no one, least of all the sufferer, would acknowledge. The need of bracing air prescribed by the family doctor, especially mountain air, was one of the reasons for Mrs. Gaskell's frequent journeys during the writing of *Wives and Daughters*.

In the daily contact with her four daughters Mrs. Gaskell found as absorbing a subject for reflection as any that could come to hand, at these critical times in their lives; and it is not surprising that in the young

[4] *GL* 551, 4 July 1864.   [5] *GL* 560, 5 Feb. 1865.   [6] *GL* 553, 25 July 1864.

heroine of her new book, Molly Gibson, she was able to portray all the phases of girlhood so unerringly. We see first the sturdy outspoken child of twelve, who preferred her pony and swinging on trees, to the detriment of her frocks, to the patronage of great ladies. Through the teenage years there is her open-hearted friendship with the Hamley brothers, leading into romantic adolescence when the language of flowers and poetry could alone express her feelings. Then she experiences the first keen acquaintance with grief over her father's remarriage, and the trials of life under a stepmother; the growth of tolerance that experience brings and, finally, the self-knowledge of first love. Molly Gibson is never otherwise than true to herself, honourable, kind, sensitive to the moods of others; Mrs. Gaskell could not go wrong in her portrayal because her very soul was bound up in her image, as the living likeness of what she most loved, her daughters.

Furthermore, knowing her daughters as she did, she could not be blind to their frailties. If Molly astounds by the truth of her delineation, no less does Cynthia, her opposite in all respects: superficial in feeling, defective in honour; seeking admiration where it may be found as the breath of life; yet wholly credible, seductive and excusable. Mrs. Gaskell seems prepared to say that even in very lovable girls there can, given her upbringing, lurk a Cynthia.

One of the most significant inclusions in the synopsis of *Wives and Daughters* is the comparison of the book's hero, Roger Hamley (Newton as he was called in the first draft), with Charles Darwin, 'who works out for himself a certain name in Natural Science',[7] because Mrs. Gaskell had just recently been staying with such a man.

On 25 January 1864 she went up to Edinburgh with Meta to stay at the home of Dr. and Mrs. Allman who lived in Manor Place in the city. Dr. Allman was Professor of Natural History in the university and was, as she described him to Charles Norton during her first visit, 'the most charmingly wise and simple man I ever met with. I mean he is full of deep thought and wisdom and knowledge and also like a child for unselfconsciousness, and sweet humility. *You* would so like and value him.'[8] Dr. Allman had married a connection of the Winkworths, Louisa Shaen, the eldest daughter of the friends at Crix, who was known to the Gaskells as far back as 1847. The subsequent marriage had in no way diminished the friendship established, nor distance prevented meetings at one or another's homes. Meta was only just recovering from a severe attack of

---

[7] *GL* 550, 3 May 1864.
[8] *GL* 546, 1 Feb. 1864.

influenza and had been ordered bracing air which, in default of mountain air, was sought in Edinburgh with no loss of time. Mrs. Gaskell took her there 'on an invalid bed', and the change of air did wonders.

The visit to the Allmans lasted between two and three weeks, and afforded Mrs. Gaskell not only a deeper knowledge of her host's delightful character, but some understanding of his special studies and tastes. While staying with him she asked Norton to get her from the States a work on birds particularly wanted by Dr. Allman and unobtainable in England. It was to come as a gift from her.

While Mrs. Gaskell's range of acquaintance was wide and included most kinds of professional men—lawyers, doctors, clergymen, teachers, and university lecturers—this appears to have been her first close contact with a naturalist and sometime explorer; and the novelty of the species to her and the character of the individual man were captivating enough for her to observe with very close interest. The conversation of such a man, his utter directness of approach ('un-selfconsciousness', as she perceived it), his keen response to information from whatever source, his informal, natural manners, appealed strongly enough to her to assimilate him into her novel as the prototype of her hero Roger Hamley. Her own appreciation of Dr. Allman and obvious ease in his presence adds piquancy to the fictional Mrs. Gibson's contempt for Roger Hamley and his scientific work as little conducive to a good income or a polished manner in society.

She had met Darwin more than once, first in 1851 on the occasion of a London visit, when he had dined at the Wedgwoods on purpose to meet her. He had been accompanied by his two sisters at what proved to be 'a large and very pleasant party'.[9] Acquaintance had been struck up, and Darwin was expected to stay at Plymouth Grove in company with one sister in October 1856, and subsequently his sister had travelled with Meta on a sketching tour in the Alps in August 1860.[10] They had found each other's company so congenial that Miss Darwin had repeatedly urged Meta the following year to arrange a similar tour.[11]

It was not, therefore, the fresh impact of a meeting with Darwin that suggested the character of the naturalist hero in *Wives and Daughters* to Mrs. Gaskell; though Darwin, the first in the field, and the most eminent of his day, was an obvious source for her to draw upon in describing her character to her publisher.

[9] *GL* 99, 100, July 1851.
[10] *GL* 476, 27 Aug. 1860.
[11] *GL* 484b, Mar. 1861.

The physical description of Roger Hamley given on his first entry in the novel, is, moreover, strongly evocative of Darwin.

He was a tall, powerfully-made young man, giving the impression of strength rather than elegance. His face was rather square, ruddy-coloured . . . hair and eyes brown—the latter rather deep-set beneath his thick eyebrows; and he had a trick of wrinkling up his eyelids when he wanted particularly to observe anything, which made his eyes look even smaller still at such times. He had a large mouth, with excessively mobile lips; and another trick of his was, that when he was amused at anything, he resisted the impulse to laugh, by a droll manner of twitching and puckering up his mouth, till at length the sense of humour had its way, and his features relaxed, and he broke into a broad, sunny smile; his beautiful teeth—his only beautiful feature—breaking out with a white gleam upon the red-brown countenance.[12]

Had Mrs. Gaskell meant Roger Hamley for Charles Darwin, it would have been a sufficient reason for not giving him a physical resemblance to the famous man and personal friend. She had too much tact to make Roger either Darwin or Dr. Allman; he was an evocation of the scientific naturalists then beginning to spring up and with whom she was making personal contact.

Such were the recognizable contributing factors to the inception of *Wives and Daughters*. A further deciding factor was the departure of Mr. Gaskell on 23 February for his two months' holiday in Rome, which allowed his wife the needed relaxation from domestic duties to advance her story. This she settled down to do—after the Edinburgh visit, and a short stay in London with Flossy to see Mr. Gaskell on his way—from mid-March until the middle of July.

George Smith had agreed to a cash payment of £2,000 for the promised work, retaining a seven-year copyright on the book. He was, as ever, most generous in the conditions he made, and when Mrs. Gaskell asked him on 25 July for an advance of £100 so as to allow her to take Meta to Switzerland to tone her up, he readily complied. Meta was in 'utter want of bracing', and yearned for the glacier air which had, on the previous trip with Miss Darwin, done her untold good. As with most of Mrs. Gaskell's journeys abroad, her decision was quickly made and their destination chosen. It was to be Pontresina, 'a cheap unknown-*ish* place' where they would stay 'en pension' for economy. Marianne, however, was essential to Meta's happiness: 'Minnie's contrast of character works so admirably on Meta',[13] her mother wrote, in a comment that illuminates

---

[12] *Wives and Daughters*, ch. 8, p. 96.   [13] *GL* 553.

much of the sisterly affection present in *Wives and Daughters*. Flossy, a 'grass-widow' at the time, and Julia must also be of the party, which in due course was joined by Flossy's husband and Thurstan Holland. Despite the size of the party and the attractions of the place, Mrs. Gaskell promised her publisher that she would write hard.

A large part of *Wives and Daughters* was, in the event, written away from home. Not only Meta's health, but her mother's, was very poor for the greater part of the time. They went to Pontresina from 12 August until early September when, on their return home, Mrs. Gaskell reported having 'such a weight of writing' on her hands that she could undertake no outside engagements.[14] She was, very shortly, so ill from overwork as to be confined to the house for the three autumn months.

The first instalment of *Wives and Daughters* appeared in the August number of *Cornhill* in 1864 and was given the place of honour at the beginning of the issue. From then on, throughout the long course of its serialization, the fear of falling behind with copy added immeasurably to the author's fatigue. No one reading this luminous tale would guess that it was produced under such constant pressure. As always, the Manchester winter greatly affected Mrs. Gaskell's spirits, and only in the spring of 1865 did she revive. 'Now, thank God!', she wrote to Norton in February, 'I am a great deal better; nearly quite strong again, I shall be when *light* comes back. I am always influenced so much by darkness, or cloudy skies.'[15]

The longing for country air, not in measured doses as a palliative for ill health, but as a permanent condition of life, was becoming obsessional with her now that Meta also was never well in Manchester. 'I long, shall long, have longed, and will ever long till I get it, for a whiff of Brighton air', she wrote to George Smith on 6 December after her illness that autumn.

She had already confided in him the great plan taking shape in her mind of acquiring a country house of her own, somewhere in the south of England, where the climate was genial and the skies undimmed by smoke, as a present refuge from Manchester in the bad weather and a future home for them all after Mr. Gaskell's retirement. She was putting aside what money she could save for the purpose. Declining Mr. Smith's prompt payment of £100 for a reprint of *North and South*, she told him in the same letter to keep it 'for the purchase of the (impossible) house'.[16] William Shaen, the family solicitor, had already £600 in hand of her savings 'towards the nest egg for the house'.[17]

[14] *GL* 555, 12 Sept. 1864.   [15] *GL* 560, 5 Feb. 1865.
[16] *GL* 557.   [17] Ibid.

While confiding in her publisher, her lawyer, and her daughters, she was not confiding the 'impossible' project to her husband, whose rooted love of Manchester, congenital antipathy to change, and dread of 'fuss' or disruption of any kind would be hard to overcome; only, she believed, faced with a *fait accompli* and the proof of the general benefit to all would he consent to rest after his labours in the charming surroundings she intended their retreat to have. He was, essentially, a domestic character deeply attached to his home.

George Smith had evidently told Mrs. Gaskell of a suitable house for sale at East Grinstead which she now deplored not having snatched-up in time. 'Oh! what a fool I was to let the East Grinstead house slip through my fingers!' she cried.[18] From that first mention of her secret purpose in December 1864, throughout the writing of *Wives and Daughters* the following year, the thought never far absent from her mind was the acquisition of the impossible house.

Her great and increasing physical fatigue, and low health and spirits in winter, were reason enough for wishing to live in more congenial surroundings than Manchester, but there may also at this time have entered into her feelings a more positive need, revived by the writing of *Cousin Phillis* and the renewed contacts with Knutsford—a homesickness for the life of the countryside and the pleasant ways she had known in her girlhood. *Wives and Daughters* may in this context be thought of as an escapist novel, a kind of sequel to *Cousin Phillis* in exploring the fuller potential of the theme of rural life, after which Mrs. Gaskell was thirsting as after a lost Arcadia.

There is such a sense of pleasure apparent in all her descriptions of the fields and lanes and copses and hedges of Hollingford; such amusement felt in the exchanges of the Miss Brownings and the mischief-making Mrs. Goodenough, speaking an English that was antiquated in Queen Anne's day; such zest in the memories of the uncouth medical students eating their huge helpings of pudding; such relish in the doctor's cool and cutting snubs at their expense; such enjoyment of the numberless subterfuges the gossips resorted to in extracting a kernel of slander from an item of news. There is excitement to be found in the daily pageant of life in the principal street, at the draper's, and the library, by leaning out of windows to see what is afoot, by chance encounters, and by observing the carriages, gigs, and country carts as they occasionally stop for an exchange of greetings. One comes to know the inhabitants of Hollingford quite intimately, and over the whole scene, Mrs. Gaskell casts a

[18] *GL* 557.

magic golden light. This is not to say that she was not acutely aware of the limitations and follies of such a way of life, and of the ridicule it must provoke. The irony does not escape her but it is muted by her memories and by the essential good nature of the people she describes. There is no real malice, nor wickedness. Mr. Preston is a cad, but he is genuinely in love with Cynthia and motivated not by greed but passion.

The residents of Hollingford are more fully realized than their predecessors in Cranford. *Cranford* is the reflection of the world she left on quitting Knutsford to get married; Hollingford is the place of her return, seen with more penetrating eyes, its busy hum heard with more acute ears, and above all absorbed by a mind matured by experience. *Wives and Daughters* is, of course, something more than a panegyric of country life. It is a long-term view, one might almost say a valedictory view, of the author's life and of life in general, particularly as it affected women in relation to every phase of family commitment, as daughter, sister, wife, mother.

It was a subject of topical and absorbing interest to her at the time, as has already been noted, with her daughters passing from girlhood into young womanhood, developing their individual characters and abilities, going their several ways, falling in love, marrying, realizing the potential within themselves. What Mrs. Gaskell hoped for them is the measure of the fulfilment she had hoped for herself. It is noteworthy that, while she secured her daughters the best education possible at the time to develop what talents they had—whether for music or painting—in order to promote their own pleasure in life and make intelligent companions of them for their future husbands, she never at any time contemplated careers for them, and by her own hard work and earnings ensured that they did not have to work for a living.

This may appear the more surprising since she herself had proved her own ability to do so. She had become a successful author almost imperceptibly, not from ambition, certainly not in a bid for independence. The success, and the consequent financial advantage, had come almost as by chance. She had written *Mary Barton* as a work of propaganda, moved to take up a cause that her geographical position at the heart of industrial distress allowed her to speak about with authority and compassion. Her success had exceeded all expectation and had, most of all, surprised herself. The eager encouragement of Dickens and the early recognition of her original talent launched her on her career as a writer. But basically she never saw herself as anything but a wife and mother, and she envisaged no more for her daughters than that they should enjoy the same fulfilment.

Had they shown outstanding talents, her hopes for them might have been different. But there was really no perceptible advance in the position of women from the time of Jane Austen to her own. If a girl of good family had to earn her living there was little or no choice. For Jane Fairfax in 1815 or for Cynthia Kirkpatrick in 1865, the choice was the same. They must go out as governesses to a strange family—only for Cynthia the horizon was broader because she had the offer of a post in Russia.

Governessing did not totally rule out hopes of marriage for a girl, as Jane Eyre is there to prove. But Mrs. Gaskell dreaded such a fate for her own daughters and it was largely because of this that she was determined to buy a family home which could be inherited in due course by those who failed to marry.

The underlying seriousness of the theme of *Wives and Daughters* may be obscured for the reader by the sparkle of the style. Never, for all the beauty and sensitivity of her previous writing, had Mrs. Gaskell been in such total command of her medium, and the gain in fluidity of style and subtlety of effect is enormous. The characters are built up from within, allowed to speak for themselves in dialogue that subtly identifies them, and Mrs. Gaskell is much more ready to efface herself and much less inclined to prompt her readers than in her earlier work. This is a sign of confidence.

Mrs. Kirkpatrick, as Molly's stepmother is called before marrying her father, is introduced to the reader only through the comment of twelve-year old Molly, who thought 'she was the most beautiful person she had ever seen, and she was certainly a very lovely woman'. Mrs. Kirkpatrick's admirable qualities, implied by a soft and plaintive voice, are suggested even by the way in which she disposes of the lunch—consisting of bread, cold chicken, a bunch of grapes, a glass of wine, and a bottle of sparkling water—destined for the child whom the heat and excitement of a day at Cumnor Towers have indisposed. It is through the child's eyes that the reader sees the expeditious disposal of the tray full of delicacies: 'Molly did as she was bid, and leant back, picking languidly at the grapes, and watching the good appetite with which the lady ate up the chicken and jelly, and drank the glass of wine. She was so pretty and graceful in her deep mourning, that even her hurry in eating, as if she was afraid of some one coming to surprise her in the act, did not keep her little observer from admiring her in all she did.'[19]

[19] *Wives and Daughters*, ch. 2, p. 16.

By this time we have a very good idea of Mrs. Kirkpatrick, but she has to be seen from other angles before any judgement of her can be safely reached. Suffering from a headache, Molly is put to bed in the great house to await her return home in the company of the old friends who had brought her; earnestly the child pleads to be called in good time to go home with them. 'Don't trouble yourself about it dear,' says the lovely lady whose name turns out to be Clare, 'turning round at the door, and kissing her hand to the little anxious Molly. And then she went away, and thought no more about it.'[20] Thackeray himself could not have punctured a character more neatly.

Molly, the heroine of the tale, is also revealed to us very largely through her own speech and conduct. The want of judgement in young creatures, positive and decided in their views, is perfectly exemplified by Molly's prejudice against Roger at their first meeting, because Roger is not the much vaunted Osborne she has been led to expect. 'To Molly, who was not finely discriminative in her glances at the stranger this first night, he simply appeared "heavy looking, clumsy", and "a person she was sure she should never get on with".'[21] Throughout this long story, the characters play out their parts like actors on a stage, apparently oblivious to their audience. Seldom is any direct appeal made to the reader.

If a character is occasionally drawn 'straight', it is by means of a witty aside. The vicar, Mr. Ashton, is presented as 'a thoroughly good and kind-hearted man, but one without an original thought in him; whose habitual courtesy and indolent mind led him to agree to every opinion not palpably heterodox, and to utter platitudes in the most gentlemanly manner'.[22] On the other hand, Squire Hamley, the fine old peppery scion of Saxon stock, reduced in the world yet too pigheaded to improve his property, who speaks a faulty and archaic English and cannot control his temper, is only very gradually discovered to have a heart of gold beneath his rough exterior. He is seen through his gestures and expletives; banging his fist on the dining-table in some access of rage and unaware that he is making his wife's heart 'beat hard for some minutes'. He adores her but is quite unable to measure her sensibility, and does not even suspect that she is dying. Lady Cumnor, who considers that her status entitles her to interfere in the affairs of other people, is as insensitive as he is, but she wounds deliberately as a prerogative of her rank. Called on to give her opinion of Mr. Preston's looks—Mr. Preston is her husband's agent—she replies: 'I never think whether a land-agent is

[20] Ibid.   [21] Ibid., ch. 8, p. 96.
[22] Ibid., ch. 4, p. 41.

handsome or not. They don't belong to the class of people whose appearance I notice.'[23]

The scope of the book as opposed to its mere length is also on a larger scale than anything Mrs. Gaskell had previously attempted. *Mary Barton*, *Sylvia's Lovers*, and *Cousin Phillis* were confined to the working or rustic classes of contemporary town, sea-coast, or village life. Their experience was limited, and their social intercourse confined to the neighbours and relatives of their immediate circle. They neither travelled nor read nor developed; they remained themselves. It was a considerable achievement on Mrs. Gaskell's part, given her background, to make the characters so convincing, so true to their environment, to re-create so accurately their various local dialects. Jem Wilson in *Mary Barton* is as living a character as Roger Hamley in *Wives and Daughters*; their differences are of an intellectual order, Roger having interests, capabilities, and ambitions unknown to Jem Wilson. In her last book Mrs. Gaskell covered the entire English social spectrum: the cottagers (the faithful old farm-tenants on Squire Hamley's land), the tradesmen, shopkeepers, and inn-keepers; the professional men, the lawyers, the clergy, the doctors; and the landed gentry and the aristocracy. All of the characters are equally authentic and faithfully observed.

Every reader must have his or her favourites, but undoubtedly the most fully realized of the male characters is the doctor, Mr. Gibson, whose very silences are eloquent and whose 'cool, sarcastic self' does not permit him to suffer fools gladly. Reticent, scrupulous, laconic, learned, totally dedicated to his work, Mr. Gibson hates ostentation, insincerity, falsehood above everything, and has the misfortune to have chosen a wife who is all these things, and some more besides: shallow, affected, vain. He is a sad man conscious of his mistake, but with enough humour to bear it with philosophy. How splendidly the qualities of mind of husband and wife are conveyed in this dialogue, worthy of Jane Austen:

'It is such a pity!' said she [Mrs. Gibson], 'that I was born when I was. I should have so liked to belong to this generation.'

'That's sometimes my own feeling,' said he. 'So many new views seem to be opened in science, that I should like, if it were possible, to live till their reality was ascertained, and one saw what they led to. But I don't suppose that's your reason, my dear, for wishing to be twenty or thirty years younger.'

'No, indeed. And I did not put it in that hard unpleasant way; I only said I should like to belong to this generation. To tell the truth, I was thinking of Cynthia. Without vanity, I believe I was as pretty as she is—when I was a girl,

[23] *Wives and Daughters*, ch. 8, p. 106.

I mean; I had not her dark eyelashes, but then my nose was straighter. And now—look at the difference! I have to live in a little country-town with three servants, and no carriage; and she, with her inferior good looks, will live in Sussex Place, and keep a man and a brougham, and I don't know what. But the fact is, in this generation there are so many more rich young men than there were when I was a girl.'

'Oh, oh! so that's your reason, is it, my dear? If you had been young now you might have married somebody as well off as Walter?'

'Yes!' said she. 'I think that was my idea. Of course I should have liked him to be you. I always think, if you had gone to the bar, you might have succeeded better, and lived in London, too. I don't think Cynthia cares much where she lives; yet you see it has come to her.'

'What has—London?'

'Oh, you dear, facetious man! Now that's just the thing to have captivated a jury. I don't believe Walter will ever be so clever as you are. Yet he can take Cynthia to Paris, and abroad, and everywhere. I only hope all this indulgence won't develop the faults in Cynthia's character. It's a week since we heard from her, and I did write so particularly to ask her for the autumn fashions, before I bought my new bonnet. But riches are a great snare.'

'Be thankful you are spared that temptation, my dear.'

'No, I'm not. Everybody likes to be tempted. And, after all, it's very easy to resist temptation, if one wishes.'

'I don't find it so easy', said her husband.[24]

Mrs. Gaskell's daughters later insisted that there were absolutely no prototypes in Mrs. Gaskell's family or among her connections for the characters in *Wives and Daughters*, but it is hard to believe that her very wide acquaintance among the medical profession—her uncle Peter Holland to start with, her cousin Henry Holland, Mr. Gaskell's brother Sam Gaskell who was the doctor chosen for her children, to name but a few—had nothing to contribute to her conception of the character of Mr. Gibson.

There are recognizable in him other resemblances as well to men in Mrs. Gaskell's closest family circle not necessarily doctors; to Mr. Gaskell himself for one—with his physical height, Scots accent that returns in moments of emotion, his half-humorous, self-deprecating manner with his little girl, even his pet appellation for her of 'Goosey' which is as far as he can go in betraying his tenderness for her. In the early years of their marriage Mr. Gaskell very often called his wife 'Goosey'.

Mr. Gibson is thus described: 'His accent was Scotch, not provincial.

[24] Ibid., ch. 60, pp. 752–3.

He had not one ounce of superfluous flesh on his bones; and leanness goes a great way to gentility. His complexion was sallow, and his hair black; in those days, the decade after the conclusion of the great continental war, to be sallow and black-a-vised was of itself a distinction; he was not jovial . . . sparing of his words, intelligent, and slightly sarcastic. Therefore he was perfectly presentable.'[25]

More convincing still is the resemblance between Mr. Gibson and Elizabeth Gaskell's own father, another Scotsman with a love of learning. The personal experience and the remembered sorrow which she introduced into her novel and which, indeed, became central to her plot, are clearly reflected in the remarriage of Molly Gibson's father and the establishment of a stepmother in her home. Mr. Stevenson's remarriage was, without doubt, the most momentous circumstance of Elizabeth's youth and one that brought her a good deal of misery. Though she was only four when her father married again, and was at that time living under the care of her aunt at Knutsford, she was seventeen, like Molly Gibson, when she was summoned to the Chelsea house to help nurse her father, and found—unlike Molly Gibson—a not particularly congenial younger step-sister and brother. The suffering of that time she never forgot, nor the sense of desolation to which a girl of that age is prone, when only the presence of 'the beautiful, grand river' seemed to bring any consolation. The intensity of adolescent feelings and the extravagance of grief, are memorably described in *Wives and Daughters* when Molly hears of her father's intention to remarry. He rides over to Hamley where she is staying with the Squire and his sick wife expressly to break the news to her. She is incredulous.

She did not answer. She could not tell what words to use. She was afraid of saying anything, lest the passion of anger, dislike, indignation—whatever it was boiling up in her breast—should find vent in cries and screams, or worse, in raging words that could never be forgotten. It was as if the solid piece of ground on which she stood had broken from the shore, and she was drifting out to the infinite sea alone.[26]

Both father and daughter dread saying something unforgivable to each other, and the inarticulate man can find nothing to say to soften the blow. 'I think it's better for both of us for me to go away now', he says, and rides off. Molly escapes into the garden where she has a favourite hidden seat on a distant terrace overlooking a 'pleasant slope of meadows beyond'.

Molly almost thought that no one knew of the hidden seat under the ash-tree

---

but herself . . . When she had once got to the seat, she broke out with suppressed passion of grief. She did not care to analyse the sources of her tears and sobs—her father was going to be married again—her father was very angry with her; she had done wrong—he had gone away displeased; she had lost his love; he was going to be married—away from her—away from his child—his little daughter—forgetting her own dear, dear mother. So she thought in a tumultuous kind of way, sobbing till she was wearied out . . . She had cast herself on the ground—that natural throne for violent sorrow—and leant up against the old moss-grown seat; sometimes burying her face in her hands; sometimes clasping them together, as if by the tight painful grasp of her fingers she could deaden mental suffering.[27]

However Mrs. Stevenson behaved towards Elizabeth or however Elizabeth regarded her (it cannot have been very cordially since she let twenty-five years elapse before seeking to see her again after her father's death) Mrs. Gaskell dreaded a similar fate for her own daughters. As will be remembered from her confidences to her sister-in-law, she feared the possibility of dying in childbed (a frequent and very real danger at that time) and leaving her little girls to a stepmother, and worried about the harm that would come to them from the deprivation of the love and sympathy to which they were accustomed. 'The want of them would make MA an unhappy character, probably sullen and deceitful,' she had written then, 'while the sunshine of love and tenderness would do everything for her.'[28] It was a situation of which she had personal knowledge, but in *Wives and Daughters* she does not use it for tragic or even dramatic effect, as one might have expected. Instead the figure of the stepmother becomes a figure of fun, a purely comic character. There was a touch of genius in this. Given the tendency to morbidity evident in the earlier novels, her decision is some indication of her progress as an artist, and her best work is linked not only with that of Jane Austen before her but with the work of George Meredith to come.

Mrs. Gibson unfalteringly and inexorably advances from folly to folly with the utmost complacency. She is self-deluding, shallow, untruthful, and affected, insensitive herself to all the finer feelings and constantly reproving her stepdaughter for want of feeling. But though she is presented as full of foibles it is not suggested that she is wicked. We are told she is good to the poor (so she is not totally heartless) and she prides herself on the total impartiality of her treatment of daughter and stepdaughter alike. This is true, and is shown as painfully unwelcome to Molly when

[27] Ibid., p. 128.
[28] *GL* 16, 23 Dec. 1841.

L

her old shabby bedroom that contains her dead mother's antique furniture is rudely renovated and the old pieces removed to match Cynthia's new and fashionable apartment. Equality in treatment for the two girls was not difficult for Mrs. Gibson as she never deeply loved her own daughter, who all too early penetrated her mother's hollow semblances of charm.

Of Molly Gibson, about whom so much could be said, what distinguishes her from her author's previous heroines is not only her class—she is a 'lady'—but the gradualness and naturalness of her growth. Her childish ignorance is delightfully conveyed by her surprise at every new discovery about life. Margaret Hale in *North and South* was unmistakably a lady too, but she was already mature and the freshness of her reactions to events, which is so much a part of Molly's charm, is missing. Mary Barton, Ruth, Sylvia Robson, were care-worn and early caught up in the struggle of life; starved of happiness they had no time in which to develop, and remained confined within the limitations of their circumstances. They could not be expected to respond to life in the same way as Molly. Molly, observed close at hand, known through and through by her creator, is patently a portrait drawn from life, not after any specific Gaskell perhaps but from an amalgam of the lot; the quintessence of young girlhood, and one of the finest specimens of her kind. The measure of Molly's growth as a girl, of her development as a character, is given in a final scene between her and her stepmother, where the impatience of childhood, the passionate dislike of untruth and artifice—of her stepmother's humbug in short—has given way to tolerance and some degree of understanding. At times, even Molly feels it in her heart to pity Mrs. Gibson for some more than usually astringent comment from her husband. Cynthia is married and gone from home, and the day has come for Roger Hamley's departure for a further six-months' expedition in Africa. Molly is now aware of his love for her but has to keep the knowledge to herself; her stepmother has no inkling of it. The infectious illness of Roger's little nephew at Hamley prevents his calling to make his farewells, which is an additional heartbreak for the lovers. Molly is sewing with her stepmother.

It was a rainy day . . . and Mrs. Gibson, who had planned to go out and pay some calls, had to stay indoors. This made her restless and fidgety. She kept going backwards and forwards to different windows in the drawing-room, to look at the weather, as if she imagined that, while it rained at one window, it might be fine weather at another, 'Molly—come here! who is that man wrapped up in a cloak—there—near the Park-wall, under the beech-tree—he has been there this half-hour and more, never stirring, and looking at this house all the time! I think it's very suspicious.'

Molly looked, and in an instant recognised Roger under all his wraps. Her first instinct was to draw back. The next to come forward, and say—'Why, mamma, it's Roger Hamley! Look now—he's kissing his hand; he's wishing us good-bye in the only way he can!' And she responded to his sign; but she was not sure if he perceived her modest, quiet movement, for Mrs. Gibson became immediately so demonstrative that Molly fancied that her eager pantomimic motions must absorb all his attention.

'I call this so attentive of him,' said Mrs. Gibson, in the midst of a volley of kisses of her hand. 'Really, it is quite romantic. It reminds me of former days— but he'll be too late! I must send him away; it is half-past twelve!' And she took out her watch and held it up, tapping it with her fore-finger, and occupying the very centre of the window. Molly could only peep here and there, dodging now up, now down, now on this side, now on that, of the perpetually-moving arms. She fancied she saw something of a corresponding movement on Roger's part. At length he went away slowly, slowly, and often looking back, in spite of the tapped watch. Mrs. Gibson at last retreated, and Molly quietly moved into her place, to see his figure once more, before the turn of the road hid him from her view. He, too, knew where the last glimpse of Mr. Gibson's house was to be obtained, and once more he turned, and his white handkerchief floated in the air. Molly waved hers high up, with eager longing that it should be seen. And then, he was gone![29]

The setting of *Wives and Daughters* is recognizably Knutsford, with the George Inn from which the coaches start for London, and the Assembly Rooms where the County Balls are held and the great folk from the Towers put in a belated appearance to please the townsfolk and tenantry whose votes they need. The doctor's house at the top of the town is, rightly, in sight of the park gates; and the park itself, entered by lodge gates at the top of the main street, with its palladian mansion among acres of old oak and beech, its ponds and conservatories, is Tatton Park, the seat of the Egerton family since Jacobean times. Hamley Hall, with its ponds and islets and desolate disrepair, is Old Tabley Hall, the scene of so many happy picnics in Mrs. Gaskell's girlhood.

The Miss Brownings' tiny habitation overlooking the principal street, ideally situated for keeping an eye on everything that is going on, belongs equally to Knutsford and *Cranford*. Many scenes, situations, and characters are related to *Cranford*, which is the only one of her previous books in which she adopted a comparably satirical vein, though the satire is much more astringent in *Wives and Daughters*. The obvious

[29] *Wives and Daughters*, ch. 60, pp. 750–1.

similarities between the two books should not be allowed to disguise the differences. *Cranford* falls short of *Wives and Daughters* in both intellectual power and technical skill. Whole scenes, like the ball at the Assembly Rooms, are admittedly almost interchangeable, and the minor characters, Mrs. Goodenough, the Miss Brownings, the medical students, could figure in either story. But when it comes to the oblique presentation of character, the reflection of conduct on character, the probing of a mind at work, the awareness of bewildered feelings, by which the stages in the narrative in *Wives and Daughters* are reached, then the reader is made to recognize how far the author has advanced in the ten years between the two books. Indeed the improvement on the more recent *Sylvia's Lovers* and *Cousin Phillis* suggests that Mrs. Gaskell was only then fully realizing her powers as a writer.

In March 1865, with the book safely launched in *Cornhill* and work on the following instalments well in hand, Mrs. Gaskell broke off to go to stay in Paris with her friend Mme Mohl who had been ill. She left home on 10 March and stayed with Mme Mohl in the Rue du Bac from 12 March to 20 April. Contrary to her custom she took none of her daughters with her, as the visit was not intended for sightseeing but for work.

It was, as it turned out, an unfortunate arrangement, as she worked too hard and under difficult circumstances. The Mohls' salon was the centre of a vast circle of callers and acquaintances, including illustrious oriental scholars, German students, international travellers, French politicians, and journalists, who appeared at all hours of the day and late into the night to interrupt Mrs. Gaskell's work and exhaust her reserves of energy. The regime in the Rue du Bac had always put a strain on her animal spirits by the peculiar character of its domestic economy. She was not accustomed to the long intervals between meals, and even to reach the Mohls' apartment on the fourth and fifth floors of a great mansion built in Louis XIV's last years was a thoroughly exhausting experience. During the first three weeks of her stay, the weather being cool, she made good progress with her book and still had reserves of energy to fall back upon. She described her situation in a long letter to Emily Shaen on 27 March:

On the fourth story are four lowish sitting rooms and Mme Mohl's bedroom. On the fifth slopes in the roof, kitchen, grénier, servants' bedrooms, my bedroom, work-room, etc.; all brick floors, which is cold to the feet. My bedroom is very pretty and picturesque. I like sloping roofs and plenty of windows stuffed into their roof anyhow . . . I have no watch, there is no clock in the house, and so I have to guess the time by the monks' singing and bells ringing (all night long but) especially in the morning. So I get up and come down into the smallest and shabbiest of the sitting-rooms, in which we live and eat all day long, and find that M. Mohl has had his breakfast of chocolate in his room (library) at $\frac{1}{2}$ past 6, and Mme Mohl hers of tea at 7, and I am late having not come down (to coffee) till a little past 8. However I take it coolly and M. and Mme come in and talk to me; she in dressing gown and curlpapers, very, very amusing, he very sensible and agreeable, and full of humour too . . . Then, after my breakfast, which lingers long because of all this talk, I get my writing 'Wives and Daughters' and write, as well as I can for Mme Mohl's talking, till 'second breakfast' about 11. Cold meat, bread, wine and water and sometimes an omelette—what we should call lunch, in fact, only it comes too soon after my breakfast, and too long before dinner for my English habits. After breakfast no 2 I try to write again; and very often callers come; *always* on Wednesdays on which day Mme Mohl receives. I go out for a walk by myself in the afternoons; and when we dine at home it is at six sharp. No dressing required. Soup, meat, one dish of vegetables and roasted apples are what we have in general. After dinner M. and Mme Mohl go to sleep; and I have fallen into this habit; and at eight exactly M. Mohl wakes up and makes a cup of very weak tea for Mme Mohl and me, nothing to eat after dinner; not even if we have been to the play. Then Mme Mohl rouses herself up and is very amusing and brilliant, stops up till one, and would stop up later if encouraged by listeners. She has not been well, but for all that she has seen a good number of people since I came.[30]

Early in April there was a sudden heat-wave as the spring burst on Paris, and despite Mrs. Gaskell's long craving for the sun it prostrated her when it came and she had something in the nature of a breakdown. She was too ill to work, to go out, or to travel, and was totally confined indoors for a fortnight. She was not fit to travel home until 20 April. Even so she had to break the journey in London and stay at Flossy's.

It was a warning of the danger ahead, of which none of her doctors seem to have given her the least indication. She was forced temporarily to take notice of her condition, feeling too ill to see friends, even George Smith and his wife. He had, however, to be informed of the situation. 'I broke down in Paris,' she wrote to him, 'and for the last fortnight could not leave the house till the day I came here. I am not strong and not able to see anyone . . . Don't either you or Mrs. Smith take the trouble to call. I am not strong enough to see anyone just yet.—Oh for a house in the country.'[31] Her illness had brought the realization of her need of rest more forcibly before her than ever before. While in London she was resolved to make good use of her time in finding the 'impossible house' in the country.

[30] *GL* 564, 27 Mar. 1865.   [31] *GL* 565, Apr. 1865.

Writing to Marianne from Flossy's on 24 April, she said:

I am not strong. I *was* so well that first 3 cold weeks in Paris; but the close over-powering heat, and the real want of food, and lowness of diet have made me so weak, I almost get out of spirits about ever being fit for anything again; which is I know nonsense, especially remembering how well I was 3 weeks or a month ago. I want to see as much as I can about houses while here. Please ask ETH [Edward Thurstan Holland, Marianne's fiancé] to send me the admission to the Wallingford House, *if it is still* unsold. But I have but little hope; I don't know why. Meta comes today at 2 p.m.[32]

From Meta's arrival until the return to Manchester on 6 May, Mrs. Gaskell had a fresh burst of energy and she and the rest of the family, apart from the unsuspecting Mr. Gaskell, were busily engaged in answering advertisements of properties for sale. She had no decided views about its location; what mattered was a rural position within reach of London. Houses as far apart as Putney, Wallingford, Bookham, even Arundel, were considered and their owners applied to. While Meta eliminated the impossible ones (too large and too expensive, like Arundel House) and visited the near-by ones (like the ones at Putney and Bookham), Mrs. Gaskell visited only one house herself, at Sunningdale, on a day's outing to Windsor with Florence, Charles, and Meta. It was a sign of the improvement in health that she was reporting to Marianne in her last letters from London. 'I am so pleased to be feeling better and stronger, I am taking Mr Mellor's tonics.' She was already planning the family summer holiday and longing for the sea. 'I hope I shall come back quite strong now. Only I *should* like some good sea air this year.'[33]

Marianne was staying at home to take the burden off her mother in finding and installing a new cook against her return; any worry of the kind was beyond her at that time. Her state of nervous debility can be judged by her refusal to face her 'Cousin Mary' (the redoubtable Miss Holland from Knutsford) who had been staying at Plymouth Grove in her absence. In that last letter from London she wrote to Marianne: 'Thank you for all the trouble you are taking for me, darling. I don't want to come home till Cousin Mary is gone. She did so snub me that day at Knutsford!'[34] She had, indeed, reached a degree of lowness if the fear of a Deborah Jenkins could so disarm her ready repartee.

Without having found a house, but more resolved than ever to do so that year, Mrs. Gaskell returned to Manchester, just two months after leaving for Paris.

[32] *GL* 566, 24 Apr. 1865.   [33] *GL* 567, 25 Apr. 1865.   [34] Ibid.

CHAPTER XXIII

THE PERFECT PLAN

MEANWHILE, serialization of *Wives and Daughters* had to go on, and advance instalments had to be written. In a long letter to her sister-in-law, Anne Robson, written almost immediately on reaching home on 10 May she reported on the work in hand:[1]

I wish Wives and Daughters were done.—It is to last till after the December No; and I have WRITTEN August No, and have four more numbers to write, and *such* a quantity of story to get in. I must set to and write hard at it; and shan't do anything else for the next 6 weeks, except house-keep, and nursing and cheering up Hearn.[2] So don't expect any more endless letters for a long time.

All the disadvantages of serial publication, even in monthly rather than the weekly parts as she had written for *Household Words*, were excessively harassing to her now. There were no margins to spare for illness, disinclination to write, or suspended inspiration. She had to supply her publisher with twenty-four pages for the *Cornhill* (considerably more in her own writing) for each month's issue, and throughout the summer it never went easily. Although the reader is unlikely to detect the constant strain under which it was written, to the author it was a crushing burden. To Marianne she made the sad admission in June: 'I have no news to tell you. I am writing away, but I hate my story, because I am not to have more money for it, I believe.'[3] The uncharacteristic sentiment and the preoccupation with money were to some extent a consequence of her frustration in not finding the house on which she had set her heart. She was tied to her task, unable to go on with her house-hunting, but avidly scanning house-agents' advertisements none the less.

There were other subjects of vexation and worry that summer, which though not connected with her work or her house-hunting, hampered progress with both. Not only Meta but Marianne and Julia had spells of ill health in early summer; anxiety enough for their mother without Hearn, the family stand-by, falling ill as well. Hearn's illness was more

---

[1] *GL* 570, 10 May 1865.   [2] Hearn was ill at the time.   [3] *GL* 572.

in the nature of a nervous depression: 'Hearn is not at all well just now,' Elizabeth told her sister-in-law, 'as much depression of spirits as anything, I think.—She wants some change of thought and scene, and we have a variety of plans for giving it her, as she has no home to go to, now-a-days. She is a dear good valuable *friend*.'[4] Mrs. Gaskell came gradually to connect Hearn's illness and the girls' ill health that summer with the defective drains of Plymouth Grove. The subject, and its remedy, runs like a leitmotiv through her letters of the time, and is seen as the immediate cause of her own prostrating illness in August. The defective drainage system of the great urban centres of the day was a frequent subject of complaint by contemporary writers: Dickens wrote eloquently about them in London, and Mrs. Gaskell had suffered acutely from them in Paris on previous summer visits. While the cleaning out of the Plymouth Grove drains was a major operation that had to be deferred until the family were from home, it can be reckoned as one of the subsidiary factors in deciding Mrs. Gaskell to find a house without further loss of time. After a summer of general family ill health, she commented at the end of August, when work upon the drains began, 'Manchester is not a place to *regain* health in'.[5]

It was with the primary aim of finding a healthy position for a house that she took up an advertisement in mid-June for a property at Alton in Hampshire, 300 feet above sea-level and within sight of the downs. She could not leave her work to visit it, but Meta and Flossy, who were acting as her scouts, went down to see it on her behalf. They had already a house to see at Bookham, and both visits may have been made on the same day; but it was the Alton house that won their hearts.

The report they sent their mother was so attractive as to decide her, without seeing it herself, to write to the owner and make an offer. Her imagination was fired by Meta's description and the agent's catalogue. The price was £2,600, of which she could find £1,600. It was George Smith who advanced her the remaining £1,000 'on an equitable mortgage', as she reported to Charles Norton,[6] which she was to pay off by future writings. George Smith had been in her confidence from the beginning about her plan to buy a house for Mr. Gaskell's eventual retirement, and for a permanent home for her unmarried daughters; but till the debt was paid off Mr. Gaskell was not to be made privy to the transaction. His horror of borrowing money and of putting himself under anyone's obligation was too well known to his wife; his disapproval would wreck

---

[4] *GL* 570. [5] *GL* 580, 31 Aug. 1865.
[6] *GL* 583, 8 Sept. 1865.

the happy effect his wife counted on when the house should become hers. She reckoned to have completed the purchase just in time for Mr. Gaskell's retirement. Till then, probably for the next three years, she planned to let it furnished until the mortgage was paid off. 'Till then', she told Charles Norton, 'it is a secret from Mr. Gaskell. When I have got it *free* we plan many ways of telling him of the pretty house awaiting him.'[7] It was the fear of never gaining that freedom that frustrated its own purpose, and by driving her even more unsparingly to work made a sick woman of her that summer.

While George Smith raised the purchase-money, the legal business concerning the house had to be conducted on Mrs. Gaskell's behalf by her barrister son-in-law, Charles Crompton, and her prospective son-in-law, Thurstan Holland, since under the existing laws regulating property no married woman could acquire or sell property without her husband's knowledge and consent. Her daughters were equally active and devoted, travelling to and fro to meet the owner, the land-agent, and the valuer to estimate the furniture to be taken over. Florence's residence in London sufficiently explained her sisters' frequent visits there should Mr. Gaskell's suspicions be roused.

The engagement of Marianne and her cousin Thurstan Holland was at last agreed to by the fiancé's parents, and Marianne spent the greater part of the Law Vacation at his home at Dumbleton, near Evesham (Mr. Holland's constituency), and Mr. Holland himself resumed his old cordial relations with his famous cousin Elizabeth Gaskell, and helped her to sell the shares she had in the Katharine Docks Co. to provide the cash she now so urgently needed.

On the face of it July was an uneventful month, the family living very quietly at home with no visitors to interrupt Elizabeth's steady programme of work. With Marianne mostly away at the Hollands and Meta frequently staying with Flossy in town, only Julia was regularly at home, and Julia like Hearn was out of health and spirits. While care for Julia, the housekeeping, and 'nursing and cheering up Hearn' were Elizabeth's only admitted interruptions, she was carrying on a vast correspondence as well as answering advertisements in *The Times* and the *Hampshire Herald* for the tenant who did not materialize. Every letter written on the subject brought threefold complications and added daily to the sheer volume of writing to an already overburdened writer. By early August the strain, the smell of drains, Hearn's continuing ill health, and the worry over her house proved too much and she was too ill to go on with

7 Ibid.

her book. She was incapacitated for three weeks. 'I've done nothing,' she wrote to Marianne in mid-August,[8] 'but lie on a sofa and be cross this last 3 weeks', an admission only wrung from her by a near-collapse— severe headaches and sleepless nights aggravating her condition.

She got so behind with her work that she was obliged to catch up during a short weekend's visit to Lord Houghton and his wife at their country house at Fryston in Yorkshire where she was invited to stay with Meta on 19 August. She was really unfit to travel, and unwilling to go, and had to force herself to try and walk a little in order to prepare herself; as she admitted to Marianne, 'I don't know how to bear the journey, and the "being agreeable" tomorrow . . . Fryston is as muggy and damp as this, in a low flat country all intersected with dykes.'[9] She had to write hard at her book, before breakfast and late at night, and came home not a whit refreshed for the change and in dejected spirits. Mercifully, Mr. Gaskell had by then started on his annual holiday and was gone to stay with his friends the Potters in the Highlands. The need to put a good face on her worries was removed and she could give free vent to her feelings. Putting through the purchase of a house at long distance was an almost impossible task, that added immeasurably to the difficulties and to her weariness. The mounting pile of business letters with all concerned caused constant misunderstandings, even with Marianne and Thurstan, who mistook the date agreed for visiting the house in her company. The strain on her nerves reached breaking-point and she wrote in another fit of irritation and unreasonableness to Marianne on returning from Fryston: 'I am sick of the whole thing and very much regret that it has all to be settled just now when I *must* save all my health and strength for writing and have no one to whom I can delegate the acting. I am very sorry indeed for your day yesterday and terribly disappointed that you have seen the house without me . . . I *am* so badly behindhand in Wives and Daughters. All these worries about Alton do so incapacitate me from writing.'[10]

As by malice intent, every small problem appeared magnified and designed to overwhelm her: 'It is very hot and distressing here', she complained. 'My old sleepless nights have begun again and Julia seems very much out of order . . . We are going to have the drains up in the yard and see if anything is wrong there.'[11] She seemed on the verge of a breakdown.

'I keep thinking of your disappointment yesterday at not finding us there', she grieved aloud to Marianne, allowing herself to be flooded by

[8] *GL* 574.   [9] Ibid.
[10] *GL* 575a, 22 Aug. 1865.   [11] Ibid.

morbid fancies; '*its an unlucky house* and I believe I was a fool to set my heart on the place at all. For it will be a perpetual worry, finding tenants and replacing furniture and worry tells on my writing power. Yet writing will be the only way to pay off the debt which the necessary purchase of furniture will largely increase . . . I shall never write up the money for the house I'm afraid.'[12]

The next moment, good sense prevailing, she took the long overdue resolution of doing something for her health. 'However,' she added as an afterthought for Marianne, 'I'm going to take a tonic (by Meta's and Hearn's compulsion) and see what I can do.' The effect, whether of the tonic or of the good resolution, or of the more cheering report from Alton that the valuer who had been holding everything up was at last expected, was a revival of spirits. Meta, accompanied by Hearn, was dispatched to meet the valuer to settle about the furniture and make lists of the wanted pieces—sizes, shapes, matching colours, price, quantity required, storage—and empowered to take all decisions on her mother's behalf. Meta and Hearn travelled up to London on 24 August, Mrs. Gaskell excusing herself to George Smith for delegating Meta for such a tricky business: 'I have had such bad head aches (before I went to Fryston), —that I am behindhand with Wives and Daughters,—wherefore I let Meta go,—I hope it is not selfish, and I hope she won't be knocked up.'[13]

In the event Meta needed her mother's backing for the major decisions, and appealed to her to join her in London. Coming on top of her own qualms of conscience at leaving such responsibility to her it was an appeal she could not ignore, though she could ill afford either the time or the money. It meant travelling the cheapest way, by excursion ticket, leaving early one morning and returning late the third day. There was no time to lose, and once embarked she threw herself into the adventure. Her accounts to Marianne of the gruelling two days' shopping in London read like the report of an athlete out to beat a record.

She went up to London on Wednesday, 30 August, by the 9.30 a.m. train. Meta and Hearn were waiting at Euston to bear her off 'to Heals directly, and staid there as long as it was light', as she wrote to Marianne that evening; 'bought all the bed-room things (Meta having wants and measurements etc) except carpets. Then came here and dined'.[14] 'Here' was Flossy's home, which was at their disposal while Flossy and her husband were on holiday abroad. The next day, Thursday, 'no time was to be lost, and we have been all day at Shoolbreds, in the City (after

[12] Ibid. [13] *GL* 576, 23 Aug. 1865.
[14] *GL* 580, 31 Aug. 1865.

carpets,—a failure—) Shoolbreds again, Heals, Copelands in Bond St. (for China and glass—Mr. Smith gets us $22\frac{1}{2}$ per cent discount there, and did not come home till 8 to dinner, *dead-beat* . . . I am quite worn out tonight.'[15]

Writing to Thurstan Holland the same night ('so tired I hardly know what I say') to thank him for negotiating the sale of her Katharine Docks shares, and to discuss the provisos of her Will respecting the new house, it is the same refrain of utter exhaustion partly alleviated by the satisfaction derived from what she had accomplished. 'I go home to-morrow after a morning's final shopping . . . We have got *all* the things at 3 or 4 shops.'[16] To Marianne, after reaching home 'nearly dead for want of food and rest', she reported on the last '*crazing* day of furnishing; going into the City—far beyond St. Paul's out of duty, being told carpets were cheaper there,—but they were coarse common things, not really cheaper, so we came back to Shoolbreds . . . Home at 8 . . . Oh Dear! I *am* nearly killed, but the *stress* of everything is nearly over.'[17]

Whatever doubts she had had about the house were now dispelled; from the moment she could be active about it herself, her spirits rose. The trip to London had perhaps been the stimulus she needed; for the first time in weeks her confidence in the wisdom of what she had done was restored, and tired though she might be she was content. Everything was under control, the house to be vacated by the Whites on 29 September, the furniture bought and stored till the removal day.

With the decisive effort now behind her, and reckoning that the journey's cost in fatigue would be cheap at the price, she turned her energies without any loss of time to planning a holiday abroad for the family that would be within her means. That they needed and deserved it after the heat of Manchester and the fatigues of acting as her aides over the house, was obvious to her; her only problem was the cost of a trip abroad. But she was resolved they should have it. '*If* the house gets let,' she wrote to Marianne on 2 September immediately on reaching home, 'and the work cleared off, I think we *may* go (with Cook's Excursion ticket 6£—6s) there and back for a month to Switzerland, Genève, Berne Frebourg Neufchatel the week after next . . . Remember, this has been our *busiest* week.' Even while making the rapid readjustment required from house-furnishing to foreign travel, she realized that for her there could be no rest from writing. 'I must however write a great deal more at Wives and Daughters first . . . My illness (3 weeks from bed to sofa

[15] *GL* 580, 31 Aug. 1865.   [16] *GL* 581, 31 Aug. 1865.
[17] *GL* 582, 2 Sept. 1865.

and vice versa—caused by drains I do believe)—threw me terribly behind hand . . . oh *how* dead I feel!—'[18]

In the event, it was not until early October that they got off on their holiday, and then only as far as Dieppe. It was everything Mrs. Gaskell needed—'the air and sky are splendid and I feel like a different creature', she reported to Marianne, while commiserating with 'Poor dear Julia' whose heart 'so yearns after Switzerland that she can't enjoy this place'.[19] Honest as ever with her daughters Mrs. Gaskell debated the pros and cons with them of staying or moving on: 'We have had a talk this morning (*very* tantalising to my dear girls,) about going there; but we have settled that the *wisest* thing is to stay near the sea.' Everything she needed to revive her was to be found there—and cheaply and pleasantly into the bargain.

We have a pleasant sitting-room au premier, *two* double-bedded rooms, (one opening out of the sitting room,—) breakfast (coffee bread and butter in our room—) lunch any time we like—chocolate, cold meat, bread and butter Neufchatel Cheese and grapes—in the Salle à Manger at a little table, and dinner at the table d'hote (10 persons only 1 gentleman which Julia finds dull—) soup, fish, 2 meats, pudding and desert—for 9 francs a piece, *service* included, Bougies, wine and fire extras. We are 2 minutes from the sea, and the house is as sweet as a nut. For ½ a franc we can go into the Establissement close at hand, hear a (shocking) out in air band and read the news. Everything is shutting up for the winter.[20]

They stayed at Dieppe three weeks, moving on from there to Boulogne for the last days before returning home.

From Boulogne she wrote to Thurstan Holland on 25 October to remind him that they expected him to join them at Alton at 'The Lawn'— naming her house very grandly for the first time and with evident enjoyment. 'You won't mind everything being rough', she wrote in great spirits. 'We can give you bread and cheese and cold meat, and "Alton Ale" and tea and bread and butter and "excellent milk" (Hearn says,) and a hearty welcome. Come sooner if you can. I want all sorts of advice about the garden etc, etc. No time for more.'[21]

Hearn was already at Alton to prepare their welcome.

The great day, so long and so anxiously awaited, was come at last, and Mrs. Gaskell, in totally relaxed mood, was launching her first informal invitation to the new house. Accompanied by Meta and Julia she went

[18] Ibid.   [19] *GL* 585, 6 Oct. 1865.
[20] Ibid.   [21] *GL* 587, 25 Oct. 1865.

directly to Alton on arriving off the boat train in London. Holybourne, her new village, was only one and a half miles out of Alton, and could be reached by local cab.

In the dusk of their arrival and in the November light of the following days, not every feature of her prize could be distinguished at once, but it was never less than enchanting to her mind, if not to her sight. Within a day or two of arriving she was already planting apple trees, and potatoes and onions for her kitchen garden, and visualizing the roses in the flower-borders. She had been trying to visualize the house ever since June when Meta had first described it to her, and now as she saw it in the late autumn it came up to all her dreams.

It was—and still remains today—a charming early Georgian house built of rose-coloured brick, plastered in the style of the time, with long French windows overlooking the lawns, and trellised walls half covered with summer climbers. The house was screened from the road by a long wall and entered by white pallisaded gates and a drive through shrub-beries, the front door being set in a side wall of the house, which made for seclusion. The surrounding garden, kitchen garden, and paddocks gave her three to four acres of ground. She had told Charles Norton in a letter of 8 September what she knew of it: 'The house is large—(not quite so large as this [Plymouth Grove]); in a very pretty garden (kitchen, flower-gardens and paddock . . .) and in the middle of a pretty rural village, so that it won't be a lonely place for the unmarried daughters who will inherit.'[22] There was bedroom accommodation for ten people (in Mrs. Gaskell's reckoning there would certainly be children helping to fill the vacant rooms) and four fine sitting-rooms on the ground floor. The drawing-room looking out on to the main lawn through three floor-to-ceiling French windows. It was a beautiful, well-proportioned room with corner recesses for china, books, and flowers, and a wide Adam-style fireplace. The entrance hall had a graceful archway dividing the front and rear portions of the house, and the large dining-room opened on to the hall by a wide archway curtained off. There was, on the opposite side of the hall, a good-sized room well fitted for a library. The stairs were perhaps the most typically early Georgian feature of the building, dividing on the first floor into two equal flights of shallow stairs leading into the two opposite sides of the house. Pointed window frames, in the neo-Gothic style dear to Georgian architects, were carried throughout the house. The servants' quarters ran over the stables and outhouses, which belonged to the oldest part of the house. It was said to have been

[22] GL 583.

the village coaching inn before a newer White Hart replaced it higher up the road. Parts of the house were reported to date from Jacobean times. The unmistakable glory of the place was the noble cedar tree fronting the drawing-room windows and already over a century and a half old when Mrs. Gaskell saw it. The garden surrounding the house on all sides sloped gently down towards the stream marking its boundaries, the Bourne, which flowed from the churchyard some half a mile away, and was said to rise from under the altar-stone.

The Lawn, viewed from within or without, was a graceful, proportioned, tranquil place, where an author might hope to live out the rest of her days in inspired peace.

The travellers' immediate concern was with the present, however, and with making the place habitable. Charwomen had been at work for the last five weeks and already Mrs. Gaskell had engaged a 'very nice servant (out of place) to come in and cook and clean the rooms we live in'[23] for the next day. Writing even in the midst of chaos she could report to Marianne on 31 October that 'It will be very nice and so complete . . . Every day we like it better and better even in the midst of all the *half* furnished state, painters, and charwomen.' She longed for Marianne to see it for herself.[24]

The principal beneficiary, Mr. Gaskell, was out of the picture for the time being, and it was never possible for the rest of the family to be together at the same time in The Lawn. Marianne had to keep house in Manchester, being the only one so far to have had a long summer holiday. Mrs. Gaskell had written to her husband almost at once on returning to England, in terms as unrevealing and as little dishonest as she could manage, to tell him that his dear ones were back. 'I did not say where from or to where',[25] Mrs. Gaskell wrote conspiratorially to Marianne, who might have to parry questions if her Papa showed any curiosity. Flossy and her husband, whose absence everyone deplored, were kept in town at the Cromptons' home by the illness and death of Charles's father—'the dear kind judge', as Mrs. Gaskell called him. Lady Crompton's need of both young people at the time was more pressing than her own, Mrs. Gaskell hastened to acknowledge.

The two families had the most cordial relationship. The Cromptons could never sufficiently spoil Florence, and Charles was not only a general favourite with the Gaskell ladies but with Mr. Gaskell, who liked him exceedingly. The death of the judge saddened them all in the midst of their new excitement.

[23] *GL* 588, 31 Oct. 1865.   [24] Ibid.   [25] Ibid.

But a happier note was struck by the ringing of the church bells to welcome the new residents at The Lawn a couple of evenings after their arrival. Amused and touched, Mrs. Gaskell reported to Marianne the men coming round to say what they had done, and the discreet exchange of half-a-crown a piece in thanks for their performance, which, Mrs. Gaskell added, no one had heard—except Hearn, who had liked it very much.[26]

The house still needed 'little bits of joinering and painting the wood-work of the window-frames—and other wood work . . . to keep all together *until* the future painting of the whole house', and Mrs. Gaskell was thinking in terms of a two to three weeks' stay until the prospective tenant (a Mrs. Moray was even then making an offer) would move in. The days were hardly long enough to place the furniture bought in town, lay the carpets (bought by the yard, and needing cutting and binding), to put the china and glass away in the cupboards, and hang the curtains. But however hard she worked, every task seemed light in the soothing atmosphere of her new house, and there was even leisure for writing. She wrote to Marianne on 31 October that she was confident now of being able to finish the book while there.[27] After a year of stress and illness and worry, it was like being back in port again after a storm at sea.

The last instalment of *Wives and Daughters* for the January issue had still to be written. Everyone knew how the story would finish now—she had often enough discussed it with her daughters. She had brought Roger and Molly to an understanding, and though he was in Africa for six months to complete his findings there, everyone knew that he must come back. Except for Mrs. Gibson, of course, whose disregard of the feelings and fears of others must continue to the last page to provide the book's purest comedy. It was with Mrs. Gibson that the author was concerned during the brief periods she could find for writing—'constantly called off', as she was, during the days at The Lawn.

Thurstan, who had joined the party as requested, and was a witness of Mrs. Gaskell's high spirits and regained health and vitality, noted in particular how 'more than ordinarily happy and full of spirits' she was, and how repeatedly she said how much better she felt than for years past and, indeed, was feeling 'years younger than she had been doing a few weeks before'.[28] In that euphoric mood it would be no licence to suppose her smiling to herself over Mrs. Gibson in those last exchanges with

[26] *GL* 588, 31 Oct. 1865.
[27] Ibid.
[28] Letter of 18 Nov. 1865 (*GL*, pp. 970–1).

Molly, where, even at that stage in the story, the freshness of the character and the inexhaustible humour of the situation never flag.

Cynthia's return from her honeymoon has been announced, and Mrs. Gibson instantly seizes on the occasion:

'Mr. Gibson, we must have the new dinner-service at Watts's I've set my heart on so long! . . . And, Molly, you must have a new gown.'

'Come, come! Remember I belong to the last generation,' said Mr. Gibson.

'And Cynthia won't mind what I wear,' said Molly, bright with pleasure at the thought of seeing her again.

'No! but Walter will. He has such a quick eye for dress, and I think I rival papa; if he's a good stepfather, I'm a good stepmother, and I could not bear to see Molly shabby . . . I must have a new gown, too. It won't do to look as if we had nothing but the dresses which we wore at the wedding!'

. . . When Mr. Gibson had left the room, Mrs. Gibson softly reproached Molly for her obstinacy.

'You might have allowed me to beg for a new gown for you, Molly, when you knew how much I admired that figured silk at Brown's the other day. And now, of course, I can't be so selfish as to get it for myself, and you to have nothing. You should learn to understand the wishes of other people. Still, on the whole, you are a dear, sweet girl, and I only wish—well, I know what I wish; only dear papa does not like it to be talked about. And now cover me up close, and let me go to sleep, and dream about my dear Cynthia and my new shawl!'[29]

Leaving Mrs. Gibson to her comfortable nap, Mrs. Gaskell would be called off yet once again by her busy household aides to settle some domestic problem, and resume, without perceptible strain, the role of housewife as she had just assumed that of author. No one can say which was her truer element.

Florence and her husband came after all for the weekend of 11-13 November, and while arranging everything for their reception on the Saturday—the first official guests to be entertained at The Lawn—Mrs. Gaskell wrote late that evening to William Shaen, her solicitor, to arrange to see him the following Wednesday. The visit concerned the Will she had asked him to draw up directly she had acquired her property. Some exchanges had passed between them already on the provisos of the Will, which she wished to be made simple and clear, arranging for the house to pass, after their parents' deaths, to her daughters—to the unmarried ones in particular. Under the existing law, the proviso must be made unequivocal, else the house would go to some collaterals of Mr. Gaskell's which Mrs. Gaskell wished to provide against. She would

[29] *Wives and Daughters*, ch. 60, pp. 754-5.

prefer, as she had already told William Shaen that 'her daughters' child-less widowers should have it'.[30] William Shaen, receiving the instruc-tions and the invitation to Alton, noted with pleasure the cheerful tone of Mrs. Gaskell's letter, which was 'full of life and spirits'.[31]

Florence and her husband arrived on the Saturday, and saw over the new house. It needed only Marianne now to complete the family circle, pending the time when the secret need no longer be kept from Mr. Gaskell, and his wife, having 'worked her passage' to freedom and paid off her debt, could confess to her latest flight of fancy and welcome him to their very own home. The thought sent her spirits soaring as, in the first flush of possession, she showed her children round the delightful place.

Being the woman she was, fundamentally religious, it was natural she should wish to go to church on the Sunday. Fatigue or no fatigue, it was part of the discipline in which she lived, and she had no prejudice whatever against the Anglican Establishment—a village church was a part of the country life she hoped to live thereafter. With Florence and Julia she went to the afternoon service while Meta and Charles Crompton took a walk. The church, whose bells had welcomed her, was a good distance away up a country lane; it was old and beautiful, standing high above its graveyard with the Bourne outlining its boundaries.

It had been decided to have an early tea, in style, round the drawing-room fire when the family reassembled—perhaps the first time furniture and fittings were all in place—and it was in the nature of a celebration, with so many of the family present, that the meal was taken. There was much animated talk, and Mrs. Gaskell, in the fullness of her own happi-ness, was grieved for Lady Crompton's sorrow, and discussing with Flossy the best way of offering her the use of The Lawn as a change of scene during her time of mourning. In the middle of a sentence she stopped, and her daughters, waiting for her to resume, saw that she was slipping forward off the couch, and only caught her from falling just in time. For a few moments they thought she had fainted, or had a stroke; and Charles and a servant ran for a doctor. When he came, and told them the truth, that she was already dead, and obviously suffered from a 'diseased heart'—a fact neither known nor suspected before—they realized that she had died without any perceptible sign of struggle or suffering. She had simple ceased to breathe.[32]

For the family there would, in time, be consolation in the manner of her dying, which would appear to them like the perfect consummation

[30] GL 581.   [31] GL, p. 783, n. 2.
[32] See GL, pp. 970-1.

of her life. She had often spoken, Thurstan Holland told Charles Norton,[33] 'of dying a sudden painless death like this and we all believe that the end was particularly happy . . . She had just got everything into order and readiness and was rejoicing in the carrying out of her wish'.

Death had, indeed, come to her like a grace rather than as a destruction; she would never now know 'the weariness of failing powers', as Meta wrote to Ellen Nussey in reply to her letter of condolence; that would have been the worst for her. 'I cannot tell you', wrote Meta; 'how beautiful a "sunset" it was—though we didn't know it was that at the time—all Mama's last days had been *full* of loving thought and tender help for others—she *was* so sweet and dear, and noble beyond words.'[34]

Mr. Gaskell had to be informed, and on Charles Crompton devolved the terrible task. Out of consideration, he decided rather to travel up to Manchester to break the news in person than to send a telegram. While he travelled north the next day (Monday) Thurstan, who had not remained at Alton, returned to stay with the girls till their father arrived.

At Plymouth Grove Charles learnt that Mr. Gaskell was gone to Altrincham for a meeting of Unitarian ministers, and telegraphed him to return home. As though Mr. Gaskell suspected the nature of the summons, he asked his friend and colleague, Samuel Steinthal, to go back to Plymouth Grove with him; where on arrival, he heard the news.

It was in such circumstances that Mr. Gaskell learnt his wife's 'terribly grand' secret, the purchase of the house that was to be their future home, and all the trouble she had gone to to acquire it for the happiness of all, as she had fondly hoped. Together with Marianne and Charles Crompton, he made the journey to Alton.

The family were unanimous in wishing Mrs. Gaskell to be buried at Knutsford, and the funeral cortège left The Lawn on the Thursday morning, 16 November, to travel north. The funeral took place on the 17th in the little Unitarian chapel graveyard, the totally unpretentious ground that she had known since childhood and described in *Ruth*. The service was conducted by her life-long friend, the Revd. Henry Green. Only the men of the family attended, Mr. Gaskell's two brothers, Dr. Samuel and Mr. Robert Gaskell standing by him, and the sons-in-law, Charles Crompton and Thurstan Holland. Though the daughters could not face the ordeal, all Knutsford was there; not out of curiosity but out of love. The return of the famous author was not marked by the presence

[33] Ibid.
[34] Letter to Ellen Nussey, 22 Jan. 1866. Shorter Collection, Brotherton Library, Leeds.

of distinguished strangers, but of her oldest friends. It was not the funeral of a celebrity, but of a traveller returned to her home.

On the Sunday following, 19 November, the traditional funeral sermon was preached at Cross Street Chapel, Manchester, in the presence of the family, by the Revd. James Drummond, who took as his text 'The Holiness of Sorrow'. The preacher, who quoted Mrs. Gaskell's favourite lines from Tennyson:

> Oh, we must hope that *somehow* good
> Will be the final goal of ill—

knew her well enough to find the illuminating train of thought by which to reach out to the hearts of her sorrowing family. 'Sorrow', he said, 'belongs to us as immortal beings. It marks our greatness, and is designed to make us greater. It lifts us towards the universal sympathy of God.'

With this gift of universal sympathy Elizabeth Gaskell had herself been peculiarly endowed. It made her what she was as a human being— charitable and kind—and as a writer—eloquent to speak with the tongues of others.

EPILOGUE

THE house at Alton never served. Mr. Gaskell, predictably, never abandoned his post at Manchester, and died in harness there at the age of seventy-nine, after fifty-six years' public service.

He lived to the end with his two unmarried daughters; the married ones, though gone from home, were never far away. Echoes of their devotion and of the close affection binding the family still persist over the years. A rare note of Mr. Gaskell's has been preserved addressed to Marianne and scribbled in the train at the outset of a journey in March 1866:

My dearest Polly,

I got off very comfortably at 9½, Florence accompanying me to the station, and so far I have got *on* very comfortably . . . and my three fellow-passengers, like true Englishmen, never open their lips nor the windows either, which is also to my liking. I have begun a similar scribble under difficulties to Meta . . .

We are now slackening speed for Rugby, and I must attack my sandwiches, *and* my brandy and water.

Leighton Buzzard

I've finished my sandwiches and my brandy and water . . . and have just been indulging in a bit of your ginger, which I found toothsome and pleasant . . .

Your loving Papa

Marianne, who married her cousin Edward Thurstan Holland the year after her mother's death, was the longest-lived of the family, dying only in 1920. She settled first at Wimbledon and finally in Hereford. Her eldest son, William Edward (she had seven children in all) was born 1867, and in the recollection of her granddaughter, Mrs. Trevor-Jones, living today, she inherited much of Mrs. Gaskell's charming and lively disposition, even into old age.

After Mr. Gaskell's death in 1884 (Florence predeceased him in 1881) Meta and Julia, the 'Miss Gaskells' as they became known throughout Manchester, carried on their mother's teaching and example, devoting much of their time to furthering schemes for higher education among the working classes, and in promoting holiday plans for women and girls. Under them, Plymouth Grove continued to be an active centre for cultural activities and social services. There was no benevolent enterprise afoot in Manchester in which they did not have a part. When Meta, the last to go, died in October 1913, eighty-one years after her parents settled in the city, the flags on public buildings were flown at half-mast; for Manchester it was the end of an era.

SELECT BIBLIOGRAPHY

I: OFFICIAL DOCUMENTS

Treasury Minutes: Memoir of William Stevenson, Book 29/87, Public Record Office.

The Annual Biography and Obituary, 1817-37, in *Treasury Officials*, ed. J. C. Sainty, 1972.

Last Will and Testament of William Stevenson, Somerset House.

John Stevenson's Certificate as Freeman of Berwick, 1822, Berwick City Council.

Unitarian Registers of Births, Deaths, Marriages, Dr. Williams' Library, London.

Registers of Dissenters, 1740-1837, Public Record Office.

Registers of St. Luke's Church, Chelsea. County Hall, London.

Registers of Brook Street Unitarian Chapel, Knutsford.

Registers of Cross Street Unitarian Chapel, Manchester.

II: ORIGINAL DOCUMENTS

Letters relating to Mrs. Gaskell in the Edward Hall Collection, Wigan Central Library, M 1006 (d) E.H.C. 205.

Autograph letters to Mrs. Gaskell from Dickens, Forster, Carlyle, etc., Shorter Collection, Brotherton Library, Leeds.

Autograph letters to Mrs. Gaskell, John Rylands Library, Manchester.

Autograph letters from Charlotte Brontë to Mrs. Gaskell, Manchester University Library.

Original documents towards a Life and Letters of Mrs. Gaskell, Shorter Collection, Brotherton Library, Leeds.

Typescript of a projected Life and Letters of Mrs. Gaskell, 1930, by Jane Coolidge (incomplete), Brotherton Library, Leeds.

Autograph letters to and from the Gaskell family, Brotherton Library, Leeds.

III: PUBLISHED WORKS OF MRS. GASKELL

The Complete Works of Elizabeth Cleghorn Gaskell, Knutsford Edition, ed. A. W. Ward, 8 vols., 1906. (This includes the anonymous publications that first appeared in periodical journals.)

My Diary, ed. C. K. Shorter, 1923.

The Letters of Mrs. Gaskell, ed. J. A. V. Chapple and A. Pollard, 1966.

Letters Addressed to Mrs. Gaskell by Celebrated Contemporaries, ed. R. D. Waller, 1935.

Letters of Mrs. Gaskell and Charles Eliot Norton, 1855-1865, ed. Jane Whitehill, 1932.

IV: CRITICAL AND BIOGRAPHICAL WORKS ON MRS. GASKELL AND HER CIRCLE

ALLEN, WALTER, *The English Novel*, 1954.

ALLOTT, MIRIAM, *Elizabeth Gaskell*, 1960.

CAZAMIAN, LOUIS, *Le Roman social en Angleterre*, 1904.

CECIL, DAVID, *Early Victorian Novelists*, 1934.

CHADWICK, ELLIS H., *Mrs. Gaskell, Homes and Haunts*, 1910.

CHITTY, SUSAN, *The Beast and the Monk: A Life of Charles Kingsley*, 1974.

CLARKE, CHARLES and MARY, *Recollections of Writers*, 1878.

FFRENCH, Y., *Mrs. Gaskell*, 1949.

Autobiography of Mrs. Fletcher, 1875.

HAIGHT, GORDON, *The Letters of George Eliot*, 1954.

HALDANE, ELIZABETH, *Mrs. Gaskell and her Friends*, 1930.

HOLLAND, BERNARD, *The Lancashire Hollands*, 1917.

HOLLAND, SIR HENRY, *Recollections of a Past Life*, 1877.

HOPKINS, A. B., *Elizabeth Gaskell: Her Life and Work*, 1952.

HOWITT, MARY, *Autobiography*, 2 vols., 1889.

JAMES, HENRY, *William Wetmore Story and his Friends*, 1903.

LUTYENS, MARY, *Effie in Venice*, 1952.

MONTÉGUT, ÉMILE, *Écrivains modernes de l'Angleterre*, 1889.

PARRISH, M. L., *Victorian Lady Novelists*, 1933.

POLLARD, ARTHUR, *Mrs. Gaskell, Novelist and Biographer*, 1965.

QUILLER-COUCH, A. T., *Charles Dickens and Other Victorians*, 1925.

RAY, GORDON, *The Letters of William Thackeray*, 1946.

RITCHIE, LADY (ANNE THACKERAY), *Chapters from Some Memoirs*, 1894.

RUSKIN, JOHN, *The Stones of Venice*, vol. ii, 1853.

SANDERS, DE WITT, *Elizabeth Gaskell*, 1929.

SHAEN, MARGARET, *Memorials of Two Sisters*, 1908.

SHARPS, J. G., *Mrs. Gaskell's Observations and Invention*, 1970.

SIMPSON, M. E., *Letters and Recollections of Julius and Mary Mohl*, 1887.

TILLOTSON, KATHLEEN, *Novels of the Eighteen-Forties*, 1961.

TROLLOPE, ANTHONY, *An Autobiography*, 1883.

WHITFIELD, A. STANTON, *Mrs. Gaskell, her Life and Work*, 1929.

Women Novelists of Queen Victoria's Reign: A Book of Appreciations, 1897.

WRIGHT, EDGAR, *Mrs. Gaskell: A Basis for Reassessment*, 1965.

V. RELEVANT WORKS

BASCH, FRANÇOISE, *Relative Creatures: Victorian Women in Society and the Novel*, 1974.

BRIGGS, ASA, *Victorian Cities*, 1968.

BUTLER, MARILYN, *Maria Edgeworth*, 1972.

CARLYLE, JANE, *Selections of Letters*, ed. T. Bliss, 2 vols., 1950.

Catalogue of the Sale of the Gaskell Property, 9 February 1914. Manchester Central Library, 1914.

CONRAD, PETER, *The Victorian Treasure-House*, 1974.

DARWIN, CHARLES, *Autobiography*, ed. Nora Barlow, 1958.

DAVIS, V. D., *A History of Manchester College*, 1932.

The Letters of Charles Dickens, ed. W. Dexter, 1928.

The Enquirer. Numbers relating to Mr. and Mrs. Gaskell in Dr. Williams' Library, London.

GREEN, the Revd. HENRY, *Knutsford, Its Traditions and History*, 1859.

HICKS, PHYLLIS, *A Quest of Ladies*, 1949.

HOLM, THEA, *Chelsea*, 1972.

HUXLEY, LEONARD, *The House of Smith, Elder*, 1923.

JOHNSON, EDGAR, *Charles Dickens, His Tragedy and Triumph*, 1953.

KROYER, PETER, *The Story of Lindsey House, Chelsea*, 1956.

LEHMANN, R., *Dickens as Editor*, 1912.

LEYLAND, F. A., *The Brontë Family with Special Reference to Patrick Branwell Brontë*, 2 vols., 1886.

LOCK, JOHN, and DIXON, W. T., *A Man of Sorrow: The Life, Letters and Times of The Rev. Patrick Brontë*, 1965.

MCLACHLAN, H., *The Unitarian Home Missionary College, 1854–1914*, 1915.

—— *The Unitarian Movement in the Religious Life of England*, 1934.

—— *Essays and Addresses*, 1950.

'Sermons and Addresses by James Martineau and William Gaskell.'

The Letters of Charles Eliot Norton, ed. Sara Norton and De Wolfe Howe, 1913.

PAYNE, GEORGE, *Mrs. Gaskell's Knutsford*, 1905.

SMITH, FRANK, *The Life and Work of Sir James Kay-Shuttleworth*, 1923.

George Smith: A Memoir, by his widow, 1902.

STRACHEY, LYTTON, *Eminent Victorians*, 1918.

TAYLOR, MARY, *Letters from New Zealand*, ed. Joan Stevens, 1972.

Transactions of the Unitarian Historical Society, 1923–6.

WADE, R., *Unitarian Chapel Histories*, 1880.

WOODHAM-SMITH, CECIL, *Florence Nightingale*, 1951.

YOUNG, G., *Victorian England*, 1957.

INDEX